Teaching in Further Education

Seventh edition

Also available from Bloomsbury

Learning to Teach in the Lifelong Learning Sector, Ewan Ingleby, Dawn Joyce and
    Sharon Powell
Reflective Teaching in Further and Adult Education, Yvonne Hillier
Teaching in Post-Compulsory Education: Learning, Skills and Standards, edited by
    Fred Fawbert

Teaching in Further Education

Seventh edition

An Outline of Principles and Practice

L. B. Curzon and Jonathan Tummons

B L O O M S B U R Y

LONDON • NEW DELHI • NEW YORK • SYDNEY

Bloomsbury Academic

An imprint of Bloomsbury Publishing Plc

50 Bedford Square   1385 Broadway
London   New York
WC1B 3DP   NY 10018
UK   USA

www.bloomsbury.com

Bloomsbury is a registered trade mark of Bloomsbury Publishing Plc

Seventh Edition © Jonathan Tummons 2013

Previous editions © L.B. Curzon 1976, 1980, 1985, 1990, 1997, 2004

First published 1976 by Cassell
Seventh edition published 2013 by Bloomsbury
Reprinted 1990, 1991 (twice), 1992, 1993, 1994, 1996, 1999 by Cassell
Reprinted 2001, 2002, 2004, 2005, 2006, 2007, 2008, 2009 by Continuum

British Library Cataloguing-in-Publication Data
A catalogue record for this book is available from the British Library.

ISBN: PB: 978-1-4411-3043-3
HB: 978-1-4411-4048-7
e-pub: 978-1-4411-5197-1
e-pdf: 978-1-4411-0704-6

Library of Congress Cataloging-in-Publication Data
Curzon, L. B. (Leslie Basil)
Teaching in further education : an outline of principles and practice / L.B. Curzon and Jonathan Tummons.-- Seventh edition.
pages cm.
Includes bibliographical references and index.
ISBN 978-1-4411-3043-3-- ISBN 978-1-4411-0704-6-- ISBN 978-1-4411-5197-1-- ISBN 978-1-4411-4048-7 1. Teachers--In-service training--Great Britain. 2. Teaching--Great Britain. 3. Professional education--Great Britain. 4. Postsecondary education--Great Britain. I. Tummons, Jonathan. II. Title.
LB1731.C85 2013
370.71'10941--dc23
2013018705

Typeset by Fakenham Prepress Solutions, Fakenham, Norfolk NR21 8NN
Printed and bound in India

Contents

Acknowledgements

Fifteen years ago, I enrolled on a City and Guilds 7307 Further and Adult Education Teachers' Certificate. My tutors on that course were Jocelyn Brooks and Jayne Moore: I continue to be grateful to both of them for their guidance and subsequent friendship.

After completing my PGCE, I went on to do an MEd in Lifelong Learning at the Open University. One of my tutors, Eileen Shaw, provided much support and inspiration during my studies.

I would like to say thank you to Lynne Paxton and Neil Arnott, who gave me my first job as a teacher educator; and to Suzanne Blake, Jacki Gill, Nick Haigh, Laura Kent, Chris Letza, Ann Metcalfe and Dean Starkey, who were good friends and (at different times) colleagues at my second FE college.

I would like to say a particular thank you to Jane Brooke, Gaynor Mount and Nena Skrbic who were such good fun to work with during my time in Leeds.

During my years in the Further Education (FE) sector, I worked as part of a large Higher Education in FE network, and a number of people who now work there have over time been both a support and an inspiration: John Aston; Liz Atkins; Roy Fisher; Kevin Orr; Lisa Russell; Robin Simmons; Ron Thompson.

I am also indebted to a small group of other people who over the years have made time for conversation, advice and friendly feedback: Andy Armitage; Helen Colley; Vicky Duckworth; Sue Wallace.

At Teesside, I would like to acknowledge the friendship and support of my former colleagues in the education section. There has been a profusion of interesting writing at Teesside during the last few years and I am both pleased and grateful to have been a part of this burgeoning culture of research and scholarship.

I would also like to thank Alison Baker and Rosie Pattinson at Bloomsbury for their patience and support: editing/rewriting/revising this book has been much more difficult than I anticipated.

Finally, of course, as always, this is for Jo, Alex and Eleanor.

Preface to the Seventh Edition

The terms of reference for the production of the first edition of *Teaching in Further Education* were: '…the provision of a text which will assist in the vital task of making teaching in the colleges of FE more efficient and effective'. This has remained the overall aim of the successive editions which have appeared during the past 35 years. This seventh edition aims to provide for teachers in training and college staff a closely-structured text which outlines key theories of learning, and examines the principal modes of formal teaching currently in use in our colleges.

As in previous editions, the text is concerned primarily with the practical activities of teaching and with those learning theories which are linked closely to successful instruction. The teacher who is aware of how students acquire, retain, access and transfer their learning is likely to be at an advantage in preparing and delivering effective lessons and lectures.

This seventh edition has involved a thorough revision of the previously published text. In particular, the following changes have been made.

- New chapters have been added, dealing with: theories of learning that draw on social psychology and social practice theories; assessment theory and practice; and the evaluation of – and reflection on – teaching practice.

- A number of chapters have been extensively rewritten in order to take into account a number of significant changes to practice in the sector since the publication of the previous edition of this book, dealing with: the implications of recent curriculum reform; provision for 14–16 learners in colleges; e-learning and blended learning; and changing modes of course delivery.

- Notes and reference material have once again been updated. As with previous editions, a large group of references to important research material noted in earlier editions remains. For this seventh edition, I have used Harvard referencing, as opposed to footnotes, as this is the convention that trainee teachers are most likely to use during their programmes of study.

I have retained the general character of the text, insofar as it continues to offer a systematic exposition of the elements of instruction common to most types of courses currently available in colleges of FE in the United Kingdom. Consequently, it does not include prescriptive advice relating to specific examinations or national certificate syllabuses; it concentrates on matters of a fundamental and overall nature which concern all members of college teaching staffs, no matter what are the precise titles or syllabus content of the courses with which they are involved.

In contrast to many other general teaching texts, this work makes no reference to either the current professional standards framework (at the time of writing, the fate of these standards had only recently been settled). This omission is not intended to signify any opposition to the standards per se (although there is an argument to be made that such frameworks serve to diminish rather than enhance professionalism). I think that the teacher-training curriculum that this book – in part – reifies and contributes to is sufficiently well-established not to need reinforcing by a framework with which it has an ambiguous relationship at best (Lucas, Nasta and Rogers, 2012; Tummons, 2011b).

Italics are occasionally employed in the text in order to bring key ideas to the reader's special attention; where they occur within a quotation, the added emphasis is entirely mine.

PART 1

An Overview of the Teaching–Learning Process

1 Education, Teaching and Learning

Since life means growth, a living creature lives as truly and positively at one stage as at another, with the same intrinsic fullness and the same absolute claims. Hence education means the enterprise of supplying the conditions which ensure growth, or adequacy of life, irrespective of age **JOHN DEWEY**

What is the purpose of the work done by FE colleges, work that this textbook seeks to inform and contribute to? Should colleges, and the learning and teaching processes that we find situated within them, be described or understood solely in terms of employability, of providing young people and adult learners with transferable or generic skills (whatever they might be) so that they are prepared for the world of work? Or should we consider the ways by which the work of colleges serves to enable students to enrich their lives more broadly, thus contributing, however modestly, to self-fulfilment and human progress?

In contrast to the best efforts of neoliberal governments (and some college principals) to reduce discourses of teaching to a series of discussions about skills or techniques and to define FE solely in terms of employability, this book rests on a series of principles that can be seen as contributing to a broader philosophy of education:

- education can contribute in significant fashion to the breadth and acuity of vision and values
- colleges of FE and similar types of institution can assist in the broadening of the nature and quality of education
- the effectiveness of the colleges can be heightened by the training of staff in the theory and practice of instruction in general, and teaching techniques in particular.

Discussions about the broader purposes or aims of education (including primary, secondary and higher education) that are framed in terms such as those offered above are perhaps unfashionable in times of recession when the number of young people aged 16–24 who are not in education, employment or training (so-called NEETs) stands at almost one million, might seem to be a luxury. Successive governmental influence – or perhaps, interference – in the learning and skills sector has resulted in an at times bewildering pace of change. New initiatives and new curricula, new funding regimes and new organizing bodies, seem to come and go at a dizzying pace: Every Child Matters; the Learning and Skills Council; subject learning coaches; the Institute for Learning; and the Learning and Skills Improvement Service are just a few of the quangos and initiatives that have come and gone over the last decade or so. Nor is this process slowing down: only very recently – at the time of writing this book – has the coalition government has decided not to proceed with the deregulation of teacher-training for the lifelong learning sector. With change such a constant part of the lecturer's life (Edward et al., 2007), it might seem difficult to justify time spent considering a personal philosophy for education in the sector when there is barely time to read through the latest revisions to a curriculum.

This book occupies a contrary position: it rests on an assumption that there is more to teaching in the sector than 'just' achievement and completion rates. This is not to deny the importance of gaining qualifications for the young people – and adult learners – with whom we work. But a relentless focus on completion rates, understood as part of a broader culture that positions education, learning and teaching as managerial processes that rests on statistics, outcomes, performance criteria and the like, risks dehumanizing the practices that make up our professional lives and that invariably drove us to become teachers in the sector in the first place: a sense that the students with whom we work are entitled to as good an education as anyone, that the FE college is not and should not be seen as the 'second best' option, that the younger 14-16 learners with whom we are increasingly expected to engage are not to be treated as 'rejects' of the compulsory school system. We need to make time and space for conversations about themes such as these, and how our practices in workshops, classrooms and tutorial rooms can embody them. It is in broader themes such as this, rather than narrow technical discussions about using quizzes with our students or how well laid out our PowerPoint slides might be, that our critical reflection needs to sit.

Introductory remarks on education

The human activity which we call 'education' (derived from the Latin word 'educare', meaning 'to lead out or to bring forth') is, in western European society, largely based largely on two processes which we know as 'teaching' and 'learning', although the relationship between these two processes is not a simple one (a theme that will be developed in later chapters of this book). The formalization of these processes, resulting in their being carried out within schools, colleges and similar institutions, has emerged from society's conscious responses to fundamental problems of adaptation and survival. Education in our culture was historically concerned with the handing on of beliefs and moral standards, accumulated knowledge and skills. In its essence it is a recognition of the fact that society's way of life must be learned – since an understanding of it is not inherited – by each individual. The process of assimilation of the experiences of earlier generations is at the basis of this task; education assists the younger generation in this process. Learning is not simply a matter of perpetuating the knowledge or skills that a society deems to be important and worthy of preservation, however. Learning also depends on the individual's experiences within, for example, her or his family, social environment and, more specifically, the educational institutions he or she is able to attend. Public examinations and certificates provide a sense of equality of educational opportunity. And yet particular sectors of educational provision are clearly perceived to be of higher status than others, in the same way as some universities are. For many years the FE sector has been referred to as the 'Cinderella sector' (Randle and Brady, 1997; Jephcote et al., 2008).

The concept of 'formal education', which features extensively in this book, should be understood clearly in a positive sense, as contrasted with the negative sense of terms such as 'formalistic' or 'formalism', which often reverberate with pejorative overtones. Lecturing in 'formalistic style', for example, is often perceived as involving rows of silent students listening to an uninterrupted address, delivered in a didactic manner. 'Formal education', in the sense in which it is used in this book, is intended to refer to an approach to teaching characterized by those recognizable structures and processes of an education system that has developed in the UK particularly since the nineteenth century, and the introduction of legislation that made schooling compulsory: colleges, examination boards, qualifications and certificates, and so forth. In particular, formal education seeks to keep in mind the significance of the history of the theory and practice of education in our community. Formal education recognizes the continuity to be perceived within the practices of teaching and its underlying principles.

Thus, when we speak of 'formal education', such as that provided in colleges of FE, we have in mind, for example, institutions, staff, curricula, programmes, community outreach classrooms and virtual learning environments: these are the means associated with the teaching–learning process. The ends with which these means are associated are a direct reflection of views of broad social aims. In these pages, the ends of education, involving its rationale, purpose and objectives, concern human growth, the signs of which include flexibility, openness to new insights, new possibilities, hospitality to novelty, to the imaginative and the creative. The educational activities appropriate to these ends also involve preparing the student to take his or her place in a changing society, a globalized, networked and increasingly local world.

At the same time, we need to be cognisant of 'non-formal' approaches to education and learning (Coffield, 2000). Research into learning in non-formal ways and contexts is of importance in its own right, opening up discussions about how, for example, apprentices learn 'on the job' when no formal intent to teach is present, or what people learn in everyday life and how this relates to what people learn in formal contexts. So, although the focus of this book remains firmly within the learning and skills sector, I wish to foreground the increasingly diverse nature of that sector and the ways in which learning outside colleges relate to learning within them.

Our study of the theory and practice associated with FE begins with a general consideration of the processes of learning and teaching.

Definitions of learning

How should 'learning' be defined? Dictionaries provide a general, if superficial, guide. 'Knowledge acquired by study' is a typical dictionary definition. More specific definitions have come from educational researchers and writers, drawing on a range of theoretical and subject positions: psychology, social psychology, sociology and anthropology. The following are examples.

(a) Any activities that develop new knowledge and abilities in the individual who carries them out, or else cause old knowledge and abilities to acquire new qualities (Galperin, 1965).

(b) A process of reorganization of sensory-feedback patterning which shifts the learner's level of control over his own behaviour in relation to the objects and events of the environment (Smith and Smith, 1966).

(c) The process by which an activity originates or is changed through reacting to an encountered situation, provided that the characteristics of the change in activity cannot be explained on the basis of native response tendencies, maturation or temporary states of the organism (e.g. fatigue, drugs, etc.)' (Bower and Hilgard, 1981).

(d) A change in human disposition or capability, which persists over a period of time, and which is not simply ascribable to the process of growth (Gagné, 1983).

(e) Learning is becoming capable of doing some correct or suitable thing in any situations of certain general sorts. It is becoming prepared for variable calls within certain ranges (Ryle, 1983).

(f) The alteration of behaviour as a result of individual experience. When an organism can perceive and change its behaviour, it is said to learn (*Encyclopaedia Britannica*, 1989).

(g) The acquisition and retention of knowledge and habits of thought in a way that permits them to be employed in a useful way after the initial exposure has been terminated (Saunders and Walstad, 1990).

(h) Learning is an improvized practice, a necessary consequence of participation in social practices, changing not only what people know, but how they speak, act and behave within different social contexts. It leads to permanent changes in not just ability or knowledge, but also identity (Lave and Wenger, 1991).

(i) The active creation of knowledge structures from personal experience (Biehler and Snowman, 1994).

(j) An enduring change in the mechanisms of behaviour involving specific stimuli and/or responses that results from prior experience with similar stimuli and responses (Domjan, 1998).

(k) Learning is any process that in living organisms leads to permanent capacity change, but which is not due solely to ageing or maturation (Illeris, 2007).

Running through definitions of this type are the following key themes: the nature of learning is inferred from changes in behaviour; learning occurs as the result of given experiences which precede changes in behaviour; learning involves behaviour potentiality (that is, the capacity to perform some act at a future time, to be able to repeat something, as contrasted with performance which concerns the translation of potentiality into behaviour); the modification of behaviour involved in learning is of a relatively permanent nature.

For the purposes of this book, we shall consider learning as 'the apparent modification of a person's behaviour through his activities and experiences, so that her or his knowledge, skills and attitudes, including modes of adjustment, towards her or his environment are changed, more or less permanently'.

At this time, it is important to note the occasionally bewildering array of types of learning that is to be found in the literature: formal learning, informal learning, non-formal learning, implicit learning, situated learning, deliberative learning and experiential learning – to name just a few. Different terms such as these tend to rest on particular theoretical perspectives or positions: for example, the term 'experiential learning' is closely tied to the work of Kolb (1984) and Schön (1983); the term 'situated learning' relates to the work of Lave and Wenger (1991) and Wenger (1998). Some of these variations lead to more profound considerations of learning and teaching processes than others, and will be considered in detail in Parts 2 and 3 of this book.

It will be obvious that not all behaviour is learned. The so-called emotional responses that have value to the human being are basically unlearned: a baby's crying is not 'learned' in the sense noted above. Some psychologists speak of 'prepared learning' and 'unprepared learning'. The former category is based on the view that we seem to be prepared in a biological sense for certain types of learning which have a high survival value, such as learning to walk and talk. Unprepared learning involves learning about the world that we live in, such as learning to read – the type of learning which seems not immediately related to survival. Behaviour resulting from unprepared learning has historically been seen to require motivational support in the form of services provided by specialized educational institutions, organized so as to produce effective learning. But other networks of influence – the family, peer groups, snack bars and cafeterias – can also encourage learning in both formal and non-formal ways and we shall need to consider these as we progress through this book.

Definitions of teaching

How then can we define 'teaching'? 'Teaching' tends to be defined in dictionaries as 'the profession of a teacher' (which at least is heartening news for those people who wish to continue to define teaching as a profession). The verb 'teach' is typically defined as 'give systematic information to a person or about a subject or skill'.

There are significantly fewer variants of the terms 'teaching' and 'teach' than there are of 'learning' and 'learn', reflecting the relatively uncontested nature of the practice, although several are extant in the literature (a number of definitions are provided by way of example in the next chapter). How a teacher behaves in the classroom or workshop has, self-evidently, changed over time as a result of not only changing societal, professional and political attitudes to the purpose and conduct of formal education but also the establishment of educational or pedagogic research as a serious component of the academy. It is a simple task to find images of the stereotypical Victorian schoolteacher and to contrast such images with the increasingly varied and fluid spaces that are characteristic of contemporary FE colleges, particularly 'new build' colleges. Despite such changes, definitions of 'teaching' remain constant, although the job role of the teacher has changed over time, to include issues as varied as pastoral care on the one hand, and the management of specific learning difficulties on the other.

Teaching and learning in the classroom

'Teaching' is a relatively uncontested term. 'Learning', by contrast, is problematic, refracted through any number of different theoretical perspectives. These perspectives do not render the definition of 'teaching' troublesome, but do problematize the relationship between 'teaching' and 'learning'. Put simply, how can we know that those activities that we do, or perform, in different parts of our workshops or classrooms 'make' learning happen? What is it that we do as teachers that gets our learners to learn?

Consider these four groups of students, typical of those to be found in a college of FE, engaged in the kinds of activities known as 'the teaching–learning process'.

Group 1: The motor vehicle workshop

The first group that we shall focus on consists of motor vehicle trade apprentices learning the fundamentals of vehicle servicing in preparation for an examination in Vehicle Maintenance and Repair, NVQ Level 2.

This class is being held in the college's motor vehicle workshop, which is equipped with appropriate machinery and tools, typical of the kinds of equipment found in the industry. Visual aids, in the form of charts and pictorial diagrams, are posted on the walls alongside more general college notices. The ten students are gathered round one of the demonstration vehicles and the instructor has explained the topic for the day's lesson – the removal and refitting of exhaust manifolds (these collect the fumes from engine cylinders into a single pipe). The lecturer has reminded the group of the work done in the previous lesson and is proceeding to an explanation of the sequence of practical steps which will constitute the procedure to be taught. 'First, after checking that we have taken appropriate safety measures, we have to disconnect…what? Yes, the battery negative lead. Let's do this. Josh, please disconnect the lead. Next we apply a considerable amount of this penetrating oil to the manifold and exhaust pipe flange nuts and bolts. Watch carefully how this is done… What has to be done next? Think carefully! Nas, can you tell us please… Correct! We unbolt any heat shields or shrouds from the manifold. Here are the necessary tools. Pay attention to how I set about this… Next, from the manifold flange we unbolt…what? Okay, if you are not sure, look at the diagram at the top of the chart on the wall behind you…'

A casual observer of this lesson will see a group of students listening to an instructor and watching his actions. To the trained observer (observations of teaching are a ubiquitous aspect of college life, both for trainees and for qualified staff) there is evidence of a carefully structured teaching–learning situation made up of a group of planned activities and based on an analysis of the separate tasks involved in mastering a series of practical skills. A clear objective has been defined and the sequence of skill activities to be taught has been arranged. A range of hands-on activities have been presented and correct responses have been encouraged and reinforced – the essence of effective instruction. The lesson ends in an innovative manner: the lecturer recapitulates by performing the task in its entirety; the class observes, while a designated student gives directions to the lecturer (who remains silent) and explains what is being done and why the activities have to follow in the particular sequence that has been taught.

Group 2: Law and retail students in the classroom

The second group comprises part-time students preparing for the examinations of the Chartered Institute of Legal Executives (CILEX – historically, legal executives were seen as occupying a lower professional status than solicitors, although recently they have increasingly begun to perform many of the same tasks as solicitors), plus other part-time students who are working towards the NVQ Level 3 in Retail and Management. They are examining problems relating to theft. The two sets of students have been brought together to share discussion of a topic which is of joint concern.

The students have attended two formal lectures on the meaning of 'theft' in law: the CILEX students are concerned with the legal implications of the Theft Act 1968; the other students are interested in the handling of suspected shoplifters. The group has heard a reminder of what is meant in law by 'stealing'. The group tutor then states that the purpose of the session is to examine in greater depth what is meant by 'dishonesty' in law. 'Let's look, first, at this short video,' he begins. 'Keep in mind what we mentioned briefly last week about "dishonest conduct".' The video, stored on the college's network drive, is shown via a data projector, and illustrates the behaviour of a customer in a supermarket: he puts two small items in his pocket and does not pay for them. On leaving the supermarket, he is stopped by a store supervisor. He is then heard telling the supervisor that the goods are of very small value and that he will pay for them there and then. The video is stopped at that point.

The tutor then speaks: 'CILEX students, please choose a spokesperson, form yourselves into a discussion group, and be ready to tell me after a quarter of an hour or so whether you think that the offence of stealing under the 1968 Theft Act can be made out. Retail and management students, please choose a spokesperson and be prepared to tell me how, as store managers, you would deal with the situation which has arisen.'

Whilst the groups are talking, the tutor moves around the classroom, listening attentively but staying silent for the most part other than to answer the occasional specific question or to clarify any point that may be confusing. But when the groups report back, it quickly becomes clear that some of the students have come to conclusions that the tutor had not anticipated. The CILEX group is clear that an offence under the 1968 Act can be made out. But the retail and management group is divided: some suggest that, based on their experience, a firm would not prosecute where items of small value are involved; others say that a firm ought to prosecute in all circumstances. One of the students points out that, in the circumstances, the police might decide not to prosecute. The tutor feels that important matters have been raised and that further discussion is essential if they are to be adequately covered in class. He decides to move away from his planned scheme of work and informs the class that the next session will be devoted to a discussion of the points raised, and, so as to prepare for the discussion, he will distribute via an email attachment and through the college virtual learning environment, a hand-out which will set out key information and provide links for further independent study on the matters which have emerged.

Here may be discerned a prepared scheme of work, based on a variety of teaching and learning strategies, and aimed at involving students in the processes of learning. As the students in both groups are part-time, they are also able to draw on their professional experience during their discussions: indeed, it was a consideration of their real-world experiences that let the retail and management students towards conclusions that their tutor had not anticipated. And in response to these, minor changes to the overall scheme of work will be made where the tutor feels that this is necessary.

Group 3: An A-level economics session

The third group for us to consider is made up of A level students engaged in studying that section of the syllabus in economics which is based on the trade cycle. The lecturer's objective for the session is to make the students aware of a quasi-rhythmical pattern and periodicity of movements in production. A data projector and smartboard is being used to display an excel spread sheet illustrating employment statistics during the second half of the twentieth century. Time has been allowed for observation of the graph, questions have been raised and answered and the teacher is developing the lesson from that point. The precise focus for this part of the lesson is for students to discuss the types of period, which make up the trade cycle. 'Look carefully at the movement of the curve between 1950 and 1990', the lecturer says. 'Note the blue arrows which I am marking in so as to show the peaks in 1959, 1971 and 1983. Note, next, the green arrows which I am using to mark troughs. Which years ought to be marked? Good! Mark them on your graphs. Now we'll watch a short extract from a BBC documentary on "Unemployment and the trade cycle". Pay attention, in particular, to the different definitions of the trade cycle from the two economists, and keep these in mind.'

In this lesson a variety of techniques is employed. Eyes, ears and the associated senses are involved in the process of receiving and interpreting information. Powers of compre-hension and deduction are being exercised and the students are moving – as the result of a deliberate plan formulated by the teacher – to a level of understanding higher than that which existed when the lesson commenced. A short-answer quiz, which the lecturer will distribute towards the end of the lesson, will measure and evaluate that level, so that lecturer and students will be made aware of progress and attainment and, where necessary, the lecturer can revise or revisit themes in future sessions.

Group 4: Health and social care students

The fourth group to be considered comprises ten 14–16 students who are working through an option module, 'social influences on health and wellbeing' as a part of their BTEC First Certificate in Health and Social Care course. The specific topic for this day's session is 'social factors influencing health and wellbeing'. The students have been divided into two groups, and each group is designing a poster presentation, based on research that they have been doing online. Whilst in one of the college PC labs, their tutor has directed the students to look at a small number of websites that she has already evaluated. Now, the students are working on their posters, adding text, drawings and photographs. The class tutor moves among the students, asking questions about the contents of their posters, and evaluating their answers; the tutor also provides additional information and ideas. The group is at times quite chatty, but the tutor is happy to allow a certain level of conversation so long as the students are all continuing to work on the tasks that they have been assignment: only once, when one of the groups is being quite noisy, does she have to intervene and ensure that a more appropriate mode of behaviour is adopted. At the end of the morning session, the posters will be displayed in the health and social care base room, and after lunch each group will talk the other group through their poster.

In this lesson, a range of resources and materials are being used, encouraging the students to develop not only their subject knowledge but also their functional skills in literacy and communication. A planned sequence of activities related to the communication of information – reception, comprehension, retention and retrieval – is the basis of this type of instruction. Classroom management has also been a conspicuous element of this session: here, the tutor has employed a 'light touch' approach, mindful of the fact that an excessively formal or disciplinarian style may well constitute a barrier to participation for a group of younger learners such as these. As long as they continue to work well, she has sensible allowed the groups to talk.

Elements of the teaching–learning process

An analysis of the teaching–learning situations described above will show the existence of the component elements of formal classroom or workshop situations (with which succeeding chapters will be largely concerned). Those elements include the following:

1. Learners or students (the two terms seem to drift in and out of fashion) whose nervous systems, senses and muscles are operating in sequences of patterned activity, which we speak of as *behaviour*.
2. A lecturer or tutor, selecting and organizing instructional methods, consciously planning and controlling a situation directed to the achievement of optimum student learning.
3. Clearly stated session topics, aims or objectives, related to the curriculum being followed and the students' anticipated and desired learning.
4. A sequence of situations affecting teacher and learner, resulting in persistent and observable changes in the learner's behaviour from which we may infer that 'learning' is taking place – differences in how the students speak, what they write, even how they look. That learning is directed by the teacher towards an enhancement of students' knowledge, skills or abilities.
5. Reinforcement of that behaviour. By 'reinforcement' we refer to an activity which increases the likelihood that some event will occur again, such as asking students to repeat elements of tasks, revise their work or explain what they have accomplished to their peers.
6. The monitoring, assessment and evaluation of the learner's changes in behaviour in relation to the aims or objectives of the learning process.

The significance of an analysis of the teaching–learning process for the teacher

The implications of what has been stated above are obviously important for the practising teacher involved in the day-to-day activities of the classroom, laboratory and workshop. Learning – often thought of as a mysterious, incomprehensible event – emerges from the definitions presented above as a very complex process, but one which, nevertheless, lends itself to analysis and which is generally amenable to rigorous and careful techniques of investigation. The activities which may be inferred as having occurred when changes in a learner's behaviour are observed have been made the subject of close and continuous enquiry. It is useful for the practising teacher to be aware of the research and conclusions of researchers in the area of the study of learning and teaching.

It is perfectly possible for teachers and trainers to come to an understanding of the learning process, to generate their own frameworks or models based on both formal study and their own experiences in the classroom or workshop. As such, learning can be planned for in considerable measure, so long as this planning process is aligned to the theories of learning (and, by extension, of teaching and of knowledge) that the teacher holds. The task of the teacher is no longer limited to the imparting of information with the hope that it will be understood in the workshop and replicated under examination conditions. Rather, her or his task has to be seen in terms of planning those conditions and activities and designing or accessing those activities, materials, tools and equipment which will result, as far as possible, in establishing an environment conducive to effective learning. The guidance of the learning process by the teacher, which comes from an analysis of its constituent elements, necessitates a range of activities based on an almost continuous cycle of planning, assessing, evaluating, adjusting and reflecting – specific tasks which are fundamental to successful teaching.

The passing on of information can no longer constitute the teacher's entire responsibility, therefore. Her or his role is understood in this book as also involving responsibility for the vital, interpersonal processes of communication which are at the very centre of the teaching–learning situation. The teacher as communicator figures prominently in some of the chapters which follow. The teacher as manager, with a direct responsibility for the planning and deployment of resources, also features significantly in these pages. And there are many other facets to the teacher's role as well. For many of us working in FE colleges (including outreach and community-based provision), the responsibilities and challenges of the role will often stretch beyond the workshop or classroom and the syllabus that is being followed. Teachers in FE colleges are invariably called up on to act as a first point of contact with any number of questions or problems, ranging from helping students to get to college using public transport, to helping a student who has a specific learning difficulty or disability (such as dyslexia) that has not been properly diagnosed in the past. These wider roles will also form part of our discussions in several of the chapters which follow.

Further reading

As might be imagined, there is a considerable amount of literature on the subject of learning. One of the very best books to explore this topic is:

Illeris, K. (2007), *How We Learn: learning and non-learning in school and beyond*. London: Routledge.
This book is recommended for its scope, its comprehensive coverage and its applicability to learning environments beyond formal schooling (which tend to be overlooked somewhat in more general literature).

Also recommended is:

Jarvis, P., Holford, J. and Griffin, C. (2003), *The Theory and Practice of Learning*. 2nd edition. London: RoutledgeFalmer.
This book lacks the theoretical ambition of the Illeris book, but is similarly broad in scope and provides the reader with a really good, and thorough, background to a variety of theoretical approaches to learning.

2 Defining and Understanding the Practice of Teaching

In this chapter we are going to consider a number of fundamental questions. Is teaching a science, an art, a combination of the two, or something else? How has what we understand 'teaching' to involve or require changed in the postmodern, networked world? What are the ethical dilemmas that surround the role of the teacher? How should we make sense of the position of theory in teaching? These are vital matters for educational theory and practice that have profound implications for not only the training of teachers (which is, of course, the central focus of this book), but also for the benchmarks or criteria that are used for the evaluation of a teacher's performance (which are, perhaps regrettably, beyond the scope of this book). We begin this chapter with a discussion about the relevance and utility of *theories*, which are understood here as suppositions that explain something, or seek to explain it, and provide us, as educators, with the ability and opportunity to explain or understand the findings of research within a conceptual framework (Tight, 2004: 399), and which in this book are positioned as a central and necessary element of professional knowledge and practice.

The relevance and utility of theories

The relevance of theories to teaching practice is not always immediately obvious to teachers. The new lecturer in a FE college, often balancing her or his new post with the demands of an in-service teaching qualification and overwhelmed by new experiences, is often unable immediately to link the reality of the classroom with the theories she or he has learned. The experienced teacher, hard-pressed to maintain standards in the face of difficult administrative decisions, may feel that there is no time for theory conceived at a far, comfortable distance from the workshop or seminar room. Such teachers epitomize those for whom difficulties in accepting theory make the reception and translation of theory into practice impossible. Yet, if teaching is accepted as even a 'partial science', theory cannot be neglected, for no valid science can be constructed without an appropriate theoretical basis. Questions are frequently posed on this topic and we shall consider answers to some of these below:

'Principles', 'axioms', 'theorems', 'hypotheses', 'theories' … What exactly do these terms mean?

These words are often used interchangeably in both books dealing with teaching theory and academic journals reporting the results of educational research, causing under-standable problems for the reader. They can be differentiated, however. A *principle* is a generalization that provides a guide to conduct or procedure, such as the principle that effective teaching demands control of the classroom situation. An *axiom* is a self-evident principle that is, apparently (although not necessarily correctly), not open to dispute, such as the axiom that lack of motivation leads to learning difficulties. A *theorem* is a propo-sition admitting of rational proof which is usually necessary to succeeding steps in some structure of reasoning, such as the theorem that it is possible to test and assess accurately the level of a student's intelligence. *Hypotheses* are unconfirmed assumptions, such as the suggestions that spatial arrangements in a classroom directly affect student learning. A *theory* is a system of ideas attempting to explain a group of phenomena, such as the processes of learning.

Why do teaching theoreticians employ so much jargon? Why can't they use everyday language?

People who use specialized bodies of knowledge tend to generate and use their own technical terminology and reproduce it in books and articles as well as in their speech. Consider, for example, the use of words such as 'energy' in physics, 'market' in economics, 'duty' in jurisprudence. The knowledge on which teaching theory rests is of a highly specialized nature. Psychology, neurology, sociology, history, anthropology and biology have all contributed to teaching–learning theory, and as a result, different expressions and phrases – terminologies – from these disciplines have found their way into the discourses of education researchers and practitioners. And there is good reason for this: it is not easy to substitute 'everyday language' for technical terms and yet maintain acceptable standards of precision of meaning.

Why is there so much fundamental disagreement among teaching–learning researchers and theoreticians? They don't agree even on the meaning of basic terms, such as 'education'.

Teaching is a complex activity, varying outwardly from one situation to another, so that it is not easy to explain or define its nature with precision – hence much of the disagreement. (Try, as an exercise in definition, to bring under one conceptual heading the modes of instruction involved in showing a child how to tie his or her shoelaces, teaching a student the use of a word processor, and explaining to an adult the concept of 'idiom'. Attempt, further, to recall how you 'learned' to tell the time, to use a calculator, to drive a car.) Not all theoreticians and practicing teachers perceive events in the same way; hence, interpretations of events differ. Disagreement is not necessarily a sign of an ineffective, sterile body of knowledge: differences in the interpretation of quantum theory have not prevented great advances in physics. Terms such as 'education' overlap several disciplines, such as the 'inexact sciences' of sociology and political theory, hence the frequent arguments as to its precise meaning. Jurists continue to dispute the very meaning of the term 'law'; economists often disagree as to the meaning of the term 'economics'. Lack of agreement on definitions does not imply total uncertainty within a discipline; it may indicate, rather, the existence of a number of approaches to the areas of knowledge embraced by that discipline.

Some teaching–learning theory seems to be based on the work of writers who lived many centuries ago. Plato, Aristotle, Locke … what relevance have they in an age which they could not have envisaged?

Contemporary educational theory did not spring into existence, fully armed with principles and axioms, in the twentieth century. Today, we as teachers and theoreticians see as sharply as we do, not because of any superior acuity of vision, not because we are wiser than our ancestors, but because, in many areas of theory and practice, we 'stand on their shoulders'. What and how *they* perceived is often interwoven with *our* thought patterns, even though we may be unaware of the debt. Today's practice and theory in educational writing cannot be understood fully without being mindful of ideas rooted in the ancestry of that theory. To provide a simple example: one of the teaching–learning techniques commonly referred to in contemporary textbooks is the *Socratic Dialogue*, (named after the Greek philosopher, who employed this technique in his own teaching), a method designed to allow students to construct meanings for themselves by being led through a series of discussion points by their tutor, who will ask questions and provide feedback in order to guide the conversation in a particular direction.

Do teachers really need theory? Surely teachers simply need to focus on classroom or workshop practice?

The simple answer to the first question is: yes. Indeed, to suggest otherwise arguably demonstrates a fundamental lack of understanding regarding the role and work of the teacher. Teaching is a rich and complex practice, requiring the practitioner to possess not only a body of knowledge that relates to her or his area of subject, craft or trade expertise, but also a further body of knowledge that relates to how this subject should be taught, how it should be reworked and repackaged in order to make it easily understandable to students. Or, to put it another way, teachers need to possess both content knowledge and pedagogical content knowledge (Shulman, 1986). In turn, if teachers are going to be able to translate what they know for their students, then they need to know something about how students learn, what motivates them to learn, and so forth. Once again, if teachers are going to know about, for example, what motivates their students, then they are going to have to understand those factors that create barriers to participation, which might be found in the home life of the student, in the student's own disposition, in the relations that the student has with her or his peers, and so on. Now, it is perfectly possible for teachers to 'pick up' some of this knowledge as they go. But an *ad hoc* approach such as this cannot satisfactorily equip the teacher with the broad bodies of knowledge that she or he needs; nor can it allow the teacher to develop the abilities to enhance their own understanding through further reading or individual classroom research, both of which it turn rest on theory. As a profession, we know what we know because of systematic research – all of which rests to a greater or lesser extent on theory.

'Teachers are born, not made, and theory can never help those who lack the innate talent to teach.' Is there any truth in this statement?

This argument has been used in its time to downgrade and devalue the work of teacher-training institutions, industrial training boards, seminars aimed at the improvement of teaching practice – and books on teaching! There is, however, much evidence to suggest that improved understanding and practice can and do stem directly from instruction in theoretical principles of teaching. The argument rests on an unwarranted belief in the existence of innate qualities of the teacher that cannot be improved through professional learning. The very concept of teaching fundamentals in any subject area as an aid to the comprehension and improvement of practical activity – the successful foundation of many generations of teaching practice – is not compatible with the idea underlying the 'born, not made' aphorism. To carry the idea to its conclusion would be to negate the very concepts of teaching and learning as activities designed to build on, and improve, our genetic inheritance.

Are the principles of teaching and learning as set out in these pages, for example, universally applicable?

This is a rather more difficult issue to unpack. At first look, it seems right to say that people learn in the same way whether they live in countries north of the equator or south of it. But the growth of a body of literature that has explored learning from anthropological and ethnographic perspectives – as distinct from psychological perspectives – has given us food for thought. Thus, if we accept that learning needs to be understood as a social and cultural practice rather than as an individual psychological phenomenon (refer to the chapters in Parts 2 and 3 of this book for more extensive discussions of such approaches), then our understanding of what learning and teaching are become more complicated.

What we mean by 'teaching', or by 'knowledge', can vary across cultural and national boundaries and these variations can be profound. Moreover, current educational research literature that draws on neuroscience, although constituting only a small percentage of research literature more generally, suggests that brain function is influenced by social and environmental factors. So, although research uses a number of conceptual tools in order to establish its wider applicability or *generalizability*, all such claims need to be approached from a critical perspective. The broader academic and intellectual context which this book, and many of the books referred to within, comes from is defined as modern, as scientific, as coming from the 'Western developed world' (whatever that might mean), and this the context in which the theories and frameworks that are explored here need to be positioned and understood.

Definitions of teaching

What do we mean when we talk about 'teaching'? Are we talking about standing and talking in front of a group of students, or helping a group of learners acquire a new sequence of practical skills? Does a one-to-one tutorial count as teaching in the same way as a whole group session does? What about other important aspects of our professional roles, such as uploading resources to a virtual learning environment for distance learners to use? When we create and upload materials to a virtual learning environment, are we teaching?

A typical dictionary definition of 'teaching' might be something like: 'causing a person to learn or acquire knowledge or skill'. The activity of teaching in this context is defined in terms of causation, with some end in view. A selection of more formal definitions drawn from pedagogical literature includes:

(a) intended behaviour for which the aim is to induce learning (Scheffler, 1960)
(b) teaching is aimed at changing the ways in which other persons can or will behave (Gage, 1963)
(c) the group of activities the teacher employs to transform intentions and curriculum materials into conditions that promote learning (Eisner, 1979)
(d) teaching involves implementing strategies that are designed to lead learners to the attainment of certain goals. In general these strategies involve communication, leadership, motivation, discipline and classroom management (Lefrancois, 1985)
(e) teaching is an interpersonal, interactive activity, typically involving verbal communication, which is undertaken for the purpose of helping one or more students learn or change the ways in which they can or will behave (Anderson and Burns, 1989)

(f) teaching is an intentional activity in which opportunities to learn are provided (Jarvis, 2002)

(g) teaching is emotional, chaotic and full of complex uncertainties (Brookfield, 2006)

(h) a teacher's work needs to be understood fundamentally as helping and supporting the learning processes of the students (Illeris, 2007).

Definitions such as these are immediately recognizable. That is to say, the activity that we refer to as 'teaching' is one that we quickly and easily find familiar, in part because we have all in some ways been through formal educational systems, and in part because popular culture is suffuse with images of teachers and teaching in feature films, television programmes and books (Fisher, Harris and Jarvis, 2008). For the purposes of this book we shall define teaching as: *'a system of activities intended to allow learning to happen, comprising the deliberate and methodical creation and control of those conditions in which learning does occur.'* But this is not to deny the potential problematization of the term, not least as debates around the differences between 'teaching', 'on-line teaching', 'training', 'facilitation', 'demonstration' and 'moderation' persist. For example: colleges may employ someone as a 'demonstrator', and therefore pay them less than they would a 'lecturer' or 'tutor', even though much of the actual work done by them in the workshop or lab is 'the same' as that done by the lecturer. Furthermore, the growth of e-learning and blended learning creates additional problems: if all of your contact with your students were to be via a virtual learning environment (VLE), would you still be 'a teacher'?

It should also be noted, therefore, that teaching needs to be understood as a *system* of activities, not a single action. Teaching assumes its distinctive character and meaning not in patterns of isolated behaviour but in sequences of interrelated activities, carefully constructed and sequenced by the teacher, and designed in such a way to afford students a series of opportunities to talk about, try out or practise using or manipulating the tools, models, concepts or equipment that the subject under discussion requires them to be able to use in order to demonstrate knowledge, competence, proficiency and understanding.

Teaching: Is it an art or a science?

Discussion with almost any group of practising teachers in a FE college or adult education centre will reveal fundamental differences of opinion on the classification of 'teaching' as an art or science. Some will insist that teaching involves a scientific application of tested theory; some will argue that it is essentially a performance on the 'classroom stage' that can be characterized as aesthetic, so that it has to be considered as a form of art (Lowman, 1984). Others will maintain that it is a hybrid, an art with a scientific basis, or a science with overtones of artistic impression; some will reject the concept of 'art' and 'science' having any place in the purely practical, day-to-day teaching activity in the colleges. And yet others will be amazed to learn that their teaching activities can be classified as either science or art in the first place!

If you observed a series of teaching activities in a typical college of FE you would almost certainly see a variety of approaches. At one level, these differences might of course be rooted in the discipline being observed: different subjects need to be taught differently, as the subject matter demands. At another level, however, these differences might be understood as being somehow bound up in the particular approach, beliefs or philosophy of the teacher.

The distinction between teaching as art and science is typified in the approaches of Highet (1977), Eisner (1979) and Skinner (1968). Highet was vehement in his denunciation of the unthinking application of the aims and methods of science to learners as individuals. For him, this has to be seen as a dangerous tendency: a 'scientific relationship' between human beings must of necessity be inadequate. So-called 'scientific teaching' will be inadequate as long as both teachers and pupils are human beings.

Eisner (1979) enumerated four senses in which teaching could be considered an art. First, it is an art in the sense that the teacher can perform with such skill and grace that for teacher and student alike the performance provides an intrinsic form of expression – the lesson has the overtones of an aesthetic experience. Secondly, teaching is an art in the sense that teachers in their professional work must exercise qualitative judgements in the interest of achieving qualitative ends. Classroom qualities such as tempo, tone, climate, pace of discussion and forward movement require the exercise by the teacher of quali-tative forms of intelligence. Thirdly, teaching, like any other art, involves a tension between routine and inventiveness. The teacher has to use his or her repertoires and routines in an innovative way so as to deal inventively and intuitively with what happens in class. Finally, teaching is an art in the sense that many of its ends are essentially emergent – they are not preconceived; they emerge in the course of interaction with students.

Such approaches adopt a perspective that contradicts behaviourist, learning-outcomes focussed approaches to teaching and learning. Skinner, a neobehaviourist theorist, argued that successful teaching can be the result only of the conscious and judicious application of scientifically validated theory to classroom situations. Successful teaching does not happen fortuitously; it emerges when the teacher has made, and interpreted, a correct analysis of student behaviour in terms of the complex interplay of elementary concepts and principles. When behaviour is understood, an appropriate instructional methodology must be sought in order that it might be modified where necessary on the basis of desired ends. On the practising teacher and the scientist investigating classroom behaviour will fall the joint tasks of observing fact, formulating theory, applying it and then reinterpreting both fact and theory. Indeed, in his novel *Walden Two*, Skinner moved beyond the classroom and theorized about how his ideas might be applied to wider social settings.

Rather like the argument that teachers are 'born, not made', the 'teaching as science or art' argument rests on a number of assumptions that are mistaken at best and false at worst. Firstly, there is the notion that to describe something as a 'science' serves to imbue it with particular characteristics such as 'rigour' and 'neutrality', as being 'based on irrefutable evidence', which therefore renders findings or conclusions 'correct' or at least 'inarguable'. But such characteristics tend to derive from popular misconceptions of scientific practice and do not reflect the reality of scientific inquiry, which – on closer look – is much messier than popular opinion might have us believe. Secondly, there is the notion that to describe something as an 'art' renders it somehow immune to systematic and rigorous (which are not the same as 'scientific') inquiry, development or theorization. People who work in the arts – graphic designers or musicians, for example – do not simply come into the world fully formed: they have to practice, to learn their craft, to understand the history, the ideas and the traditions that underpin and inform their own work.

Fundamental to this book, therefore, is the belief that the practice of teaching ought to move to a position in which it can be seen as based openly on an application of theory reflecting the reality of the classroom and its environment; such theory and practice ought to be subjected to continuous, severe criticism. The critical, methodical appraisal of teaching principles and practice, informed by a similarly critical reading of research literature, would seem to be a prerequisite for the construction of a comprehensive theory of teaching. One thing, however, is almost certain – teaching, because of its very nature, can never be an *exact* practice, not least as the exact relationship *between* what we do in seminar rooms and workshops – teach – and what our students do – learn – is difficult to define.

Teaching styles

If we allow for the fact that teaching is an inexact practice, then it stands to reason that what we call teaching can happen in different ways. That is to say, different teachers can do different things in their workshops or seminar rooms, but it will all still count as teaching. At one level, these different kinds – or styles – of teaching practice will rest on the particular theoretical perspectives that the teacher in question subscribes to. Teachers who align themselves to a *neobehaviourist* theoretical perspective (as discussed in Chapter 4) will plan, prepare and practice in the classroom in a quite different way to those teachers who subscribe to a *communities of practice* perspective (as discussed in Chapter 10). The nature of the curriculum provides a further variable when considering the style that a teacher adopts. Some subjects or topics necessarily – and naturally – lend themselves to particular kinds or styles of learning activity, which in turn will require particular styles of teaching. A teacher's style of teaching might also be based on more nebulous factors such as personal preference or even personality.

This book is not arguing that teaching styles constitute a theory any more than learning styles can be seen as being a robust theory (which it categorically is not (Coffield et al., 2004)). But one useful way of thinking about teaching styles is from the point of view of *metaphor* (a device which is used to a significant extent in educational research and writing). Perhaps the best series of metaphors to describe the different styles that a teacher might adopt come from Apps (1991), although we have to remember that any individual teacher may combine different elements of style or move from one style to another when appropriate:

(a) lamplighters – teachers who seek to enlighten their students
(b) gardeners – teachers who grow the minds of their students by providing nourishment, controlling the climate and removing weeds; once everything has been prepared, they can sit back and watch them grow
(c) muscle builders – teachers who provide exercise for unfit minds
(d) bucket fillers – teachers who pour knowledge into empty containers
(e) challengers – teachers who question the assumptions that their students bring with them to class
(f) travel guides – teachers who help their students negotiate pathways to learning
(g) supervisors – teachers who monitor the processes of learning, both inputs and outputs
(h) artists – teachers who see learning as an artistic process
(i) applied scientists – teachers who plan their teaching through the application of educational research
(j) craftspeople – teachers who use a variety of skills.

We shall find as we proceed that the metaphors that Apps offers to us are identifiable from a theoretical perspective as well as from the perspective of everyday experience. Apps' metaphor of a teacher as a gardener, carefully tending to young green saplings that will eventually grow into strong and self-sufficient trees, is not so far removed from another metaphor used to refer to a particular theoretical perspective: the teacher providing both the scaffolding and tools that a student needs to be able, eventually, to work independently. As the student develops and learns how to use their tools, the teacher does not need to provide so much scaffolding support until, eventually, the student stands by themselves. This is – in an admittedly simplified form – an account of the teaching–learning process that rests on the theories of Lev Vygotsky (as discussed in Chapter 8).

So what is meant by 'teaching style', if indeed it means anything? Perhaps the most thorough recent account of teaching styles is provided by Jarvis (2006), who proposed a number of styles of teaching, each resting on particular theoretical perspectives:

(a) didactic teaching styles, based on formal lecturing

(b) Socratic teaching styles, based on two-way dialogues between teachers and students that are designed to reveal the knowledge and understanding of the latter

(c) facilitator-style teaching, based on creating environments in which students can have a voice in the direction and pace of their learning

(d) experiential teaching, based on giving value to and accounting for the experiences of students as resources for learning

(e) mentor-style teaching, based on nurturing processes that allow the student to grow and develop at their own pace.

Categorizations such as these certainly allow us to think more critically about what we mean when we talk about teaching, but rarely do they allow us to divorce the idea of 'teaching' from the idea of 'learning'. The five perspectives listed above (which, like Apps' metaphors, are not necessarily meant to indicate approaches to teaching that are mutually exclusive) only make sense if they are considered in tandem with a relational theory of learning. Thus, as we proceed through an exploration of several different theoretical approaches to learning, beginning in the chapter that follows this one, different implications for the role of the teacher, in relation to the theoretical approach in question, will emerge.

The ethics and problematics of teaching

A consideration of the *purpose* of education might at first glance seem to be outside the scope of this book. Such a conversation would encompass a range of philosophical and political topics and controversies. Indeed, the philosophy and politics of educational structures constitute complete academic disciplines in themselves. But to attempt to ignore the broader political issues that surround the role of the teacher is difficult if not impossible, not least as there is so much interference by politicians in the working lives of teachers and trainers in the FE sector – a pace of political change that has in the past been described as endless (Edward et al., 2007), and which in recent years has shown no sign of slowing down – a pace of change reflected by the changes made to the various government departments and other regulatory or funding bodies that are responsible for different aspects of education and training within the sector. And at the same time, wider philosophical debates are readily identifiable at a day-to-day level. For example, the ways in which colleges are influenced by free market models, in terms of funding and management, might be explored through a consideration of *neoliberal* ideologies in education.

The ethics of teaching are similarly complex, and similarly visible within the workshop or seminar room with the application of a critical perspective. Debates around the ethics of teaching range from issues around duty of care (which includes not only more 'obvious' issues such as safeguarding but also more nuanced problems such as the extent to which teachers might challenge the existing knowledge and understanding of their students) to issues around the broader *purposes* of education. If, as teachers, we understand education to be a vehicle for meaningful and critical social emancipation, such a perspective would undoubtedly influence our attitudes towards widening participation initiatives and other similar outreach programmes. If, by contrast, we understood education to be a vehicle for social and cultural reproduction, we might instead feel that the educational structures that we work within served to restrict and diminish, rather than widen, the opportunities available to the students with whom we work.

Such debates might seem to be abstract at best, but to dismiss them as such would be a mistake. It is in fact entirely reasonable, and quite believable, to imagine the practice of adult education tutors as being informed by a broader commitment to the educational, social and economic welfare of their students rather than by a simple desire to report high levels of student retention and achievement in an annual evaluation report. Lecturers working with young offenders or with prisoners (many if not all of whom engage with formal programmes of study during their periods of incarceration) are self-evidently working within a professional and ethical framework that is rather different from that occupied by a lecturer who is working with 'mainstream' 16–19 students in a FE college. Is the critically aware, reflexive lecturer who considers that the students with whom she or he is working are not necessarily best suited to the course that they have been offered merely being cynical when suggesting that the work-related skills of a group of diploma students are not being sufficiently developed, or is she or he in fact making a legitimate point regarding the nature of the curriculum in the learning and skills sector at a time of recession?

This book is not a philosophical work; nor does it deal extensively with the ethics of teaching. But this book rests in part on the notion that the themes and problems such as those outlined above are unavoidable, and as such they need to make themselves felt in the text from time to time.

Teaching in a postmodernist world

The final theme to be considered in this chapter concerns the ways in which teaching, as a necessary component of education, might be understood from a postmodernist perspective. A critical exploration of postmodernism would require a entire book in its own right, but here can be usefully (albeit briefly) summarized as an intellectual movement that challenges dominant explanations and theories, and distrusts ideologies, drawing critical attention to conventional modes of explanation.

A challenge to the primacy of the teacher in the classroom would be symptomatic of the postmodern culture of the present (in which both institutions and individuals in authority are almost routinely problematized). Put simply: what is the point of the teachers and on what foundations does the authority of the teacher rest? If a student was to challenge a teacher over a point of knowledge or application of skill, should such a challenge need to be considered as a behaviour management issue or as an example of a meaningful, and therefore legitimate, critique of the teacher's role more generally? To put it simply (and rather crudely), the expertise and hence authority of the teacher is only a Wikipedia search away from being overturned.

Autodidacts – people who teach themselves everything there is to know about a subject through extensive reading and private study – are not a new phenomenon, but the ease with which people are able to access considerable bodies of knowledge and scholarship through the use of appropriate technology (a laptop computer, a smartphone or a tablet) has had a profound impact on formal educational systems and structures. This is not to say that traditional modes of scholarship are now no longer valued (any reader who doubts this should try submitting a PGCE/CertEd assignment with no references other than from Wikipedia), but the body of knowledge which, in part, the historic authority of the teaching profession rested on can now be seen to be much more widely distributed.

If subject knowledge is now no longer the exclusive preserve of the teacher, then what is? Where, and on what basis, does the expertise and authority of the teacher reside? Drawing on the work of Shulman (1986), the argument presented in this book is that it is in what Shulman referred to as *pedagogical content knowledge* and *curricular knowledge*. If content knowledge is what teachers know about their subject or area of competence or expertise (for example accountancy, electrical installation or horticulture), then pedagogical context knowledge is a variation of this, and refers to the ways in which teachers translate their content knowledge into a form that can then be taught to their students. *Curricular knowledge* allows teachers to make meaningful links between the courses or programmes that they work with, and the wider curriculum that their students are exposed to as a consequence of their participation in formal education and training systems. For Shulman – and for this book – it is in pedagogical content knowledge and curricular knowledge, which therefore should be at the centre of all teacher-training curricula, that the professional expertise and authority of the teacher reside.

Summary

The role of the teacher has quite clearly changed over time, and this should not cause any surprises or upsets. In a culture where information is more readily available than ever before, the position of the teacher as the fount of all knowledge is clearly untenable. Similarly, in a culture where theories of learning, and by extension of teaching, are many and varied, it might seem that to study such theories would be a needless task. This book takes the opposing view, and argues that the study of theory is an essential element of the professional development and knowledge of the teacher. It is through a critical and theoretical understanding of why the work of the teacher is what it is, that properly informed perspectives on learning, on assessment and on curriculum emerge. The exact relationship between teaching and learning may continue to be a point for speculation, but this is not the same as saying that such speculation should be discouraged or avoided. Teaching is sometimes a complex and difficult task, but it is also a rewarding one: it should not be a surprise to learn that the study of teaching is also sometimes complex, and sometimes rewarding as well.

Further reading

The theory and practice of teaching has been an established area of philosophical and scholarly enquiry for many centuries. Perhaps the best single book that provides an account of different modes of teaching, as well as something of the theory and philosophy that underpins them, is:

Jarvis, P. (ed.) (2006), *The Theory and Practice of Teaching*. Second edition. London: Routledge.

Theories of Learning: Psychological Perspectives

3 Behaviourism

The chapters that are presented in this section of the book, and the section which follows, all provide different approaches to the deceptively simple question: *how do we learn?* In Part 2 of this book, we shall draw on *psychology*, defined by William James, in 1890, as the science of mental life, both of its phenomena and of their conditions; it is concerned with what James refers to as 'feelings, desires, cognitions, reasoning and the like'. Its study has produced a variety of approaches to the phenomenon of the mind, and it has given rise to several well-established schools of thought. In this section of the book, we shall explore the following schools of learning theory:

- *Neobehaviourism*. Psychologists who believe that behaviour is generally purposive in that it is directed to a goal are known as 'neobehaviourists': they seek to study how behaviour, often directed by anticipations of consequences based on past experiences, can be related to the nature of goals to be sought and the means to attain those goals.

- *Gestalt theory*. The significance of organized forms and patterns in human perception and learning constitutes the main concern of the Gestaltists. The very essence of learning is to be found in an understanding of relationships within organized entities of thought.

- *Cognitivism*. Cognitive psychology is concerned with the various mental activities which result in the acquisition and processing of information by the learner. Its theories involve a perception of the learner as a purposive individual in continuous interaction with his social and psychological environment.

- *Humanism*. Humanistic psychology calls for a quality of teaching which allows students to make conscious choices in an environment characterized by 'freedom'. Concern for human values and 'authentic relationships' among teachers and students features in the humanistic approach, which is directed to spontaneity, creativity, mental health and self-fulfilment.

And in this chapter, we shall begin with:

- *Behaviourism*. This involves a mechanistic, materialistic view of psychology, involving a close study of observable, objectively measurable behaviour. It teaches that the explanation, prediction and control of behaviour are possible without reference to concepts involving 'consciousness'.

Behaviourism

Classical behaviourism was essentially a reaction against theories based largely on data derived from introspection (that is to say, subjects' verbal reports of their reactions and perceptions). Behaviourists insisted on the necessity to discard introspection in favour of a study of *the objectively observable actions* of persons. In this way the science of psychology would become an 'objective experimental branch of natural science'.

Several interlocking concepts were common to the research writings associated with the development of behaviourism in its heyday around 1913–35.

1 Consciousness, mind, mental states were examples of ideas that were to be rejected *because they could not be verified*. The early behaviourists rejected mind–body dualism, saying that the problems of human nature could be explained in *purely mechanistic terms*.

2 The philosophy of reductionism, which suggested that human activities could be explained in terms of the *behavioural responses of the lower animals* (such as rats and dogs), was seen as offering a valuable approach to the solution of problems involving human behaviour.

3 All behaviour was to be investigated and understood solely in the context of *responses to stimuli*. Hence the behaviour known as 'learning' might be defined in terms of changes in responses made to stimuli on the basis of the learner's past experiences.

4 The circumstances in which stimuli become linked to overt responses must be a key subject for study. Hence the process of *conditioning*, whereby relationships of responses to stimuli are modified in order to change behaviour, is also an important subject for investigation.

5 Behaviour might be explained as a *function of environmental influences*.

6 The methodology of behaviourism required a *formal, quantitative basis* if scientific method (as it was understood at the time) were to characterize psychology.

7 Behaviourism in its early stages has as its objective the *prediction and control* of human behaviour.

Pavlov, Watson, Thorndike, Guthrie and Hull were writers and researchers who all made very important contributions to the behaviourist school, and the key ideas of each are considered in turn below.

Pavlov

Pavlov (1849–1936), the celebrated Russian physiologist, was primarily interested in the circulation of the blood and the processes of the gastro-intestinal system. The study of the nervous systems of animals led Pavlov to methods of investigation from which he discovered the techniques of the *conditioning of behaviour*. On the basis of these techniques was erected a new structure of the investigation of aspects of human behaviour and, in particular, the study of aspects of the learning process. For Pavlov, *all* human learning is due to conditioning. 'Conditioning' is a process whereby the behaviour of an animal becomes dependent on the presence of environmental stimuli; learning will involve, therefore, a large number of conditioned responses. His work on the process of conditioning continues to rank very high in the list of contributions made by scientists to an understanding of learning.

According to Pavlov, so-called 'mental phenomena' could be dealt with objectively and scientifically only if it were possible to reduce them to observable, measurable physi-ological quantities. Behaviour in all its varieties was, according to Pavlov, essentially *reflexive*; it was determined by specific events. *Unconditioned* reflexes or responses were inborn types of nervous activity, transmitted by inheritance. But *conditioned* reflexes or responses were acquired by an organism during its life; they were not normally inheritable, according to Pavlov. Human beings learn as the result of *conditioning*, and it was this hypothetical process which formed the basis of Pavlov's research.

The process of conditioning studied by Pavlov was derived from the results of his well-known investigation into salivation in dogs. Pavlov inverted the parotid salivary gland of a dog so that its secretions could be accumulated in a cannula (calibrated glass) and measured externally. The animal was placed in a harness and then presented with a stimulus such as the sound of a metronome, bell or tuning fork. Initially, the sound did not seem to elicit any observable response. Later, a powdered meat was presented to the dog after a short interval of time following the sound and its salivary fluid was collected and measured. After further trials, in which the sound of the metronome or bell was invariably followed by the presentation of food, the sound alone produced an *anticipatory salivary response*. The dog had learned that a meal followed the sound of the bell.

This conditioning process was seen by Pavlov as a possible explanation of certain aspects of the organization of behaviour. Most environmental stimuli can become condi-tioned stimuli with direct effects on behaviour. The techniques of conditioning, it was suggested, could be applied to the training of human beings. Human behaviour might be amenable to the process of moulding on the basis of the controlled establishment of conditioned responses.

Pavlov's work and the teacher

The mere suggestion that Pavlov's work might have positive lessons for the practice of classroom instruction is rejected firmly by many teachers. Research derived from experiments on animals should, it is argued, have no application whatsoever to human learners. The atmosphere of the animal laboratory is, and must remain, a world away from that of the classroom and the purposes of the activities therein. Further, it is felt by many that the entire concept of conditioning, with its all-too-familiar connection with 'brain-washing' (that is, the deliberate influencing of behaviour patterns in persons so as to make them conform to the demands of a political ideology), must have no place in educational activity. The freedoms which must characterize the classroom are incompatible with the philosophy and technology associated with conditioning.

Others, however, see in Pavlov's work a possibility of evolving techniques which, when refined, can be used consciously and conscientiously to shape human intellectual development – an important objective of teaching activity. The excesses of those who have deliberately misused conditioning techniques ought not to be advanced, it is argued, as reasons for forbidding the use in all circumstances of some of those techniques. For Pavlov, learning was inseparable from association; hence, *what* teachers do, *how* they do it, in what *surrounding circumstances* and to what *ends* become significant for the study of instruction.

Environmental stimuli provided *intentionally and unintentionally* by the teacher's performance in the process of instruction may become associated with undesired responses – the authoritarian instructor who arouses a dislike for his subject area and, in so doing, conditions students to a permanent dislike for closely associated subject matter, is an example. The moral for the teacher seems clear: ensure as far as possible that stimuli provided by teaching performance become associated with appropriate and desired positive responses by students. This means considering the lesson, its planning and delivery, in all its aspects, as a totality.

Watson

Watson (1878–1958), professor of experimental and comparative psychology at Johns Hopkins University, Maryland, began his career as a researcher into animal behaviour. Psychology, according to Watson, ought to be a purely objective, experimental branch of natural science, and concepts such as 'sensations' and 'feelings' were to be cast aside. The concept of memory was also rejected by Watson; instead of using the term, a behaviourist should speak of how much skill has been retained and how much has been lost in a period of no practice. The principal method of study should be *objective observation and experimentation*. This required a new vocabulary from which subjective terminology would be eliminated; references to 'introspectively observable phenomena', such as sensation, thought and intention, which were said to intervene between stimulus and reaction, would disappear.

According to Watson, human beings are born with some few reflexes and emotional reactions, but no 'instincts'; all other behaviour is the result of building new stimulus–response (S-R) connections. Habit formation may be analyzed in terms of constituent units of conditioned reflexes. Learning, as an aspect of human behaviour, can be studied in terms of the formation of connections in the learner's muscle groups. When stimuli and responses occur *at the same time*, their interconnections are strengthened and the eventual strength of the connection will depend largely upon the *frequency* of their occurring together. A stimulus produces activity in a part of the brain, and a response emerges as the result of activity in some other part; stimulus–response neural pathways are strengthened when the two parts of the brain are simultaneously activated. But learning produces no new connections in the brain – they exist already, as part of the learner's genetic constitution, and learning may merely make functional a connection that has been latent. Hence our behaviour, personalities and emotional dispositions are all *learned* behaviours. The human being is no more than the sum of his or her experiences.

Given this analysis, conditioning was seen as fundamental to learning. The conditioning of the learner through environment and experiences, in which the teacher may actively intervene, is the central process in the building of habits, and will determine his or her acquired patterns of behaviour. Heredity and instincts counted for little in Watson's scheme as contributions to human behaviour. Learning becomes an all-important factor in the development and modification of an individual's behaviour.

Watson embodied Pavlov's findings into his theory of learning. Watson believed that young children had no reason to fear animals. In a famous experiment involving conditioning, he showed an 11-month-old child some tame white rats, an experience which the child apparently enjoyed. Later, a rat was presented shortly after a loud noise which frightened the child. After several repetitions of the experience the child showed fear of the rat even in the absence of the distressing noise. Fear was displayed also in the presence of other furry objects. Watson showed later that, by feeding the child with his or her favourite dishes, and introducing the feared animal very gradually into the background and then into the child's direct view, the fears could be extinguished.

Watson's work and the teacher

The behaviourism propagated by Watson and others who share his views has become an object of unceasing criticism by psychologists and teachers. His work is said to have suffered from an absence of data and over-generalization. It has been condemned as reductionism which reduces the complexities of human development to mechanistic, deterministic and over-simplified formulae.

Others, however, view the behaviourists' emphasis on the significance of environment and experience as stressing the *positive role of the teacher*. The possibility of the student being conditioned to respond favourably to the circumstances in which he learns – his class environment, his instructor, the content and overtones of the lesson – reminds the teacher of *the importance of planning the learning environment and lesson content with care*. Each part of the lesson ought to be examined in the teaching-planning stage, and evaluated during class activity, as a contributory factor to the eliciting of those responses which make up desirable criterion behaviour. 'What type of response will be elicited from my students as the result of my teaching activity?' Questions of this nature ought to be posed by the teacher in the preparatory stages of a lesson, and the answers ought to affect subsequent lesson content and development.

Teachers in FE ought not to forget the possibility of students' attitudes to their lessons being formed as a result of the conditioning process of which Watson wrote: stories of students who feel dislocated or even hostile to formal learning provision as a result of earlier, negative experiences at school are all too common. Watson's work can also act as a reminder to the FE teacher in turn to take particular care to avoid creating, intentionally or unintentionally, the anxieties and hostility which may emerge later as a wide, fixed response to formal instruction of any type.

Thorndike

Thorndike (1874–1949) was one of the dominant personalities for many years in the study of learning. Almost all his professional life was spent on the staff of a teacher training college. His output was prodigious: a recently compiled list of his works showed more than 500 titles. His main interest was animal psychology and, in particular, intelligence, learning and understanding. The basis of Thorndike's approach to problems of behaviour lay in his beliefs that behaviour and, therefore, learning were explicable through an understanding of the bonds between stimulus and response. The task of the psychologist was to discover how those bonds are created.

Thorndike's theories emerged largely from experiments with cats, chicks, dogs and monkeys, but he believed that some universal laws of behaviour could be derived from that work. A human being, in his view, differed from the other animals only in degree and merely in the *number and frequency* of the associations that s/he develops between environment and her/his corresponding reaction. Human superior intelligence was little more than a reflection of the capacity to form stimulus–response bonds. Degrees of human intelligence were quantitative, not qualitative, and signified varying speeds of bond formation; the more intelligent person has more bonds at her/his disposal to enable her/him to deal with problems.

Thorndike's contribution to the theory of learning may be summarized by a statement of his major and subsidiary laws. The *law of effect* was defined thus: an act which results in an animal experiencing satisfaction in a given situation will generally become associated with that situation, so that when it recurs the act will also be likely to recur. Thorndike defined satisfaction as a state of affairs which the animal does nothing to avoid, often doing things which maintain or renew it. The opposite state of affairs is one which the animal does nothing to preserve, often doing things which put an end to it. An act which results in discomfort tends to be dissociated from the situation, so that when the situation recurs, the act will be less likely to recur. The greater the satisfaction or discomfort experienced, the greater the degree to which the stimulus–response bond will be strengthened or loosened. Pleasurable effects, therefore, tend to stamp in associations and unpleasant effects tend to stamp them out.

According to the *law of exercise*, a response to a situation will generally be more strongly connected with that situation in proportion to the number of times it has been so connected and to the average strength and duration of the connections. Regular exercise or practice therefore strengthens the bond between situation and response (for example, in repeating times tables or formulae in order to 'learn' them 'off by heart'.) This law, too, was later modified when Thorndike announced that it was of minor importance. The *law of readiness* suggests that a learner's satisfaction is determined by the extent of their readiness of action; this refers to the dependence of the rate with which a connection is developed or the extent to which it corresponds to the learner's current state.

The *law of multiple response* states that a response which fails to produce satisfaction will trigger off another until success results and learning becomes possible. According to the *law of set*, learning is affected by the individual's total attitude or disposition; hence a student's cultural background and present environment are of importance in determining her or his responses. What the learner brings to the learning situation is significant. The *law of selectivity of response* suggests that as a person learns, so she or he becomes capable of ignoring some aspects of a problem and responding to others. The *law of response by analogy* emphasizes that a person's response to a novel situation is determined by innate tendencies to respond, and by elements in similar situations to which she or he has acquired responses in the past. The *law of associative shifting* suggested that a learner responds first to a given stimulus, then she or he may *transfer* the response by association to a different stimulus which acquires the capacity to elicit the same response.

Thorndike's work and the teacher

Thorndike's theories have been criticized as crude and over-simplified. In particular, his stimulus–response bond explanation of the basis of learning has been condemned as a mechanical and restricted interpretation of some few aspects of the complexities of human behaviour. His *law of effect* has been criticized on the grounds that it pays no attention to the internal information processing which must be going on during the learning event. The law is too vague about the temporal conditions involved. It seems to ignore the causal relationship which must exist between actions and outcome. The role of insight in learning seems to have been rejected.

Criticism has been directed against those aspects of Thorndike's work which were derived specifically from his experimental work with monkeys. The fallacy of attributing higher cognitive functions to animals has been noted repeatedly by those who warn against interpretations of animal behaviour that attempt to transfer such findings to humans. Thorndike, it has been argued, was much given to far-ranging extrapolations of his animal studies which, in the event, vitiated the force of his theories concerning *human* responses to stimuli.

Many psychologists and teachers, however, see Thorndike's work as that of an important pioneer, mapping a route for others who followed. Thorndike's general view of the relationship of psychology to teaching is significant. He viewed psychology as part of the necessary basis of a scientific approach to the practice of teaching, and there is much in Thorndike's work which is of relevance to the day-to-day tasks of the class teacher. Its emphasis on the significance of the stimulus–response bond reminds the teacher of the importance of viewing *all* his activities (intended and otherwise) as contributions to the learning process. An orderly classroom, learning objectives based on progress from simple to complex concepts with appropriately sequenced assessments and a 'dominant' teacher using positive control, would characterize a Thorndike-type teaching-learning situation. It should resemble the real world outside the classroom as far as possible: it should accommodate the teaching of skills which will be useful outside the classroom, and which will reflect the stimuli and responses of the wider world. Lesson planning, instructing and evaluation of attainment emerge in the light of Thorndike's analysis as related directly to those responses which make up learning. Assessment and feedback must be swift, so that a student's incorrect responses to certain stimuli may be corrected in order that they will not be reinforced by practice.

Thorndike's *law of effect*, which stressed external reward as a more effective factor than punishment in the modification of a learner's behaviour, has an obvious lesson for the teacher. Further, the *law of exercise* suggests the importance of 'doing' and of repetition in the learning process, remembering that repetition without reinforcement will not enhance learning. The *law of readiness* stresses the importance of preparation for learning and serves to remind the class teacher of the vital part played in the learning process by *motivation* and of her or his responsibility for the strengthening of a student's readiness to learn. A student's interest in their work, and in improvement, can be conducive to learning; significance of subject matter to the student can affect that interest. The need for learners to be flexible in their approach and the value of learning through trial and error emerge from Thorndike's *law of multiple response*. The *law of selectivity of response* underlines the importance of arranging instruction so that students can discriminate among lesson components on the basis of selective attention.

Learning is incremental, says Thorndike. It occurs in small steps rather than in large jumps; it is direct and not mediated by reasoning in the form of ideas. The technique of attempting to instruct by mere lecturing can be unproductive and the commonest error of the inexperienced teacher is to expect pupils to know immediately what they have been told.

Guthrie

Guthrie (1886–1959) was professor of psychology at the University of Washington. He had been influenced by philosophical writings which suggested that a number of the more important problems concerning 'mind' could be translated into concepts of behaviour and comprehended accordingly. His definitive work was *The Psychology of Learning* (1935). Learning, said Guthrie, could be defined as the alteration in behaviour that results from experience. Observable and nameable events have to be studied in order to understand learning. In particular, knowledge of the fundamentals of learning required an awareness of the nature and interplay of stimuli and responses.

Guthrie's theory of learning is based on the concept of there being one kind of learning only, and on one general principle, that of *simultaneous contiguous conditioning*: if someone does something in a given situation, the next time they are in that situation they will tend to do the same thing again. Whether the response emerges as the result of an unconditioned stimulus or in any other way is of no matter, according to Guthrie. Provided that the conditioned stimulus and reaction occur together (that is to say, in contiguity), learning will take place.

In order to explain what happens when stimuli precede responses (so that they are *not* in contiguity), Guthrie proposed the concept of movement-produced stimuli (MPS). The presentation of a stimulus elicits a *miniature* response which in turn acts as a stimulus for another response, and so on until finally an *observable* response is elicited, demonstrating that learning has taken place.

A further law states that a stimulus pattern gains its full associative strength on the occasion of its first pairing with a response. The implications of this are clear: reinforcement plays no part in the learning process, and practice adds nothing to the strength of the stimulus–response bond, which is of the all-or-nothing type. A bond is there or not there, and no intermediate variation in its strength can be inferred. In answer to the comment that 'practice makes perfect' (a phenomenon that we have all witnessed, even if we cannot necessarily theorize it), Guthrie's response would be that all that practice can do is to ensure that a response will occur under a *variety* of differing circumstances. Mere repetition is futile if the stimuli are the same from one test to another.

Forgetting is interpreted by Guthrie as a case of the failure of response to a cue. The teacher can presumably make forgetting happen by creating a situation in which the student makes a new response to the same set of stimuli. Once she or he has made the new response, the student replaces the old response with the new response. Forgetting is not, therefore, a passive fading of stimulus–response associations over time, but requires *active unlearning*, which consists of learning to do something else in the circumstances. Put simply, all forgetting must involve new learning.

Guthrie's work and the teacher

Guthrie has not escaped the general criticisms levelled at behaviourists. Critics point to the real-life complexities of behaviour, particularly in the classroom, and argue that such behaviour is not explained satisfactorily by contiguity theory. (Guthrie stressed the importance of practising acquired skills in the *exact conditions* under which tests will take place.) Not all teachers are convinced that if a learner does something in a given situation, he or she will tend to do the same thing again when next in a similar situation.

But the significance of Guthrie's concept of learning should not be overlooked in its entirety. His insistence on particular responses to particular stimuli serves to remind the class teacher of the importance of the *combination of stimuli* resulting from a carefully arranged classroom environment and teaching activity. It emphasizes, too, the overall significance of presenting stimuli in a *planned* way. Essentially, the teacher should act so as to ensure that students behave in a particular way and, while they are doing so, the appropriate stimuli to be associated with that behaviour should be presented.

Guthrie stresses the importance of attempting to elicit desired patterns of behaviour in specific situations. Preparation for a formal test, for example, involves practicing and relearning in a situation which should have a close resemblance to that of the actual examination, such as through the provision of examples of past papers and allowing students to see work done by previous student cohorts. Simulation-based assessments, which require a precise analysis of stimuli and responses, can play a very important role in those activities related to preparation for particular situations in the workplace. Indeed, an implication of Guthrie's theory might be that, if we accept the necessity to plan instruction so that it should approximate as closely as possible to likely, future real-life circumstances, then perhaps teachers are too dominant a part of the instructional process. Where a teacher dominates, the students' responses will be cued to the sight of the teacher and the sound of his or her voice. In the teacher's absence the desired response, in content and strength, might not be elicited. It seems, therefore, that the teacher ought to be as small a part of the stimulus situation as is consistent with class control requirements.

Guthrie's views that rewards and punishments are of little significance, since there is no important place in his theory for the concept of reinforcement, and in that themselves they are neither good nor bad, are also of immediate practical importance in the seminar room or workshop. Whether they are effective or ineffective will be determined by what they cause the learner to actually do.

On the subject of class control, Guthrie has useful advice for the teacher, who should remember that each time she or he gives an order and something other than obedience follows, 'associative inhibition' tends to attach to that order. If a teacher makes a request for silence in the room and it is disregarded, the request actually becomes a signal for disturbance.

Guthrie's observations on the process of learning continue to have much relevance for the teaching-learning situation in FE colleges. If we learn only through what we ourselves do, then students, in solving problems, must engage in activities other than watching. Students do not learn what was in a lecture or a book. They learn only what the lecture or book caused them to do. What a person does is what a person will learn.

Hull

Hull (1885–1952) was an American psychologist, although an engineer by training, who worked firmly within the behaviourist tradition as it applied to adaptive behaviour. He taught at Yale and later headed a team at the Institute of Human Relations where he directed research on the place of learning in the conduct of social affairs. His theoretical roots were in the Pavlovian stimulus–response system and its explanation of learning. Hull's major writings are *Principles of Behaviour* (1943), *Essentials of Behaviour* (1951) and *A Behaviour System* (1952).

An important aspect of Hull's work is its quantitative, deductive character. He was concerned with the use of scientific method in his enquiries. Thus, a hypothesis would be put forward, and this would in turn be used to generate a number of deductions that could be tested out through carrying out a body of empirical research. This research process might confirm, reinforce or modify the hypothesis; it might fundamentally alter it or even cause it to be rejected. The job of the theoretician would be to formulate hypotheses in a manner which would produce exact, precisely stated deductions. Hull believed that a significant offshoot of all theoretical research was the empirical research that it generated, and his work dominated the psychology of learning in America between 1930–50.

The fundamental function of behaviour in an animal, said Hull, is to enable it to deal with its biological problems. Needs (for example, for food) produce a reaction in the form of *activity*. The particular behaviour that results, which reduces those needs, is gradually learned so that adaptation by the animal to its environment is assured. Basic physiological needs such as hunger or cold produce *drives,* the psychological counterparts of those needs, which Hull in turn divided into primary or secondary drives. *Primary* drives are those which are immediately necessary if the animal is to survive. *Secondary* drives emerge as offshoots from the process of satisfaction of primary needs. In an emergency situation, therefore, inborn response tendencies act as an automatic adaptive behavioural mechanism. The *capacity to learn* is a secondary mechanism, which according to Hull consists of a slightly slower means of adapting to acute situations. *Habits* are formed when drive-reduction (which reduces organic needs and follows the attainment of a goal) is perceived as rewarding. The strength or intensity of a habit is determined by the strength of the associations between stimuli and responses. Reinforcement is effective because it tends to reduce a learner's drive state, enabling the learner to return to the state of *homeostasis* – the maintenance of his equilibrium – which had been disrupted temporarily by the arousal of the need, culminating in the drive.

Hull found the simple stimulus–response model unsatisfactory. He instead suggested that in order to explain fully the relationship between a stimulus and a response, it was also necessary to consider the significance of *variables*, which will affect the nature, shape and intensity of a response to a stimulus. Examples might include the history of any prior training of the organism in previous similar situations, or the amount of reward available.

Learning should be viewed, therefore, in terms of the *habit* which may be considered as a function of *reinforcement*. Drive reduction, with its accompanying satisfaction, is an important reinforcer – the process of repeated drive reductions will reinforce the learning that is taking place. Learning does not take place following a single episode: indeed, a number of episodes may be found necessary before the results of that learning move beyond the threshold and are recognized in the learner's performance.

Hull's work and the teacher

Hull's drive theory, based on the concept of the existence within individuals of relatively intensive internal forces which motivate most types of behaviour, and his view of the strength of stimulus–response associations as dependent on innate habit strength and acquired habit strength, have a number of implications which can straightforwardly be extended to the classroom. Thus, the motivation of behaviour is seen as resulting from *intense arousal*; the ability to produce the arousal necessary for learning can be developed by *appropriate environmental stimuli*. Here is a rationale for the activities of those teachers who aim deliberately at the arousal and maintenance of interest in a lesson by a planned, structured environment. The perceived value of rewards, Hull suggests, clearly influences the intensity of behaviour. The teacher who is considering the utilization of a system of rewards as a reinforcement of desired behaviour will be interested in Hull's controversial view of reinforcement and drive reduction as almost synonymous.

Hull's work also reminds the teacher of the need for distributed practice so that inhibition will not appear during the process of learning. Topics to be taught should be placed in the timetable so that the subjects that are most *dissimilar* will succeed one another. In this way learner fatigue should be reduced.

Many practising teachers think of behaviour in the learning situation as an outcome of drive and cognitive processes. Hull emphasizes the drive component and notes the importance of variables in the process of learning. *Anxiety* might be considered as a vital drive component. An excess of anxiety would tend to disrupt learning; too little anxiety would reduce the perceived need to learn. Mild anxiety, according to Hull's approach, tends to produce the appropriate attitude for learning (a sentiment that many of the teachers with whom this author has worked would reject). In terms of the behaviourist tradition which Hull enriched, he extended the analytical value of the S-R behavioural model and paved the way for a deeper understanding of the drive stimuli which he held to be at the basis of the phenomenon of learning.

Summary

During the first half of the twentieth century, behaviourist psychology occupied a dominant position within what would today be referred to as 'educational research'. Rightly or wrongly, they continue to occupy significant space within teacher-training curricula today. But the central criticism remains: too much of the research work done by these writers was conducted with animals, not with people, and in laboratories, not educational contexts. Some of these concerns were addressed in turn by the *neobehaviourist* school, and it is to these writers that we shall now turn.

Further reading

Behaviourist theory continues to be a mainstay of many education and teacher-training, as well as psychology, curricula. Almost every general textbook relating to teacher training in the further education sector contains a chapter on behaviourism. The *Encyclopedia of Informal Education* contains a very good essay which is recommended as an additional introduction to the topic:

Smith, M. K. (1999), The behaviourist orientation to learning. *The encyclopedia of informal education.* http://infed.org/mobi/the-behaviourist-orientation-to-learning/ [accessed: 15 May 2013].

An up-to-date book that provides a focus on the learning of adults, as opposed to children, which is also recommended, is:

Tennant, M. (2007), *Psychology and Adult Learning*. Second edition. London: Routledge.

And a final good, and up-to-date, text, with lots of practical advice (although not specific to FE) is:

Woollard, J. (2010), *Psychology for the classroom: behaviourism*. London: Routledge.

4 Neobehaviourism

The neobehaviourists, exemplified by Skinner (the *theoretician* concerned with the principles of learning) and Gagné (the *practitioner* concerned with the design of instruction), moved away from the approaches of the behaviourists with whom the preceding chapter was concerned. Skinner's work was, in effect, a break with traditional psychology. Neobehaviourism insisted that truth was to be found in observations, rather than in the interpretation of observations. Behaviour, he argued, is controlled very largely by the environment. Gagné, through his writing, stressed the importance of contiguity and reinforcement, and the effect on individual human development of systematically designed instruction. Together with Tolman, these writers offered an account of educational psychology that included a consideration of the impact of environment and that sought to counter what were defined as the mechanistic approaches of the 'classical' behaviourists.

Tolman

Tolman (1886–1959) taught psychology at the University of California. Because of his highly individual, eclectic approach to the study of behaviour and his findings, he is claimed by both behaviourist and cognitive schools (discussed fully in the following chapter) as an advocate of their teachings. He opposed the views of the stimulus-response fundamentalist associationists: for him, the stimulus-response association was not an objective fact, it was no more than an *inference*. The act of behaviour had to be studied from the top down, not the bottom up. As a behaviourist he rejected introspection as a mode of inquiry, but the mechanistic views of the early behaviourists seemed too simple for an adequate explanation of behaviour, which he saw as *holistic*, as being capable of explanation in terms of the whole system, including contextual and environmental factors.

His major work, *Purposive Behaviour in Animals and Men* (1932), emphasized his view of behaviourism and purpose in behaviour. His argument was that the motives which lead to the assertion of behaviourism are simple. All that can ever actually be observed either in human beings and or in the lower animals is behaviour. Human beings do not, however, merely respond to stimuli. Rather, they move towards goals related to their beliefs and their attitudes. As educational psychologists, we can understand behaviour only by examining an entire *sequence* of varied behaviour with some predictable end; we have to examine the whole so as to understand how the sequence is put together and the end achieved. Early behaviourists had viewed anything intervening between stimulus and response as itself in the nature of a response. Tolman rejected this as too simple an explanation, and viewed the determination of behaviour as not only a result of environmental stimuli and physiological states *but also* due to the intervention of variables such as appetites and demands (which he, somewhat confusingly for our purposes, termed 'cognitions'). Cognitions, demands and appetites combine so as to produce responses. Behaviour is flexible and not invariant, and adaptable to changing circumstances. But Tolman stressed that purposive behaviour was none the less a behaviourism, arguing that stimuli and responses, and the behaviour-determinants of response, require study.

When thinking about something, a person uses what can be termed a *cognitive map*, that is, a general appreciation of the *relationships* among different stimuli and a set of *expectancies* about the meaning of those relationships. Such a map constitutes a symbolic representation of the person's environment – physiological, psychological and social – and her or his possible relations to it. The map would be constructed on the basis of the person's specific goals or purposes. Goal objects have motivating qualities; the presence of a preferred goal object may result in a performance superior to that elicited by the presence of a less desirable goal object – therefore, the *expectations* concerning a goal object are of great importance.

Learning, according to Tolman, was the *acquisition of expectancies*. By expectancy he meant that, in the presence of a certain *sign*, a particular behaviour will produce a particular consequence. We learn when we establish a series of expectations concerning the contiguity of events based on repeated past experiences of their appearance in sequence. In short, the student learns 'what leads to what'. As a person becomes aware of novel behaviour and unsuspected relationships, new behaviour will appear (a learning process very similar to the Gestaltist concept of 'insight', which is discussed in the next chapter) and described by Tolman as 'inventive ideation'. Essentially, said Tolman, learned behaviour comprises performances or acts which can be understood in terms of end results.

In contrast to the classical behaviorists, Tolman argued that reinforcement was *not* necessary for learning to take place. He suggested instead that the learner's expectations will not be transformed into behaviour unless she or he is *motivated*. Motivation (please refer also to Chapter 20) performs two functions: first, it creates a state of deprivation which in turn produces a desire for a goal object; secondly, it determines those features among the environment to which the learner will attend. According to Tolman, the simultaneous experiencing of events will suffice for learning to happen; reward may affect *performance* where it motivates a learner to show previously learned behaviour, but it will not affect the actual *process* of learning itself.

Different kinds of learning

Tolman argued that there are six different kinds of learning:

1 *Cathexis* (from the Greek word *kathexis*, meaning "retention"). This is based on a learned tendency to seek one goal rather than another when a certain drive is present. When a goal object satisfies a certain drive a cathexis is formed; the organism has acquired a positive disposition. When the organism has learned to avoid some objects while in a drive state, a negative cathexis is said to have been formed.

2 *Equivalence beliefs.* Where either a reward or a punishment is found in a certain situation, the situation itself is *equivalent* to the reward or punishment and is, therefore, *in itself* rewarding or punishing. It is evident where a student's sub-goals have the same effect as his or her main goal.

3 *Field expectancies.* These are built on cognitive maps, based on anticipations about the environment in which we function and resulting from repeated experiences. They make possible short cuts and round-about routes in learning.

4 *Field-cognition modes.* These are biases towards learning one thing rather than another, resulting from the discovery of principles and the changing of one's frames of reference. They make possible new strategies of perceiving, inferring and remembering.

5 *Drive discrimination.* This involves a learner's ability to distinguish one kind of internal drive stimulus from another. When learners' needs are not clear, their goals are also unclear and their behaviour may be inappropriate. An ability to understand one's *drive state* is needed for effective behaviour.

6 *Motor pattern acquisition.* This involves learning by contiguity, which can be viewed in terms of simple conditioning, based on stimulus-response connections.

According to Tolman's theories, students need to be granted a variety of opportunities in which to try things out, to test their ideas and presumptions. The role of the teacher, therefore, is to assist by constructing a variety of test situations and providing positive and affirmative feedback when the students' ideas and assumptions are shown to be accurate. In this way students will develop their own cognitive maps, allowing them to pursue their activities meaningfully. This is a practice that can be achieved in the classroom or workshop, although smaller work or tutorial groups may be more effective for learning strategies of this nature.

Tolman's view of behaviour has drawn the attention of teachers to the need for *an overall approach to class behaviour*, which is not to be viewed in simple terms. He argued

Neobehaviourism

that a wide range of factors influenced learning within the classroom or workshop, including not only biological factors such as the age of the student, but also social factors such as the previous educational history of the student. The importance of Tolman's work – which constitutes a significant break with the classical behaviourists – lies in reminding us, as teachers, that the learning that is taking place in the classroom is not the only factor that influences overall behaviour and that student reactions have to be understood in wider terms than those constituting the simple stimulus-response schemes of earlier psychologists.

Gagné

Gagné (1916–2002) was an educational psychologist who held the chairs of psychology at the Universities of Princeton and Florida. His work was concerned largely with a consideration of the general processes of learning, so that the design of instruction might be improved. His most important books are *The Conditions of Learning* (1965), *Essentials of Learning for Instruction* (1974) and *Principles of Instructional Design* (1988), in which he offers a rationally consistent basis for the design of instruction in the classroom.

Gagné defined instruction as a series of events that affect learners in such a way that learning is facilitated. Learners may, in fact, be able to initiate and manage some instructional events themselves. The planning of instruction is undertaken so as to support the process of learning. Learning must be linked with the design of instruction through consideration of the different kinds of capabilities that are being learned. That is to say, those activities, which we call 'instruction' and which require the teacher to arrange the conditions of learning that are required, must have different characteristics depending on the kind of change in performance that is the focus of interest.

It should be noted that some of Gagné's critics suggest that his work does not constitute a *theory* of learning (although the word 'theory' is frequently misapplied), and that it provides, at best, little more than a combination of instructional methods. Many teachers who have drawn heavily upon Gagné's work as a guide to course preparation, respond to criticism of this nature by explaining that Gagné provides not only a methodology of instruction, but an account of the underlying principles, derived essentially from observations of student learning behaviour: the result, theorefore, is a combination of both practical advice and learning theory.

Gagné saw learning as a process taking place in the learner's brain, comparable to other processes such as digestion and respiration. People do not learn in any general sense, but rather in the sense of changed behaviour that can be described in terms of an observable type of human activity. The change in a student's performance is what leads to the conclusion that learning, which may lead to an increased capability to achieve a particular task or a changed attitude or disposition towards something, has occurred.

Characteristics of learners

Gagné theorized that there are eight *characteristics* of learners (not including innate qualities such as eyesight, for example) and learning which in turn affect instructional design:

1   *Intellectual skills*. These refer to the capacity for *new learning* of concepts, rules and such like, involving in turn both cognitive strategies and verbal information (see below).
2   *Cognitive strategies*. These are internally organized capabilities which the learner makes use of in guiding her or his own attention, learning, remembering and thinking. They comprise procedures that govern the selection and utilization of intellectual skills. New learning (see above) requires these.
3   *Verbal information*. Ideas and concepts, according to Gagné, are the main ways by which human beings transmit accumulated knowledge. New learning, in turn, requires the recall of propositions, meaningful contexts and the recall of key ideas (which may involve other related ideas and contexts as well).
4   *Attitudes*. These are acquired internal states that influence the choice of personal action. Gagné theorizes that internal states affecting choices of personal action are affected strongly by situational factors – the revival of memory of a situation may also involve revival of the *attitude* associated with it. New learning will involve the activation of the learner's motivation.
5   *Motor skills*. These make possible the precise, accurately timed execution of the type of performance involving the use of the learner's muscles. New learning in this area demands the recall of sub-routines and part-skills.
6   *Schemas*. These are organizations of memory elements (e.g. images) representing a set of information pertaining to some general concept. In essence they are organized bodies of knowledge, allowing the learner to facilitate the retrieval and utilization of acquired information for future problem solving. New learning necessitates the activation of related networks of propositions.
7   *Abilities*. Gagné sees these as fundamental, stable characteristics, persisting over long periods and not easily changed by instruction or practice. New learning involves the adaptation of instruction to levels of abilities.
8   *Traits*. These are the tendencies of learners to respond in characteristic ways to a variety of situations. New learning involves the adaptation of instruction to differences in a learner's traits.

Types of learning

Following these, Gagné in turn theorized that there are eight *types* of learning, each requiring its own teaching strategy. Each type of learning relates to a different type of knowledge, which will produce a new capability for performance.

1 *Signal learning.* Here the learner associates an available response with a new stimulus. A generalized response to stimuli is made.
2 *Stimulus-response learning.* Here the learner acquires exact responses to discriminated stimuli.
3 *Chaining.* The learner acquires a number of stimulus-response bonds, such as the sets of motor responses needed to change a toner cartridge in a laser printer, set up a CNC milling machine, or finger A-flat on the oboe.
4 *Verbal association learning.* Here the learner acquires verbal chains, selecting the links from her or his previously learned repertoire. The chain cannot be learned unless the individual is capable of performing the individual links.
5 *Multiple discrimination.* The learner acquires the capacity to discriminate among apparently similar stimuli and to make the correct response.
6 *Concept learning.* The learner is able to make common responses to classes of stimuli that appear to differ widely from one another and to recognize relationships, known as classes.
7 *Rule learning.* The learner is able to form chains of two or more concepts. Knowledge of a rule is an inferred capability that enables the individual to respond to a class of stimulus situations with a class of performances. New rules are discovered when previously acquired rules are used so as to produce new capabilities. Knowledge of a rule involves much more than the ability to repeat it with accuracy. Effective learning involves the student being able to *apply* a rule to a variety of circumstances and to retrieve the constituent parts of the rule from memory.
8 *Problem-solving.* This is an extension of rule learning, which is characterized by discovery of relationships between and across rules.

Phases of learning

According to Gagné, any act of learning (irrespective of length, timing, complexity and so forth) comprises of eight different *phases*. The role of the teacher is therefore to provide those different types of external stimulation, which will affect the processes of learning.

1 *The motivation phase*. This initial phase involves the identification of students' motives and channelling them into activities that accomplish the educational goals that have been set.

2 *The apprehending phase*. The teacher's task here is the direction of attention, so that the learner is ready to receive appropriate, prepared stimuli. This is accomplished through engaging the learner's short-term memory (as discussed in Chapter 19). The highlighting of aspects of presentation – by repetition, through using audiovisual aids and through verbal or visual emphasis – establishes a 'foundation' for learning.

3 *The acquisition phase*. This phase involves transforming information into a sequence appropriate for storage in the memory. The role of the teacher here is to provide learning guidance and to stimulate the recall of prior knowledge and understanding and other supportive material from the learner's long-term memory through asking questions or requiring students to demonstrate skills or tasks that they have previously practised.

4 *The retention phase*. Memory storage, following storage entry, is the essence of this phase. Teaching strategies designed to ensure retention – practice, assessment and feedback – are necessary here.

5 *The recall phase*. Here, the job of the teacher is to provide a variety of opportunities for learners to draw on and apply prior learning. Thus, the learner may be required to apply what she or he has learned to new types of problem, or in different contexts, to what she or he has studied before.

6 *The generalization phase*. This phase centres around the transfer of learning (as discussed in Chapter 19). The role of the teacher is to facilitate this transfer. Gagné argued that transfer of learning required both lateral and vertical movement. *Lateral transfer* is a process of generalizing that 'spreads over' situations at approximately the same level of complexity, such as where the acquired ability to recognize parts of speech is carried over from English to, say, French. *Vertical transfer* involves the use of learned capabilities at one level of learning at a higher level, as where the knowledge of handling clay is utilized in the design of pots.

7 *The performance phase*. In order for the teacher to be able to assess the extent to which the learners have met their learning objectives, an appropriate performance has to be planned for. Typically this will involve formal formative or summative assessment (as discussed in Chapter 30).

8 *The feedback phase*. This final phase, in which the learner is made aware of the degree to which his performance approaches required standards, acts as a reinforcement, strengthening newly-learned associations and their recall.

Through his *theory of instruction*, Gagné sought to establish a rationally-based relationship between the events constituting instruction, how they affect the learning process and how that process results in a learning outcome. The following four concepts should underpin the theory.

1   Learning ought to be thought of in terms of sets of processes which are internal to the individual learner and which result in the transformation of stimuli from his or her situation into information which will be lodged in long-term memory, resulting in qualitative improvements to her or his capacities.
2   A learner's capacities include intellectual skills, cognitive strategies, verbal information, attitudes and motor skills; all are differentiated in ways allowing their differentiated assessment.
3   Different learning outcomes necessitate differentiated instruction.
4   Three principles derived from classical behaviourism would also inform this theory of instruction. These include: the principle of *contiguity*, so that the stimulus situation should be presented simultaneously with the desired response; the principle of *repetition*, allowing the frequent repetition of the stimulus situation and the desired response; and the principle of *reinforcement*, based on the view that the occurrence of a new act is learned more readily when followed immediately by an earlier-learned act.

Gagné sees the teacher as a designer and manager of the process of instruction and an assessor of learning outcomes. He emphasizes, above all, the importance of the systematic design of instruction based on intended learning outcomes and linked with awareness of the internal conditions of learning. Gagné's view of the hierarchical nature of the learning process serves as a reminder to the teacher that learners must be adequately prepared to enter a particular phase of instruction. The teacher must ensure that relevant lower-order skills and abilities have been acquired before the learning of the related higher-order skill is undertaken. The first job for a teacher is to find out what the student already knows. The second job, then, is to begin teaching from that point.

The importance of feedback in the classroom is stressed by Gagné. This necessitates communication to the student, as swiftly and accurately as possible, of the outcome of her or his performance and calls for careful and regular assessment in the classroom. The planning of feedback is one example of the design of instruction – with the learner in mind – which characterizes the neobehaviourism of which Gagné is a powerful and influential advocate.

Gagné's work is of particular importance to teachers because it has, at its centre, the practical problems of class instruction. His theories, and the research which underpins them, relate to the everyday activities of staff and students. He warns against research into learning which is based on a variety of sources, not all of which relate to education, and emphasizes that a learning theory which does *not* take into account the formal processes of instruction in schools and colleges may be of restricted value to the teaching practitioner.

Skinner

Skinner (1904–90) graduated in English and entered Harvard as a graduate student in psychology in 1928. His doctoral thesis investigated the concept of the reflex; his specific interests led to work on operant behaviour, which was carried out in the biological laboratories at Harvard. During the war years he worked on a project involving the training of pigeons to guide missiles. In 1945 he became chairman of the Department of Psychology at Indiana University, returning permanently to Harvard in 1948, where he held the chair in psychology until his retirement in 1974. The period from 1974 until his death in 1990 was marked by a prodigious output of books and articles, many of which were designed specifically for practising teachers, with whom he maintained close links. He wrote prodigiously, and his major works include *The Behaviour of Organisms* (1938), *Science and Human Behaviour* (1953), *Verbal Behaviour* (1957), *The Technology of Teaching* (1968), which deals with topics such as the science of learning and the art of teaching, motivation and teaching machines, *Beyond Freedom and Dignity* (1971), and *About Behaviourism* (1974). Perhaps surprisingly, what might be seen as the most concise account of his theories can be found in his novel, *Walden Two* (1948).

The experiments associated with his name were based upon the use of the 'Skinner box', an apparatus which allowed him to study the responses of a variety of animals. A hungry (but unconditioned) animal, for example, a rat, is allowed to explore the box. When the rat spontaneously presses a small brass lever, the experimenter drops a pellet of food from a container into a tray, thus allowing the animal to eat. This is repeated on several occasions until the rat acquires the habit of going to the tray when it hears the sound made by a movement of the food container. Later, the lever is connected directly to the container so that the rat's pressure results in the presentation of a food pellet. Conditioning then follows rapidly. Skinner used accumulated data on the animal's rate of response in his formulation of the effect of reinforcement in learning. These techniques were later refined and used as the basis of continued experiments in the modification of behaviour by operant conditioning which, for Skinner, is synonymous with the essential characteristic of the learning process.

Much of Skinner's work concerns the functional analysis of behaviour, of which learning is just one type. 'Learning', according to Skinner, is manifested in changes in a learner's responses. According to Skinner, the experimental analysis of behaviour, most of which is a product of *operant reinforcement* (see below), constitutes the creation of an effective technology applicable to education.

Learning results in most cases from a process which he termed *operant conditioning*. An operant is a series of acts which constitute a learner's doing something, such as picking up a pen or opening a web browser on a PC; these are voluntary responses emitted by the learner, whose behaviour operates on the environment so as to generate consequences. Operant reinforcement improves the efficiency of the learner's behaviour; the most significant stimulus for the learner will be that which immediately follows the response.

Skinner distinguished between operant and respondent behaviour. Operant behaviour involves voluntary, emitted responses which are not elicited by any identifiable external stimuli. Respondent behaviour, in contrast, involves responses elicited by known stimuli, such as when someone blinks in the presence of excessive light.

Skinner's analysis of the learning process is based on his view of the importance of conditioning the learner's operant behaviour. For Skinner, units of learning are sequences within which a response is followed by a reinforcing stimulus. The strength of a learned response – the probability of its recurrence – is generally determined by the amount of reinforcement it receives. Operant conditioning is, therefore, a type of learning that will result in an increase in the probability of a response occurring as a function of reinforcement.

Reinforcement is the process of increasing the frequency of occurrence of a low-frequency behaviour, or maintaining the frequency of occurrence of a high-frequency behaviour. Skinner distinguished between positive and negative reinforcement. Positive reinforcement occurs when a stimulus is presented which, when added to a situation, increases the probability of occurrence of a response, for example when praise is given to a person when the desired behaviour occurs. Should the learner not perform the response, he will not receive the reinforcing stimulus. Negative reinforcement occurs when an unpleasant stimulus is used, for example when something is taken away from a person upon occurrence of a behaviour that is being discouraged.

Skinner's advice to teachers rests on the necessity to understand the role of reinforcement in the learning process. To begin, the teacher must define the behaviour that she or he wishes to build, remembering that operant behaviourism necessitates *teacher-centred* instruction. The teacher should then select as reinforcers those objects and events which, in the context of the class, with its given social and intellectual background, will have reference to the maintenance of desired behaviour. The types of reinforcer should be varied and symbolic reinforcers (such as a smile of recognition or a nod of approval) might be used. When desired consequences fail to emerge, the types of reinforcer should be changed. Reinforcement should be considered as a means to an end: the end is that quality of behaviour from which the acquisition of learning may be inferred. Thus, through a process known as *shaping*, the teacher can set about the process of reinforcing a student's correct responses to a series of planned stimuli.

Skinner's work and the teacher

Skinner's view of the learning process has attracted trenchant and persistent criticism. His fundamental belief that psychology must become a precise science has been rejected as a mirage, and he has been accused of coming to conclusions that were not actually supported by the data that he constructed. His generalizations concerning human behaviour have been attacked as reflecting the study of animals which are totally unlike human beings. The shaped behaviour of a pigeon or a rat in a skinner box has been held to be irrelevant at best to an explanation of the complex activities which form human behaviour. Nor, it has been argued, should the conditions of the operant conditioning chamber be used as the basis of suggestions concerning the conditions which ought to exist in the classroom.

Other critics directly attacked Skinner's experimental work. He was charged with failing to take into account the natural behaviour of animals in their normal surroundings, or of what has been termed the *unique species-typical* behaviour of animals. Skinner's views on punishment have also been criticized. Skinner argued that punishment ought to be avoided. Appropriate behaviour should be reinforced, and inappropriate behaviour should be ignored. The elimination of inappropriate or objectionable behaviour merely requires the teacher to study the source of reinforcement of that behaviour and to attempt to remove it: behaviour which is not reinforced will simply disappear. Skinner's condemnation of punishment has been criticized as being inefficient and ineffective, perhaps even leading to a broader decline in social standards.

Skinner replied repeatedly to many of these criticisms and reasserted his views. Teaching remained, for him, the arrangement of contingencies of reinforcement under which behaviour changes. This is a view which has important implications for the class teacher. Teaching, he reminds us, should not be a random, hit-or-miss affair, nor is it an unfathomable mystery. Instead, it is a process which is amenable to investigation, and which requires the methodical application of techniques based in part on the results of the experimental analysis of behaviour. If a student has been taught something, then this means that she or he has been induced to engage in new forms of behaviour and in specific forms on specific occasions. The teacher's task is to shape behaviour and this requires an awareness of objectives and the techniques of assisting attainment. Lesson objectives must be defined behaviourally. It requires, additionally, a knowledge of the basis of reinforcement, of results of types of reinforcement scheduling, and of the particular importance of a partial reinforcement schedule. Indeed, the infrequency of reinforcement was regarded by Skinner as the most serious criticism of contemporary classroom practices (immediately dismissing a number of teaching strategies – formal lectures being the most obvious). In essence, the teacher's role should be that of the practitioner of a technology designed to maximize the inherent potential of each student, with consequent benefits for society at large.

Skinner set out a number of interesting views for teachers who are considering the problems involved in teaching students 'how to learn'. For Skinner, it was important that students should learn to solve problems by themselves, explore the unknown, make decisions, and behave in original ways and that these activities should, as far as possible, be taught. But there should be no attempt to teach 'thinking' while subject matter is being taught. Instead, it should be possible to teach the behaviour known as 'thinking' by using material which is already available in areas such as psychology, scientific method and logic (a perspective that is clearly in opposition to current and recent trends towards teaching 'thinking skills').

In his final years, Skinner continued to defend his point of view by vigorous condemnation of what he termed a 'conspiracy of silence' about teaching as a skill. In an article entitled 'The shame of American education' (1984) he set out his responses to a report that in the preceding year, the average achievement of American high-school students on standardized tests was lower than it was a quarter of a century earlier. Skinner saw the spread of what he described as 'the fallacies of cognitive and humanistic psychology' (discussed in the following chapters) as an important contributory cause of this state of affairs. His solution was simple and precise: teachers must learn how to teach; all that is needed is for teachers to be taught more effective ways of teaching. What needs to be done is this: be clear about what is to be taught; teach first things first; allow students to advance at their own rate; plan and sequence the subject matter carefully. Give students and teachers better reasons for learning and teaching.

Skinner continued to emphasize that a really effective educational system cannot be constructed until the processes of learning and teaching are properly understood and accepted. Human behaviour, he insisted, is far too complex to be left to casual experience or even to organized experience in a classroom environment which is, by its very nature, restricted, and in which too great an interval exists between student behaviour and its reinforcement. Skinner's words affirm the importance for the class teacher of practice based firmly on tested theory. Education, for Skinner, involved the establishment of behaviour which will be of advantage to the individual and to others at some future time. The role of the teacher is the creating of that advantageous behaviour.

Summary

In contrast to the classical behaviourists, the neobehaviourist perspective presented in this chapter offer a more immediately meaningful approach to the practice of the FE lecturer, whether in a workshop, a tutorial or a seminar room. The importance of motivation in understanding learning (as proposed by Tolman), the notion that different types of subject matter require in turn different types of teaching (as proposed by Gagné), the central role played by a pedagogy that has been systematically researched and analysed (as proposed by Skinner) – themes such as these are quite common in teacher education curricula for the FE and lifelong learning sectors, although they are invariably accompanied in contemporary accounts by other theoretical perspectives.

However, the essential features of the neobehaviourist school are held in common with the classical behaviourists, in particular the centrality of the stimulus-response relationship, which can be made more or less sophisticated (for example, by considering how environmental factors might impact on the relationship between a stimulus and a response), but which continues to focus the theorization of learning on the *individual* and to understand learning as leading to *observable* changes in behaviour. For some theorists and researchers working in the middle of the twentieth century, these neobehaviourist accounts were enough. For other theorists and researchers, however, it was those very problems that behaviourists and neobehaviourists alike dismissed from the remit of their research – one being the impact of environment and the learner's relationship to it, and the other being the process of thinking or *cognition* – that would be at the heart of their inquiries. In the two chapters that follow, therefore, we shall consider how these two important themes were conceptualized and researched by scholars working in two quite distinct academic traditions: the gestalt school, and the cognitive school. And it is to the gestalt school that we shall now turn.

Further reading

The works by Smith (1999), Tennant (2007) and Woollard (2010) recommended in chapter 3 are also recommended here. Readers who are interested in a more expansive account of Skinner's work are recommended to read his novel, which was written in order to provide an account of how not just education but social life more generally might be organized according to his principles:

Skinner, B. F. (1948, 1976), *Walden Two*. Indianapolis: Hackett Publishing.

5 Gestaltism

Gestalt psychology takes its name from the German word *Gestalt* – a configuration, structure, pattern; it is a 'form' psychology. It stands in total opposition to the principles, methods and conclusions of the structuralist and behaviourist schools of psychology, and states uncompromisingly that the phenomenological experience (that is to say, that which is perceptible to the senses) is different from the parts that make it up. Gestaltist theories concerning the nature of thinking, understanding and learning have found their way into classroom procedures, particularly into teachers' concepts of instruction and its component elements.

The Gestaltists built upon the work of von Ehrenfels who, in 1890, had researched into the fact that a melody is recognizable when sung in any one of a variety of keys. He had concluded that over and above the sensory ingredients of a tune (or a painting) there must be what he termed a 'form quality' (in German, *Gestaltqualität*) which describes that which is possessed by the tune (or painting) and which is not explicable merely in terms of component tunes (or colours).

The basic theories of the Gestaltists were formulated and elaborated by three other psychologists: Koffka, Köhler and Wertheimer. Koffka (1886–1941) graduated from the Universities of Edinburgh and, later, Berlin. He emigrated to America in 1924 and taught at the University of Winsconsin until his death. His book *Principles of Gestalt Psychology* (1935) is a compendium of Gestaltist theories and findings. Köhler (1887–1967) received his doctorate from Berlin University in 1909, but left Germany in 1934 and taught in America for the rest of his life. His most important work is agreed to be *Gestalt Psychology* (1929). Wertheimer (1880–1943) was a professor at the University of Frankfurt in 1929. He left Germany in 1934 and settled in America, where he taught at Columbia University. His work *Productive Thinking* (issued posthumously in 1945) attempted to distinguish the laws of logic (based on imitative behaviour) and the laws of thought (creative acts of thinking).

Gestaltist objections to structuralism and behaviourism

Structuralists such as Titchener (1867–1927) had attempted to understand mental states and processes by examining and analyzing their composition and arrangement. The Gestaltists condemned this 'atomistic' approach, insisting that any analysis of the mind which merely attempted to reduce it to component elements was misleading. Mental patterns could not be reduced, they claimed, to combinations of smaller elements, to 'bundles of sensations'. The components of an individual's mental life, such as learning and thinking, could be analysed successfully only when viewed as organized, complete structures. Attributes of component parts could be defined only by their relationship to *the* system as a whole in which they are functioning.

Behaviourism, and specifically the classical behaviourism of, for example, Watson (as discussed in Chapter 3) was also rejected by the Gestaltists. The reduction of human behaviour to stimulus-response patterns was criticized as over-simplified. In its place the Gestaltists offered a concept based on a pattern characterized as stimulus-organization-response. According to this theory, the relationship between a stimulus and a response is mediated by what they termed *perceptual organization*, a process by which the individual organizes or makes sense of the stimulus in relation to the environment within which she or he is in. Geslaltists maintained that individuals do not merely respond to their environment, but they have transactions with the environment. A person experiences her environment, her world, by imposing on her perceptions simplicity, regularity, symmetry and stability: this is a key to an understanding of the Gestaltist approach. The Gestaltists also rejected the behaviourists' denial of the importance of introspection as an analytical tool. Indeed, said Koffka, the trouble with the behaviourists is that (perhaps ironically) they leave out too much behaviour from their analysis, and generally ignore the purposive nature of much human behaviour.

To cut to pieces living and thinking processes in an attempt to get at the elements of thinking, was to blind oneself to the significance of structure as a whole. It was to the pattern and meaningfulness of the mental process as a whole that the Gestaltists turned their attention. Their guiding thesis was formulated by Wertheimer, thus: there are contexts in which what is happening in the whole cannot be deduced from the characteristics of the separate pieces, but conversely, what happens to a part of the whole is, in clear-cut cases, determined by the laws of the inner structure of the whole.

The essence of the Gestaltist approach

The whole transcends the sum of its parts; we are dealing with wholes and whole-processes possessed of inner intrinsic laws: this is the essence of the Gestaltist approach to a study of the phenomena with which psychology is concerned. Some scholars perceive in this approach the influence of the philosopher, Leibnitz (1646–1716), for whom the whole was *prior* to the parts: according to Leibnitz, there is a unity of mind from which constituent parts are differentiated as development takes place. It is the total structured form of an individual's mental experience with which the psychologist and the teacher ought to be concerned; the attributes of the whole are not entirely deducible from an analysis of constituent elements. The whole itself, as well as its individual components, may be considered as possessing its own properties. So, for example, the structural form of a Beethoven piano sonata is 'greater' than the totality of the notes of which it is made. The structure of a screw-cutting lathe is 'greater' than the mere sum of the carriage, spindle, cutting tool, etc., of which it consists. The rectangle is 'greater' than the sum of the four lines from which it is constituted. The complex perceptions which are involved in thinking and learning are much more than mere bundles of sensations of which they are said to be constituted. A learner's experience has a pattern, a wholeness, which is more than the sum of its parts; it is a structure of psychological phenomena with properties which cannot be understood by a mere summation of those phenomena.

A basic Gestalt formula was enunciated by Wertheimer who suggested that a coherent whole possesses properties that are not discoverable in its individual isolated parts. Further, a part, when in a coherent whole, possesses properties which it does not possess when it is in isolation (or when it is a part of some other whole). The character of a whole may determine the properties of an individual part; hence the part has to be understood as a dependent property of its whole.

In the process of learning, how do we understand? According to the Gestaltists, understanding necessitates awareness of some required relations between facts. The relations will seem to follow on from the facts themselves. But an understandable relation between two terms is not an added third term; given any two terms, a third may be demanded by the situation. Gestaltists have suggested that understandable relations between terms possess a character of requiredness. Thus, when a learner is faced with an incomplete situation, the gap in understanding of that situation has a property of its own that will produce a tendency towards completion.

Productive thinking, according to Wertheimer, is the development of new structures, new organizations. The solution to a problem – a gap, as it were – involves a process (not a single act), which begins with a situation and a goal that, at a given moment, cannot be reached. The learner's thinking in relation to this incomplete situation leads, it is suggested, to an urge to bridge the gap; this leads to a re-examination of the problem and its component material. The learner reorganizes the material. New relations emerge and lead to a transition to a new, more coherent, point of view. The learner works and reworks features of that view and builds a structure from which he or she derives detailed steps leading to a solution to the problem. What began with a perception causing the learner to have to stop and think, to work out a solution or resolve a problem, ends in a new balance, based on a new, organized structure of perception. The learner now looks at their environment anew, with the 'answer' or 'solution' now a permanent feature of their perspective.

Past experiences of the learner also contribute to the process of understanding and learning (a feature which is common in theories of adult education generally) but, according to Gestaltists, thinking is much more than the mere recall of prior knowledge or practice. Rather, these experiences need to be selected, manipulated and reorganized if new structures of perception are to be constructed.

An individual's experiences and his or her behaviour are therefore not explicable, argued the Gestaltists, by 'atomistic' theories. Phenomena such as learning have to be studied as complex, highly organized structures. The aspect of behaviour which is known as 'learning' is, in this view, a pattern of activities characterized by *organization*. And fundamental to an understanding of these activities is the Gestaltist concept of *insight*.

Insight

Insight is a common word, but it is used by Gestalt psychologists in a very specific sense. Insight is said to emerge when the learner suddenly becomes aware of the relevance of her or his behaviour to some particular objective and is the result of an unforeseen reorganization by the learner of her or his field of experience. The learner experiences a flash of inspiration, or has a new idea – a 'brainwave'. But insight should not be confused with the random lucky guess. There can be no insight in the absence of appropriate prior knowledge. That is to say, such moments of inspiration rest on meaningful and serious bodies of prior experience and knowledge.

Insight, according to the Gestaltists, does not result from separate responses to a series of separate stimuli; it is a complex reaction to a situation in its entirety, a perception of a whole group of relationships, a discovery of a previously unrecognized but fundamental unity in a variety of phenomena, in effect, a suddenly occurring reorganization of the field of experience. Insight and thought are, in this sense, virtually synonymous.

Köhler's study of insight learning in chimpanzees (an issue that will be commented on a the end of the chapter) involved tests of the animals' abilities in the solution of problems, some necessitating the use of tools and other equipment. In one of these experiments, the animal under observation appeared, at one stage, to act very suddenly (giving the impression of carrying out some plan of operations) in order to reach bananas suspended out of its reach. It placed boxes on top of one another, climbed them and seized the fruit. In another experiment, it put together, after many attempts, some jointed sticks which it then used to reach fruit placed outside its cage. Köhler interpreted these actions as being discontinuous with the animal's previous trials and errors. Instead, he saw them as exhibiting a pattern of learning which he recognized as insight, transferred to conceptually similar situations. The animal seemed to have made a discovery in thought. It should be noted, however, that later critics of Gestalt theory drew attention to other experiments suggesting a lack of evidence indicating insight on occasions when the animals in the experiment had been brought up in captivity. Köhler's animals had been captured in the wild, and their past environments may have provided opportunities for them to use sticks in the manner described here.

On a very much higher level the phenomenon of insight might be observed in the learner who is struggling to find the correct solution to a mathematical problem. She may seize on an apparently important feature of the problem and reformulate it in terms of that feature. Eventually her perception becomes sufficiently structured to allow him to 'see into' the problem and to solve it. The sudden 'I have it! I need to multiply the square root by three, and there's the answer' is not a fluke or a lucky guess or a fortuitous assembling of the elements of the problem in their correct order. Instead, according to Gestalt theory it is the result of the learner having perceived the structural essence of the total situation posed by the problem. The learner has made an imaginative leap from present facts to future possibilities. The learner sees things that she could not see previously. And finally, it is important to note that this leap, this ability to 'see' the answer, comes from insight that is entirely from within: a teacher cannot 'give' insight to a student.

Gestaltists hold that, in general, learning resulting from insight is characterized by the following features:

(a) the solution to a problem comes suddenly and completely

(b) the solution can be repeated subsequently and without any error, on the presentation of further problems of the same type

(c) the solution can be retained for long periods of time and be transposed to problems which possess the same basic features as the original problem, but which are in very different contexts

(d) generalized insight is equivalent to 'understanding'.

The laws of Gestalt psychology

The basic laws of Gestaltist psychology arise from the belief that the fundamentally biological process of perception is governed by principles of organization, so that any human being imposes on their physical environment a certain *Gestalt*. These laws may be summarized as follows:

1 *Law of figure-ground relationship.* This involves perceiving selected parts of a stimulus so that they stand out from other parts. An individual's perceptions are organized into 'figures' which tend to stand out from their background. Consider, for example, the letters which are printed on this page: they stand out from the spaces which separate them. Yet, although both figures and space form the field of perception, the spaces are not perceived by the reader. Similarly, the pattern in which acts take on their meaning from their context in time and place is based on relationships of this nature. The effect of expectations is also important. When the learner attends to one aspect of their environment, that becomes the 'figure', and everything else becomes the 'ground'; which aspect of the learner's perceptual field is figure and which is ground is merely a matter of attention.

2 *Law of contiguity*. Things tend to be perceived as a unity according to their proximity in time or space. The closer they are, the more likely are they to be perceived as 'grouped'.

3 *Law of similarity*. Items which are similar to one another in some way, for example, in terms of their shape, tend to be perceived in a group or pattern, other things being equal.

4 *Law of significance*. Perceptions tend to produce the best patterns possible under the prevailing controlling circumstances, that is, figures will be perceived in their best possible form, in the shapes most characteristic of form or structure. Wertheimer considered this law as of the greatest importance. He emphasized that grouping will tend to maximal simplicity and balance, that is towards the formation of a good form; the brain tends generally to interpret a form as an integrated whole.

5 *Law of closure*. Figures and actions which are incomplete may be perceived as though symmetrical or complete, for instance, gaps in a learner's visual field tend to close in order that she may recognize complete units. (The behaviour of Köhler's chimpanzee could be interpreted as a 'closing of the gap' in its field of perception.) Tension in the learner impels her towards the completion of an incomplete task. IN addition, there may be a mental tendency to organize one's perceptions so that they 'make sense', since closed areas are perceived as more stable than unclosed ones. That is to say, there is an inherent mental tendency to solve problems.

6 *Law of transposition*. Patterns may be changed or distorted without their recognizable identity disappearing. For example, if the Ukulele Orchestra of Great Britain played a version of the 'Coronation Street' theme tune, it would still be recognized as the Coronation Street theme tune even though the 'original' is played a different speed and using different instruments. In explaining this mental phenomenon, Köhler referred to perceptual constancies, defined as moments when we tend to see an object as the same object under a variety of circumstances.

Learning and productive thinking

Learning, therefore, is no mere linking of associations or the workings of formal logic in the mind of the learner; it is a special case of perception, a cognitive phenomenon. Indeed,

Wertheimer referred to the rules of traditional logic as reminding him of 'an efficient police manual for regulating traffic', consisting of rules that undoubtedly explained logical processes but that could not explain or enhance understanding. Learning, according to Gestalt theory, results from the learner's restructuring and reformulating his perceptions of situations involving problems. Emotions, attitudes and intellect will also enter into these perceptions, which lead to a sudden solution based on insight and reflect the learner's cognitive understanding of the relevant relationships. This type of learning will persist for a long period and can be applied to other, similar, problems – it can be *transferred*. Learning is a dynamic process, not constituted by mere bundles of discrete stimulus-response events that are transformed, somehow, into new concepts acquired by the learner. The acquisition and retention of insight, according to the Gestaltists, form the core of the learning process. Persistent changes in knowledge, skills and attitudes constitute learning, but this is not always or necessarily reflected in a learner's observable behaviour. Learning by doing is not recognized by Gestaltists, except where a learner's doing assists in changing his cognitive structures. In these situations, learning results where the learner (the doer?) is aware of the consequences of his or her acts.

Koffka defined learning in precise terms based around the concept of the *trace*. A trace, according to Koffka, is the inferred effect of an event on a person's memory. Where events are connected in some way they form a unit and, in turn, a *unitary* trace. Any future stimulation of some part of this trace, for example, through triggering a memory of a particular event, will spread to the whole trace. The stronger the trace, the stronger will be its influence on the memory processes as a whole. Consequently, the improvement of a skill through practice reflects the influence of a relevant trace or unitary trace on the skill pattern. It is as if the process has become 'hard-wired' into the learner's brain.

Koffka, writing in *Principles of Psychology*, describes and analyzes the learner's 'trace system' in terms that are of considerable significance for the teacher. Take learning to type, for example. When we learn to type, Koffka suggests, our individual lessons are soon forgotten, and the clumsy movements which we originally carried out will, at some later stage, become impossible. This means that traces of those first lessons have been altered by the *aggregate* of subsequent traces which has been produced through practice and repetition and which is responsible, therefore, for the general improvement in our typing skill. Koffka sees a parallel in what happens when we stay in a room for any period of time so that we obtain many impressions of the room by moving about or merely letting our eyes wander from one object to another. But, in the event, no more than a few of those impressions can be recalled in the future.

An aspect of learning which was of much importance in the theories of the Gestaltists, particularly Wertheimer, was so-called productive or creative thinking. The uncritical and unthinking use of formulae that have been memorized off by heart in order to find an answer to a problem are contrasted here with what Wertheimer called the dynamic and creative process in which learners apply themselves to the discovery of a solution, based on understanding such formulae and applying their growing awareness of the structure of the problem to the finding of an answer. Wertheimer's experiments led him to conclude that although a potential capacity for this creative thinking may be present in many learners, it is often unrealized and goes to waste because of the blind, drill-like, learning by rote procedures of piecemeal instruction to which they have been subjected. Productive solutions are usually related, said Wertheimer, to the whole characteristics, and not the isolated aspects, of problems. Productive thinking, he asserted, necessitated the learner's grasping the essential relationships within a problem, grouping them into wholes and restructuring the problem.

Productive thinking was analyzed by another Gestalt theorist, Wallas, who suggested that thinking of this type usually involves four stages:

1 *preparation*, in which the learner explores the problem and defines it

2 *incubation*, in which the learner rests and, in effect, dismisses the problem from her conscious thoughts

3 *illumination*, in which solutions may occur to the learner in an unexpected manner

4 *verification*, in which the solutions are investigated and checked by the learner.

And in turn, the Gestaltist position as it relates to thinking as an element of student learning can be summarized as follows (Chaplin, 1978):

1 productive thinking may take place when the learner encounters an original problem with which he or she is unable to deal by the application of habitual methods

2 thinking, in the face of a new problem with which the learner is confronted, involves a stepwise transformation of the thought processes so that the learner's attempted solutions become more specific

3 the process of thinking involves the learner in perceptual reorganization based upon concentrating on the gaps in the possible solutions to the problem and filling them

4 the readiness with which the learner discovers solutions is linked directly to his or her perceptual field, motivation and previous learning attainment

5 the eventual solution results from sudden 'jumps' from one possible solution to another, reflecting sudden transformations of the learner's field of perception

6 where the learner has been able to achieve 'insightful solutions' to problems and has grasped fundamental principles, there is then the possibility of a high degree of transfer of learning to the solution of similar problems.

Gestalt psychology and the teacher

Gestalt doctrine has been criticized by psychologists from other intellectual traditions who argued that its laws were never properly systematized or fully explained. There may be much agreement with Koffka's comment that measurement is not the sole source of valid evidence; but the broader lack of quantification in expositions of the foundations of Gestalt psychology suggests, for some investigators, an absence of hard, empirical fact.

The concept of insight, which is at the heart of Gestalt psychology as it applies to learning, has brought criticism from some psychologists and teachers. It has been suggested that the solutions to some of the Gestaltists' experimental problems arose out of the subjects' *transfer* of prior learning and current knowledge and understanding (as discussed in Chapter 19), not as a result of any insight or 'gestalt' episode. It may therefore be the case that what seems to be insight is in fact the result, not of a sudden understanding of the essence of the problem, but of the recall of past learning. Perceptual functioning, in relation to learning, seems to teachers to require an appropriate foundation of prior experience. Teachers have pointed out also that no insight appears necessary for the learning of many things, such as simple facts. The student of history does not learn the names of the six wives of Henry VIII by insight. Psychologists such as Gagné (as discussed in Chapter 3) have reminded the Gestaltists that insight is not a prototype for a great deal of learning which people generally undertake.

Further criticism of Gestalt theory focuses a perceived confusion surrounding the use of the key term 'insight'. Critics argued that the term 'insight' was used indiscriminately, particularly by Köhler, so that on some occasions it refers to intelligence, judgement or understanding, and on other occasions it is used in connection with the sudden acquisition of new understanding. In some instances, Köhler writes about 'insight' as characterized by the appearance of a complete solution with reference to the whole layout of the environment; in others he writes of the dawning of a solution and of useful errors made during the process of reaching a solution, a far more haphazard-sounding process. Other critics focussed on the concept of 'suddenness' as a criterion of insight, arguing instead that the overwhelming body of experimental evidence pointed instead to the conclusion that a new insight consists of a recombination of pre-existent, mediating processes, not the sudden appearance of a wholly new process.

In spite of these and other criticisms of the fundamentals of Gestalt psychology, the concept of learning outlined by the Gestaltists has found a sympathetic response in the practice of some class teachers who are aware that, in order to understand the responses of students, it is necessary at first to consider a multiplicity of facts. Learners often mentally organize the components of a task and perceive with 'sudden vision' the solution to a problem (or, as teachers and students sometimes put it, 'the penny suddenly drops'). This is a common experience in classroom teaching. Learners often select from new material that which seems important, so that new terms emerge, leading to insight. Insight becomes more highly structured until it produces a solution to the problem. To plan a lesson, to arrange a problem situation, to organize the elements of separate exercises into meaningful wholes, so that the learner is able to move to the discovery of patterns, relationships and solutions, is often a difficult, but necessary and worthwhile, task. To prepare students for the possible emergence of novel concepts during contemplation of a problem is to assist in the development of insight.

The Gestaltists' approach to learning emphasizes for the teacher the importance of so arranging lesson structure that learners find the route to the solution of a problem and see their efforts as directed to that end. Considerable progress may be made in lessons in which learners are brought to a particular point and then asked to examine and explain how they have arrived at that point and how they see their work as linked to the next steps in the solution of the problem. In these cases learning will be facilitated where an overview is presented and the interrelationships of course topics have been explained. Conversely, the presentation of disconnected scraps of information in a lesson is to be avoided.

Wertheimer's warnings against mechanical and blind drill based upon rote learning are echoed in those lesson structures based deliberately on comprehension and under-standing as opposed to mere memorization of facts and rules. Understanding rather than memorization should pervade lesson objectives. Those teachers who have arrived at similar conclusions intuitively or as the result of careful and direct observations in classroom, laboratory and workshop, will be encouraged to note that their conclusions are supported by much formal research.

The retention and transfer of knowledge – important objectives of the teaching process (though see also the discussion in Chapter 19) – appear in the light of Gestalt theory not as the product of repetitive drills, but as the result of the learner's discovery of patterns, relationships and principles and their effective transposition to a new, wider range of situa-tions. In short, Gestalt theory suggests that the teacher should aim to elicit productive thinking based on the perception of phenomena as integrated wholes to which parts are related. The teacher's task is, in the light of this theory, the arranging of the conditions of learning so that perception of this nature is facilitated. A variety of teaching techniques can contribute to this end, provided that they allow for student–teacher interaction.

The Gestaltists stress the importance of practice: they suggest that teachers should consider the advisability of providing for students continued opportunities for the observation of novel patterns and relationships. Awareness and understanding of those relationships can be translated by the teacher into a series of planned, systematic exercises, so that problem-solving can be carried out sensibly, structurally, organically, rather than mechanically.

Gestalt theory: Some final comments

One of the more fundamental critiques of Gestalt theory, in common with many of the theories that have been presented thus far in this book, relates to the experimental base on which these theories were initially established, which involved animals and not people. Put simply, to what extent can a series of experiments with monkeys trying to obtain bananas that have been purposefully placed out of reach, satisfactorily explain the complexities of human learning? Other critiques have argued that Gestalt theory is essentially descriptive rather than explanatory, and offers no meaningful conclusions regarding how learning happens and how it might be encouraged by teachers. But perhaps the most powerful critique is also the most straightforward: there is simply an insufficient body of sound educational research, based on Gestalt, which can allow meaningful generalizations or theses to be drawn. This is not to deny that the language of Gestalt, taken at a metaphorical level, has contributed to research-led and theoretical discussion more generally, because it has, particularly in relation to neuroscience. But this is not the same as saying that the empirical foundations (that is to say, the sound, critically-researched knowledge base) of Gestalt are reliable and generalizable enough to be used to inform a broader approach to learning and teaching processes. Thus, in order to find a more robust critique of the classical behaviourists and neobehaviourists, an alternative approach is needed. Such an approach can be found in *cognitivist* psychology, and it is to this that we shall now turn.

Further reading

Gestalt theory occupies a diminishing role in the teacher-training curriculum for further education, although in other areas (informal education, counselling) it continues to be used. For those readers who do require additional introductory material, a number of general teacher-training books continue to cover this approach, such as:

Wallace, S. (2011), *Teaching, Tutoring and Training in the Lifelong Learning Sector*. Fourth edition. Exeter: Learning Matters. Chapter seven.

For a discussion that relates this approach to practical classroom application, the following is also recommended:

Gould, J. (2012), *Learning theory and classroom practice in the lifelong learning sector*. Second edition. Exeter: Learning Matters.

6 Cognitivism

Among the behaviourist psychologists were many who doubted the very existence of mind and consciousness: these were, at best, redundant concepts, having no place in a scientific explanation of human behaviour. Cognitive psychologists hold, on the contrary, that these concepts are necessary for an understanding of the human being.

The process of cognition is perceived as involving the overall functioning of a complex system of unobservable mental abilities (remembering, reasoning, and so forth), which are the key to the manipulation of information. The tenets of the cognitive school involve a rejection of those of the behaviourists. It is the learner, not the learning task, which is of significance; the emphasis in any explanation of learning has to be placed on mental structure, strategy and organization, not on the stimulus-response model; and internal processes and innate factors must be emphasized in discussions on learning.

Cognitivism makes wide use of analogies in order to explain the processes of cognition. A popular analogy is that of *information processing* and the input-output capacity of the computer. The learner is viewed as an information processor who discriminates among the input of stimuli to his or her sensory organs, detects regularities in accordance with his or her patterns of experience, and uses these regularities to solve problems in a manner which renders possible the coding of any further input. The 'cognitive product' is the direct result of 'cognitive processes' transforming, reducing, elaborating and storing cognitive input. This concept is known as the computational theory of mind.

Cognitive processing can be inferred as applying to all types of information. Therefore, students' learning can be analyzed in terms of a single model. Further, in the teaching–learning context, the relation between cognitive processing and environmental events is *reciprocal*. Students are, therefore, not merely passive recipients of information: they create what teaching means to *them*, so that it is incorrect to view their achievements as resulting solely from the teacher's activities. The role of mental structure and its organization should be seen as vital in the learning process. By structure, cognitivists mean the properties of intellect that are inferred as governing behaviour. Learning is viewed as the modification of these structures.

The key elements of cognitive psychology have an immediate appeal for many teachers. The teaching environment does appear to convey information which students process. It seems as though students act so as to make sense out of their environment by selecting important stimuli; some aspects of the environment are rejected, some are utilized. Cognitive characteristics, such as prior levels of student attainment, general mental abilities and developed memory functions do appear to account in large measure for levels of achievement. If teachers wish to understand the processes which are presumed to take place privately within the student, the analogy of information processing does appear to offer some assistance. For cognitive psychologists, the task of the teacher is seen as related directly to the development of cognitive strategies within the students, so that they may improve their capabilities in selecting and modulating their internal processes of thinking, perceiving and learning.

Skinner (discussed in Chapter 4) made a sustained attack on the conceptual basis of cognitivism, which he believed to have set back serious research into educational problems. He argued that cognitive scientists were speculating about processes which they had no real means of observing, and that their speculation was characteristic of metaphysics and literature, being couched in terms which were suitable enough in those areas but inappropriate for science.

Dewey

Dewey (1859–1952) became one of America's best-known educationists and made outstanding contributions to several areas of knowledge. His work on education reflects an era of transformation in social, political and technological thought. As a philosopher, he occupied the chairs of philosophy at the Universities of Chicago and Columbia and was one of the founders of *pragmatism* – the philosophy based on the doctrine that the only real test of the truth of philosophical principles or human cognitions is their practical result. As a psychologist, he was a founder of the school of *functionalism*, which viewed mind in terms of its adaptive significance for the organism, emphasizing its mediating function between the environment and the organism's needs. As an educationist he helped to mould American thought and practice in the classroom through a prodigious output of articles and books.

Dewey viewed education as intelligent action, characterized by the learner's continuous evaluation of his or her experiences, the eventual product of which is a redefinition of purposes. An educational process has two sides, one psychological and one sociological; the former is probably the more significant. Indeed, without the educator's insight into the psychological structure and activities of the student, the educative process can be only haphazard and arbitrary. Education should train one's powers of reflective thinking. Genuine freedom, says Dewey, is intellectual; it rests in the trained power of thought, in the ability to turn things over, to examine a problem in depth. Reflective thinking is based on five steps between the recognition of a problem and its solution: *suggestions* for a solution; *clarification* of the essence of the problem; the use of *hypotheses*; *reasoning* about the results of utilising one of the hypotheses; and *testing* the selected hypothesis by imaginative or overt action.

A sound educational theory is essential for sound educational practice, according to Dewey, if one accepts his concept of education as a conscious, purposive and informed activity. There are four central notions involved in education, each requiring deep theoretical analysis. First, *the aim* of the activity – educational ends and immediate aims had to be postulated with care, but the exact aims of instruction could not be 'legislated' because they depended on groups of variables unique to particular times and places. The second notion concerned *the teacher*, whose task was to prompt with enthusiasm ideas of development in the student by providing a setting which would be conducive to learning and to the acquisition of good habits of thinking. The third notion concerned *the learner*, whose desires, interests and purposes 'fired and sustained' the educational process. The fourth and final notion concerned *the curriculum*, the means by which educational aims were achieved, and this was to be based, not on the dictates of tradition, but on the principle of relevance of live issues that would stimulate orderly thought.

Dewey argued that the behavioural act in a reflex movement does not remain a 'meaningful' act if reduced merely to its sensorimotor elements. Rigid distinctions between sensations, thoughts and acts were to be avoided. Reflexes and all other types of behaviour had to be interpreted in the light of their significance for *adaptation*; isolating single units for study is valueless if the purpose of behaviour is ignored.

According to Dewey, the focus on an individual stimulus-response as a precursor to a specific form of learned behaviour was valueless if the *purpose* of that behaviour was going to be ignored. Instead, the study of the human organism *as a whole*, functioning in its environment, was the proper subject matter for psychologists. All human behaviour, he argued, is the result of events and is guided by anticipation of consequences and other intervening variables. That behaviour also determines events which follow it. Learning has to be viewed as part of a whole, as part of an interaction of the learner and his environment.

Learning is learning to think. The process of learning involves the exercise of the intelligence and the comprehending of information so that it can be used in new situations. Learning by doing is impossible, unless the doing effects a change in the learner's cognitive structures; routine or rote learning fails to develop the ability to understand, even though it promotes skill in external doing.

Dewey argued against the notion that learning was related to physical maturation. He also warned against the tendency of practical and technical programme of study being purely mechanical. Mere imitation, dictation of steps to be taken and mechanical drill may indeed give quick results, but they will not promote reflective thinking. The true learning of skills necessitates their acquisition as the result of the use of the mind, not just the use of fine muscle control.

Dewey's views on education also rest on a particular conception of growth, as a characteristic of life more generally. Our power to grow, Dewey argued, depends upon two elements, which are at their peak in adolescence: first, a need for others; and secondly, a quality that he termed 'plasticity'. Dewy defined 'plasticity' as the power to learn from one's experience, leading in turn to the formation of habits which allow people to control their environment for their own purposes. For Dewey, the true criterion of the value of education rests in the extent to which it creates a desire in people to learn to control their environments and to readjust one's activities to meet new situations, all of which he referred to as 'growth'.

Dewey's work and the teacher

Dewey places great emphasis on the role of the teacher as a stimulus to response to intellectual matters. Everything a teacher does in the classroom, as well as the manner in which he or she does it, will encourage the student to respond in some way or other and each response tends to set his or her attitude in some way or other. The teacher's influence is paramount, even in learner-centred situations in which the student's personal desires, level of attainment and motivations are taken carefully into account. The teacher's responsibility for the development of reflective thinking (not to be confused with reflective practice) in students is also emphasized. More radical is Dewey's stress on the importance of curriculum content, which he argued should be related to the student's environment and his or her intellectual needs rather than the demands of tradition. Teaching is a process not simply of the training of students but of the formation of social life. The real end to be sought by teachers and learners is not the accumulation of abstract bodies of knowledge, but growth (as defined above). Classroom activity is not set apart from society's progress; it is a prerequisite of that progress. Translated into practical terms, this necessitates a curriculum and modes of instruction designed consciously with the learner's purposes and the aims of society in mind.

Ausubel

Ausubel (1918–2008) carried out much of his work in the City University of New York in which he directed the Office of Research and Evaluation. The principles of his thought are set out in *Educational Psychology – A Cognitive View* (1968); his other important writings include *Theory and Problems of Adolescent Development* (1964) and *The Psychology of Meaningful Verbal Learning* (1963). Educational psychology, according to Ausubel, should be concerned primarily with the nature, conditions, outcomes and evaluation of classroom learning, not with topics such as the nature and development of needs, animal learning and conditioning. Further, it should take into account *only* those kinds of learning that take place in the classroom.

Ausubel theorized that learners' cognitive structures were hierarchically organized, with a foundation of facts and informational data supporting more complex concepts and arguments. Such structures could not be brought about through rote learning, however, which he dismissed as being the memorization of isolated facts that learners would not be able to refer to or make use of in any meaningful sense.

The principal factors influencing meaningful learning and retention are, according to Ausubel, the substantive content of a learner's structure of knowledge and the organization of that structure at any given time. If cognitive structure is unstable and disorganized it will inhibit meaningful learning; if it is stable and well organized it will assist in such learning. To have appropriate background knowledge of concepts and principles is essential for problem solving. Prior experience with related problems is necessary for a learner to deal successfully with novel situations.

Ausubel differentiated carefully between what he called reception and discovery learning. In reception learning a learner is presented with the entire content of what is to be learned in its final form; the presentation is meaningful if it allows her to integrate new ideas with existing knowledge schemes and reproduce it, with understanding, at some future date, but it will not be meaningful if it does not assist in the creation of new understanding. The presentation of a geometrical theorem in a way that gives the learner an opportunity to comprehend its structure, is an example. Discovery learning involves the learner discovering independently the principal content of what has to be learned before it can be incorporated meaningfully into already existing cognitive structures. Ausubel suggested that a condition for optimal learning is the placing of newly learned facts within a context for meaning. Following such learning, the student's capacity to transform facts and integrate them into previously acquired experience will be increased.

Ausubel did not accept that *all* discovery learning is meaningful, however (in contrast to Bruner, who is discussed below). Indeed, he believed that students who have reached the early stages of cognitive development learn more effectively by reception techniques. Problem-solving ability, he argues, is not necessarily transferred to situations outside the context in which it was acquired. Further, the discovery approach is not always linked to intrinsic motivation. He poses a rhetorical question to those who urge the use of discovery learning in all learning situations: is it intended that a student shall rediscover *every* principle set out in the subject curriculum?

Ausubel emphasized meaning as involving 'cognitive equivalence': there can be no meaning for the learner without the existence of a related cognitive structure. In learning, the student absorbs and integrates material to her cognitive structure. As a result of methodical expository teaching, students are able to proceed directly to a level of abstract understanding that is qualitatively superior to the intuitive level in terms of generality, clarity, precision and explication.

For Ausubel, meaningful learning – to which classroom activity should always be directed – involved the acquisition of new meanings. New meanings allow a learner to relate and anchor new material to the relevant and inclusive concepts in his or her existing cognitive structure and to integrate the essence of new experiences with existing patterns. By contrast, rote learning does not result in the acquisition of new meanings, it involves no logical perception, no comprehension of relationships, but only arbitrary constructs. But for meaningful learning to happen, two prerequisites are needed. First, the learner must be disposed to relate new information to a prior structure in preference to engaging in rote learning. Secondly, the new information presented to the learner must be relatable to his prior knowledge on a non-arbitrary basis: that is to say, the new information and that which is constituted in the learner's prior knowledge must be related conceptually.

Ausubel's work and the teacher

The principal function of the teacher was seen by Ausubel as the art and science of presenting ideas and information meaningfully and effectively so that clear, stable and unambiguous meanings emerge in the process of instruction and are retained by the learner over a long period of time as an organized body of knowledge. Ausubel's emphasis on meaningful learning necessitates the careful design of programmes of learning with that end in mind. His stress on linking units of instruction to form a continuous process necessitates a programmed approach to classwork so that sequential learning might be achieved and the learner assisted in the discrimination of old and new ideas.

Ausubel suggested that learning can be improved through use of the technique of what he termed progressive differentiation. The most general concepts of a subject discipline should be taught first, followed by less general concepts, thus setting the stage for the teaching of specific information and themes. Ease of assimilation and retention of information should result, since the learner's cognitive structure will then contain stable 'hooks' on which new material can be placed. The learner must be helped to discriminate between old and new ideas; this may require the paraphrasing of new ideas. Concepts must not be taught in isolation; the teacher must provide a framework related to the learner's existing knowledge into which new concepts will fit with relative ease. New ideas must be integrated with those previously learned during a course: it is unhelpful to students to devote one lesson, early in the course, to a discussion of ideas and concepts and to fail to refer to those concepts at later stages of the course, which would introduce barriers between subject elements and relationships. There should be reference throughout the course to previously learned ideas, definitions and principles, so that they are integrated into course content as a whole. Throughout these processes, the provision of feedback is seen by Ausubel as an essential component of encouraging learning. Feedback can confirm appropriate meanings, correct mistakes and misconceptions and indicate how well the learning task has been mastered.

On the matter of teacher responsibility for the content of the curriculum, Ausubel took an uncompromising stand against the advocates of a system in which student decisions are used to determine that content. The direction of the curriculum should always be the responsibility of the teacher, notwithstanding those arguments made in terms of democracy or progressivism. The content of the curriculum should take into account the students' needs, but its formulation remains, however, the responsibility of the teachers, not the students.

Bruner

Bruner (b. 1915) graduated from Duke University and Harvard, where his experimental work in psychology convinced him that the effective instruction of human beings involves leading them through sequences of statements of problems or aspects of knowledge which cumulatively increase the ability to group, transform, and transfer what is being learned. He became professor of psychology at Harvard in 1952 and established and directed the influential Centre for Cognitive Studies. In 1973 he was appointed professor of experimental psychology at Oxford. Bruner's special interest in the craft of teaching led him to a long-term programme of empirical research in schools and colleges and to a lasting interest in the role of the teacher and the relationship between insight, under-standing and competence. Among Bruner's many writings, the following texts will be of particular interest to college tutors: *A Study of Thinking* (1990), dealing with the formation and use of concepts; *The Process of Education* (1960), reporting a congress on teaching for understanding; *On Knowing* (1962), essays on the phenomenon of human knowledge; *Toward a Theory of Instruction* (1962), perhaps Bruner's most influential text; and *The Culture of Education* (1999).

Bruner positions learning as being the creation of the developed human being, not simply as the accumulation of knowledge. The institutions in which formal learning takes place – schools, colleges, universities – are responsible for what he termed the 'amplification of intellectual skills', which must involve instruction concerning the place of students in the culture of their society. Cultural variations produce variations in modes of thinking so that a student's cognitive growth will be influenced directly by social patterns.

Students should be trained to develop their capacities to the full. Understanding of principles should be developed if students are to be given confidence in their capabilities. They must be taught how to analyze problems. What students should be learning is not 'particular performances', but competence, and central to the attainment of that end is the acquisition of correct modes of thinking. Bruner's cognitive development theory is concerned with how what one wishes to teach can best be learned; it takes into account both learning and development.

Learning, therefore, is a cognitive process involving the learner acquiring new information, transforming his state of existing knowledge and checking the adequacy of that state of knowledge against the demands of new situations. We learn best, not by committing a body of knowledge to mind, but by participating in the process that makes possible the establishment of knowledge. Knowledge is a process, not a product. The acquisition of knowledge is an active process and depends for its effectiveness on the learner relating incoming information to previously acquired frames of reference. Learners gradually acquire internal models, giving them a pattern of meaning for their experiences and an awareness of predictability and regularities so that they are able to extrapolate on the basis of that pattern. They construct hypotheses to explain incoming information and test them so as to produce meaningful interpretations of reality.

Learners construct mental models of the external world and those models will be determined largely by the culture of the society of which those learners are a part. An adequate model will not only explain objective reality, but will also predict how the world might be. As such, the models become 'expectancies', allowing the learner to make short-cuts and leaps from partial evidence, reflecting the human tendency to organize, sort and categorize.

The construction of these categories involves the learner's ability to create sequences of mental events related to goal, a process that consists of three elements. The first is the *informational situation* which will determine whether more information needs to be gathered by the learner before he arrives at a conclusion. The second factor is the *certainty of cognition*, that is, the intensity of the thinking needed to arrive at a conclusion. The third factor is the *general consequence of failure*, that is, the risk involved in the result of cognition. These factors interact to produce a learner's strategy of movement towards a learning goal.

Growth in learning capacity is not, according to Bruner, a gradual collection or reinforcement of associations or stimulus-response connections. Rather, it is a more uneven process, involving period of both activity and rest. Nor does learning necessarily depend on the learner's age, but rather on his or her ability to organize incoming information within frames of reference and models of reality. The development of that ability is one of the teacher's principal tasks. But the difficulties of this task should not be underestimated.

In Bruner's view, education is concerned with the intensification of cognitive skills related to the principles and needs of the community's culture; it should be linked closely to an understanding and development of those technologies and their tools which are a vital part of cultural expression. The purposes of education may be categorized as follows:

1 The development of the student's confidence in his or her innate capacities and their potential for development. This involves a curriculum which will encourage the student to explore strategies of learning through *problem-solving*.

2 The development of the student's confidence in his or her ability to solve problems of a new type through *use of the mind*. The development of understanding and knowledge of transforming one's powers of cognition will be of much importance.

3 The motivation of the student to operate on his or her own with confidence. Location of the form of a problem is important and this requires the study of *techniques of interpretation*.

4 The development of *economy in the use of the mind*. This will necessitate training directed at the skills needed to search for relevance and structure, what Bruner calls *reflective* learning.

5 The development of intellectual honesty in the student. It is the task of the teacher to insist upon *rigour* and *self-discipline* in the attainment of goals in the various disciplines of our culture.

Bruner's work and the teacher

A theory of instruction appropriate for our day and our type of society must be, according to Bruner, both prescriptive and normative. It must involve the enunciation of rules concerning effectiveness in attaining knowledge and must provide for the evaluation of modes of teaching and learning. Criteria for instruction must be considered. Such a theory can be built around five essential features:

1 It must specify the experiences which will most effectively predispose students to learn. Effective learning will involve a rigorous exploration of alternatives, leading to learning how to learn.

2 It must specify ways of structuring knowledge so that students might attain comprehension at the best possible or achievable level or scale. A general understanding of the fundamental structure of a subject necessitates grasping its inner significance by comprehension of basic, generalized principles, so that knowledge that is of significance can be extracted from information that is less so.

3 It must specify the optimal sequences of presentation of the material to be learned. (For the significance of sequencing, please refer to Chapter 23). Different subject matters have their own appropriate forms of representation, allowing knowledge of their principles to be converted into comprehensible structures.

4 It must specify the nature and pacing of reinforcement in the processes of teaching and learning. This involves assessing and giving feedback to the learner during the instructional process in a fashion which will make it possible for him or her to take over the corrective function, thus avoiding the danger of establishing in the learner a permanent dependence upon a scaffolding of reward and a rewarder. This will necessitate *appropriate feedback of results to the student*. It should come at that point in a problem-solving episode when the student is comparing the results of his or her try-out with some criterion of what he or she seeks to achieve.

5 It must seek to take into account the fact that a curriculum ought to reflect the nature of knowledge, and the nature of the knower and the knowledge-getting process.

Interpreting the cultural patterns of society for the learner and assisting him or her to achieve mastery of the processes inherent in creative thinking are key tasks of the teacher, according to Bruner. Students must be taught in a manner which allows them to comprehend single instances in terms of broad generalizations and principles. Bruner stresses that the student learning physics is, in effect a physicist, and it is easier for her or him to learn physics behaving like a physicist than by doing something else. The class teacher has the responsibility of ensuring that methods of teaching are *realistic* in that they allow discovery activity; purely expository teaching on its own is of little value, according to Bruner, in helping a student to acquire the capacity to think creatively and critically.

Bruner's call for discovery learning (or, as he occasionally refers to it, 'inquiry training') reflects his belief that the curriculum of a subject should be determined by the most fundamental understanding that can be achieved of the underlying principles that give structure to that subject. Teaching will be most productive where the subject matter is 'gutted' so that its bare bones – its structural elements – are revealed and made a foundation for the acquisition of principles. A student who knows the principles of a discipline has the power to investigate and solve problems within its terms. In addition, the student is more likely to remember information associated with these principles: If information is to be used effectively, it must be translated into the learner's way of attempting to solve a problem.

In discovering the meaning of principles, a student is learning concepts and relationships. Bruner suggests that the activity of discovering has *four* advantages. First, there is a growth in intellectual potency – the student acquires the ability to develop strategies in approaching and analysing patterns in his or her environment in an organized manner. Secondly, intrinsic motivation becomes a preferred alternative to extrinsic rewards – the student achieves satisfaction from discovering solutions on his or her own (motivation is discussed in depth in Chapter 20). Thirdly, the student who has mastered the techniques of discovery learning is able to apply them to the solution of real problems outside the classroom. Fourthly, improvements in memory seem to be associated with the organization of one's knowledge – retrieval of information stored in the memory (an issue discussed in Chapter 19) becomes easier where the student has organized her knowledge in terms of her own system.

Building on Bruner's views, Taba (1963) outlined some general steps in discovery learning. First, learners should be confronted with a problem that initiates a feeling of bafflement. The teacher should offer no important generalizations at this stage; learners must be encouraged to explore the problem for themselves. Next, they should be prompted to utilize previously acquired knowledge so as to understand new patterns and structures from which will emerge solutions to the problem facing them. They should then be given an opportunity to demonstrate, in relation to other problems, the principles they have now acquired. In this way the teacher has provided the conditions facilitating the learner's discovery of organising principles.

Mastery of specifics is essential if the student is to make progress and it is the teacher's task to ensure such mastery. Lower-order regularities must be mastered if there is to be movement towards higher-order learning. Students must be given an opportunity to master specifics by developing skills related to immediate problems in which their knowledge may be put to use. The exploration of alternatives must be part of the instructional process and it should be linked with a general understanding of the structure of subject matter. The acquisition of a generalized set of basic ideas is an important aim of classroom instruction. Indeed, according to Bruner, one of the true tests of learning is whether the student has grasped, and can use, the 'generic code' he or she has been taught. Speed of learning, resistance to forgetting, transfer of learning, creation of ability to generalize and to create new hypotheses are some of the criteria of instruction. A curriculum built on rudiments acquired at an early age, moving upwards and circling back to previous understanding is essential for the successful structuring of subject matter. Such a curriculum ought to be built around the great issues, principles and values that a society deems worthy of the continual concern of its members. Development and redevelopment of the learners' capacities, so that they are able to deal with problems at advancing levels of complexity, are the prerequisites of successful learning and this necessitates appropriate planning of instruction in the classroom.

Bruner argues also in favour of students being given training in recognizing the 'plausibility of guesses'. Educated guesses, which may possess the elements of an intuitive leap (although this is not to be confused with Gestalt) are not to be discouraged. To repress guessing is, in effect, to check some of the cognitive processes inherent in discovery.

From the variety of teaching techniques suggested by Bruner, Dembo (1981) selected four which, taken together, could constitute an effective teaching model for many courses in FE:

1 first, teach the basic structure of the subject, emphasizing concepts, fundamental principles and relationships

2 next, experiment with discovery learning techniques so that students are motivated and assisted in the acquisition and retention of principles

3 thirdly, consider the advisability of commencing sessions with a problem that calls for the utilization of previously acquired knowledge in order to assist students in the search for solutions at a new level of knowledge

4 finally, pitch the instruction at a level appropriate to a student's overall cognitive functioning so that concept formation is encouraged.

Cognitivism

On the teacher's role in reinforcement of learning, Bruner is categorical. He calls for a de-emphasis of extrinsic rewards. Intrinsic rewards should be emphasized instead. The teacher's task is to arrange instruction so that there is a challenge to their students to exercise their mental powers fully and to heighten their inner sense of accomplishment. The danger of creating dependence upon rewards is to be avoided. In the absence of external rewards, students need continuous knowledge of their progress, which involves effective feedback.

Instruction, Bruner reminds the teacher, is, after all, an effort to assist or shape growth. It is the responsibility of the teacher to seek to understand growth as development, and to link this understanding to an appropriate theory of knowledge and instruction.

Summary

Cognitivist perspectives continue to be influential. Although classical behaviourists and neobehaviourists might complain that cognitivist psychology lacks a sound and broad experimental base, cognitivists in turn might argue that behaviourists – of all hues – have positioned their own theories on a fundamentally mistaken premise: that the behaviour of animals in laboratory settings in some way equates to the behaviour of humans in classrooms and workshops (or, indeed, anywhere else for that matter). Cognitivist perspectives provide the teacher with ways of thinking about classroom interactions, about the role of assessment and feedback, and about the nature and construction of the curriculum. Put simply, these perspectives start to offer meaningful commentary about educational processes more generally, rather than internal learning processes more specifically. The focus on the environment or context of learning – though still restricted to formal educational systems – is also of immediate relevance to college tutors and lecturers. Also new is the emphasis placed on how the individual learner might become part of the society in which she or he lives through the educational process. How such processes might impact on the learner as a person, as an individual, however, is not considered. In order to think about these questions, a different approach is needed: humanism.

Further reading

Tennant (2007), recommended for chapter 4, is also recommended here. Other works, in addition to those in the bibliography, that would inform a more extensive analysis of this body of theory include:

Parkin, A. J. (2000), *Essential cognitive psychology*. Hove: Psychology Press.

Woolfolk, A., Hughes, M. and Walkup, V. (2008), *Psychology in Education*. Harlow: Pearson.

And again, there is a useful and well-informed essay at the *Encyclopedia of Informal Education*:

Smith, M. K. (1999). 'The cognitive orientation to learning', *the encyclopedia of informal education*. http://infed.org/mobi/the-cognitive-orientation-to-learning/ [accessed: 15 May 2013].

7 Humanism

Humanistic psychology emerged in America largely as a deliberate reaction against behaviourism, which was condemned, along with psychoanalysis, as having reduced essentially human qualities to mere physical entities. The leading proponents of the humanistic theory of learning, Maslow and Rogers, advocate principles based on the 'self' as the essential characteristic of the human being, on the growth, worth and dignity of persons, and on the need for teachers to facilitate the processes which will lead to the 'self-actualization' of students. Education has the task, according to the humanistic school, of helping each person to become the best that she or he is able to become.

Maslow developed a theory of self-actualization which allows a person to grow to his or her optimal stature. Rogers fashioned the idea of experiential learning (a concept taken up by other educational researchers as well), which would give to education a humanistic orientation, leading to true freedom and self-fulfilment. These ideas have been perceived by some – teachers, policy makers and researchers – as a clear challenge, even a threat, to the practice of formal, structured instruction as administered in schools and colleges. Perhaps because of this perceived challenge, they have arguably had a greater impact amongst practitioners in adult and continuing education.

Maslow

Maslow (1908–70) was professor of psychology at Brandeis University and pursued research which resulted in a distinctive contribution to theories of motivation and to a novel view of psychology which stressed human potential and aspirations. *Motivation and Personality* (1954), *Toward a Psychology of Being* (1968) and *The Farther Reaches of Human Nature* (1971) set out his perception of the tasks of psychology and education as the development of the real self. What he referred to as 'scientific' psychology has given to the subject a narrow, sterile and dehumanized basis, focusing on the mechanics of behaviour rather than the person in themselves. Maslow instead demanded an approach to psychology based on the person as a whole, which would recognize her higher nature and dignity. Human beings have needs, he argued, which must be analyzed, understood and gratified if full growth is to result. It is the task of the psychologist to uncover the foundations of those needs. By extension, it is the task of the teacher to assist in the development of students toward their full worth. The need gratification which Maslow had in mind was perceived by him as the most important single principle underlying all development.

In his study of motivation, Maslow arrived at a formulation based on a 'hierarchy of needs' (see below). A person's behaviour in the classroom, factory or home is dominated at any given moment by those needs which have the greatest potency. Motivation is to be understood in terms of an individual's striving for growth. In the context of education, motivation for learning may not arise until certain basic needs have been satisfied; that motivation should be recognized as being internally-driven – as being intrinsic.

Maslow defined learning according to two paradigms: *extrinsic* learning and *intrinsic* learning. He defined extrinsic learning as 'learning of the outside, learning of the impersonal, of arbitrary associations, of arbitrary conditioning, that is, of arbitrary (or at best, culturally determined) meanings and responses'. Such learning is extrinsic to the learner and his personality because it comes, quite literally, from outside or beyond him: as a result, such learning cannot have meaning for the learner because it's content or subject matter is alien to him. The learner, conditioned by his teacher, is merely collecting habits, associations and pieces of information, just as he might accumulate objects which he puts in his pocket. What he has collected may be largely irrelevant to the particular, individual, idiosyncratic human being he is. Intrinsic learning, on the other hand, rejects the generality of repetition, of learning by drilling and involves, primarily, learning to be a human being in general and, secondly, learning to be a particular human being (that is to say, learning to be ones self). This necessitates the development of wisdom and life skills. Such learning will not only reflect the goals of the teacher, but will also be based on the values and perceived objectives of the learners themselves.

The teacher who wishes to assist in the process of intrinsic learning must see herself as a helper, counsellor and guide. She must be receptive rather than intrusive; she must accept the student as he is and assist him to learn what kind of person he is. She must acquaint herself with the student's style, aptitudes and potentialities. She will concern herself, above all, with the student's growth and self-actualization.

Optimal persons and peak experiences

Maslow studied the lives of a number of historical persons who, he claimed, had fulfilled their basic potentialities and had grown into self-actualized people. They included Thomas Jefferson (the third president of the United States of America), Henry David Thoreau (an American philosopher, author and poet), Eleanor Roosevelt (delegate to the United Nations and chair of the committee that drafted the Universal Declaration of Human Rights) and

Albert Einstein (the Nobel physicist). These 'optimal persons' had characteristics in common – they had been dedicated fully to causes outside themselves; they had reacted to experiences selflessly, with full concentration and total absorption. They had been spontaneous, independent, and in tune with their 'inner beings'.

Few persons, according to Maslow, would experience self-actualization in its full sense in the manner that the outstanding individuals listed above would have done. But many more people would have enjoyed occasional moments involving what he termed 'peak experiences', such as the vision to be derived from listening to classical music (Maslow, 1968). The teacher whose advice and guidance can assist in movement toward such experiences is assisting students in their real growth and in the realization of their inner potential. The emotional reactions which accompany peak experiences have, according to Maslow, 'a special flavour of wonder, of awe, of reverence, of humility and surrender before the experience as before something great'.

Peak experiences have prologues and consequences of which a teacher must be aware. These experiences may be triggered in a variety of ways and in a variety of contexts, whether studying music or studying mathematics. Acceptance of this concept will involve the sympathetic teacher in a continuous search for modes of classroom delivery that will lead a student to experience the real pleasure to be derived from discovery. The consequences of peak experiences may involve being changed, seeing things differently, or having different ideas or opinions about things. No teacher, says Maslow, can afford to ignore the significance of changes of this nature.

The hierarchy of needs

In his research, Maslow produced a hierarchy of human needs which affects the pattern of behaviour designed to achieve a goal – we refer to this as 'motivation'. Observing one student with a conspicuous drive to work hard and to perform well, and then comparing this with another student who's work habits are sporadic at best, can best be made sense of through reference to some kind of internal process which moves these two students to satisfy their perceived needs in such different ways.

Maslow's hierarchy of needs

These differences reflect different *levels* of need, which are commonly visualized as a pyramid (see Figure 7.1, below):

(a) At the base of the pyramid are *fundamental physiological needs*. For example, thirst and hunger lead to the need and desire for water and food. Survival depends on the satisfaction of these needs. Temporary deprivation may override other drives.

(b) The next level is made up of *safety needs*, such as a desire for protection, physical and psychological security, which must be satisfied.

(c) The third level comprises *belonging needs* or social needs, such as friendship, affection, or affiliation and a sense of membership.

(d) The fourth level is based on the *need for self-esteem* which, in turn, reflects a desire for adequacy and competence, and for attention, recognition and prestige.

(e) At the very top of the pyramid is the need for self-fulfilment or *self-actualization*. This need may be met by internal cognitive growth – to which the teacher can contribute much – as well as by other rich and varied experiences.

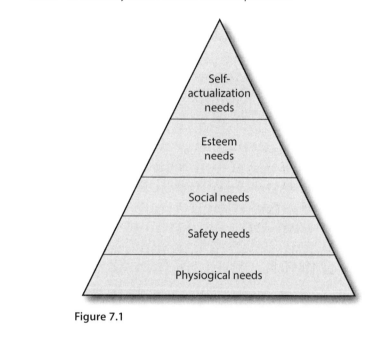

Figure 7.1

The first four levels of needs (a)–(d) are referred to by Maslow as deficiency needs. They motivate the student to engage in activity only when they remain unmet to a significant degree. In the classroom, the satisfaction of physiological needs may call for comfortable seating, appropriate ventilation. Safety needs may include respect for students' privacy or demonstrably fair treatment. Social needs may relate to interaction among students and staff. Esteem needs may relate to self-respect, or praise in appropriate circumstances. Self-actualization is seen as a 'growth need': students strive continuously to satisfy it. In his earlier writings, Maslow appeared to suggest that self-actualizing needs would emerge and be activated automatically following the satisfaction of the fourth level of needs (that is to say, level 'd'). He commented later that the move to the level of self-actualization level (level 'e') depends not only on the satisfaction of lower needs, but on an acceptance of certain types of value implicit in both *cognitive* needs (to know and understand) and *aesthetic* needs (such as the need for order and accord).

Maslow's model throws some light on motivation in the classroom. Students' basic needs have to be satisfied before effective learning can take place. For example, the lack of motivation apparent in a student who is physically tired or who is hungry has to be accepted as a temporary phenomenon only. Students who feel threatened by an environment which they perceive as hostile, or who interpret the demands of instruction as an unacceptable restriction on their freedom may be experiencing a need for security. Class members who esteem acceptance by their peer group as more important than academic achievement may be demonstrating an apparent lack of motivation which reflects no more than the significance they attach to self-esteem and recognition. For the FE lecturer, Maslow's message is clear: do not accept the absence of motivation in a student as an unalterable state of affairs. Motivation can often be analyzed adequately in Maslow's terms; it can, therefore, be understood and modified to the advantage of student and teacher.

Maslow appears to suggest that, when the need for self-actualization arises, a person will not always choose his or her course of action wisely: a student may, at this stage, make a bad, even seemingly self-destructive choice. The teacher can assist, according to Maslow, in ensuring that the student's choice is at least in the right direction, by ensuring, as far as is possible, that learning situations are not perceived by the student as dangerous, valueless or threatening. The growth choice must be presented so that it is perceived by the student as leading to a desirable outcome. It is for the teacher to help in situations of this nature by urging the student to choose by making the growth choice positively attractive, and less dangerous, and by making the regressive choice less attractive and more costly (refer also to the discussion on motivation in Chapter 20).

Maslow's work and the teacher

The fundamental tenets of humanistic psychology as expounded by Maslow, his emphasis on realizing human potential, of developing personality and understanding, are immediately attractive to many teachers – and quite understandably so. It is, however, partly the difficulty of interpreting the precise nature and practical applications of the theory which has created a degree of scepticism. Much of Maslow's theorizing appears to be based on insubstantial speculation rather than thorough and robust research (an issue that will be returned to at the end of the chapter). It has been said that his theory relies for its underpinnings on colourful anecdotes, selective case reporting and inconclusive observations. The belief that a person's essential nature is 'pressing to emerge' has not been validated; the catalogue of exemplary 'optimal persons' and their characteristics has been interpreted as reflecting little more than American white middle-class aspirations, values and morality of the 1950s and 1960s (Illeris, 2007).

So is it still a worthwhile exercise to take account of the general argument of Maslow's work? Defenders would argue that his motivation model assists in explaining, albeit only in a pragmatic rather than theoretical manner, the nature and quality of some types of student drive in the classroom. His insistence on the value of intrinsic learning should remind those teachers who are responsible for curriculum design and syllabus construction of the significance of insight learning, as opposed to the mechanical acquisition of facts, and of the importance of the enunciation of educational goals that are understood by students, in terms of learning more about themselves and their relationship to others. Also of understandable importance are the arousal of curiousity among students, the explanation of the significance of what is to be learned, the use of verbal praise where it is appropriate, the provision of swift feedback on student progress, and the careful delivery of properly planned and engaging sequences of sesisons or lessons. In sum, those who are assisting the educational growth of students should understand the basis of maximizing and maintaining student motivation if their classroom practice is going to be successful.

Rogers

Carl Rogers (1902–87) occupied chairs in psychology at Ohio State University and the University of Wisconsin. His work in therapy became the foundation of a theory of learning which was outlined in *Freedom to Learn* (1969), which was later revised as *Freedom to Learn for the 1980s* (1983). Rogers' thinking on education was similar to that of Maslow: he opposed much of the educational practice that surrounded him, and the psychology on which it is based; he called instead for student-centred education based on active discovery, in contrast to the essentially passive, conformist, accumulation of stored knowledge that constituted the dominant approach of his time.

The humanist approach to education marked out by Rogers placed emphasis on feeling and thinking, on the recognition and importance of a student's personal values, on interpersonal communication, and on the development of positive self-concepts. Human beings, he argued, are innately good and are oriented to growth. Their perceptions of reality determine their patterns of behaviour. Each person has an 'actualizing tendency' which maintains and enhances her or his experiences and potentialities. As they grow, so they develop self-concepts. The task of the educator lies in the construction of situations that will allow freedom to learn, and the provision of those conditions in which learning can be generally facilitated. The goal of the educator should be to facilitate the growth and development of a fully functioning person who is dependable in being realistic, self-enhancing, socialized and appropriate in their behaviour. The outstanding quality of the successful teacher, according to Rogers, is *empathy* – the ability to see someone else's problems through one's own eyes, and to communicate understanding with clarity and care.

The background to Rogers' attitude to contemporaneous, formal education systems, which have produced institutions which he perceived as traditional (here used as a pejorative term), rigid, bureaucratic and resistant to change, is to be found in his educational psychology based on the concepts of *organism*, *self* and *congruence*. The organism is the total person, with a need for positive regard by others. When its needs are met, it will develop a self, which is in congruence with (that is, in alignment, agreement and sympathy with) those needs and the environment. Lack of congruence will result in inner conflict, alienation and hostility to the outside world. It is an essential task of education, therefore, to assist students in dealing with manifestations of incongruence. In order to achieve this, teachers need to create a climate of trust in the classroom, ways by which students can paticipate in decision-making, and a culture of excitement of intellectual and emotional discovery.

A theory of experiential learning

Rogers rejected learning which is primarily directed, cognitive and basically concerned with the fixing of certain associations. Such learning is often very difficult to acquire and is forgotten swiftly. In contrast, experiential learning is meaningful and significant. It arises from the student's appreciation of what he is learning as satisfying his real needs and wants.

Experiential learning has the following important elements: it possesses a quality of personal involvement and stimulates the feelings and cognitive aspects of personality; it is self-initiated, in that the impetus to learn comes from within; it is pervasive and can affect the learner's entire personality; it is evaluated by the learner as satisfying a need; its essence is meaning.

Learning to learn and active involvement in a process of change should be the primary aims of an education based on experiential learning. But, Rogers argued, the assumptions implicit in current educational practice deny the possibilities and value of such learning. It is assumed by those in charge of educational institutions at all levels that students cannot be trusted to pursue their own learning, so that guidance along approved paths becomes necessary. Learning consists of the presentation of facts which are built, brick by brick, on a foundation of clearly defined knowledge. Such assumptions, argued Rogers, are faulty and dangerous. When made the basis of practice, they result in a denial of freedom, a stunting of intellectual growth, and the formation of behavioural patterns which are flawed and which prevent the flourishing of students' actualization. Instead, an experiential approach is required, characterized by the flexible use of space, student choice of activity, and the sharing of control with a class with students in a structured multi-task fashion, which in turn gives the students the chance to develop responsibility, autonomy and higher-level thinking skills.

The humanistic approach to education

Rogers advocated a humanistic orientation which should characterize an approach to problems of education. The principles of this orientation are set out below. (Rogers' own words appear in quotation marks):

Humanistic approach to teaching

1 'Human beings have a natural potentiality for learning.' They are 'ambivalently eager to develop and learn'. This desire to learn and discover can be made the foundation of a new approach to education.

2 'Significant learning takes place when the subject matter is perceived by the student as having relevance for his own purposes.' Learning takes place more rapidly when a student sees his or her learning environment as relevant to the achievement of his or her desired objectives.

3 'Learning which involves a change in self-organization is threatening and tends to be resisted.' Reappraisal of one's own values or prior knowledge or becoming aware that previously held opinions or beliefs have been mistaken, is often painful to the learner.

4 'Those learnings which are threatening to the self are more easily perceived and assimilated where external threats are at a minimum.' The encouragement of self-evaluation and the freedom to work at one's own pace are relevant here.

5 'When threat to the self is low, experience can be perceived in differentiated fashion and learning can proceed.' An environment which assures students of personal security will enhance their learning processes.

6 'Much significant learning is acquired through doing.' The exploration of problems which one is currently experiencing, and their solution as the result of 'experiential confrontation' with practical issues, will enhance learning.

7 'Learning is facilitated when the student participates responsibly in the learning process.' Participative learning, in which students decide their own course of action, is more effective than passive learning.

8 'Self-initiated learning which involves the whole person of the learner – feelings as well as intellect – is the most lasting and pervasive.' This kind of learning may occur in the discovery of a new, self-generated idea or in the acquisition of a difficult skill.

9 'Independence, creativity, and self-reliance are all facilitated when self-criticism and self-evaluation are basic and evaluation by others is of secondary importance.' Creativity involves an atmosphere of freedom and, if creative work is a goal, external evaluation is largely fruitless. The student must come to his or her own conclusions and decide on appropriate personal standards.

10 'The most socially useful learning in the modern world is the learning of the process of learning, a continuing openness to experience and incorporation into oneself of the process of change.' The survival of our culture depends on our ability to develop persons for whom change is a central fact of life 'and who have been able to live comfortably with this central fact'.

11 'Significant learning rests not upon the teacher's lectures and presentations but upon certain attitudinal qualities which exist in the personal relationship between the facilitator and the learner.' That is to say, it is somewhere in the inter-personal relationship between the lecturer and the student that learning happens.

The teacher as facilitator

The translation of Rogers' humanistic approach into a process of teaching involves a total reappraisal of the role and functions of the teacher. Rogers understood the role of the teacher as being not a controller or director of learning, but a facilitator of learning. He put forward the following guidelines for the *teacher-as-facilitator*:

Teacher as facilititator

1   the teacher should be involved with setting the initial mood or climate of the group or class experience, from greeting students as they enter, to establishing an appropriate physical environment

2   the teacher should help to elicit and clarify the purposes of the individuals in the class as well as the more general purposes of the group. Time should be allowed for students to establish their own reasons and aspirations for learning

3   the teacher should rely on the desire of each student to implement those purposes that have meaning for her or him, as the motivational force behind significant learning

4   the teacher should look on himself or herself as a flexible resource to be utilized by the group, not as an unquestionable authority figure

5   the teacher should attempt to organize and make available the widest possible range of resources for learning

6   the teacher should, in responding to expressions from the class group, accept intellectual content *and* personal feelings. If learning is about the whole person, then the emotional as well as intellectual development or growth of the person needs to be accommodated

Humanism

7. the teacher should become a participant learner and a member of the class group
8. the teacher should share his or her feelings and thoughts with the group
9. the teacher should remain alert to the expression of deep or strong feelings
10. the teacher should endeavour to recognize and accept his or her own limitations.

Rogers' work and the teacher

Rogers' perspectives raise a number of fundamental challenges to established educational structures and philosophies. Current educational provision is hopelessly inadequate, he argued, because it is derived from false premises and a simplistic view of students. In the name of a wider freedom and the continuation of our culture, the education system must be changed and the teacher must rethink his or her role. In particular, the teacher must examine the extent to which he exercises, consciously or unconsciously, decisive control over his class so that students are prevented from making choices and managing their own learning.

The response of teachers to this challenge has been mixed. Relatively few have adopted Rogers' tenets in their entirety; some, however, have attempted to organize 'free schools', 'discovery areas' and 'student-centred learning experiences'. The liberal tradition of adult education also provided an environment that was receptive to Rogers' approaches (Wallis, 1996). The kinds of criticism levelled against Maslow have also been applied to Rogers. In Rogers' work, there is an absence of compelling scientific evidence in favour of experiential learning, which is justified in broadly rhetorical rather than empirical terms. The vagueness of terms such as 'fully functioning person' and 'participative learning' makes interpretation and application of principles difficult, if not impossible. Rogers' view of 'freedom in education' is believed by many commentators to be based upon a misunderstanding of the concept of 'freedom' in relation to the classroom. In *Learning to be Free* (1963), Rogers articulated his beliefs that people are 'essentially unfree in a scientific sense', that 'self-initiated student learning' is critical for freedom, and that it is essential 'to initiate a process in the classroom of learning to be free'. Put simply, many of Rogers' key tenets are insubstantial and impressionistic.

One of the most trenchant and coherent bodies of criticism of Rogers' work came from Skinner (discussed in Chapter 4). In *The Free and Happy Student* (1973), he argued against the idea of 'the free classroom', and proposed that Rogers' failure to acknowledge the undeniable benefits that the formal provision of education and training – no matter how imperfect they might be (and Skinner by no means fully endorsed the educational structures of his day) – constituted a serious weakness in his argument. Rogers' teaching model, he argued, implied that only what is relevant to the present is of significance. It made no explicit preparation for the future. Indeed, the very concept of a 'free school' is a myth. If students are 'freed' from the control of their teachers, then they simply come under the control of other conditions that still need to be researched in terms of both cause and effect. In *The Selection of Behaviour* (1989), Skinner argued that Rogers and Maslow felt threatened by the objectivity of scientific knowledge and its so-called 'impersonal' workings. By contrast, Skinner argued that social action based upon a scientific analysis of human behaviour is much more likely to be humane than not.

The positive side of Rogers' work is viewed by some practising teachers as being related to his call for the humanization of the classroom. His reminder of the paramount importance of the student in the education process, his opposition to the sterility of dogmatic instruction, and his insistence on questioning not only what we teach but also why we teach it, have all acted as an incentive to some teachers engaged in the rethinking of the curriculum. The humanist emphasis on individual free will and a balanced curriculum attuned to the student's social environment and his personal, intellectual and emotional needs, on the integration of studies so that insight might emerge, on activity leading to understanding, and on growth as a desirable educational end, should not be overlooked. Teachers in FE who do not subscribe fully to Rogers' views of the essential good nature and trustworthiness of human nature and the need for self-actualization, may, nevertheless, share his belief in the maximum development of human personality as a worthy educational goal (although this is a goal that is by no means unique to Rogers' writings). They will empathize with his beliefs that humanistic education should assist in helping teachers to grow as persons, finding rich satisfaction in their interaction with learners and uncovering the excitement in intellectual and emotional discovery which leads students to became lifelong learners.

Summary

The theories of both Rogers and Maslow are undoubtedly attractive to some practitioners, particularly in post-compulsory settings (including both further and adult education). Elements of the humanist approach such as the focus on the broader growth or development of the whole person (as distinct from a narrower focus on learning as a feature of cognition, of mental or intellectual work), or the focus on intrinsic as opposed to extrinsic motivators for learning, resonate strongly with those practitioners in the FE sector who define it as a 'second chance' sector, and who see their students as having been in some way failed by compulsory schooling. Defining the role of the teacher in a facilitative rather than didactic manner can easily be seen as being appropriate for such students who may well have had only negative experiences of formal schooling: if they are going to be successful in their FE colleges, these students will need to establish a new mode of relationship with their teachers, and facilitative models such as those presented here might be appropriate.

Criticisms of these theories, however, are both numerous and profound. Just as Gestalt theories were dismissed as being descriptive rather than analytical or predictive because they were not based on any serious research, so have humanist approaches been criticized for being partial at best and anecdotal at worst. The idea that a meaningful, generalizable theory of learning and teaching can be built from a study of isolated historical figures such as former US presidents, Nobel prize winners and United Nations representatives is no more convincing than the idea that such a theory might be generated from studies involving monkeys, rats or pigeons. Like gestalt, so humanism speaks to practitioners in such a way as to reinforce and thereby (erroneously) justify their philosophies or practices, rather than to meaningfully explicate them.

Maslow's hierarchy of needs stands as perhaps the best example of a hypothesis (as it is most certainly not a theory in the correct sense of the word) that has been misapplied and indiscriminately used. It is a theory that attempts to categorize motivation as a discrete, transferable quality or characteristic of the human being, whereas instead the focus of educational research ought to be on different groups of learners and what factors – environmental, social, political – motivate or demotivate them. At a more prosaic level, it is quite easy to find everyday examples in FE colleges and adult education outreach centres where Maslow's hierarchy can be demonstrated to be false. Illeris (2007) provides the example of people who defy social relations to achieve something that is of greater importance to them, giving the (admittedly extreme) version of suicide bombers as an example. For the purposes of this book, the frequency of marital break down amongst mature students who are returning to further or higher education is a readily recognizable, and more palatable, example of motivation to participate in learning that counters Maslow's hierarchy. But if Maslow's theories are to safely be passed over, Rogers offers something more substantial to the practitioner, not in terms of a robust theoretical perspective, but in terms of an analysis of the relationship between student and tutor that offers a meaningful and positive model for classroom or workshop dialogue and behaviour and as such continues to be a worthwhile topic for discussion.

Further reading

Humanism, as a branch of educational psychology, has, arguably, been more closely associated with adult education as distinct from further education, and this is reflected in works such as:

Rogers, A. and Horrocks, N. (2010), *Teaching Adults*. 4th edition. Maidenhead: Open University Press.

Rogers, J. (2007), *Adults Learning*. Fifth edition. Maidenhead: Open University Press.

Also recommended is a book that focuses on training and workplace learning, but is straightforwardly applicable to mainstream FE as well:

Heron, J. (1999), *The complete facilitator's handbook*. London: Kogan Page.

PART 3

Theories of Learning: Social and Cultural Perspectives

8 Learning as a Social Practice

This part of the text seeks to expand on, and in some ways move away from, the theoretical discussions that characterized the previous part. The differing schools of psychology that are represented in part 2 of this text have in turn generated theories and frameworks of learning which occupy what can be defined as a dominant position within teacher-training curricula. Chapters about humanism, andragogy or Bloom's taxonomy of learning in the cognitive domain are common features of the textbooks which are written for students on CertEd/PGCE or PTLLS-CTLLS-DTLLS programmes (Armitage et al., 2012; Gould, 2012; Hillier, 2011; Ingleby et al., 2010; Reece and Walker, 2007; Scales, 2012; Wallace, 2011). Part 2 of this text is no exception. However, it is proposed that a consideration of a quite different body of theories of learning – often referred to as 'social practice' or 'sociocultural' theories of learning – can offer significant insights into the practices of both teachers and students in the FE sector. These are offered in this part of the text as a counter-argument to the perspectives that have preceded them.

Social practice theories are based on a broad tradition that can be seen as starting with the work of Lev Vygotsky in the early part of the twentieth century. Vygotsky (one social practice theorist who has managed to find his way into the mainstream teacher-training curriculum for the FE sector), discussed in the following chapter, deviated quite radically from the approach of many of his contemporaries in focussing on the social and environmental contexts in which learning and teaching occurred. This approach, often labelled social constructivism, has influenced a number of other theorists and researchers, some of whose key works and concepts of learning and teaching are explored in the following chapters.

At this time it is worthwhile to explain the structure of this part of the text. In the present chapter, the discussion will be restricted to a brief account of the wider themes of social practice theory. In the three chapters that follow this, some key theorists, and some practical applications for their frameworks and concepts in the FE sector, are briefly outlined and critiqued. And in the final chapter of this part of the text, a brief account will be given of two recent research projects that have been conducted in the FE sectors in England and Wales, and which drew on social practice theory. It is suggested that these two research projects are of considerable importance to practitioners in the sector, and are therefore of relevance and importance to the overall argument which is presented in this section of the text.

Researching the real world: Moving away from classical psychology

From the point of view of social practice theory, a number of aspects of classical psychology are significantly problematic (Lave, 1988):

1 The first such problematic area rests in the laboratory. The research done by psychologists and the conclusions that they draw are assumed to be straightforwardly transferable from laboratory settings to the outside world (to real life, as it were). Traditional cognitive experiments are conducted on a variety of subjects, and the results of these are assumed to be generalizable. Cognitive processes are assumed to be transferable across contexts or settings.

2 The second problematic area can be found in the relationships that exist between academic psychology and formal schooling. Psychological theories shape both educational theories and educational practices. The psychologists' focus on cognition effectively serves to foreground intellectual work and, thus, the academic curriculum.

3 A third problem can be found in the construction of this academic curriculum, which rests on the notion that if people study particular subjects, then these studies will form a mental discipline that will – in general – improve the minds of the students. Because cognition is assumed to be transferable, the knowledge that the individual student will have acquired can be carried from the educational context into life after school or college.

4 A fourth problem rests in the artificial distinction that has been made over time between 'scientific' knowledge and 'everyday' knowledge. The knowledge that is said to be contained within formal academic curricula is assumed to have a higher status than the 'everyday' knowledge of peoples' family or working lives.

5 A final problem rests in the geographical and historical roots of classical psychology. The research and theories that stem from psychology come from a specific western, intellectual culture that can be dated back to the Age of Enlightenment – a period in history that saw the emergence of 'scientific thought'. In the past, this same intellectual tradition drew on 'scientific thought' to argue positions that today are seen as entirely untenable – for example, that women have weaker cognitive abilities than men purely on the grounds of their gender, or that some societies are 'civilized' and others are 'primitive' (and, of course, that the civilized societies are superior).

Social practice theory rests on a very different approach to doing research. Instead of being rooted in the laboratory, the social practice researcher conducts her or his work in the real world, drawing on anthropology and ethnography rather than psychology. Anthropology is the study of human societies and relations, including how and why people live in the ways that they do, how societies are organized, how cultures reproduce themselves and so forth. Ethnography is the study of cultures and societies from within, on their own terms. Both anthropology and ethnography use very different methods to psychology. Instead of laboratory-based tests of human behaviour (often based on the notion that there is a 'right' answer), anthropologists and ethnographers rely on long-term observational studies within the communities that they are researching.

For researchers who are interested in how and why people learn, how people are taught things and what kinds of knowledge or ability are valued within societies, this social practice tradition has raised a number of interesting issues:

- The kinds of types of knowledge that are valued in particular societies or cultural settings are very variable, and depend on that social or cultural setting. It is not the case that some kinds of knowledge are 'better' than others (for example, in the way that the academic curriculum in the UK is perceived as being superior to the vocational curriculum).

- If it is accepted that knowledge is specific and linked to the setting or context in which it is found or used, ideas about the transfer of learning need to be reconsidered.

- There is more to knowing things than simply having lots of qualifications. The things that people know can be seen in how they work, how they live with their families and friends, how they go about all kinds of activities in work and at leisure.

Thinking about learning from a social practice perspective

Researchers and writers who draw on social practice perspectives do not explore learning from the point of view of the stimulus-response, or from what might be happening 'in the head' of the learner. They share with classical psychologists an interest in observing changes or differences in learned behaviour, but always seek to do so within authentic and meaningful social and cultural concepts. For social practice theorists, being knowledgeable can be seen not in terms of examination results or qualifications, but in terms of what people do, how they talk, behave and act, and how they use tools, books or other artefacts. A cycle mechanic can be seen to be knowledgeable in the way that he or she selects the right tools for the job, correctly diagnoses a mechanical problem simply from the sound that a cycle makes when ridden, and asks a colleague to pass a particular spare part from the workshop shelf. It might be possible to create a written examination in order to assess the theoretical knowledge that the cycle mechanic possesses. A typical question might be asking where on a bicycle would one find left-handed threads, instead of the more usual right-handed threads? (Two places might be offered: the thread on the left-hand pedal and the thread on the right hand side of the bottom bracket, which is where the crank arms are connected to the bicycle frame). But what use would this knowledge be when written down on a test paper? The knowledge only makes sense when the cycle mechanic is fitting new pedals or replacing the bottom bracket. And when the mechanic is able to calculate which type and size of bottom bracket is needed (there are many varieties) simply by looking at the bike frame and crank arms in question, another kind of knowledge is being used or enacted, but one that only makes sense because there is also a bicycle there (which needs new parts), a mechanic to fit them, and a board upon which is hanging a selection of tools that have been specifically manufactured for this particular job.

The extensive research that has been carried out across different contexts and cultures over time has led social practice theorists to question the relationship between learning and formal educational structures such as FE colleges. If it is the case that people can be seen as being knowledgeable despite not having received formal instruction (defined here as based on a formal pedagogy and delivered in an educational institution), then an important question arises: how do people learn, if not through being taught in colleges?

Researchers and writers working from the point of view of classical psychology tend also to divide learning in terms of 'formal' and 'informal' learning, echoing the distinction that is made between 'scientific' knowledge and 'everyday' knowledge – the former assumed to be superior to the latter. From a social practice perspective, there is no difference between scientific and everyday knowledge – it is all, simply, knowledge and no one kind is better or different than another. Rather, different kinds of knowledge are more or less useful depending on the context or situation. Knowing is not a purely or solely mental process, but a process that has an impact on the whole person – how they think, talk, act, use tools and interact with their environment. And there is no such thing as formal and informal learning – learning is always the same process, in terms of how the learner changes, grows and can do or say new things or use new tools or objects.

According to social practice theory, learning happens as a consequence of practice. Different social practice theories explain this in rather different ways (as discussed in the chapters that follow this one), but a common theme that can be found across these theories is the importance of authentic practice. Put simply, people learn things from being able to take part in authentic practice, to try things out. Being able to ask other, more experienced people, how things are done, which tool or procedure would be used and when and so forth is an important part of this practice – but this is not quite the same as 'teaching', because the more experienced person is not defined as, let alone trained as, a teacher. It is simply another version of a similar conversation that might take place whenever somebody who doesn't know something asks a question of somebody who does. The role of such conversations – such forms of dialogue – is a crucial element of social practice theory, which argues that learning is always a social, shared process, and never an individual one. Whatever people learn, there are always other people involved – whether it's a person to talk to, a book that someone has written, a skype conversation or email exchange or a tool that someone has designed. The important central theme is that nothing happens in isolation.

These conclusions are quite profound and raise significant challenges to educators across all sectors. According to social practice theory, classical psychology relies on the concept of learning transfer to provide a plausible explanation for the relationship between formal education and the rest of society (the workplace, peoples' everyday lives at home and with their families and so forth). But if this concept does not work and is based on a series of false assumptions, what then for pedagogy and for formal education and training? At the same time, these theories do not (as shall become clear in the chapters that follow) provide entirely trouble free accounts of education and learning. Whilst it is easy to imagine that people learing how to use their new smartphones manage to do so – and in the process acquire a lot of new knowledge and skill that is in parts quite complex – without the need for formal instruction, it seems clearly incorrect to assume that someone could learn how to become a doctor simply by spending time with other doctors, assisting them in their work, trying out some procedures and learning the specialist vocabulary of their profession (Lemke, 1997).

Social practice theories offer ways of thinking about learning which are quite different from the ideas expressed in Part 2 of this book. The combination of the focus on knowing in practice (in 'the real world'), the questions that are raised concerning learning transfer, the move away from the laboratory as a place of research and, by extension, the move away from a science that historically based theories about human learning on experiments conducted with animals, can all be seen as rendering classical psychology as problematic. It is not the case, however, that social practice theory seeks simply to prove classical psychology wrong or to provide a different account of how knowledge might be constructed by the individual. Instead, it provides an entirely different – and unrelated – perspective on learning and knowledge that does not seek to explore mental function and behaviour (the focus of classical psychology) but instead seeks to explore how people behave in different social settings or contexts, which of necessity must include how people learn what to do and how to do it, whether they are working as welders or midwives, attending a club or society meeting for fellow hobbyists, or learning how to use a new computer.

Summary: Social practice, theory and the break with the classical tradition

The three chapters that follow this one are each devoted to a single theoretical perspective. These three theories have been chosen because, it is suggested, that they provide examples of both the diversity of social practice theories, of how they might be applied to an under-standing of the work done by teachers and students in colleges of FE, and of the limitations or restrictions that such theories carry with them. They are not positioned as infallible and straightforwardly applicable. The focus of chapter 10 is on situated learning in communities of practice – one of the more popular social practice theories (though, arguably, a theory that is often insufficiently well explained and only employed at a surface level). The focus of Chapter 11 is on activity theory and expansive learning, a less well-known approach (in terms of the FE sector), though one which raises interesting questions about the work of the FE teacher as much as that of the student. The first theoretical framework to be explored in the social practice tradition of the work of Lev Vygotsky and his theory of scaffolded learning within a Zone of Proximal Development. This is a quite well-known and highly regarded body of theory, and is positioned as the first social practice theory to be followed because of the way in which it provides a bridge between classical psychology and social practice.

Further reading

Social practice accounts of learning are starting to appear in general texts, alongside the growth of more specialist works on the subject. Another introductory chapter can be found in:

Gould, J. (2012), *Learning theory and classroom practice in the lifelong learning sector*. 2nd edition. Exeter: Learning Matters.

And a more general discussion can be found in:

Pritchard, A. and Woollard, J. (2010), *Psychology for the classroom: constructivism and social learning*. London: Routledge.

9 Social Constructivism

Constructivism is a psychology of learning that assumes that people make their own meaning about things in a unique manner. The branch of educational theory known as social constructivism takes this notion and at the same time expands it to include the social contexts in which this meaning making takes place. It is most widely associated with the work of Lev Vygotsky. Although he changed some aspects of his approach during his lifetime (in some cases quite radically), and although his theories have been widely interpreted and reinterpreted, there is nonetheless a core body of ideas that are, it is suggested, of relevance and importance to the FE teacher.

Lev Vygotsky (1896-6–1934) was a researcher at the Psychological Institute in Moscow. His work there was interrupted by a period of serious illness and later by his own decisions to change the focus of his research. During his life, his work was criticized, and after his early death, his work fell into disfavour not only as a consequence of the prevailing political attitudes of the country but also because of disagreements with other psychologists. In Europe and America, his theories were effectively rediscovered as a consequence of new translations of his work, which were published around 35 years ago (Vygotsky, 1978). Since this time, Vygotskian scholars have continued to dispute aspects of his theories and to offer a range of perspectives that contain some significant variation although on a number of key points (which are explored in this chapter) a level of consensus can be observed (Daniels, 1996; Langford, 2005).

Key components of Vygotsky's theory

An initial exploration of Vygotsky's work reveals a number of key components or themes that need to be understood when considering his perspectives on learning and teaching. These are briefly explored here. It is important to note at this time that as Vygotsky's research was predominantly focussed on children, and is reflected in the discussion that follows, although the more generic term 'student' has been used where appropriate. The transferability of these theories to the teaching and learning of young adults in FE will be returned to in more detail below.

1 Language

As an aspect of human development, Vygotsky argued that language was generated as a consequence of the human being's need to communicate, and was integral to the development of thinking. He suggested that as a child learns a language (which is understood to be an example of a tool (discussed below) which is external to the child, not inbuilt), two forms of speech develop – one internal and the other external. A younger child would at first use external speech in order to interact with the world (including both people and tools) around her or him but over time, speech would be internalized. This inner speech would then develop in a manner unique to each individual and would be the tool by which the child would learn and manipulate mental concepts. So, the younger child would literally 'think out loud' until inner speech developed. From this point onwards, any dialogue with another person would involve the individual having to, in effect, translate their inner speech into external speech. The answers given or comments made by the other person would then be translated back into inner speech so that it might be made sense of.

2 Tools

For Vygotsky, the use of tools by human beings (whether the tool in question is a hammer or a computer (or both)) is an integral aspect of his research. Following the theories of Karl Marx (who was an influence throughout his life), Vygotsky argued that tools started out as extensions of the human body for activities such as hunting, and then became more sophisticated over time as humans develop (it is important to note, however, that he changed his ideas about human development during his lifetime). He proposed that there were two types of tools: psychological tools and technical tools. Technical tools are the kinds of tools that a person uses in order to change an external object (such as using a plane on a piece of wood). Psychological tools are the kinds of tools that impact on mind and behaviour (such as language, texts, mathematical formulae or any other form of sign or symbol that carries meaning). Vygotsky argued that the reasons why different cultures exhibited different cognitive practices was due to the differences in psychological tools that existed between them.

3 Cultural mediation

An integral part of all forms of learning is, according to Vygotsky, social interaction, which is a necessary, permanent and unavoidable aspect of being alive. Through interacting with at first parents and later teachers and other adults or older children, younger children learn about the world around them. These social interactions will of necessity involve speech (a psychological tool) together with any other tools that are relevant to the situation and will allow the student to construct knowledge. This knowledge is at the same time unique to each child and shared within the social context. The other people with whom the student speaks will help her or him to come to know about whatever it is that is being discussed. Because this learning involves both people and tools, learning is said to be mediated (which means to be reconciled or brought together) in a cultural context. Put simply, the understanding of the student is always developed through not only their interaction with the world but also through their interactions with other people and objects in the world.

4 Internalization and appropriation

Internalization is a term with a broad application in both psychology and sociology. It refers to the ways in which individuals take on board particular attitudes or understandings, thereby making them part of the self so that they will influence how people think, act or work. For Vygotsky, internalization explains the process by which children come to know how to do something. For example, building a tower with building blocks is a task, which is at first outside the child. As the child practices with the blocks, she or he will come to know how to build a tower – which involves not only manipulating the blocks (which are a form of technical tool) but also learning about how they might be balanced on top of each other, how they might wobble and fall over if the tower is too high and unstable (which are psychological tools). Mindful of social context, the process of internalization will be rather different if one child has been left to stack blocks on her own, and another is being shown how to stack blocks by a parent. The social dimension of playing with building blocks, however, is not restricted solely to the building of the tower (or any other shape). Should the child decide to behave inappropriately with her building blocks (by throwing them against a wall, for example), the admonishments of the parent would help the child learn the social and cultural rules that surround the use of the blocks.

However, this does not mean that there is 'only one way' to play with the blocks. Should the child decide to invent her own construction with the blocks, instead of following the instructions that came with them, this would be seen as an example of appropriation – the moment when a child takes a tool and in some sense personalizes it or makes it more-or-less distinctive to them.

5 Scaffolding

When discussing the learning of younger children (usually up to the age of seven), Vygotsky advocated the use of individual assistance in order to help each individual child to learn. An analogy can be used to illustrate this approach: as a new building is constructed, the builders, engineers and architects surround the building-in-progress with scaffolding. This is because it would be very difficult, if not impossible, for the builders to access some parts of the building without the support of the scaffolding. Moreover, the builders might need to access slightly different parts of the building to the engineers: as a result, the engineers might need a different arrangement of scaffolding.

For Vygotsky, the learning of younger children could best be facilitated through such an approach, which is referred to as scaffolding. However, it is important to note that as a concept, it occupies only a very small place in Vygotsky's writings and was taken up and explored in depth by other theorists. It is also important, and interesting, to note that Vygotsky advocated a more regimented teacher-led pedagogy for older students (Langford, 2005).

6 Zone of proximal development

The zone of proximal development (ZPD) is the difference between what the child can already do, and what she or he can do with help (that is, with scaffolding). The more formal definition that Vygotsky himself provided of the zpd was: 'the distance between the actual developmental level as determined by independent problem solving and the level of potential development as determined through problem solving under adult guidance, or in collaboration with more capable peers' (Vygotsky, 1978: 86). The ZPD, therefore, forms the social and cultural space in which the individual and the social are brought together, and in which psychological tools are used to help make meaning through the processes of cultural mediation. It is important also to note here that a ZPD is unique to each student within a group. That is, a zpd should not be seen as a way of conceptualizing a classroom or workshop of students, but rather as a way of conceptualizing the past and potential learning on the individual student. As a result of this, the scaffolding that will be required in each case will be more-or-less different.

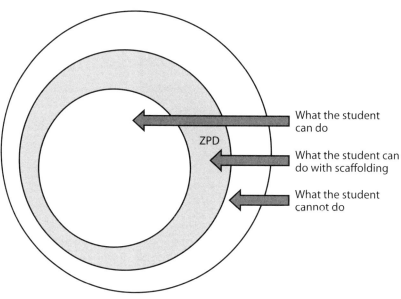

Figure 9.1

Vygotsky's perspectives on pedagogy

A reading of Vygotsky's own writings would suggest that he proposed quite different approaches to pedagogy depending on the age of the student. For younger children (under the age of seven), he advocated what would in contemporary terms be referred to as a facilitative approach on the part of the teacher, underpinned by discovery learning. Discovery learning (a term originated by Jerome Bruner (discussed in Chapter 6) covers a wide range of teaching and learning strategies, but is commonly used to refer to methods of instruction which provide a series of questions and a series of resources for the student, who will then explore the resources provided in order to establish answers to the questions provided. Examples include running a series of experiments, or exploring a theoretical question through recourse to a series of published documents.

For students over the age of seven, Vygotsky advocated an approach to pedagogy that is more characteristic of a teacher-led approach. The first stage of this approach consists of formal instruction in a series of principles that are to be applied, or rules that are to be followed. The second stage of this approach consists of a series of activities that allows the students to test out the principles or rules that they have learned, and (importantly) to apply them to real-world situations. This style of pedagogy is familiar to the FE teacher who might, for example, provide a demonstration of a mechanical procedure and then require students to replicate the processes that they have been observing.

The individual nature of the zpd poses particular problems when considering the dominant form of whole class teaching – that is, of a single teacher having responsibility for the instruction of a group of students. Vygotsky's solution to this was to put students into groups according to their current level of performance (the principles underlying the assessment of this performance in Vygotskian terms will be considered shortly). There are three ways of achieving this.

1 streaming – putting students into groups according to their overall level of progress
2 setting – putting students into different groups for each of the subjects that they are studying;
3 mixed groups – having students in mixed groups, and then taking smaller subgroups of students who are progressing at a similar level for separate instruction.

Vygotsky's perspectives on assessment

Assessment is a complex topic for discussion and is discussed in depth in Chapters 30 and 31. For the purposes of this discussion, it is sufficient to note that there are two dominant form of assessment in FE colleges: formative assessment (often referred to as assessment for learning) and summative assessment (often referred to as assessment of learning).

Formative assessment is defined as a form of assessment that primarily aims to help the student to learn; summative assessment is designed to assess what the student has learned (Tummons, 2011a).

For Vygotsky, there were three main functions of student assessment:

1 what is the developmental potential of the student?
2 what is the zpd of the student?
3 therefore, what stream or set should the student be placed in?

In contrast to contemporary summative assessments, which are used to make judgements about a student's potential future performance based on their past individual performance, Vygotsky proposed that assessment should be carried out through giving students problems to solve that were within their zpd, not their current level of performance. That is to say, the assessment would deliberately consist of items or problems that were beyond the current ability of the student. The application of the assessment would involve help from the teacher in the form of scaffolding. The extent to which the student is then able to solve the problem and complete the assessment, with scaffolded help, indicates what is termed their 'zpd index'.

Although there is a body of research that suggests that such an approach to assessment provides a valid and reliable indicator of students' potential learning, the implementation of such a regime at a summative level is far outside the established practices of the FE sector (and, indeed, of formal education and training in the UK more generally). However, it is suggested that such as approach might be practicable as a form of formative assessment in allowing teachers to develop detailed profiles of their own students.

Vygotsky's perspectives on knowledge

Vygotsky subscribed to a view of knowledge that is widely shared amongst social practice theorists (including Lave and Wenger, and Engeström, who are discussed in the following two chapters). He rejected the individualism that was current in the wider psychological trends of his time (and that is a key characteristic of the classical psychology discussed in Part 2 of this text), and this rejection informed not only his approach to learning as being mediated by social and cultural practices, but also to knowledge as a social practice. He argued that knowledge was created through social practice – through the interactions, dialogues and mediated activities of people – over time. In this sense, he advocated what can be referred to as an evolutionary approach to knowledge. He acknowledged changes in knowledge over time and the differences in knowledge that would be held within primitive societies as opposed to advanced societies. But he did not equate these different bodies of knowledge with different levels of kinds of learning and cognition. Instead, he argued that whether the tasks at hand were more primitive acts of agriculture or hunting, or more advanced acts of engineering or scientific study, they would be approached through objective and logical thinking and learned about in the same way.

Extensions of Vygotskian theory

A number of other researchers and writers have either articulated or expanded on Vygotsky's theories. A powerful criticism of this outpouring of research and writing is that Vygotsky's own ideas have become lost sight of and somewhat dissipated (Daniels, 2001; Langford, 2005). Here, a selection of ideas from later writers are provided in order to not only illustrate some of the criticisms of Vygotsky's approach but also to provide a more detailed account relating to what might be termed a Vygotskian pedagogy.

* Facilitating learning in the zone of proximal development

   Vygotsky himself was quite vague in describing the kinds of teacher-led practices or interactions that would help to develop facilitative learning within the zpd. Later researchers who have drawn on the Vygotskian tradition have identified the following methods, many of which are familiar aspects of the FE sector (Tharp, 1993):

1 Modelling

   Modelling involves offering patterns of behaviour that students are expected to imitate. The model that is offered – in terms of performance, information or motor skill – serves as a performance standard.

2 Feedback

   Feedback involves providing information on progress towards the required standard (this is discussed in more depth in chapters 30 and 31). Ensuring feedback is the most common and most effective form of self-assistance that can be provided for the student.

3 Contingency management

   Contingency management involves the reinforcement of behaviour and any appropriate steps that need to be taken to manage unwanted behaviour

4 Instructing

   Instructing refers to the provision of specific request for action on the part of the students. Teachers should provide clarity, offer relevant information and allow students an element of decision-making.

5 Questioning

Asking questions entails requiring a verbal response from the student that in turn assists in producing a mental operation that the learner wither would not or could not produce if in isolation. A second benefit of asking questions is in providing feedback to the teacher in relation to the student's developing understanding.

6 Explanations.

Explanations provide structures that help students to organize, justify or evaluate new learning or new perceptions.

7 Structuring

Tasks should be structured into segments or chunks. Ideally these chunks should suggest themselves to the teacher according to the components of a larger sequence of operations, or similar. If an entire task is beyond a student's zpd, it might be the case that chunks of the task are within it.

- Understanding power relationships in the zone of proximal development

Theorists and practitioners have over time, taken up the social constructivist model of teaching and learning across the further, higher and adult education sectors. The facilitative approach that sits within the concept of the zpd has made Vygotsky's work attractive to practitioners who hold to a liberal and/or democratic philosophy of education. The dialogic nature of the Vygotskian classroom was assumed to remove power imbalances from the teacher-student relationship as the teacher guided the students – in their individual ZPD – towards their own, individual, constructions of knowledge.

However, such an approach does not hold up to close scrutiny. Although Vygotsky himself did not write extensively on the power relationships of the classroom, a number of inferences can be made if his theories are explored through to their logical conclusion and if the different elements of his wider writing are thoroughly incorporated into the analysis (that is to say, if the analysis considers not only the zpd but the other elements of Vygotskian theory that have been outlined in this chapter).

One of the more thorough critical readings of Vygotsky was that of Basil Bernstein (1924–2000), who was professor of sociology of education at the Institute of Education in London. Bernstein's analysis centred on the role of language in Vygotsky's work. Because language is grounded in culture and practice, he argued, it was necessarily subject to the influences of power and discursive regulation. (Discursive regulation occurs when possibilities for expression and/or representation – through talking or writing, for example – are restricted or controlled). Thus, the ways in which students might express themselves in relation to the curriculum that they are following will always be restricted, for example, by the specifications of the curriculum or the requirements of the assessment regime (Bernstein, 1990, 1996).

- Understanding the motivation to learn

  Vygotsky's conceptualization of motivation, and its relationship to learning, was another area of fundamental revision during his lifetime (Aidman and Leontiev, 1991). In his earlier writings, the focus was on motivation, cognition and development. He argued that motivation was important for cognition for several reasons:

1 In early life, cognition is linked to survival. Motivation at this stage is therefore linked to physical factors such as hunger or tiredness. Motivation is, at this stage, necessary.

2 As children mature, motivation begins to focus on means rather than ends. For example, when an older child is hungry and sees some food, he or she might start thinking about how s/he might obtain that food. The motivation becomes linked to the goal of the activity rather than to the activity itself.

3 Upon entering young adulthood, motivation becomes clearly attached to higher cognitive function. It continues to be as a result of necessity (as before), but also now of structure, use or content. Content provides a straightforward example: if someone is interested in a topic, they will know a lot about it (that is, they will have acquired a lot of content).

In later writings, however, he evidenced a more optimistic approach of human nature. Instead of explaining motivation in relation to survival, he argued that from a young age, children had a natural inclination to desire knowledge. This desire translates into motivation and provides an overall impetus for development. Humans have an 'instinctive drive' to seek greater knowledge through developing themselves. However, these changes in the understanding of motivation were not due to the analysis of any empirical research. Rather, Vygotsky's analysis of motivation changed over time as a result of his own reading and of the authors and books that grew to influence his thinking as his career progressed, leading to motivation being described as his most 'vulnerable' area (Langford, 2005: 239).

Applications of Vygotskian theory in further education

Having provided an outline of the key themes of Vygotskian theory, it is now possible to explore how these concepts can be used to illustrate teaching and learning processes in the FE college. Here, two worked examples of typical sessions from the FE curriculum will be explored from the social constructivist perspective, with reference to the key themes of Vygotsky's approach that have been discussed above.

1 A social constructivist analysis of an entry to uniformed services programme: The NCFE Level 2 Diploma for Entry to the Uniformed Services

a. Language

Learning involves not only the use of language in dialogue between the students and the teacher, but the acquisition of language as well. This might include new words or phrases, new uses for words and phrases that are already known, or new rules governing language use. Examples of new words might include 'witness testimony' or 'professional discussion' (which are two permitted forms of evidence which students can put into their portfolios of assessment). New meanings for already known words might include 'drill' (here used in a military sense). New rules governing language use might be acquired through studying the 'exploring equality and diversity' unit.

b. Tools

The kinds of tools that students might learn to use will depend upon the specific units that they choose to study. Typical examples for students on unit 5 – 'carrying out map reading and navigation' would include maps and magnetic compasses. These provide excellent examples of tools which work at both a technical level (a map is a device which allows one to navigate; a magnetic compass is a device which allows one to orientate a map) and a psychological level (a map is a symbolic device that contains signs, words and shapes that in turn require perception, memory and understanding).

c. Cultural mediation

Learning on this Diploma programme happens as a consequence of the social interaction between students and teacher: the experience and biography of the teacher provides what might be termed a vicarious source of knowledge and practice in relation to the curriculum. But other forms of cultural mediation are also at work. The curriculum itself acts as a cultural mediator, in introducing 'the uniformed services' (with all that this entails) into the environment of the FE college.

d. Internalization and appropriation

As the course progresses, the students will begin to internalize key concepts, attitudes, behaviours and knowledge, relating to the curriculum. They will learn how to read a map confidently, standing to attention and dressing by the left when performing drill, terms of address to use when addressing officers, and so forth. Some aspects of the course do allow students some degree of autonomy and flexibility – that is to say, some degree of appropriation. For example: in the map reading and navigation unit, candidates can plan their own route. The 'working as a volunteer within a chosen organization' unit gives the student the opportunity to select the type of organization that she or he would wish to work in.

e. Scaffolding

Changes in the scaffolding structures employed by the teacher would become visible over time. In the early stages of the programme, for example, drill work might be slowed down and might involve repeated explanations of what particular instructions mean. When marching, students might be helped to keep to time if the teacher counts out loud. In later stages of the programme, drill work will be speeded up and instructions will be kept to a minimum. When marching, students will be expected to keep to time without a count from the teacher.

f. Zone of proximal development

For each student, the ZPD will be different. For some, map reading may be difficult to learn whereas others may have already been orienteering in the past. Some students may find basic health training more arduous than others. And some students may find difficulties in identifying the relevance of studying health and safety in the workplace. For the teacher, different levels or styles of intervention will be needed, therefore, to ensure that learning is facilitated for all of the students. Buddy groups might be employed to facilitate peer learning and support. Differentiated activities might be designed to help teach students who are new to map reading how to remember the different symbols that are used.

2 A social constructivist analysis of a health and social care programme: the BTEC Level 1 First Certificate in Health and Social Care

a. Language

Again, language is both a vehicle for teaching and learning and a cultural tool that will be acquired and used by the students. Some of the terms – and their underlying concepts and debates – that will be studied on this programme include 'genetic inheritance' (in relation to health risk factors), 'positive and negative self-esteem', and 'safeguarding and duty of care' (in relation to the physical and emotional safety of others).

b. Tools

The health and social care course is rich in complex symbols, concepts and frameworks that in turn help to encourage the development of the students' own psychological functions of memory, perception and attention. For example, the concept of 'the effects of socialization on the health and wellbeing of individuals' could involve the use of tools as diverse as: magazines, television programmes and social networking sites. The study of 'health promotion' might involve looking at leaflets from a local doctor's surgery, changing personal hygiene routines such as hand washing, or stopping smoking.

c. Cultural mediation

As with the uniformed services programme, the teacher provides the initial focus for cultural mediation, bringing the real world issues that are covered in the curriculum into the classroom through her or his choice of resources, PowerPoint slides and worksheet activities. The curriculum specifications from the awarding body provide a framework within which the teacher can operate. The curriculum content affords students the opportunity to explore a number of broad themes relating to social policy, health, nutrition and personal relationships. In order to make the curriculum more meaningful (that is, more relevant), the use of guest speakers such as healthcare workers and service users is recommended by the awarding body: however, not all colleges will be able to provide this.

d. Internalization and appropriation

As students progress through the curriculum, they will begin to use new forms of language or other specialist terminology to display changing attitudes towards some of the issues covered in class (such as personal safety or diet, for example). The internalization of the key themes and concepts of the course will become apparent through the way that they talk (with their teacher and with their peer group). As students complete their assignments, they will find that they have increased opportunities for personalization of the style and exact coverage of their written work, thereby allowing a limited degree of appropriation (for example, students may choose to design their assessment for the equality and diversity module on one overarching task or on a smaller number of tasks).

e. Scaffolding

Scaffolding strategies will be utilized by the teacher according to the needs of the students, the demands of the curriculum and the resources that are available. For example: if the teacher wishes students to investigate the ways in which a local NHS trust publicizes campaigns to help people stop smoking, she or he might ask students to go online and look up relevant information. This might also require a brief conversation regarding staying safe when online – an issue of particular importance if the student group was a 14–16 group rather than a 16–19 group. On subsequent occasions, less such support might be needed and students might be able to offer each other advice about where to search online in order to get the best results. Alternatively, it might be possible for the students to visit a local surgery and to see what facilities are offered to people who wish to stop smoking, and perhaps even speak with a healthcare professional who is involved. When visiting a workplace setting for the first time, it is possible that some members of the group may be shy and not wish to speak. Subsequent visits may help ease this problem.

f. Zone of proximal development

Again, the ZPD for each student will be more or less different, requiring different forms of dialogue between teacher and student (for example, in relation to the specialist terminology that the teacher might use), different classroom strategies (for example, one approach might be to divide students into small groups according to current levels of ability) or different assessment strategies (for example, a choice of case studies might be offered to students who would be able to make a selection based on personal interest/motivation).

Summary: Vygotsky and the zpd as a framework for further education teaching and learning

The single most important contribution that Vygotsky made to the study of learning and knowledge was in foregrounding the social and cultural contexts of learning. Not all of his ideas were fully formed at the time of his (premature) death, and prevailing political conditions meant that his work remained relatively unknown outside the former Soviet Union for almost half a century. Although some of his more enthusiastic supporters have not always read his work as thoroughly as they ought to do (and it should be noted that this chapter can only hope to provide a brief summary and not a thorough critique of his work), the key concepts of his theory – of learning as socially mediated, of the ZPD as an individual characteristic – are aligned to two of the fundamental characteristics of the FE college – the provision of authentic, work-related and work-based opportunities to learn, and the provision of personalized, differentiated learning – that as a framework for exploring teaching in the sector it is difficult to ignore.

Further reading

Vygotsky's work has become the subject of a renewed enthusiasm in recent years, and a number of excellent books have been published that combine a critical exploration of his work with an appreciation of his wider influence in educational research. The following are all recommended for the reader who wishes to explore further:

Hogan, K. and Pressley, M. (1997), *Scaffolding student learning: instructional approaches and issues*. Cambridge, MA: Brookline.

Long, M., Wood, C., Littleton, K., Passenger, T. and Sheehy, K. (2010), *The Psychology of Education*. 2nd edition. London: Routledge. Chapters 7 and 8.

Ormrod, J. (2006), *Human Learning*. 5th edition. New Jersey: Princeton. Chapter 5.

10 Communities of Practice

The singular contribution made by Lev Vygotsky to understanding learning, as discussed in the preceding chapter, arguably revolved around his exploration of the social dimension of learning. Unlike many of those psychologists who came immediately before him or who were his contemporaries (such as the behaviourists) or indeed many who followed him (such as the cognitivists), Vygotsky understood that learning could only be understood through exploring the social and cultural spaces or contexts in which learning happened. Some of the social learning theorists that are current at the time of writing this book position themselves as what might be termed 'direct descendants' of the Vygotskian tradition (one example of this is cultural-historical activity theory, which is discussed in the following chapter). Other theoretical traditions are clearly informed by and owe a debt to Vygotsky's work, and that of his followers, but takes an analysis of learning as a social practice in a rather different direction. One such example is *situated learning theory*, or *learning as situated within communities of practice*.

The concept of the 'community of practice' as a way of explaining the social and cultural spaces in which learning happens first appeared in a book (by now recognized as highly influential) called *Situated Learning: legitimate peripheral participation* (1991), co-authored by Jean Lave and Etienne Wenger. Jean Lave is currently professor of education and geography at the University of California, Berkeley. She is a social anthropologist and ethnographer who for many years has been carrying out research into how skills are learned in informal settings (an account of, and reflections on, her research appeared in a book published in 2011 titled *Apprenticeship in Critical Ethnographic Practice*). In addition to Situated Learning, her other publications include an edited volume which is now considered to have made a landmark contribution to theories of learning and social practice, *Understanding Practice: perspectives on activity and context* (1993, with Seth Chaiklin); and *Cognition in Practice: mind, mathematics and culture in everyday life* (1988). Etienne Wenger, formerly a research scientist at the Institute for Research on Leaning in Palo Alto, California, is an independent researcher and consultant, and his work revolves around social learning theory in both organizational contexts and lifelong learning. In addition to Situated Learning, his other books include *Communities of Practice: learning, meaning and identity* (1998), and *Cultivating Communities of Practice: a guide to managing knowledge* (2002, with Richard McDermott and William Snyder).

When first used by Lave and Wenger, the term community of practice was left relatively unexplored, and it was not properly defined in their book. Instead, it was left as a 'largely intuitive notion' that required further investigation (1991: 42). Arguably, the term was introduced as a by-product of their more sustained analysis of learning as a social process that they referred to as *legitimate peripheral participation* (which was in fact the focus of their 1991 book), in order to create some sense of the kinds of cultural and social places where learning might happen. How a community of practice might be identified, described or defined, or questions relating to what the constituent components or characteristics of such communities might be, were only later explored in depth by Wenger (1998 – this is discussed in depth below). Subsequently, a qualitatively different perspective on communities of practice was presented by Wenger et al. (2002), focusing on how the development of communities of practice within organizations might lead to improved economic performance (Barton and Tusting, 2005: 5–6). This later work maintained the framework that had been established in the earlier books, but with a focus that was quite narrowly concentrated onto organizational learning. For the purposes of this discussion, however, it is the earlier works (that is, Lave and Wenger (1991) and Wenger (1998)) that shall be referred to in order first to explain what communities of practice are, before going on to define learning as an aspect of participation within them.

The structure of communities of practice

Communities of practice are everywhere. Everyone is a member of multiple communities of practice, some of which overlap with others. They are usually pretty easy to identify, and it is often easy to work out who might be a member of a particular community, perhaps on account of the clothes that they wear, the tools or objects that they use, or the vocabulary that they employ in their writing or their conversation. Sometimes, people are not even aware that they are members of a particular community, not least because only a very few have been subject to methodical, critical scrutiny (invariably by academic writers in books, journal articles or theses). People engage in all kinds of activities – *practices* – as part of their 'everyday' lives, interacting with other people, sometimes in close proximity and sometimes at a distance or by proxy: at work, at play, with families or with friends. In order to take part in these various practices people come together in *communities* so that they can talk about their practices, share them and learn more about them. These *communities of practice* can be found in formal, institutionalized settings and in informal, vernacular ones. Lave and Wenger's examples include tailors, midwives and butchers (1991). Wenger's examples include amateur radio operators, recovering alcoholics and office-based computer users (1998). Other examples that are of particular relevance to readers of this text include adult learners in a basic skills class (Harris and Shelswell, 2005), teachers of mathematics

(Cobb and McClain, 2006), hairdressing apprentices (Billett, 2008), education researchers (Hodkinson, 2005) and trainee FE teachers (Tummons, 2008).

In some communities, members will meet and talk on a regular basis; but in others, they will meet only infrequently. Some communities have existed for a long time, and others are relatively new. Some communities establish and sustain close relations with others, sharing aspects of their practice, whilst others are relatively self-sufficient. All communities of practice, however, irrespective of their size, their membership or their age, share specific structural qualities. There are three attributes that are described as maintaining the coherence of practice within a community, and these shall be discussed in turn. The three attributes are: *mutual engagement, joint enterprise* and *shared repertoire* (Wenger, 1998: 73–85).

1 *Mutual engagement.* This is the term used by Wenger to refer to the ways in which members of a community of practice interact with each other and do whatever they do. This might be face-to-face, or via email, in a meeting or through a large social gathering. Members of a community might engage with others in a complementary manner or an overlapping manner, depending on the relative competence and positions that they occupy. Because working together creates differences as well as similarities, differences and similarities of opinion or fact can be seen. Things can be done, argued over or spoken about in various ways so long as these are, at the end of the day, reconcilable to the shared work of the community of practice.

2 *Joint enterprise.* This is the term that Wenger uses to refer to the shared work or endeavour of the community of practice. The joint enterprise of a community of practice can be seen as being the 'goal' or 'focus' or 'raison d'etre' of the community.

3 *Shared repertoire.* This is the term that Wenger uses to describe the habits, discourses, routines, ways of talking, tools, structures and other artefacts that over time have been created or adopted by a community of practice. Members of a community draw on the shared repertoire in order to engage in practice. Such artefacts serve a number of functions. They allow the members of a community to make statements about their practice, to express their identities within the community, and they represent the history of mutual engagement within the community. Reflecting the different ways in which members engage in practice, for example as members move from being 'newcomers' to being 'experts', so members draw on the repertoire of the community in differential ways as they learn.

Learning in communities of practice

For Lave and Wenger (1991) and Wenger (1998), learning is a consequence of engagement in social practice. Learning is 'the same' whether or not any kind of educational structure has been established to provide a context for it: there are no contrasts between 'formal' or 'informal' learning, for example (Lave and Wenger, 1991: 40). Other terms which are quite common in the FE sector, such as 'work-based learning' or 'community learning' also have no place within communities of practice theory. This is because terms such as these imply that the 'quality' or 'worth' of learning is somehow different in different contexts. Lave and Wenger were concerned to establish a theory of learning that did not divide learning up according to where it happened, reflecting the idea expressed in Lave's earlier work (1988) that learning in formal institutional contexts is – erroneously, she argued – valued more highly and seen as more important than the learning that happens in everyday life.

As people engage in practice, they learn about that practice at the same time. Indeed, they can't help doing so. And this is because participation in a practice or activity always affords people the opportunity to learn about that practice. There is no need, or room, for 'formal instruction' or for 'pedagogy' (a problem that shall be explored later in this chapter). Lave and Wenger argued that a 'language of formal instruction' would only ever serve as a barrier between the learner and the practice that she or he wants to participate in and hence learn. Rather than *talking about* practice, they argued that people needed to *engage in* practice in order to learn.

However, it is not simply enough to engage or participate in practice in order to learn. The nature of that practice is also of importance, as is the nature of the participation. In order to learn, people need to be given the opportunity to engage in *authentic* practices, not in simulations. Learning things requires being able to try things out on real life. And at the same time, people need to be allowed to participate at first in only a small way, before being allowed over time to engage more fully (a concept that demonstrates clearly the ways in which Lave and Wenger drew on earlier apprenticeship models in their work – these are discussed in Chapter 12). Or, to put it another way, participation needs to be *legitimate* (that is, authentic) and *peripheral* (that is, deliberately small in scale) in order for learning to happen. In Lave and Wenger's work, therefore, learning is a process that they refer to as *legitimate peripheral participation*.

Learning happens, therefore, when people participate in practice. But it is important to note that learning is not a phenomenon that occurs solely in the head. In common with other social practice theorists (please refer back to the discussion in Chapter 8), Lave and Wenger did not concern themselves with what might be happening in people's minds or memories or brains, and this is a reflection of the research methods that they both used whilst formulating their ideas (both Lave and Wenger conducted in-depth ethnographic research over considerable periods of time). Rather, they concerned themselves with learning as a practice that leads to changes to the whole person, and how she or he acts and moves within the social world. Learning changes how people think, act and speak: one of the ways by which learning can be observed to be happening, (perhaps ironically, social practice theorists have this one theme in common with behaviourists and cognitivists – that learning leads to changes in behaviour that can be *seen*) is in how people talk, how they use things and how they behave as they go about the business, the practice, of their communities.

As members become more expert in the practice of the community over the course of time, they draw on the repertoire, tools and artefacts of the community in an increasingly fluent and expert manner. Their participation, within the community, becomes more full. But this does not imply that the time will eventually come when a member has 'finished' learning, that there is no more learning to be done, or that there are no more things that need to be learned. This is because communities of practice do not themselves stand still. In fact, they are constantly (sometimes quite quickly, and sometimes at a very slow pace) moving and changing. This might be because new ideas or tools come into a community from outside, causing the practice of the community to change. Or it might be because members of a community have new ideas or find new ways of working with existing tools or artefacts that cause the community to shift. As a result, a community of practice is never 'finished' or 'complete'. Consequently, the ways in which the members of the community move around and work are also never finished: there is always something new to do – something new to learn.

Moving and learning across community boundaries

Communities of practice do not exist in a vacuum. Sometimes, communities of practice might share things such as tools, ideas or routines that can travel across the boundaries that exist between communities. Consider the *teacher-training* communities of practice that many of the people who read this book will be members of. These different communities will be found in FE colleges and universities across the country, but they will often use the same resources such as textbooks and journal articles. A community of practice of *hairdressing apprentices* who work in a training salon in a FE college will share many aspects of their work with a similar community that is located in a commercial salon. And people as well as objects can move across communities as well. When the trainee teachers leave their Certificate in Education classes and go to teach their own students, then they move into another community where they are the teachers, not the students. When the hairdressing apprentices at a FE college finish their portfolios and receive their certificates, then can then move to commercial salons and thereby enter a different community of hairdressing practice.

Although communities can be relatively self-sufficient, some of them establish and sustain close relations with others, and might even share aspects of their practice, therefore. Indeed, the practice of one community may be influenced quite strongly by the practice of another. In order to explain how practices, objects or even people from one community might be able to move up, down or across into other communities, carrying meaning and intention with them, Wenger explores the nature of the *boundaries* that exist between communities. Elements from one community of practice can be introduced into another in two ways.

1 *Boundary objects*. Boundary objects are particular kinds of objects that can in some way connect people to communities of which they are not, or not yet, members. They will carry with them some aspect or element of the practice of that community, which can be made sense of or used by non-members. Such an artefact might have been specially designed to be a boundary object, or it might simply be an object from the everyday practice of the community that has been made in such a way that it can also serve as a boundary object. A course prospectus is an example of a specially designed boundary object, sending information about a particular programme of study to people who are not yet part of that programme but who may choose to be so in the future. A course textbook is an example of an object from the everyday practice of a community that might also work as a boundary object. People may choose to read a book about a particular subject and then choose to enrol for a programme of study during which this book would be used by all of the students on the course.

2 *Brokering*. Brokers are those members who are able to coordinate activity and meaning across communities of practice boundaries, creating new networks and connections between them. Sometimes, members of a community will act as 'specialist brokers', and they are those members of a community who are particularly adept at maintaining a presence at the boundary of their community, whilst sustaining their own engagement in practice. At other times, members of a community may be asked to do some brokering but they will then return to their 'usual' or 'accustomed' places within the community. An external verifier (EV) for an awarding body is a good example of a specialist broker. The job of an EV is to represent the interests of the awarding body – City and Guilds, for example – at the colleges where City and Guilds programmes are offered. When the college lecturer responsible for a programme of study has to prepare work for the EV to look at (as part of the quality assurance cycle), she or he is taking on a temporary brokering role – by acting as a 'go-between' between the college and the awarding body – before returning to her or his 'main' role as a lecturer within one of the communities of practice in the college.

From these examples, it can be seen that both objects and people can move across community boundaries, to help create a *constellation* of practices, which may be kept together by people, or shared repertoires, or artefacts, or any combination of these.

Membership of multiple communities of practice, and the transfer of learning

It is important not to confuse brokerage with *multi-membership* (Wenger, 1998: 159). This is the concept used by Wenger to explain how people participate in multiple communities. According to Wenger, the ways in which people will participate will vary according to the community of practice in question. Somebody can be a long-established expert within one community and a newly arrived novice in another. Therefore, it is important to consider the ways in which these different forms of participation impact on the *identity* of a member (this issue will be returned to shortly) as she or he moves within and across these different communities of practice. That is to say, the ways in which the member participates in one community (whether fully or peripherally) are shaped or influenced by the ways in which she or he participates in others, as a consequence of multi-membership.

The extent of the impact of multi-membership on participation depends on the kinds of communities of which someone is a member. If someone is a member of several communities of practice that have little or nothing in common – that is to say, if the experience of multi-membership is of highly disparate communities – then there will be little opportunity for a member's practice in one community to be influenced by her or his practice in another. On the other hand, if a person is a member of several communities that are arranged in a constellation, then opportunities for alignment between these practices become much greater.

The concept of multi-membership and the ways by which the learning that people do in different communities might be aligned, allows the communities of practice theorist to address the troublesome concept of *learning transfer* which is rejected by Lave and Wenger. Behaviourist or cognitivist theories, they argue, work on the assumption that learning results in new knowledge being 'poured into' people and that this new learning can then be carried around like a toolkit from place to place. Instead, Lave and Wenger argue that learning is *situated*, that it is closely related to the contexts and places in which it happens. When people are members of a community – that is to say, when they are learning within a community – it is not simply the case that this learning leads to more knowledge. Rather, it leads to changes in the *identity* of the learner – how they act, how they speak and how they think. Learning involves the whole person.

Whether people go somewhere new and leave a community of practice (when they start a new job after finishing a college course, for example), or whether they become members of a new community whilst staying in an existing one (when going on a work placement as an integral component of a college course, for example), it is not simply the case that what they have learned will transfer from one place to the next. Instead, Lave and Wenger suggest that the person will start to learn anew once they have become a member of that new community of practice. If the new community is closely aligned to an existing one, then learning within the new community may (it is important to remember that this is by no means guaranteed) be easier, more straightforward or more easily negotiated. Rather that focusing on how knowledge might be transferred, communities of practice theory instead focuses on how people move about, carrying their understandings, their expertise and their abilities with them and then re-learning these if necessary in order to participate in a new community.

Communities of practice in further education

Within any FE college, therefore, it would be a straightforward task to identify multiple communities of practice, each with their own routines, stories, ways of doing things, shortcuts and processes (Avis et al., 2009; Viscovic, 2005; Viscovic and Robson, 2001). These communities are situated within staff rooms, workshops and classrooms. Some of these communities relate to the administrative and managerial practices within a college, and many more relate to the different vocational, technical and professional curricula or courses that are offered within a college. They have their own practices, their own artefacts, systems and routines and their own shared histories, all of which serve to both bind a community together, to create a boundary around it, and to exclude others who do not belong. They even have their own shared sense of humour which, like many other aspects of a community's repertoire, helps to mark out the boundary of the community, to indicate who is a member and who is not. One of the authors of this book, when conducting his research into trainee teaching in FE, was struck by the fact that across all of the colleges where he carried out his research, there was always a similar level of mutual – and, it is important to remember, affectionate – teasing between teachers of electrical installation and teachers of plumbing.

Thus, the payroll department is a community of practice; the functional skills department is another; the electrical installation department is a third, and the business management department is a fourth. And there are many others, all of which overlap to a greater or lesser degree to form a constellation of communities that can be seen as being circumscribed by the boundaries of the institution itself (Wenger, 1998: 127). Put simply, a FE college can be seen as a constellation of communities of practice.

Pedagogy in communities of practice

Much of the research that has been done with communities of practice theories has understandably, and quite correctly, focused on what is often termed 'informal learning'. As has already been noted in this chapter, this is emphatically not because communities of practice theory suggests that there is a distinction between 'formal' and 'informal' learning, however. Rather, this is a reflection of the fact that communities of practice theory rejects the notion of pedagogy. According to Lave and Wenger, there are no special forms of discourse in a community of practice aimed at apprentices that 'correspond to the lecturing of college professors'. But if there is no such thing as pedagogy, no such thing as a language of instruction, then this makes things rather difficult if a communities of practice approach is to be applied to the FE sector (or, indeed, to any other formal educational context). As such, it is necessary to turn to the later work of Wenger (1998), and to move away from the earlier work of Lave and Wenger (1991), in order to find a satisfactory solution.

Wenger provides a concept that allows for a community of practice to emerge or develop as a consequence of the establishment of a *learning architecture*. A learning architecture is a design for learning. There are four issues that always need to be addressed if a learning architecture is to be designed successfully so as to allow the best possible chance for learning to happen:

Principles for designing learning architectures

1   learners need to be able to use resources that authentically represent the practice of the community
2   the design of the learning architecture has to be aware of the different ways in which learners will talk about and work with the resources that have been provided for them. Not everyone learns the same things in the same way
3   relationships with other communities of practice need to be included in the design of the learning architecture. No community exists in isolation
4   learners need to be able to play a meaningful role within the community if they are to participate and hence learn. If possible, elements of the work that learners do should be negotiated rather than imposed.

A learning architecture, therefore, consists of a collection of components that may allow learning to take place. Such a collection of resources will usually consist of a place (rooms, workshops, libraries, IT suites), tools and equipment (textbooks, materials, machinery, handbooks, reading lists), people (lecturers, teachers, technicians, students, support workers) and activities (demonstrations, seminars, tutorials, practical tasks, assignment tasks), all designed to create a place or environment within which learning can take place. One of these resources is *teaching*, which is understood as being *part of the learning architecture*, rather than a separate process that stands outside it. Therefore, it follows that teaching becomes part of the *repertoire* (see above) of the community of practice, to be employed by those members of the community who have the appropriate expertise to access it: the teachers.

Criticisms of communities of practice theory

The position of teaching within a community of practice (as discussed above) has long been considered to be a significant problem relating to communities of practice theory. There are two other problematic aspects of the theory that also need to be considered at this time. These two problems are, however, related to each other and can both be satis-factorily answered using the same theoretical solution. When describing the journeys that people make through a community of practice (which are referred to as *trajectories*) both Lave and Wenger (1991) and Wenger (1998) rest their analyses on two assumptions. First, they assume that *full membership* is the assumed consequence of increased participation. That is to say, they assume that if people join a community of practice, then they want to become full members of that community. Secondly, they assume that mastery of the practice can be had *solely* by participating in that practice. That is to say, they assume that you can only learn something or become good or skilled at something by taking part in the practice in question.

But both of these assumptions are clearly flawed in a number of ways. If someone is a hairdressing student at a FE college or, to put it another way, is a member of a community of practice of trainee hairdressers, it is because she or he wants eventually to become a member of a community of practice of hairdressers – to get a job in a commercial salon. Their membership of the trainee community is only every going to be a temporary one. And at the same time, somebody different could do an apprenticeship in the workplace, by being employed as a shop junior and then doing all of their training in the commercial salon. But if someone wanted to be a cardiac surgeon, they would not be able to just get a job at a hospital and 'work their way up'. Instead, they would have to spend substantial amounts of time learning in other communities of practice that would be preparing them for a job as a cardiac surgeon.

Jay Lemke, another theorist whose research and writing has focussed on social learning theories, identified this problem in his reading of Lave and Wenger's work. In order to find a solution to this problem, he suggested that people might need to spend time learning in one community of practice *before* they were able to enter, and therefore learn in, another community (Lemke, 1997). For example, if somebody wanted to join a community of practice of motor vehicle teachers, they would *first* need to spend time in a community of practice of teacher-training. This process – of having to spend time in one community before being able to join another one – provides a coherent theoretical explanation of the learning trajectories of students in FE (and, indeed, in other educational contexts as well), and has been taken up by a number of other communities of practice theorists, including writers who have used communities of practice to explore teacher-training (Malcolm and Zukas, 2007; Tummons, 2008; Viskovic, 2005).

Consider a group of students who are taking a course at a FE college: this might be a course in plumbing, a course in book-keeping, or a course in teacher-training. Once these students have successfully completed their programmes of study and have received their certificates, then they can demonstrate that they have successfully learned all of the things that the curriculum has required them to learn. But this is not to say that once in employment, a newly qualified plumber now no longer needs or want to learn anything else about plumbing, or that a newly employed book-keeper will never learn anything new that will help them to do their job, or that a newly qualified teacher in their first post has already learned everything that they needed to learn in order to teach.

In all three of these examples, the people in question have *first* spent time in a community of practice within an educational context which has then allowed them *secondly* to become members of other communities of practice which relate to, or are *aligned* to the careers that they were seeking to establish for themselves. Moreover, through exploring these three learning journeys from a communities of practice perspective, the importance of providing new employees with continuing opportunities to learn once they begin their employment clearly emerges. At the same time, it becomes equally clear that employers who argue that college leavers should be 'ready' to start work at once are not entirely correct in their assumptions. There will *always* be more things that the new employee will need to learn once they start their working – as opposed to studying – lives.

Summary

It is important to remember that in Lave and Wenger's original work, it was legitimate peripheral participation, which is a theory of learning, and *not* the community of practice, which was the main focus. Or, to put it another way, it is important to remember that a community of practice is a place where learning happens – it is a means to an end and not an end in itself.

The term 'community of practice' remains problematic because it is so often misused or misapplied. Not every gathering of people is a community of practice. Unless learning is taking place through legitimate peripheral participation, as described above, then there can be no community of practice. Similarly, if the three key characteristics – mutual engagement, joint enterpsie and shared repertoire – cannot be identified, then there is no community of practice. And if something is a community of practice, then it needs to be properly described as such, in terms of not only the three key characteristics but also in terms of legitimate peripheral participation, boundaries, brokerage, constellations and so on. It is to be regretted that a not inconsiderable number of textbooks and academic articles use the term 'community of practice' very freely indeed, with scant regard for the kind of detailed explorations that a community of practice deserves and requires – a level of detail that echoes the research approaches of Jean Lave and Etienne Wenger that informed the writing of their book.

However, if it is used thoughtfully and thoroughly, a communities of practice approach can provide useful insights into formal education and training contexts such as FE colleges and adult education or community learning centres. It can help the teacher or trainer to think about the ways in which students learn how to use the 'tools of the trade' (although these might not be tools in the literal sense), how to 'talk the talk' of the subject or curriculum, and how to behave in ways that are appropriate to the workplace or occupational communities of practice that they aspire to become members of once their college studies are completed.

Further reading

Very few textbooks for the further education sector provide any meaningful coverage of communities of practice theory. Two books that do have relevant chapters are:

Avis, J., Orr, K. and Tummons, J. (2010), Theorising the work-based learning of teachers. In Avis, J., Fisher, R. and Thompson, R. (eds) *Teaching in Lifelong Learning: a guide to theory and practice*. Maidenhead: McGraw Hill.

Ferguson, B. and Strong, A. (2010), Belonging and collegiality: the college as a community of practice. In Wallace, S. (ed.) *The Lifelong Learning Sector reflective reader*. Exeter: Learning Matters.

Etienne Wenger's own website contains a useful introduction, and this is at:

http://wenger-trayner.com/resources/what-is-a-community-of-practice/ [accessed 15 May 2013].

An older article by Wenger, *Communities of Practice – learning as a social system* – can be found online at:

http://www.co-i-l.com/coil/knowledge-garden/cop/lss.shtml [accessed 15 May 2013].

11 Activity Theory and Expansive Learning

Activity theory can be understood as a direct descendant of the theories of Lev Vygotsky (as discussed in Chapter 9). It is not specifically a theory relating to formal education, in contrast to Vygotsky's original work. Instead, activity theorists are interested in a wide range of subjects that are all related to learning (in a widely defined sense), such as language acquisition, the nature of knowledge, the relationship between individuals and their social environments, and so forth. Whilst there is a number of researchers and writers who are using activity theory in their research, the main focus of this chapter will be on the theories of Yrgö Engeström who uses activity theory as part of a broader theory of expansive learning (Engeström 1987, 1993, 1999, 2001; Engeström et al., 1999). Yrgö Engeström is Professor of Adult Education at the University of Helsinki, with interests in learning and knowledge at work and in organizations. His work on expansive learning and activity systems was first published 25 years ago in a ground-breaking work titled *Learning by Expanding: an activity-theoretical approach to developmental research*. A later volume, co-edited with Reijo Miettenen and Raija-Leena Punamäki (also at the University of Helsinki), titled *Perspectives on Activity Theory*, brought together work from a wider range of scholars who all broadly follow a Vygotskian tradition. Engeström recognizes that activity theory and expansive learning are just two examples of a wider body of social practice theories that have emerged during recent times, including situated learning and communities of practice, many of which look back to the work of Vygotsky in some way. Before continuing, it is important to note that Engeström's theories have been applied to learning at work as opposed to formal educational systems. It is proposed therefore, in the first instance, to focus on the work of the FE teacher in order to provide examples of activity theory in practice. Ways in which the learning of students might be explored using this framework are considered later. The reader is asked to note that the account presented here is (in common with other theoretical discursions in this text) somewhat simplified. The references provided will allow the interested reader to pursue the ideas presented here in more depth.

First theoretical component: The activity system

A single activity system makes up the basic unit of analysis of activity theory. It is a way of thinking about the places and spaces in which people go about their work, what tools or equipment they have to use, what other people else are involved, and so forth, in order for learning to happen. There are a number of different elements to an activity system, all of which are linked together, and the easiest way to explain an activity system is through a worked example. The elements are:

1 Subject.
   The subject is the person or group of people who are engaged in the activity, that will lead to learning, which is being explored.

2 Rules.
   The rules are the norms, accepted ways of working, regulations and so forth that shape the environment being explored. The subject has to work within and towards these rules.

3 Tools.
   Tools are the artefacts, equipment, texts, notices and so forth that are used, manipulated or referred to by the subject. It is important to note that tools are not necessarily physical objects, but might also include routines, processes and ways of doing things.

4 Community.
   Community refers to the wider group of people who are also involved in the same physical or social space of work – other members of staff, colleagues and so forth.

5 Division of labour.
   Division of labour refers to the ways in which work done by the subject will be differentiated from the work done by other people in the space of work or activity system.

6 Object.
   Object refers to the focus or target of the work that the subject is engaged in.

All six elements are interconnected in an activity system. That is to say, each element relates to, refers to or is otherwise linked to all of the others. The activity that is being explored cannot happen without all six elements being identified and drawn on as appropriate. Thus, an activity system can be depicted in diagrammatic form as a triangle with a series of interconnected points.

Inside a FE college, there will be any number of different activity systems at work, located across different departments, curriculum areas, and so forth. (In this sense, the theory works in a similar manner to communities of practice theory as discussed in the

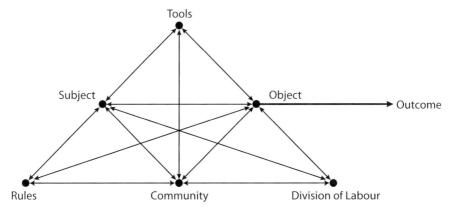

Figure 11.1

previous chapter). A college will already have lots of activity systems in it: it is simply a question of identifying them by looking for the six elements of any system as specified above. For example, if exploring the technical or vocational curriculum, the following elements might be discerned:

1 Subject.
A teacher of electrical installation.

2 Rules.
The funding regulations that surround the FE sector. The specifications of the curriculum awarding body. Relevant occupational standards and regulations such as those published by the Institute of Engineering and Technology (IET).

3 Tools.
The equipment in the electrical installation workshop. Registers, timetables, portfolios and health and safety notices. Whole group teaching session and one-to-one tutorials.

4 Community.
Other teachers of electrical installation. Other ancillary staff who are involved in the delivery of the curriculum such as technicians or assessors. Support staff.

5 Division of labour.
Occupational roles are distinguished between the staff involved. For example, technicians will help in setting up equipment but would not make assessment decisions relating to students' progress. (The wider role of support staff is discussed in Chapter 27).

6 Object.
The successful delivery of the electrical installation curriculum/qualification that has been specified, leading to the achievement of the students who have enrolled on the programme who will then be occupationally qualified and thereby certificated so that they can work as electrical installers.

An example from the professional and academic curriculum would be as follows:

1 Subject.
   A teacher of childcare studies.

2 Rules.
   The regulations that surround the FE sector. Legislation relevant to safeguarding. Relevant occupational and sector standards such as the Early Years Foundation Stage (EYFS).

3 Tools.
   Classroom resources such as textbooks, games, portfolios and posters. Seminars and one-to-one tutorials. Work placements. Observations.

4 Community.
   Other teachers. Assessors and observers. Placement officers. Safeguarding officers. Staff working at placement locations. Parents.

5 Division of labour.
   Division of responsibilities between members of the teaching team.

6 Object.
   The successful delivery of all aspects of the curriculum, leading to the achievement of the students who have enrolled on the programme, who will then be certificated to enter the early years workplace.

Having outlined the component characteristics of any activity system, it is important to note that activity theory rests on five underlying principles. These can be summarized as follows, and contextualized through referring back to the two case study activity systems that have already been proposed (electrical installation and childcare) (Engeström, 1999):

1 The activity system is the main unit of analysis within activity theory. Individual activities or goals can only properly be understood when explored against the backdrop of a collective activity system. The work of a college teacher only makes sense when considered in the context of the curriculum being taught, the FE sector as a whole and the sector of the economy that the students will go to work in after completion fo the course.

2 Activity systems always contain multiple points of view and perspectives – they are not homogenous. Participants have different points of view depending on how their labour is divided. Different rules that have accumulated over time will offer different perspectives, as will the different tools that are used within the activity system. Participants will need to work through these different points of view as part of their own activity. Different teachers like to do things in different ways. They have particular aspects of their curricula that they favour and others that they question. They may

have their own routines and habits that are more-or-less in alignment with the processes established across the college as a whole.

3 Activity systems do not appear overnight: they take time to become established and take shape. The history of any activity system becomes an important issue, therefore: what happened before in relation to the activity system may still be of relevance to current participants. FE colleges in their current form (as incorporated bodies) can be dated back to the early 1990s, but of course the history of technical and vocational provision dates back to the mechanics' institutes of the nineteenth century (Walker, 2012).

4 Changes occur within activity systems as a consequence of a specific type of process called a contradiction. Contradictions within activity systems are those moments when, for example, a new process or technology is introduced. When the new technology causes conflict with the existing rules or tools of the activity system this is referred to as a contradiction. Contradictions such as these become resolved as new ways of working emerge to accommodate the changes. Curriculum change due to new professional or occupational standards would cause a contraction within an activity system. The implementation of a new attendance monitoring system within a college would provide a smaller contradiction.

5 Over time, the work done by activity systems can change, and these changes can be profound. Contradictions can accumulate and aggravate the work of the activity system, and this can lead individual participants to work on a collective basis to change the object of the activity system. An example might include the decision not to offer a particular qualification, or to withdraw an entire curriculum from a college's provision.

Second theoretical component: Expansive learning

Expansive learning is the theory of learning that underpins activity theory, in a similar manner to the way in which communities of practice theory is underpinned by a theory of learning called legitimate peripheral participation (as discussed in the preceding chapter). Expansive learning theory seeks to address four themes:

1 who are the subjects of learning, and how are they defined and located?

2 why do they learn? What motivates them to make the effort to learn?

3 what do they learn? What is the content of their learning? What are the outcomes?

4 how do they learn? What are the processes or actions that are central to their learning?

It is important to note that these four themes are integral to the theory of expansive learning and always need to be considered together. That is to say, according to activity theory, there is no 'separate' consideration of motivation apart from the other elements listed such as content or processes. All of these four themes are bundled together as one. This is because it is not possible to describe or make sense of the learning that is happening without taking all of these into consideration.

Any cycle of expansive learning is made up of seven actions, which are referred to by Engeström as epistemic (which means relating to knowledge or cognition). Expansive learning always takes place within activity systems. Therefore, when providing any account of expansive learning at work, attention should be paid to all of the elements of the activity system.

The seven epistemic actions (Engeström, 1999):

1   Questioning
    This action consists of asking questions, raising criticisms, rejecting accepted practices or previously held ideas or notions. These will have been raised or stimulated by contradictions (as described above).

2   Analysis
    Analysis, at the most basic level, involves asking the question: why? This might refer to practical or theoretical matters, and the aim of the analysis stage is to find out the causes or reasons behind something, or the explanation for something. There are two types of analysis. The first relates to the origins or evolution of something – this is called historical-genetic analysis. The second relates to the construction, current state or understanding of something – this is called actual-empirical analysis.

3   Modelling the new solution
    This action consists of constructing a model (not a literal model – it might be a series of answers, a set of procedures or a series of actions, and so forth) that explains and offers a solution to the problematic situation that has raised the questions in the first place.

4   Examining the new model
    This action involves running the model that has been constructed (providing the series of answers, following through the new procedures, taking the newly-defined actions and so forth). This is done in an experimental manner, so that the potential of the model can be explored and any limitations can be worked through.

5   Implementing the new model
    This action involves the full implementation of the model, providing practical applications in order to 'fix' the new model into a solid form.

6   Reflecting on the process
    This action involves reflection on and evaluation of the new model and any processes or practices that the new model has entailed. The total experience of the new model should be explored and evaluated at this stage.

Teaching in Further Education

7   Consolidating the new practice
    This final action involves acting on any issues that have been raised during the
    reflection/evaluation stage, and then consolidating these into the new model which
    can then become a new and fixed or stable element of practice.

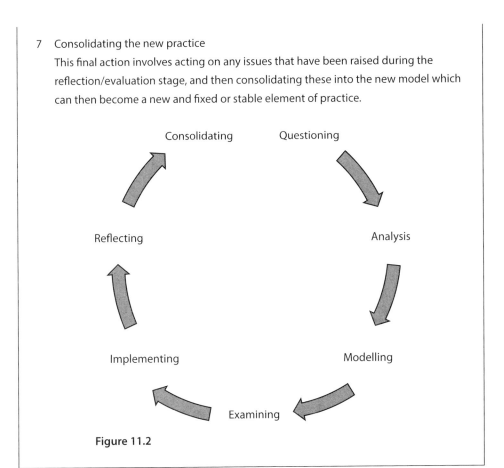

Figure 11.2

The expansive learning of teachers in further education

In the first place, as indicated at the beginning of this chapter, activity theory can be used
to explore the expansive learning of teachers of FE. Once any contradiction (as defined
above) can be identified, the sequence of epistemic actions that lead to expansive learning
to resolve the contradiction can be explored, making reference as and when necessary to
the different elements of the activity system.

The contradiction that is going to be explored here is not a new phenomenon in
relation to the sector as a whole, but it is a contradiction that not all teachers in FE will have
had direct experience of. Because it is a relatively complex topic, but also a very current one,
it provides a worthwhile case study of expansive learning. The contradiction that will be
explored is the provision for 14–16s in FE within a specific curriculum area (such as trowel
occupations, for example).

To begin, it is necessary to consider the elements of the activity system in question. These can be outlined briefly as follows:

1 Subject.
   A teacher of trowel occupations in a mixed FE college. The teacher has worked at the college for several years, teaching 'traditional' 16–19s. in the past he has also taught adult learners but this area of provision has been scaled back over recent years due to changes in funding systems (this constitutes another contradiction in itself).

2 Rules.
   In addition to the framework established by the curriculum that is being followed, institutional and national policy relating to the teaching of 14–16s in FE colleges will need to be considered (to cover issues such as safeguarding).

3 Tools.
   Workshop tools and resources. Strategies for teaching 14–16s. Behaviour management strategies.

4 Community.
   Learning support workers. Safeguarding officers. Parents.

5 Division of labour.
   Division of responsibilities between members of the teaching and support teams.

6 Object.
   The provision of a curriculum that successfully engages a group of students who have been labelled 'at risk' of disengagement from formal education and training, and enables them not only to work towards a qualification but also to reengage with their education.

A consideration of the activity system allows us to consider how all of these elements are inter-related, and that in isolation they cannot help in an understanding of the work that is being done – that is, the work of delivering a course to the 14–16s (Harkin, 2006). The teacher works to a set curriculum, much as he would when working with a more traditional FE group, but has to be mindful of the particular differences that result from working with 14–16s in terms of behaviour, level of qualification and so forth: all of these constitute the rules of the particular activity system in question. The tools that are used to deliver this curriculum range from actual tools in the workshop, to registration procedures that ensure that all of the students are present and that any additional learning support is provided. The community can be defined in quite a broad sense in this instance, and can conceivably include not only college staff, parents and funding bodies, but also policy makers at regional and national levels who are interested in ensuring that the young people in question do not drop out and become NEET (not in employment, education or training). Within this activity system, labour is divided in a pattern that is typical across the FE sector, with the delivery of the curriculum (including teaching, assessment, verification and so forth) being the responsibility of the teacher. Pastoral issues provide a new area of work although many of these issues will come under the purview of learning support workers.

Having established a brief outline of the activity system, it is now possible to provide an account of the expansive learning of the teacher, following the structure outlined above.

1 Questioning

The contradiction – the new phenomenon of teaching 14–16s in a FE setting – will be a familiar one across the sector as a whole (including the curriculum for the training of teachers for the sector), even though only a minority of teaching staff will have been involved.

2 Analysis

The historical-genetic analysis of the contradiction might involve the following key questions: why are 14–16s now expected to come to college instead of staying at school? What are the expectations of the students, of their parents and wider families, of the college management and of the local education authority? What are the wider implications of 14–16 provision for the FE sector? The actual-empirical analysis might consider: how will teaching 14–16s differ from working with 16–19s, and how will it be the same? What aspects of teaching style are best suited to working with this group, and are behavioural difficulties anticipated? How will the learning support assistants best be employed within the workshop environment?

3 Modelling the new solution

In order to meet the challenges posed by this contradiction, the teacher will initially design a new scheme of work and series of lessons with aims, outcomes, resources and assessment strategies that meet the needs of the curriculum but at the same time address the individual needs of the student group. Consulting with other members of the college teaching staff, who have prior experience of working with 14–16s, might yield useful feedback regarding lesson planning, behaviour management and classroom conduct.

4 Examining the new model

Once the new course has been designed, delivery can begin. At this stage, the teacher will be delivering the course on a 'trial' basis: as this is the first time that he has taught a 14–16 group, he has no direct prior experience and knowledge upon which to draw.

5 Implementing the new model

As the course becomes established, patterns of behaviour – on the part of the teacher and the students – will become normalized and routinized. The teacher is, at the same time, creating an infrastructure that can be used for the delivery of a similar course in the future. Resources, tools, assessments, appropriate teaching and learning strategies and appropriate behaviour management strategies will all become part of the professional repertoire of the teacher.

6 Reflecting on the process

Formal evaluation processes will be embedded into the curriculum as a consequence of not only the awarding body regulations, but also the quality assurance systems of the college (this topic is discussed in detail in Chapter 32). Informal evaluation and reflection by the teacher will be ongoing throughout the delivery of the curriculum. The results of both of these processes will feed into any revising or redesigning of the curriculum in advance of the arrival of a new cohort of students.

7 Consolidating the new practice

With the processes of planning, delivery and evaluation of the new 14–16 curriculum now completed, this aspect of college provision becomes fixed and stable. A new set of tools, systems, procedures and ways of working has been established, accompanied and reinforced by the new experience and workplace knowledge of the teacher who has delivered the course.

In conclusion, it can be said that the contradiction – the new provision for 14–16s at the college – has now been addressed. Within the activity system, new rules have been established (for example relating to safeguarding) and new tools have been created and used (such as new activities in the workshop). The community has been widened (by learning support workers and by the new cohort of students themselves) and a new division of labour between the required staff has been established. The object – the delivery of the curriculum to the new group – has been accomplished.

How, then, can the expansive learning of the teacher be understood? Because activity theory is a social practice theory, expansive learning is concerned with not what happens in the head (which is the preserve of psychologists or possibly neuroscientists) but with what people do in practice, in the real world: how they act and talk whilst resolving contradictions, how they interact with the tools and artefacts of their social context and so forth. For the FE teacher, the expansive learning which has led to new understandings and new forms of practice is located within his new 14–16 curriculum, his new understanding of the needs of 14–16 students and the ways in which he works with the learning support assistants: put simply, this episode of expansive learning has led to a significant shift in the professional knowledge, expertise and practice of the teacher.

Classrooms and workshops as activity systems

Although Engeström's work has focussed on expansive learning in work environments, other researchers and writers have used activity-theoretical perspectives to explore formal education contexts as diverse as history teaching, mathematics teaching, language learning and drama. Activity theory has also been used to provide a critique of formal educational practice as lacking sufficient application to or alignment with society at large. According to this perspective, schools are isolated from other societal activities: the focus of school learning is the memorizing, repeating and reproducing of the texts that are being studied. If the object of learning at school is going to be redefined according to the perspectives offered by activity theory, then three changes to the way that schooling is organized need to be accomplished (Miettinen, 1999):

1 bringing reality into school in the form of materials and tasks taken from real life, work environments
2 have students study activities and objects outside school
3 apply models studied in school to problems outside school.

Ideas such as these three (perhaps gratifyingly) will appear to be familiar to most teachers in FE:

1 Bringing reality into school in the form of materials and tasks taken from real life, work environments
   Curriculum provision in FE colleges satisfies this idea in a number of ways ranging from the ways in which teachers create their materials and resources using authentic case studies and examples, to the provision of training restaurants or training hair and beauty salons.
2 Have students study activities and objects outside school
   Many courses in the FE sector maintain links with local employers in order to further establish authenticity of provision. Site visits and study trips all contribute to students' learning by allowing them to study beyond the institutional confines of the college.
3 Apply models studied in school to problems outside school
   The work placements that are characteristic of many of the course offered in colleges provide opportunities for the learning that has taken place within the college being applied outside. For example: students on childcare courses will learn the importance of developing good observation skills in the classroom, and then have the opportunity to actually use these observation skills when on placement.

At the same time, if an activity system is to be accepted as the unit of analysis for the theory as a whole, then it follows that if, for example, a car mechanics' workshop or an access to higher education programme (or a certificate in education for FE teaching) can be shown to consist of all of the elements of an activity system, then the expansive learning of the subjects within it can be ascertained.

The example that was provided above (the 14–16 trowel occupations group) positioned the teacher as the subject. Here, it is suggested, the students might be positioned as the subject. In this way, activity theory can be used to explore student learning in FE as well as the professional learning of teachers at work.

The expansive learning of students in further education

Returning to the model of the activity system that has already been described, an application that focuses on the students as subject can be considered in the following ways:

1 Subject.
   A group of students who are enrolled on a City and Guilds Technician Diploma in Motor Vehicle Systems at a FE college.

2 Rules.
   A number of frameworks exist that impact on the students in different ways. At college, college-wide codes of conduct are applied, which, together with the City and Guilds specified curriculum, shape much of the students' working day. Although they are less formally structured, there are also particular rules that apply to the workshop, specifically, a small number of habits that the teacher requires of the students: particular rules about when the radio is allowed on, when the workshop and the tools should be tidied up, and so forth.

3 Tools.
   The tools of this activity system include actual tools (screwdrivers, vernier calipers, spanners and so forth) and larger pieces of equipment (car chassis, diagnostic computer equipment, posters on the walls showing cutaway sections of car part). The City and Guilds documentation is another tool, as are the assignments that the students are completing.

4 Community.
   Beyond the student group, the most immediate members of the community are the teacher, the technician and (if necessary) the learning support worker or functional skills teacher. Beyond this immediate group are found other students on similar courses, other members of college staff who provide services that the students may need from time to time (counselling staff, financial advice and so forth).

5 Division of labour.
   The work of the different members of the community is clearly marked out in this example through the clear identification of the students as 'students', and the teacher as 'teacher'.

6 Object.
   In this activity system, the object is the successful accomplishment of the curriculum.

This entails successful study, regular attendance, hard and effortful work, and diligent application to the assessments. Put another way, it entails practice. The wider consequences, beyond certification, include employability, the possibility of future study, the possibility of independent living once work has been obtained, and so forth.

And the learning of the students can be understood as follows through exploring the seven epistemic actions that make up the expansive learning cycle (as discussed above):

1 Questioning
In this context, questioning can be taken to refer to the ways in which students interrogate the themes, topics or routines that they are studying or practicing. In the context of a motor vehicle course, this might refer to how to use a tool correctly, how to carry out a specific procedure correctly, or the fact that a number of procedures have to be carried out in a fixed sequence.

2 Analysis
In this context, the 'why' questions that might be asked will be similarly varied, ranging from questions about why one rather another method, tool or diagnostic should be used, to more fundamental questions about the mechanics and engineering principles of the combustion engine. In this way, the analysis includes both the immediate learning environment (the actual-empirical) as well as allowing students to begin to explore the wider background and history of motor vehicle engineering and maintenance (the historical-genetic).

3 Modelling the new solution
At this stage, students will be beginning to grasp key issues, fundamental points and to practice basic motor and cognitive actions. These actions will still be conditional, even hypothetical and will rely on guidance and feedback from the teacher.

4 Examining the new model
In this context, this refers to the students' developing motor and cognitive skills which can be used to solve problems or resolve tasks of increasing complexity that have been set by the teacher. At this stage, students' responses and solutions may be more or less tentative and competence and understanding may still be reinforced through dialogue with the teacher.

5 Implementing the new model.
At this stage, students are problem solving more or less independently of their teacher (although their peer conversations will be characterized by more 'on-task' critical commentary, peer support and peer feedback). Repeated applications in practice help routinize and enrich what has been learned.

6 Reflecting on the process
At this stage, students discuss their progress – amongst themselves as well as with

their teacher. For example, as the workshop is tidied up as the end of the day, tools are cleaned and tasks are signed off, conversations may range across that day's work, the work that is going to be done tomorrow, which tasks still need more practice, how these new practices fit into the wider curriculum, and so forth.

7 Consolidating the new practice

Over the coming days and weeks, what were once new tasks or new bodies of knowledge become firmly and deeply entrenched in the practices of the students.

In this example, the expansive learning of the students can be understood in terms of: their greater knowledge and understanding of how to perform particular mechanical or diagnostic operations on vehicles; their gradually deepening understanding of the broader cultural, social and historical context of their studies and of the industry that they are seeking to enter; and their deepening participation within the culture of the FE college more generally (as a consequence of their attendance, learning and activity over a period of time). All of this learning can be seen as being in response to the initial contradiction of wanting to work in the motor vehicle industry, but being unqualified and hence incapable of doing so. As such, Engeström's theories can be seen to provide a useful framework for thinking about not only what teachers learn whilst working in FE, but also what students learn whilst studying.

Critiques of activity theory and expansive learning

Activity theory is not used to the same extent as communities of practice theory which of all the social practice theories under consideration has probably been the most influential, even if the application of the theory is sometimes flawed (Illeris, 2007; Tummons, 2012). Nonetheless, some critiques of activity theory have been made and are briefly noted here (Ashwin, 2009; Avis, 2007; Davydov, 1999):

- Is the subject a named individual, a group of individuals or an abstraction (such as 'general practitioner' or 'dental nurse')? Does this make a difference to how the rest of the activity system might be defined?

- If teachers occupy one activity system – as subject – and students occupy another, should these be combined or linked together if the pedagogic processes are to be properly explored? (Engeström has argued that systems can be combined so that any analysis will always start with at least two minimally interacting activity systems (Engeström, 2001: 136)).

- How closely is each element of the activity system defined? Does a curriculum constitute a rule, a tool or can it be both?

Summary: Activity theory in further education

As with the other theories presented in this text, activity theory is proposed as just one possible framework through which aspects of learning and teaching practice can be explored. It does not offer the same kinds of answers as other theories that have already been discussed – nor should it. Activity theory is not concerned with stimulus-response or self-actualization: it is a framework that seeks to join together the work done by people who are learning through their work, with the environment, cultures, tools and histories that surround them. Activity theory reminds the teacher that the work that they do is just a small part of a much richer social context. Learning needs not only to consider what might happen at the psychological level, but what happens at the social, cultural and environmental level as well. Activity theory provides one way for the FE teacher to think and reflect on just these themes.

Further reading

Activity theory is derived in part from the theories of Vygotsky but has yet to receive such wide coverage in teacher-training literature. There are some websites that provide an outline of activity theory. An excellent example can be found at:

http://www2.warwick.ac.uk/fac/soc/ier/glacier/tlrp/qualitative/chat/ [accessed 15 May 2013].
This is a website relating to a larger scale research project in a UK setting.

A significant focus of research in this area is at the University of Helsinki, and their website is also recommended:

http://www.helsinki.fi/cradle/index.htm [accessed 15 May 2013].

A very helpful critique of activity theory from a HE perspective – the conclusions of which are transferable to FE – can be found in:

Ashwin, P. (2009), *Analysing Teaching-Learning Interactions in Higher Education: accounting for structure and agency*. London: Continuum.

12 Social and Cultural Perspectives on Further Education

In this final chapter of Part 3, we shall briefly outline the key aims and findings of two recent research projects that explored a number of aspects relating to teaching and learning in FE in England, Wales and Scotland. Both of the research projects that are discussed here formed part of a much larger research strand, the *Teaching and Learning Research Programme* (TLRP) which was funded by the Economic and Social Research Council (ESRC). It is suggested that these research projects, both of which draw on social practice theories, have much to offer the FE teacher and as such deserve much wider consideration amongst practitioners, teacher educators and trainee teachers than they currently receive.

Transforming learning cultures in further education

The transforming learning cultures project is the largest research project ever undertaken in the FE sector. It ran from 2001 to 2005 and was based on a case study approach of teaching and learning at 19 different sites across four FE colleges (in Leeds, Coventry, Bristol and St Austell). The design of the research project acknowledged the low status that FE colleges enjoy in comparison to schools and universities (historically, FE was referred to as the 'second chance' sector or the 'cinderella sector') and highlighted the unstable funding regimes, managerialist cultures and rigid quality assurance and audit regimes that makes the working lives of teachers more difficult (Gleeson et al., 2005). Resting on an understanding of learning as being a social practice (that is to say, of being something that is shared, not individual, and is practical and not merely mental), the project highlighted four main findings:

1 learning in FE colleges is shaped by complex cultural relationships
2 what counts as good teaching varies across different contexts (institutional, and subject-based)
3 learning outcomes are numerous, and are highly variable. They are not all

beneficial to the student. (For example: nursery nurses achieve a qualification and become practitioners, but are as a result identified as low-status and low-paid workers)

4   learning in FE is being damaged by unstable and inadequate funding regimes and by an over-emphasis (driven by audit and inspection cultures) on measureable learning outcomes.

In turn, the project highlighted four corresponding implications:

1   changing learning cultures would be the most effective way to improve learning

2   for learning in FE to improve, the sector needs to receive sufficient funding on a more stable basis, more consistent and less rapidly-changing policy objectives, and enhanced staff professionalism

3   a greater range of learning outcomes (including those articulated by students) should be recognized

4   there should be a move towards greater professional autonomy and expertise for practitioners in the sector.

But what does a cultural view of learning look like in this context? Drawing on social practice theories, the project team argued that (James and Biesta, 2007: 28):

- learning cultures are not the contexts in which people learn, but the social practices through which people learn

- individuals influence and are part of learning cultures just as learning cultures influence and are part of individuals

- learning cultures are not the same as learning sites. Learning sites have clear boundaries, but the factors that make up the learning culture(s) in a particular site do not

- a learning culture will permit, promote, inhibit or rule out certain kinds of learning. This means that the key issue is how different learning cultures enable or disable different learning possibilities for the people that come into contact with them.

In this sense, the project can be seen quite clearly as resting on social practice theories of learning and teaching, making explicit and integral the links between people (students and teachers), places (colleges, different departments, different parts of the country) and the curriculum. Based on the four drivers of student interests, teachers' professionalism, pedagogy as an art and the cultural view, the project suggested the following as key principles for improving learning cultures in FE:

1 Maximizing student agency

The motivations and dispositions of students in FE are diverse, above and beyond the goal of achieving the qualification that has been signed up for. This diversity should, the project concluded, be reflected in the monitoring of provision at regional and national levels, as well as in the workshop or classroom, where teachers should do more to support students for whom the qualification is not the main concern and also acknowledge and address the negative effects of learning.

2 Maximizing teacher professionalism

The project argued that teacher professionalism should be recognized in different ways, mindful of the different contexts in which FE teachers work. It suggested that professionalism should be understood in terms of teacher autonomy, creativity, innovation and expertise in judgement making. Workplace practices should be adjusted so that teachers have the time and space to develop meaningful professional learning, peer support and exchange.

3 Improving pedagogy

The project demonstrated very clearly that effective pedagogy varies significantly between different learning cultures and between different teachers. With these broad themes in mind, the project recommended that a more expansive debate concerning what counts as 'good' pedagogic practice should be facilitated, acknowledging that a national audit or inspection system will never be able to capture adequately these diverse practices. Teachers should – having been given the time and resources – work to be creative in their approaches to teaching and learning, and develop critically reflective approaches to their own pedagogy.

4 Enhancing positive aspects of a learning culture

All of the themes mentioned above are understood to contribute to the positive aspects of learning cultures. In addition, a number of other issues were raised. Government and college management should recognize the negative as well as positive impact that they have on teaching and learning and seek to minimize these, and should work to create more stable and less volatile environments for teachers and students. Teachers, in turn, should work to improve the effectiveness of teaching by maximizing positive learning processes and outcomes, and minimizing negative processes and outcomes.

Literacies for learning in further education

The literacies for learning in FE project ran from 2004 to 2007, and was based on a combined case study approach across two FE colleges in England (one in Lancaster and one in Preston) and two in Scotland (one in Glasgow and one in Perth). Because the project aimed to explore the literacy practices of teachers and students in FE, the theoretical framework that was used related to literacy specifically, rather than learning more generally. However, the framework used – literacy as social practice, also known as the new literacy studies – is in part derived from and shares much ground with the social practice theories that have been discussed up to this point.

According to the new literacy studies, literacy is best understood as a set of social practices, which can be inferred from events, which are mediated by written texts (Barton, 1994). Such events arise from literacy practices, which are those general ways that people use written language in all sorts of social contexts, whether at work, at home or elsewhere. Literacy events are relatively straightforward to observe. Literacy practices are not, however, and this is because they involve how people feel about, or the extent to which they value, the literacy in question. However, literacy is not the same across contexts: there are different literacies, wrapped up in different literacy practices, which are identifiable and which belong to different social contexts or domains. For example, the ways in which students on an access to higher education write their essays are quite different from the ways in which – when they are at home – they write emails to their friends, for example. And just as literacies vary across contexts, the ways in which meaning can be taken from written texts vary as well. Readers bring knowledge to their reading of a text, and the meanings that the reader makes will be mediated by this knowledge. It is also important to recognize that much literacy learning takes place within relationships of unequal power, where some forms of literacy are acknowledged and encouraged (these are referred to as dominant literacies) and others are marginalized or deemed inappropriate (these are referred to as vernacular literacies). Arguably, the dominant genre of academic writing that is of most relevance to this research is *essayist literacy* (Gee, 1996; Lillis, 2001). This term is used to describe the ways in which students are expected to write their assignments. At the same time, students also use vernacular literacies during their studies: during email exchanges with their tutors, for example, or when establishing peer support groups on Facebook.

The literacies for learning project rejected the transferable skills approach to literacy, therefore, arguing instead that there are many different kinds of literacies, and that these need to be understood in terms of their social contexts and in terms of the social practices that the users of literacy employ. For example: a student who was perceived to have 'literacy problems' or a 'literacy deficit', might in fact be highly adept in using other kinds of literacies outside their college life: writing a diary, reading the Highway Code when learning to drive or using the internet to create a family tree, for example. Indeed, during the research period, the project team ascertained that the ways in which students used literacy in their everyday lives (as opposed to their college lives) was highly complex. Students' literacy practices were:

- multi-modal – involving pictures, symbols, music and colour
- multi-media – combining electronic and paper media
- shared – were interactive, participatory and collaborative

- non-linear – offering varied reading paths
- agentic – students had control over what they read and when
- purposeful – the literacy practices had meaning and relevance for the student
- self-determined – students could choose the type of activity, the time and the place
- varied – not repetitious.

On the basis of this theoretical position, the project focused on three key findings:

1 public conversations about poor functional literacy fail to account for the rich and varied literacy practices that students use in their daily lives.

2 teachers often ignore the communicative aspect of learning – for example, by rarely explaining what 'critical analysis' actually mans and entails.

3 teachers feel constrained to use the assessment processes set by awarding bodies, even though making changes to them would be beneficial to students' learning.

In turn, the project highlighted three corresponding implications:

1 when teachers in FE 'tap into' their students' daily literacy practices, then student learning is enhanced

2 the communicative aspects of learning need to be made more explicit

3 students should be assessed on their capacity to engage in authentic literacy practices that are related to the actual vocational or academic programmes that they are engaged in.

An increasing amount of research has been done that has built on the approaches taken by the literacies for learning project (Ivaniç et al., 2009). Examples include the exploration of the literacy practices of the catering and hospitality curriculum (Brooke, 2013), adult basic education and skills for life (Barton et al., 2007), the relationship between literacy learning and playing computer games (Gee, 2004), and the ways in which trainee FE teachers are assessed (Tummons, 2008). As for the project itself, the practical implications of its findings for the teacher in the workshop or classroom can be summarized as ensuring that the literacy practices of students are rooted in the subject matter being taught. The literacy practices of the motor vehicle workshop (completing a job sheet, ordering spare parts, completing an inventory) are not the same as those of the catering students (creating and writing menus, writing down customers' orders, making a note of table reservations). But because these are all authentic literacy practices, they are meaningful to the student and therefore more likely to be engaging and to lead to learning, in contrast to the standalone key skills/functional skills curriculum.

Summary: Researching further education from a social practice perspective

The two research projects that have been briefly reported here have been selected on the basis of their relevance and applicability to the readers of this text. (At the same time, it is important to note that the TLRP funded a small number of other projects relating to the FE sector: topics included policy, community-based FE, Welsh/English bilingualism and FE teacher professionalism). These research projects are based on substantial bodies of robust research conducted over several years and as such constitute a valuable and highly authoritative resource for teachers in FE, and further reading around these project areas is recommended not only because of the pertinent and immediately practical conclusions that are raised, but because they demonstrate the insights offered by social practice theories, supported by real world research.

Further reading

The two projects referred to in this chapter have now concluded, but many of the publications and presentations written by the researchers involved are still available online. Together, these constitute two excellent collections of materials and demonstrate how the internet *should* be used by students when preparing their assignments!

The *Literacies for Learning in Further Education* project is at:

http://www.lancs.ac.uk/lflfe/ [accessed 15 May 2013].

And the *Transforming Learning Cultures in Further Education* project is at:

http://education.exeter.ac.uk/tlc/homepage.htm [accessed 15 May 2013].

PART 4

Communication and Control: The Essence of the Teaching–Learning Process

13 Communication in Teaching and Learning

The work that goes on in classrooms and workshops in FE colleges – indeed, in college buildings more generally – cannot be properly understood without a consideration of those complex sets of relationships between teachers and learners that result from *communication*. The process of communication is explored from a number of different perspectives in this chapter, and is explained, at its most basic level, in terms of the exchange of meanings between teachers and learners, without which effective instruction is impossible.

Much of this chapter is taken up with an outline of models and analogies of the process of communication; these are no more than conjectures based on theoretical and simplified representations of aspects of the real world. Abstraction can lead to over-simplification, and it should be clear to the reader by this stage of the book that theoretical perspectives possess varying degrees of robustness and reliability, but it may assist in rendering more comprehensible a formal analysis of common events in the classroom.

What is communication?

A typical dictionary definition of the verb 'communicate' would include: transmit or pass on by speaking or writing; impart non-verbally; and share a feeling or understanding or relate socially. For teachers and trainers in a FE college, such a definition is immediately identifiable: teachers speak with their students in a seminar room, indicate agreement or acknowledge progress through a nod or other gesture in the midst of a busy and noisy workshop, and offer sympathetic advice and guidance in a tutorial accompanied by a reassuring smile. Clearly, the ways in which teachers communicate with their students are varied. As such, they are worthy of investigation so that ways of making these lines of communication as effective as possible might be established.

The essence of communication is the transmitting and receiving of information through a common system of signals and symbols, whether in the form of writing, images, logos or other signs, expressive movements or gestures, or the spoken word. For example: a table is called a 'table' because the symbol made up of the letters t-a-b-l-e has over time come to be used to refer to those objects of varying sizes that we sit at in order to type on our laptops, eat our breakfast or produce an architectural drawing. A word can be a symbol. So can an image or a picture such as an emoticon.

Communication in the teaching-learning process

A number of definitions of communication have been put forward by different researchers and writers, a selection of which is presented here in order to provide more critical and comparative perspectives on communication as an element of a wider learning-teaching process:

(a) when two corresponding systems, coupled together through one or more non-corresponding systems, assume identical states as a result of signal transfer along a chain (Schramm, 1954)

(b) the achievement of meaning and understanding between people through verbal and non-verbal means in order to affect behaviour and achieve desired end results (Mondy, 1983)

(c) the transfer of information from the sender to the receiver, with the information being understood by the receiver (Koontz, 1985)

(d) the process by which people attempt to share meaning via the transmission of symbolic messages (Stoner, 1989)

(e) communication is the transactional use of symbols, influenced, guided and understood in the context of relationships (Duck and McMahan, 2012).

An important characteristic of human beings (as distinct from animals, reinforcing scepticism regarding the use of educational theories based upon animal experimentation) is their capacity for the expressive vocalization, which we call *speech*. It may be that the early growth of civilization depended in large part on a person's ability to communicate with his or her neighbour by speaking, and the later stages of civilization have reflected, in some measure, the invention of more complicated media of communication, such as the printing press, the telephone and the internet. The development of formal teaching, in particular, is linked to the qualitative expansion of communication methods. From the spoken discourse to the printed textbook, from television programmes for schools and colleges to computers, ipads and websites, the teaching process has depended on the ability and technique of the teacher to convey to the learner, in an appropriate form, the fruits of human thought – that is, to communicate.

In a teaching environment, communication by the teacher is generally intended to influence the learner's behaviour in some way, perhaps to direct attention to a specific resource, to check prior understanding through question-and-answer, or to manage potentially disruptive behaviour. Its mode will be determined, therefore, by the particular situation which will reflect the objectives and content or theme of the lesson. To that end, communication in the workshop or classroom may be verbal or non-verbal, formal or informal, one-way or two-way, designed to elicit a verbal or non-verbal response, or intended to state a fact or pose a problem. Its primary function in the teaching and learning process is the creation and maintenance of a commonality of thought and feeling which will lead to learning.

The nature of communication

Theorists and researchers provide different frameworks or concepts for understanding communication. Two such frameworks are presented here. First, there is the work of Duck and McMahon (2011) who analyze the nature of communication from a number of perspectives.

Duck and McMahon's communication model

1 communication involves *symbols*. Verbal communication involves language, and non-verbal communication involves all other symbols

2 communication requires *meaning*. Symbols have the potential for multiple meanings, and take on meaning over time in social contexts

3 communication – verbal and nonverbal – is different within *different cultural contexts*

4 communication is *relational*. All forms of communication involve not only a 'content level' but also a 'relational level'. The way people communicate depends in part on their relationship

5 communication involves *frames*. Basic forms of knowledge that serve to limit conversations, focus attention and help people understand their role in the conversation

6 communication is a *transaction*. It involves the construction of shared understandings or meanings between two or more people.

This framework is readily applied to a typical workshop or classroom context within the FE sector. Examples of *symbols* include textbooks, portfolios, posters and such like. The ways in which *meaning* varies according to social context is reflected in the ways in which different subject areas use the same words to mean different things: for example, in hair and beauty, the word *block* has a quite specific meaning (it refers to the dummy heads that students practice with). *Cultural* differences are easily seen in considering working with diverse groups of students: for example, a student may not shake hands with their tutor if to do so would be to go against their cultural or religious traditions. The *relational* aspect of communication can be seen in the ways in which the nature or pattern of tutor–student conversations develop as each gets to know the other over time. The role of *frames* in classroom or workshop conversations can be seen in the ways by which particular elements of the subject being taught become the focus around which conversations happen. And the *transactional* nature of communication can be understood through considering the fundamental shared purpose of classroom talk – the 'doing' of the course or subject, involving the student coming to know and understand what she or he has to do and when, in part through guidance and structure provided by the lecturer or tutor.

An earlier (but still relevant) body of research by Halliday (1973) set out seven *functions of language* which indicate the purposive nature of communication. Purpose in communication is generally thought of as the creation of understanding in the speaker's audience, often with the intention of involving the audience in further action. Again, this theoretical model is readily applied to practical settings.

Halliday's communication model

1   The *instrumental function,* which causes events to happen. This might be something as simple as when a tutor tells her students to open their portfolios or clean some tools.

2   The *regulatory function,* which controls events and maintains control. This might refer to an event such as when a tutor talks his students through the schedule of work that they are going to do that day.

3   The *representational function,* which involves the use of language to convey facts, to explain things, or to represent reality, as one perceives it. A typical example would be when a tutor informs students of the date for a practical exam.

4   The *interactional function,* which helps to ensure social relationships are sustained by keeping open channels of communication and facilitating social exchange. An example of this at work would be found when a tutor uses humour in classroom conversation in order to encourage participation.

5   The *personal function,* which allows speakers to express emotional or personal feelings that denote individuality. A typical example would be when a tutor told a group of students that he was proud of what they had achieved in their most recent assessments.

6   The *heuristic function,* which involves the use of language for the acquisition of knowledge. A question and answer session is a typical example of such language function.

7   The *imaginative function,* which assists in the creation and reception of ideas. An example might include the use of an example drawn from everyday life to illustrate a key point of knowledge or debate for the students which might otherwise not be understood.

These functions are not mutually exclusive. The use of language in class by students and teacher may involve a number of simultaneous linguistic functions. In considering linguistic communication in the classroom its *purpose* must be kept in mind. Similarly, in analyzing a failure of communication in the classroom it is always useful to consider the purpose of the failed message and to examine the degree of correspondence of function and form of the message used.

Communication in relation to teaching

Whether pointing to a PowerPoint slide, standing quietly and still to attract attention or asking a subtle question that demands interpretation and insight for its solution, the teacher is engaged in the process of communicating. Consider, for example, the following situations in typical FE contexts:

1   Plumbing students are being instructed in the maintenance of household toilet cisterns. Their tutor is pointing out the need to check the fitting of the cistern inlet valve, and uses a diagram, projected onto a screen, to talk the apprentices through the operation. He ensures that he has been understood by asking a variety of questions following his presentation before moving on to a practical demonstration.

2   Business administration students are studying a variety of documents. A data projector displays an example of a bill of exchange (a legal document usually used in international trade to transfer money). The teacher says "this obviously isn't a standard cheque, which we looked at a few minutes ago. What differences do you notice?' Answers are then elicited and considered by teacher and class.

3   Economics students have been listening to one of their group delivering a short presentation titled 'problems relating to Britain's adoption of the Euro'. She has reached her conclusion: 'I believe that I have shown that this is really a political, and not an economic, question'. The students turn their attention to the tutor, awaiting her reaction. She in turn raises her eyebrows in mock, exaggerated surprise. The students observe, and interpret, her reaction; some express disagreement with the speaker by shaking their heads; others nod their heads in agreement.

In these examples we can discern a variety of patterns of communication, and a similar variety of resources. They include statements of fact, expressions of opinion, comment on opinion, questions, replies to questions, and the posing of problems. The media and channels of communication used here include the voice, gestures (pointing, facial expressions, other gestures, often referred to as *proto-linguistic* signs and which are of great importance in the classroom) and visual aids. In each of these varied examples of classroom communication the following elements may be discerned:

(a) an *objective* (for example, to achieve an understanding of the functions of a bill of exchange)

(b) an *awareness* by the class teacher of the path to that objective

(c) the *creation of a link*, or channel, between teacher and class, the effectiveness of which will be determined in large measure by the teacher's skill and the learner's initial motivation and continuing interest

(d) the adoption by the teacher of appropriate *modes* of communicating his or her 'message', calculated to elicit responses and modify behaviour

(e) the *reception* and *comprehension* of the message, of which the teacher becomes aware.

Communication in the classroom is, therefore, not merely a matter of an instructor addressing a class; it is the outcome of a number of interrelated activities. Where any one of these activities is omitted, the effectiveness of the communication will be vitiated or destroyed, so that the probability of successful learning is reduced accordingly.

Communication theories

Several attempts have been made to analyze the basis of information transmission so as to formulate a general theory of communication. Here, a number of different theoretical perspectives will be briefly explored and then considered in the context of learning and teaching contexts.

The mathematical theory of communication put forward by Shannon and Weaver (1949) draws on information theory to present an explanation of communication systems, and it has important analogies with the teaching process. The aim of information theory (Hamming, 1986), is the discovery of laws, capable of reduction to mathematical terms, concerning systems designed to communicate or manipulate information. The concept of 'information' is used in a highly technical sense to mean that which reduces uncertainty and it can be measured in terms of changes in probability. It is not to be confused with 'meaning', which refers to making sense of information. In less formal terms, Paisley (1980) describes information as denoting any stimulus that alters cognitive structure in the receiver.

Consider a very simple system of communication, for example that which exists where teacher speaks to student. The system includes the following three elements:

(a) a *source* (or transmitter) – the speaker (that is to say, the teacher)

(b) a *channel* – the sound of the speaker's words travelling through the air

(c) a *receiver* – the listener (that is to say, the student).

Such a system may be represented by the simple diagram in Figure 13.1:

Figure 13.1

Schramm designed a more complex model, illustrated in Figure 13.2 (Severin, 1988; Stanton, 1996). This diagram illustrates Schramm's belief that what is communicated is only what is shared in the fields of experience of the message source (the teacher) and the destination (the learner). It is only that portion of the signal *held in common* by the teacher and the learner that can be said to have been communicated. Schramm argued that it was the responsibility of the teacher, in initiating a communication, to be aware of the steps to be taken so as to ensure that the communication system in his or her classroom is working optimally. Because communication rests on the prior knowledge, experience and social and cultural background of both the teacher and the learner (referred to as a 'field of experience'), the teacher needs to ensure that what is said and how it is said has been properly understood in the way that was intended, and not misunderstood due to, for example, differences in prior experience.

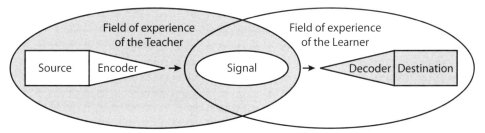

Figure 13.2

A number of general features can be found in the above models. First, communication is viewed best as a process or a series of sequential activities directed to some end. Secondly, communication involves interpersonal relationships. Thirdly, communication involves the use and exchange of symbols which, by their very nature, are mere approximations to the concepts intended to be transmitted. And finally, communication, if it is to be effective, necessitates an accepted commonality of meaning attached to its symbols.

Shannon and Weaver (1949) designed a relatively simple model of the communication process. A message flows along a selected channel from source ('transmitter') to receiver. Emitted signals are decoded by the receiver. In modelling information flow in this way, the problems to be answered are: who says what, in which channel, to whom, and with what result? Osgood (1954) believed that the Shannon and Weaver model was not suitable to explain the complexities of human communication in the home or the classroom, for example. Human beings function as sources *and* destinations; each person in a communication event is both transmitter *and* receiver, and each is a complete communicating system. Osgood's model includes all aspects of behaviour. So, for example, when the teacher talks face to face with the learner, the teacher's words, postures and so forth are of relevance because they are parts of the message being sent to the learner. Moreover, other parts of the teacher's behaviour, such as his reactions to the *learner's* posture, for example, are also important. A message, therefore, is much more complex in structure than it appears to be. Shannon and Weaver, by contrast, stressed the generality or transferability of their theory, which they argued was as applicable to written documents or spoken words as it was to pictures or even music.

Figure 13.3 represents fundamental features in the communication process based on Shannon and Weaver, and is made up of the following components:

(a) An *information source* (the sender) from which the message material originates (the teacher);

(b) A *transmitter*, which transforms or encodes the message into a form suitable for the channel. This is the teacher's voice (for verbal communication) and her or his hands, arms or other elements of posture (for non-verbal communication);

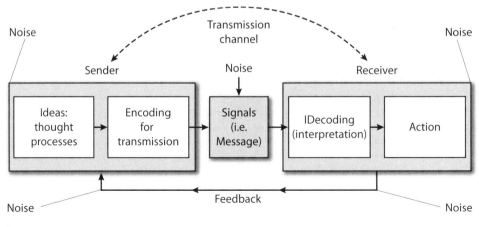

Figure 13.3

(c) A *noise source* which interferes with the flow of information between transmitter and receiver and reduces the probability of the message being received correctly to less than one. According to Shannon and Weaver pointed out, the efficiency of a communication system as a whole is defined in part by the probability that noise will change the information content of the message. This might refer to disruptive behaviour that 'masks' the message or to a style of speech that 'distorts' the message (for example, a particular verbal tic that serves as a distraction);

(d) A *receiver* which decodes the message encoded by the transmitter (the students' ears (for verbal communication) and eyes (for non-verbal communication));

(e) A *destination* for the message (this is the student who may be required to think about, act on or speak about some aspect of the message);

(f) *Feedback* so that the sender can ascertain the extent to which the message has been understood.

Shannon and Weaver identified three different problems that might affect communication:

1 the problem of *technique*. With what accuracy can the very symbols of a message be transmitted?

2 the problem of *semantics*. With what precision do the symbols convey the meaning of the message?

3 the problem of *effectiveness*. With what effectiveness do the received and perceived meanings affect behaviour?

These in turn can be considered by the teacher through analyzing a lesson and seeking answers to the following questions:

1 how accurately have I conveyed the meaning of the lesson, and did I employ the appropriate mode of communication?

2 how precisely, in practice, did the lesson content resemble that which I had in mind?

3 how did perception of the lesson content modify the behaviour of the students as judged by their responses, and, in general, how effective was I?

Communication theory and the classroom

How, therefore, might the various elements of the communication process, as they appear in the theoretical models above, be considered in relation to the classroom? We shall consider these themes in turn:

The information source (the communicator or sender)

The teacher-communicator in the classroom is a single individual (not a group or collective entity, as in the case of, say, a newspaper or TV programme). The communicator's initial step is the formation of an idea, such as a perceived need demanding some activity, such as a deficiency in class response, or a recurring error in class work, both of which require remedial instructional activity. It should be noted that communicators are also receivers (see Figure 13.3). An effective teacher will be receiving and monitoring listener responses at all times – even though the roles of teacher and student are separately defined.

The message

A message refers to some object in the environment of communicator and receiver. It requires *a community of experience* amongst teacher and students. For example, it may be intended, in the classroom context, to assist in the reduction or removal of ambiguity. The teacher, as communicator, is conveying information which can create uncertainty reduction in the signals (that is to say, the *symbols*) which constitute the message. That message need not be verbal; it can be in any form or style than can be experienced and comprehended through any of the receiver's senses.

Encoding

In the classroom, as elsewhere, encoding involves *converting* the communicator's ideas into appropriate message form. The teacher should use a message form based on a plurality of signs which have a *common signification* to a number of interpreters (McQuail, 1984). Therefore, he or she can consider sign systems other than normal writing or speech, such as pictures or even objects. The rules of encoding demand an awareness of classroom conventions and of the necessity of matching the teacher's intentions with the students' abilities in swift, correct interpretation. A search for 'the right word' may be essential.

Channels of transmission

The effective transmission of communication within the classroom demands not only media of communication (speaking, writing or video, for example) but also means of transmission. The selection of appropriate channels for the carrying of messages is deter-mined in part by institutional or cultural rules or expectations – for example, FE teachers are expected to distribute handouts (Tummons, 2010a). Where the teacher is free to select channels, he or she will keep in mind the best possible way, in the circumstances, of gaining and holding the attention of the students for whom the message is intended.

The receiver

In some formal models of communication in the classroom the receiver (the student) may appear to be playing only a passive role – he or she reacts or responds. In practice this is not so: the student is often also the initiator of messages and of processes of selection, inter-pretation and action. Were this not so, classroom communication would be impossible: the student is expected to discriminate among stimuli (including formal messages), to interpret them and to act. Similarly, the communicator, in interpreting feedback, is acting as receiver.

Decoding

The receiver, that is the teacher or student, must first perceive the message intended for him or her and then act so as to interpret it. The process of decoding is often complex: it is affected directly by the receiver's previous experiences, assessment of the symbols which constitute the message and, above all, the degree of commonality of meaning with the sender. The level of effectiveness of communication will be in direct relationship to the match between the intentions of the sender and the decoding of the receiver.

Feedback

In the classroom, feedback (refer also to Chapters 30 and 31) is a process which begins with a reaction to aspects of the initial message as received by the student. That reaction may be a verbal or non-verbal response which is transmitted to the teacher. The student's response is interpreted as indicating the level of understanding between parties to the communication. Without responses, the teacher cannot evaluate the effectiveness of his or her communication; with it, the teacher can *adjust* the content and mode of his or her activities. Feedback is, therefore, essential to good classroom communication; it exerts a measure of control over the activities of teachers in their role as communicators.

Noise

The best-planned lesson can fall flat and there must be few tutors in FE who have not suffered the chagrin which arises from the confrontation of a teacher, anxious to present a carefully prepared lesson, and a class, apparently indifferent and unwilling to participate. It is undeniably frustrating for the tutor who, having prepared what she or he thought was an excellent presentation accompanied by relevant informal assessments and a number of extension activities, finds her or his group of students to be unresponsive, or even to misunderstand.

The effectiveness of communication in the classroom may be weakened by the deficiencies of the source and transmitter, by noise and competition from a variety of sources, and by inadequacies of the receiver. Often, the very environment in which the class works can act as a noise source which can interfere with and distort reception of the teacher's message. Physical conditions, such as lighting (flickering fluorescent light tubes are a particular bugbear), temperature and seating, may be such as to distract from, and therefore weaken, reception of the message. A badly set out room in which the teacher can be neither seen nor heard properly is a common source of interference with information flow. Where a college classroom is set out in rigid school style, with chairs and tables in rows, the recall of earlier, unhappy experiences or of failure associated with compulsory schooling may interfere with the effective reception of communication by adult students. Controlling the teaching environment – in the sense of ensuring that it does not function as a noise source – is an important task for the class tutor. This is not to be taken as implying that effective communication and teaching cannot take place save in a carefully illuminated, thermostatically controlled room. On the contrary, it is well known that extremely efficient instruction has taken place in ill-ventilated huts or in badly illuminated laboratories overlooking noisy railway shunting yards. In analysing the reasons for poor communication, however, it is necessary to consider the effect on the class of *all* types of noise, including the physical environment.

The source and transmitter (that is, the teachers themselves) may be responsible for the creation of noise if they put up – knowingly or otherwise – *barriers* to effective communication. Their personality and mannerisms may obtrude on the communication process. An aggressive manner, a nervous disposition (which may reflect inadequate knowledge or poor lesson preparation) or the examples of body language which are swiftly interpreted by students as evidence of hostility or lack of interest in the subject matter, may block the pathway to learning. Students are quick to detect insincerity, or lack of conviction or motivation, so that there is unlikely to be effective learning where tutors reveal, by an inflexion of voice or a display of indifference in response to a question (which are examples of proto-linguistic symbols) that they are out of sympathy with the class or the purpose of the lesson. An incorrect choice of the medium of communication – a long verbal explanation of the contents of a document, for example, rather than a discussion using those contents projected on a screen – may weaken the effectiveness of message transmission. A lesson pitched at too high a level or out of sequence with previous lessons will similarly cause confusion, so that real communication is impossible. A rate of delivery which is too swift for comprehension and assimilation of the message, or too slow to maintain interest, can prevent effective transmission. A badly structured, disjointed lesson plan may produce signals so erratic that no part of the intended message reaches the class.

The learner – the receiver and destination of the message – may function in a manner which introduces noise and weakens or renders meaningless the communication. He or she may be incapable of receiving or decoding (that is to say, comprehending) the content of a lesson because of inadequate preparation or insufficient prior knowledge or experience. Where effective interpretation of messages received by the senses is impossible because of lack of acquaintance with the phrases, terms or ideas being employed, noise is intensified and comprehension of the message is impossible. Where there are variations in the learner's level of intensity of interest, the reception of information is influenced directly: there is no real communication where the learner's mind is elsewhere.

Noise may be produced where a teacher is unaware that the language he is using is, by reason of its structure, style or overtones so far removed from that to which the class is accustomed that the disjunction of transmitter and receiver is almost total. Trainee teachers often raise the question of communication difficulties likely to emerge when they and their classes use differing *registers* of speech, in which vocabularies and modes of expression may produce mutually exclusive patterns of comprehension.

Paralanguage

In every workshop or seminar room, non-verbal communication is so frequent and important that every teacher or trainer needs to understand it and how it works (Brosin,1961). The totality of a spoken message communicated in the classroom will consist of words, gestures, facial expressions, posture and so forth. Sayings such as 'actions speak louder than words' and 'it's not what you say, it's the way that you say it' might sound like clichés, but are in fact highly informative.

We have already made reference to proto-linguistic symbols: these abound in any lesson and form a part of the subject matter of *paralanguage*, which consists of all of the non-verbal elements of communication that nonetheless are used to convey meaning, such as pitch, tone and other forms of inflection. For the teacher, communicative competence involves the skilled use of paralanguage, and that the effective direction of classroom instruction necessitates an awareness of one's own and students' non-verbal communication (Pennycook, 1985).

There are several aspects to paralanguage. *Kinesics* is the study of the communication that takes place through facial expression, gestures and movement. Signals emitted and received during a lesson (referred to as kinesic markers) include – in addition to spoken words – head movements, eye blinks, gaze and gestures which will be interpreted by students. *Cultural context* is, of course, a vital feature of interpretation of a message; thus, direct eye contact is expected in most European classrooms, whereas in some countries in the Far East it is rarely acceptable; bowing before or after a formal conversation is acceptable in Japan, whereas in Europe it may be considered as evidence of unacceptable obsequiousness. It is for the teacher to interpret and react to the overt, non-verbal signals from the students, and to be aware that, according to some researchers, we have less control over our non-verbal behaviour than over our verbal behaviour (Duck and McMahan, 2012). The teacher as communicator has the special task of ensuring that, as far as possible, his or her gestures, posture and other movements shall be appropriate to the nature of the communication.

Paraverbal features involve the non-lexical aspects of speech – intensity, pitch, intonation, rhythm, speed, pronunciation and vocabulary, for example (Hargie, 1997). They may have a decisive effect on the reception of a message in the classroom. Audio recordings of the teacher's voice made during a lesson can be analyzed so as to assist in the improvement of vocal delivery. Constructive – as opposed to judgemental – lesson observers can also provide useful feedback in this area. Again, cultural setting is critical: where a message is enunciated in a style or with a vocal pattern which, in the circumstances, widens any perceived teacher–student gulf, the partnership necessary for communication disappears, often to be replaced by a growing antagonism.

The fundamental messages from research into paralanguage seem to be: we do not communicate in words alone; our paralinguistic signals confirm, contradict, or are irrelevant to our words; the effective use of paralanguage can be of positive assistance in understanding students; the silent yet thunderous impact of nonverbal language requires study by teachers and those who train them. Abercrombie's words (1960) express the essence of paralanguage and provide a reminder to teacher in our colleges: 'we speak with our vocal organs, but we converse with our whole body'.

Summary

The importance of thinking about the ways in which teachers communicate their students cannot be underestimated. Irrespective of whether we are considering how teachers talk with their students, how they prepare handouts or PowerPoint slides for their students or how they decide which objects or pieces of equipment to use with their students (discussed in Chapter 28), it is important to foreground the necessity of communication that is clear, unambiguous and therefore meaningful. Teachers and trainers need to talk with their students and apprentices in different ways at different times: the context of a pastoral tutorial in which the teacher needs to provide additional support for a vulnerable student, for example, is quite different to the context of a portfolio workshop in which the teacher is going through the assessment requirements for a module or unit of study. Similarly, a seminar room where tables are arranged in an open horseshoe pattern so that learners – and the teacher – all share open sightlines, or a workshop where learners can gather around a central work surface for a demonstration without being crowded out, will both render communication more effective. For the teacher, there is a lot to consider – how she or he dresses or moves around the classroom, how the workshop is laid out, which words or technical terms to employ – in ensuring that communication is as interference-free as is practicable. And it is arguably the most central component of the teachers' professional knowledge and competence: without good communication, there can be no good teaching or learning.

Further reading

For the new reader, these books will prove to be invaluable:

Appleyard, N. and Appleyard, K. (2010), *Communicating with learners in the lifelong learning sector*. Exeter: Learning Matters.

Duck, S. and McMahan, D. (2012), *The Basics of Communication: a relational perspective*. 2nd edition. London: Sage.

And other general texts also have useful chapters, particularly:

Scales, P. (2013), *Teaching in the Lifelong Learning Sector*. 2nd edition. Maidenhead: McGraw Hill. Chapter two.

Wallace, S. (2011), *Teaching, Tutoring and Training in the Lifelong Learning Sector*. 4th edition. Exeter: Learning Matters. Chapter two.

14 Controlling and Managing Teaching–Learning Processes

Without effective communication, teaching is impossible: this is the central argument of the previous chapter. But good communication skills – both verbal and non-verbal – will not be enough in themselves to create an environment for effective teaching and learning. The teaching process, of which communication is a vital part, has to be directed to some desired end. This might be coverage of a specific topic or body of knowledge, or the demonstration and practice of a series of mechanical operations. Movement towards such objectives requires a carefully planned progression, a sequence that might involve tasks, activities, carefully selected resources and so forth. The use of a strategy of instruction designed to attain a learning objective requires *control* of the teaching process – the alternative could be a circuitous meander which may, or may not, bring the learner to that objective. Control, its elements, its application to classroom teaching and, in particular, its relation to the concept of *information feedback* (or 'knowledge of results') will be examined in this chapter.

The argument that is going to be put forward here, which seeks to consider control of the specific process of instruction in terms of control of a general system, is based on an extended *analogy*. An analogy is a way of explaining something by drawing parallels between known or familiar ideas or themes, and new ones. The use of analogy can assist in the assimilation of new ideas to old concepts, and can aid comprehension of the unfamiliar in terms of the familiar. Where we attempt to correlate a relatively abstract, intangible process with one whose structure is obvious and well known, understanding may be improved. In studying this chapter and its underlying analogy, teachers should keep in mind the workshops and classrooms *that they are familiar with*, with their sometimes unpredictable natures, instabilities and transient features.

Terms such as 'control' or 'manipulation of the environment' are not generally welcomed by teachers, for they are often associated with undesirable circumstances such as loss of autonomy or denial of human rights. Terms such as 'student-centred learning', the focus on 'the voice of the learner' and concepts such as 'learners as stakeholders' all contribute to a workshop or classroom culture that would seem at first look to be a place where such strong terms as 'control' would be unwelcome at best. Certainly, many practitioners in adult and community education (who continue to represent a significant minority of the workforce in the learning and skills sector) would in all likelihood resist such ideas. At a time in which the very legitimacy of authority as such is being questioned fundamentally (not least as a product of the postmodernist turn) there will be no ready acceptance by teachers of any principles which appear to further threaten student independence. But the argument presented below turns on the belief that in *any* organized system, such as that constituted by a class and tutor, some control is essential, and some manipulation of environmental factors is needed if organizational objectives are to be accomplished efficiently. Here, control is not to be understood as a term that carried negative connotations: it is simply being used to reflect that aspect of the teacher's work that requires her or him to perform effortful work in the workshop or classroom so that the shape or direction of travel of the entirety of the session in question is organized and sequenced so that an environment that is conducive to learning can be established and then maintained.

The perception of classroom processes considered below involves an understanding of, and respect for, the student for whom the provision of effective learning conditions is the essence of teaching activities; the processes are not based on any belief in the need for suppression of individuality, but are intended to assist in the expression and furtherance of individuality within the context of learning. If students are indeed to become autonomous or independent, it must also be the case that they need to be able to participate in learning episodes that are structured and resourced in such a way that appropriate opportunities for learning are available to them. As such, the argument presented in this chapter rests in part on the notion that it is the professional responsibility of the teacher or trainer to work to provide such environments.

Controlling and managing teaching–learning processes: The basis of feedback

Information feedback, which is an essential ingredient in any system of control, may be considered as the return of a signal which indicates the result of an action and which can be used to determine future actions. Here it is important to note that the use of the word 'feedback' in this context is rather different from the use of the term when discussing the theories and practices of assessment (as discussed in Chapters 30 and 31). Driving a car provides a clear example of this kind of information feedback at work. Consider, for example, seemingly simple feedback actions such as those of a car driver becoming aware of a change in the contact between the car tyres and the road surface, thereby sensing the presence of ice and immediately reducing speed. The presence of ice on the road may require the driver to adjust the way in which they are steering. The sounds made by the tyres on the road may change as the surface ices over. Put simply, different kinds of signal are fed back to the driver, who adjusts their driving accordingly.

Investigation of any system which is purposive or adaptive (such as driving a car, which has both a purpose – the need to drive somewhere in order to complete a journey – and an adaptive aspect – the ways in which the driver adapts their driving to suit the prevailing conditions), reveals some *circularity of action* between its parts, so that the system's output can be assessed and the input modified, creating a feedback loop. A car driver, to continue our example, is continually receiving signals relating to their driving environment and adjusting their riving behaviour accordingly: it is not simply the case that once the presence of ice on the road has been accounted for, the driver will therefore stop paying attention to the conditions that they are driving in.

The basic principles of feedback – which will be considered later in relation to classroom practice – can be illustrated further by considering analogically two processes which, outwardly, seem totally different from each other: the steering of a vessel and the lifting of a pencil.

Consider, first, a helmsman steering his craft through a turbulent sea, his eyes fixed now on the stars, now on the faint outline of land ahead, sensitive to each movement of his vessel which he is guiding to a selected harbour. Helmsman and craft form a *system* which has a *goal* (reaching the harbour). The process of *control* (steering the craft) is determined by the *response* of the helmsman to the information which reaches him (that is to say, his *assessment*) concerning his environment (stars, sea, craft, land).

Consider, next, a student intending to lift a pencil from her desk. Hand and eye, brain, nerves and muscles which regulate movement form a *system* which at that moment has a specific *goal* (lifting the pencil). The hand is *controlled* and guided to the pencil by muscles which act on *signals* coming from the body's central nervous system. Signals from nerve endings in the retina of the student's eye result from *responses to information* presented by the position of the pencil (how far it is from the desired position) and are fed back to the brain, which *assesses* them and *regulates* the action of muscles in the arm and hand. Here is an example of *informational feedback* by which the student learns the effect of her responses on the environment.

The information feedback system that is presented here can be seen as resting on the following key elements:

(a) It is a characteristic of a goal-seeking system. A typical FE setting provides a straightforward example. The students, teacher, curriculum, institution and so forth constitute the system, and the shared educational aim of the different members of this system constitutes the goal that they are seeking.

(b) It arises where a system is furnished with continuous signals as to its environment and it's functioning within that environment. Teachers receive constant signals from their students – motivation, engagement, attendance, progress through the curriculum, developing skills and knowledge, and so forth. Other part of the environment also provide signals – course evaluation reports, retention and achievement statistics and such like all provide teachers with information relating to the ways in which students are working towards their goals.

(c) It allows the system to respond to information provided by signals. The progress made by students, the attitudes with which they approach their studies and the overall extent to which course outcomes, benchmarks and so forth are met all allow the teacher – and the institution as a whole – to evaluate the extent to which the curriculum goals are being addressed.

(d) It enables a response to be made which results from an assessment of signals and an adjustment of activity in relation to the system's goals. Such responses might include a change in teaching strategy, the procurement of new resources, the provision of new forms of leaning support or the restructuring of assessment tasks.

Positive and negative information feedback

Feedback may be classified as *positive* or *negative*. However, it is important to note that these qualifiers do not constitute value judgements concerning their desirability. Commonly found statements such as 'after the lesson there was positive feedback, indicating that the level of learning had been high', or, 'negative feedback suggested that the lecture had failed in its objectives' represent both misunderstanding and misuse of the terms. Thus, just as it is necessary to avoid confusing the use of feedback when discussing assessment ('assessment feedback') with the use of 'feedback' in the context of this chapter, when discussing control ('information feedback'), so it is necessary not to confuse different uses of the terms 'positive' and 'negative', which instead need to be understood in context.

Positive feedback is understood here as being the kind of feedback that has a reinforcing effect on the activity or practice about which that feedback is being provided. It is positive in the sense that it strengthens or perpetuates the practice or activity in question. Sayre (1976) gives an example of immediate interest to the teacher: an insecure student who incites teasing from his class because of his apparent vulnerability, leading to an increase in his feeling of inadequacy, leading to intensified adverse attention of his class, and so on. In cases of positive feedback there is an increase in the rate of some pattern of activity resulting from performance of the activity; in effect, the activity is reinforcing its own performance.

Negative feedback, by extension, is understood here as being the kind of feedback that has an opposing effect on the activity or practice about which that feedback is being provided. That is to say, it is the kind of feedback that serves to lessen or cancel out – to *negate* – the activity in question. A familiar classroom example may be found in the swift reaction of an experienced teacher to a question and answer session, the results of which indicate a total misunderstanding by the class of a section of the lesson. The content and presentation of the remainder of the lesson would be adjusted immediately so that the teacher has the opportunity to revise or rework the content that had been misunderstood. It is important to note, in this context, that the cause of the misunderstanding is a separate issue to the misunderstanding itself. It may have been the case that the teacher assumed that the students had a greater level of prior knowledge or experience than was in fact the case. Or it may have been that the teaching strategies that were chosen did not in practice serve to engage the students.

Feedback in further education workshops and classrooms

A typical workshop or classroom, therefore, can be considered in terms of *a system* – a set of *interrelated elements*, characterized by a particular structure and particular kinds of behaviour. In terms of *structure* it consists, in essence, of a teacher or trainer and a group of students, each reacting to the other as they work through, talk or write about their programme of study, work with relevant resources and materials and work through their assignments. The *behaviour* of this system is that of a goal-seeking body, the goal being, at any given moment, a predetermined set of learning objectives or outcomes. The goal in this sense might relate to the outcomes that the teacher has established for a particular session or lesson, the outcomes that students are working towards as part of an assignment or the overall objectives or outcomes of the curriculum or programme of study that is being worked towards. The goal of a system can to some extent be set from outside that system. The teacher's activities are directed to the *control* and *transformation* of the system of which he or she is a part. In this case, the control of the system refers to all of those actions that the teacher carries out in order to help bring about the successful planning and delivery of the curriculum which in turn leads to transformation, to an appropriate level of attainment on the part of the students. This level of attainment can be defined here as learning which is aligned to the curriculum in question and which therefore leads to appropriate certification or qualification.

Any teaching activity may be viewed usefully in system terms, in the way that has been demonstrated above. A workshop designed to teach electrical installation apprentices how to fit a junction box, a class discussion on the problems of safeguarding children's welfare, a lesson designed to reduce the apprehension felt by some mature returners to studying in a formal institutional context – each of these typical FE classes may be interpreted as a directed process intended to alter some element of the system's components. A directed process, however, demands that the director be continuously aware of the state of the system, its approach to and deviation from its goal. According to this analogy, therefore, the exercise of control of the teaching system (that is to say, the teacher and class) requires that the teacher shall know its state and its rate of progress towards its goal through the constant evaluation of information feedback.

The nature of the lesson in question may make such flow of information feedback more or less difficult, or even impossible. When, for example, engaged in delivering a formal lecture (as discussed in Chapter 25), it is difficult for the teacher to find ways to obtain verbal feedback in order to check on the progress of the lecture and of the students: instead, she or he will need to rely on non-verbal communication (as discussed in the preceding chapter). The teacher who is working with a large seminar group of 25 students will find it more difficult to evaluate the students' different reactions throughout the lecture or lesson, in comparison to a colleague who is working with a small group of 12. Circumstances such as these, which in both theory and practice reduce the general possibility of feedback and control to a relatively low level, require the teacher both to maximize opportunities for feedback (for example, by breaking larger groups into smaller groups for part of a session and going round them in turn, or by interspersing formal lecture content with more inter-active activities and opportunities for discussion (as discussed in Chapter 26).

There is the additional problem for the teacher of recognizing the adequacy or repre-sentative nature of feedback signals in the classroom. A common teaching method used by teachers – in both workshop and classroom settings – is the use of question and answer in order to assess student's progress or understanding. A demonstration of a workshop procedure or a short classroom-based presentation may be followed by a series of questions posed by the teacher in order to ascertain the extent to which the demonstration or presentation has been understood. If the group are working well the teacher may then move on to the next topic. If some aspects of the work done so far are proving difficult, these difficulties will emerge in the students' answers, and the teacher can pause and repeat or revise topics as necessary. But how many questions should be asked? How many correct answers are sufficient to indicate that the group is indeed ready to progress? If the teacher asks ten questions to a group of 15 students, does this indicate adequate or representative feedback? How many correct answers are required before she can be assured of 'appropriate' feedback? Have the questions been phrased so as to test the students' understanding without the possibility of guessing? Careful questioning and representative samples of answers may provide the sole indicators of the value of responses as feedback in the classroom in a situation where the size of the student group, the style of the teaching session or the time available to the teacher prevents more in-depth assessment.

But the lesson which does *not* allow for the testing of progress, which omits the use of any corrective device allowing the teacher to 'keep on course', has a limited chance of success – if that success is to be evaluated by attainment of a desired goal – an achieved learning outcome or a completed assignment. Explanations interspersed with tests, the evaluation of the body language of a class, recapitulations and revisions followed by question and answer sessions – these are some of the methods of obtaining the *timely* signals of progress which the teacher or trainer needs to ensure that her or his control of the classroom environment is sufficient, and that an environment that is conducive to learning has been established.

Control defined

The process through which the teacher ensures that learning performance conforms to the level of desired performance – this defines what control in the classroom is *intended to achieve*. But what is also required is an indication of what control is or how it should be defined. The following, based on Mockler's (1972) explanation of management control is suggested as a working definition: control in the classroom is a systematic effort to set performance standards, to design feedback systems, to compare actual performance with those predetermined standards, to determine whether there are any deviations and to measure and assess their significance and to take any action required to assure the attainment of learning objectives in the most effective and efficient way. This definition suggests four steps in classroom control:

Types of teacher control

1 Setting standards (usually in reference to the curriculum being followed) and deciding on methods of assessing the learners' performance (which will be more or less under the purview of the teacher, depending on the curriculum being followed);
2 Measuring those standards and assessing the significance of the results by a process of feedback;
3 Deciding on the acceptability or non-acceptability of performance (a decision which will be informed by a number of factors including the overall profile of the group, individual student profiles or a consideration of 'distance travelled' (that is, a student may not yet have reached the required level of performance, but may nonetheless have made good progress, allowing for their starting point));
4 Taking any appropriate adjustive action (which might include revision of key topics, changes to assessment activities or the rearrangement of the scheme of work).

The elements of control

The overall work of the teacher which is presented in this text is based on a number of different roles which the teacher might need to occupy at different times in her or his working week. These roles include working as a *manager* (perhaps at course or even curriculum level – it is not uncommon for even very new teachers in a FE college to be given responsibilities for module or programme leadership), as a *planner* (when designing the delivery patterns, teaching schedules and assessment timetables for a module or course, for example), and as a *controller*. As controller, the teacher undertakes the direction of the individual session, with a series of defined teaching objectives as a goal, and a strategy aimed at attainment of these objectives. To that end the teacher requires feedback which enables him or her to adjust future conduct by reference to past performance. The control function is not an end in itself, rather it is the general means by which the teacher and students are able to perform a specified function – the achievement of the lesson objectives.

From a consideration of the different processes mentioned in both this chapter and the preceding one, the essential constituents of a control activity, whether in the classroom or elsewhere, can be understood as consisting of three inter-related elements:

(a) *measurement*

(b) *assessment*

(c) *adjustment.*

Control (that is to say, direction) cannot be effective in the absence of any one of these activities. For example, the successful driving of a car (an exercise in precise control) involves continuous cycles of measuring distances, assessing speeds, looking in mirrors, adjusting the position of levers and on, so that the car's direction and speed are controlled. Effective staff promotion policy in a business organization necessitates a process of measuring staff performance, assessing that performance in relation to potential and the adjusting responsibilities, so that total performance is more effectively controlled. In much the same way, it can be argued that effective teaching (remembering that effective *teaching* is not to be conflated with effective *learning* – as discussed in Chapter 2) demands a process of *measuring* learning performance, *assessing* it in relation to class objectives and *adjusting* teaching plans where necessary.

Where possible, therefore, the teacher must first *measure* the attainment of the students against the objectives that have been established. This does not necessarily involve absolute precision (indeed, precision may be difficult if not impossible to achieve) although the more precisely he or she is able to measure a learner's level of attainment at any moment, the more effective will be the quality of the teacher's control. The measurement must focus on *critical aspects* of a performance and must be both valid and reliable (these key concepts are discussed in Chapter 30).

The teacher must then *assess* the significance of her or his measurement – not always an easy task. What if a student who usually scores over 75 per cent in tests suddenly plummets to 20 per cent? What if only half of the members of a class respond adequately to a series of snap questions posed in mid-lesson? What if a workshop demonstration patently fails to engage or inform the students how a specific practical task should be performed? The assessment of the significance of this kind of signal requires a knowledge of the lesson, subject and curriculum objectives, of the students' abilities and of those boundaries of toleration which indicate whether a student is ready for their assessment or whether they have yet to meet the required performance level. What the teacher does next will depend on assessments such as these.

The final stage in a cycle of control procedure is reached when the teacher decides to *adjust* the situation and takes steps to do so. This may require additional work for an individual student or a swift adjustment of the lesson plan or scheme of work as it relates to an entire student group. Control demands that the teacher shall act to reinforce success and correct shortcomings. It is the ability to react swiftly and appropriately to a changing classroom situation that marks out the teacher who has mastered the technique of lesson control.

The types of controls necessary to give the teacher effective control can be considered in relation to the specifications favoured by Drucker (1972):

1 They should be *economical*. The fewer controls in the teaching–learning situation, the better.

2 They should be *meaningful*. What is to be measured and assessed must have significance. Trivial events can be ignored. Controls should be related only to the major activity within the workshop or classroom – learning.

3 They should be *appropriate*. Controls in the classroom should indicate the real structure of events therein. Hence the need for carefully constructed tests, which can analyze as far as is possible the general level of class attainment.

4 They should be *congruent*. A teacher's controls must be congruent with what he or she is attempting to measure. This is an important principle in relation to phenomena such as student interest, motivation and other highly subjective matters.

5 They should be *timely*. Controls which provide information only after a fairly long interval of time may be of little value to the tutor. Information concerning the nature of class responses has to be available swiftly if it is to assist in immediate control.

6 They should be *simple*. Assessment based on a complicated array of grades, indexes and deviations is rarely appropriate for control in a swiftly changing classroom situation where assessment decisions need to be made much more quickly. Complexity and ambiguity must be avoided if learning is to be monitored effectively.

7 They should be *operational*. This involves controls centred on activity, which give results from which necessary changes may be put into operation.

To sum up, the effective direction of a system involves its overall control by means of an appropriately designed group of controls. In terms of classroom activity, and the demands of the formal lesson, control is the *sine qua non* of attainment of learning objectives, and among the necessary controls is the establishing of conditions which will allow *swift adjustment* of the teaching–learning system, based on *feedback* (Stoner and Freeman, 1989). A system of performance appraisal is essential; where information indicates that performance is deviating in unacceptable fashion from the standard, appropriate corrective action must be taken swiftly.

Summary

In this chapter we have set out the theoretical basis of *information feedback* as an element of *control* in the teaching–learning system. It is important not to confuse information feedback with assessment feedback: assessment feedback is a component of formative and summative assessment practice; information feedback, as discussed here, is an element of the control process that, we have argued, is necessary for the teacher to be able to establish an appropriate environment for teaching and learning. It is not to be confused with classroom or behaviour management (which is discussed in Chapter 21). And at the same time control is not, in the present context, intended as a negative term: it is simply being used to indicate the level of control that the teacher needs to have over their professional environment – the workshop or classroom, and the students with whom they are working – in order to be able, simply put, to do all of the things that as a teacher she or he needs to do. Put another way, everything that the teacher has to do in order to be able to provide learning opportunities for her or his students can only happen or be put into practice after an appropriate level of control has been established. In this sense, the establishment and maintenance of control, as much as lesson planning, designing assessments or the selection of appropriate resources, is a crucial element of the teaching process.

At the heart of the control process is a well-planned lesson, a lesson which the teacher has taken time and care to plan and prepare for so that realistic learning aims have been established, links to the curriculum as a whole have been taken into account, and timely and authentic assessment tasks have been designed. And it is the specific process of lesson planning that will be discussed in the next chapter.

Further reading

The literature relating to the management of learners and learning has expanded significantly during recent years. It is, understandably, a key topic for the FE sector. The following are strongly recommended:

Ginnis, P. (2001), *The Teacher's Toolkit*. Camarthen: Crown House.

Wallace, S. (2007), *Managing behaviour in the lifelong learning sector*. 2nd edition. Exeter: Learning Matters.

15 Aims, Objectives and Outcomes in Planning for Learning

The careful planning and preparation of a lesson – whether in a workshop or a classroom – is at the same time one of the most important and the most bureaucratic tasks that teachers – and trainee teachers – in FE are required to be involved in. The paperwork that surrounds lesson planning can indeed be bewildering, but it is important for the teacher to maintain a distinction between the process of lesson planning and the writing of a lesson plan. The latter is in essence a bureaucratic task, nothing more. The former is an important aspect of the role of the teacher. Stories regarding teachers who 'do not need' to plan are easily found, but there is no substitute for the careful planning and preparation of a teaching session. There are a number of themes that need to concern the teacher as she or he plans a lesson: the current progress of the student group; the specific topics that need to be covered that day; impending assignment deadlines; resources and access to them; and the requirements of the curriculum or awarding body. All of these issues come into focus when considering one specific aspect of planning: the actual learning that the teacher plans to facilitate or encourage, and then to assess: the learning outcomes or objectives (we shall discuss the variations in terminology below) of the session that is being planned.

This chapter, therefore, focuses on the formulation of learning outcomes or objectives, the attainment of which provides markers along the road to understanding and mastery. Advocates of the use of outcomes or objectives argue that their nature and composition help the teacher to plan instruction based on logical sequences of thought or practice, to set out patterns of productive class activities and to specify assessments so as to determine whether learning has occurred. Critics of this approach claim that the model of learning upon which outcomes and their related assessments are based can rarely assist in the actual *processes* of learning. What is set out below, then, is the theory and practice associated with one method of seeking to specify with relative precision the outcomes of the teaching-learning situation. This approach requires exploration due to its ubiquity: the majority of FE colleges and adult education providers (the latter, particularly, since the introduction of RARPA – Recognizing and Recording Progress and Achievement) require staff to plan lessons using learning outcomes or objectives. Nonetheless critiques of this approach will also be considered in the discussion that follows.

Aims, outcomes, objectives – defining terms

Teachers – and teacher-trainers – as well as curriculum documents and college managers often use the terms 'aims', 'outcomes' and 'objectives' without differentiating between them. In a way, this is hardly surprising, as they broadly refer to the same thing: the learning that the unit or module or programme of study, to which the outcomes or objectives in question refer, has been designed to bring about. Consequently, it is hardly surprising that trainee teachers express confusion and even frustration when trying to delineate between these terms. Three examples, drawn from readily accessible and current curriculum documentation, can demonstrate this conceptual confusion quite easily:

(1) Health and Social Care
The first example is from the current (September 2012) specifications for the *BTEC Level 1/ Level 2 First Certificate in Health and Social Care*. This BTEC document uses the term *learning aims*. For unit 2, *Health and Social Care Values*, there are two learning aims:

(a) explore the care values that underpin current practice in health and social care;

(b) investigate ways of empowering individuals who use health and social care services.

These learning aims are in turn mapped on to relevant content and appropriate assignment specifications. The assignment specifications – in common with BTEC provision more generally – are divided according to pass, merit and distinction criteria, with students required to complete more detailed assessed work in order to meet more detailed criteria. The document describes the work that students need to do in terms of *achieving* the learning aims.

(2) Electrical Installation
The second example comes from the current (February 2008) City and Guilds *Level 3 Certificate in the Certification of Electrical Installations*. In this document, unit *aims* are used to set out the rationale for the unit in question. In unit 301, *technical knowledge of the inspection, testing and certification of electrical installations*, the rationale is as follows: 'the aim of this unit is to enable the candidate to develop the necessary technical knowledge and understanding about the inspection, testing and certification of electrical installations'. In turn, the unit is described as having three *learning outcomes*. 'There are three outcomes to this unit. These include a knowledge and understanding of: preparation for inspection and testing; inspection; testing.' Content is subsequently linked specifically to each outcome. Each body of content is prefaced by the term 'for each topic the candidate

will be able to', followed by the specific outcome in question. Outcome 3.7, for example, reads 'state the effect of temperature on a conductor'.

(3) Counselling Skills

The third example comes from the current (February 2011) *NCFE Level 2 Certificate In Counselling Skills*. The introductory section of the document makes reference to the *aims and objectives* of the qualification, as follows:

This qualification aims to:

- introduce learners to the use of counselling skills in everyday life and work and some of the approaches that underpin the use of these skills.

The objectives of this qualification are to help learners to

- develop counselling skills
- understand the different approaches involved in the use of counselling skills
- appreciate the importance of self-development.

For each unit in the qualification, both *learning outcomes* and related *assignment criteria* are given. For unit 1, *Using Counselling Skills*, the learning outcome is 'know what counselling skills are', and the assignment criteria are 'identify core counselling skills' and 'describe how core counselling skills can be used in a counselling relationship and in other helping activities'.

FE colleges also contribute to this conceptual confusion. During the course of his research into the assessment of trainee teachers, one of the authors of this book looked at the lesson plan templates that were in use at four different FE colleges (Tummons, 2010b). Each college used slightly different terminology in their lesson plan, echoing the variations in practice within the curriculum documents referred to above. In turn, each college used the following terms:

1 learning outcomes
2 learner outcomes
3 learning aims and learning objectives
4 aims and objectives.

A close analysis of these terms could lead to a number of complex and far-reaching conclusions. For example, if outcomes are defined in terms of learning, rather than the learner (as in the first two instances given above), does this make a difference? Should outcomes focus on course or curriculum content, or on the learners – the students – themselves? Should they in some way define the role or actions of the teacher or trainer? Such conversations would not be without merit or interest, but they would also risk overcomplicating the discussion. Arguably, the interchangeable use of these terms is more to do with personal and institutional habit than with theoretical perspective. In the discussion that follows, therefore, the term 'outcome/objective' will be used. This is a deliberate step that is intended to acknowledge differences in professional and contextual use, but also to stress the essential agreements over definition and usage (though refer to the discussion regarding the work of Gronlund (1981), below, for a detailed exposition of the use of objectives and outcomes as two separate aspects of the lesson planning process).

The essence of learning outcomes/objectives

Bearing in mind the definitions of learning which have been explored in this book (in Chapter 1), a learning event may be said to culminate in a change in the learner, and the result of that change may be observed (and learning may be inferred) by noting what the learner can now do, as compared with what he or she was unable to do before the learning event. By 'do', we refer here to actions on the part of the learner in a broad sense: it might be the case that a learner can now thread spokes into a hub, lace them into a rim and build a bicycle wheel. Or it might be that a learner can now give a definition of the term 'jurisprudence'. To put it another way, the content or *domain* (refer also to the discussion of taxonomies of learning in Chapter 16) of learning is immaterial: what is important is that a learning event has taken place.

Learning outcomes/objectives are usually worded as statements which describe what a learner will be able to do on the completion of a series of planned teaching and learning processes. There are *three* principal teaching functions of outcomes/objectives, based on their construction and use in the context of classroom teaching. First, they impose on the teacher the discipline of selecting and formulating in unambiguous style the steps that he or she considers necessary in the process of instruction. Secondly, they provide him or her with an overall view of the structure of the instructional task. And thirdly, they present him or her with the basis of a suitable assessment and feedback process in relation to the topic, content or activities that the session in question is about.

The statement of specific outcomes/objectives for a lesson, usually written on a lesson plan (which is invariably provided in a pre-approved format by an institution), presupposes a planned series or sequence of precise instructional steps. Each step has to be seen as a link in a process; each should be considered as starting from an ascertained level of student performance; each should be planned so as to contribute to a movement of that performance to a higher level. This is not an easy task since it involves the teacher posing and answering repeatedly many questions, including: 'What is the student able to *do* before the session commences?' 'What do I want her to be able to *do* after the session?' 'What resources will be available to the student group?' and 'What constraints – such as time available, staffing, or access to equipment or resources – do I need to account for?' Without answers to questions of this kind, the defining of learning outcomes/objectives will be problematic: a learning episode cannot be satisfactorily planned for without taking into account, for example, the availability of necessary tools or equipment. Through following a series of 'planning steps' such as these, it is a straightforward task for the teacher – or trainee teacher – to outline the structure of the lesson, designed to achieve the defined instructional ends.

The formulation of learning outcomes/objectives

From the outset, it is important to remember that the specific formulation of learning outcomes/objectives – the specific statements that refer to the students' learning that the planned session has been designed to bring about – must always be considered alongside *assessment* (as discussed in Chapters 30 and 31). If a planned learning outcome/objective (of whatever kind – this might refer to a student's ability to identify correctly a number of symbols that are used on an electrical circuit diagram, or to a student's ability to prepare correctly a surface prior to painting) is not going to be assessed, then the formulation of the outcome is meaningless. There is no point in drawing up learning outcomes/objectives for an individual session if an appropriate assessment of that outcome has not also been drawn up.

Outcomes/objectives of lesson plans

There are a number of factors to consider, therefore, when drawing up learning outcomes/objective as part of a lesson plan:

1. they should be worded unambiguously
2. a different outcome/objective should be formulated to cover each of the planned learning topics or goals for the session
3. the number of outcomes/objectives should be realistic and should be dictated by the requirements of the curriculum and/or scheme of work: there is no 'right number' of session outcomes/objectives
4. the session plan should always include details about assessment and, specifically, the assessment activities should be mapped onto the session outcomes/objectives.

It should be noted, however, that these factors presuppose an acceptance of those conceptual or theoretical perspectives that position the use of learning outcomes/objectives as an appropriate strategy for teaching and learning. We shall consider some criticisms of this below.

Theoretical foundations in the statement of outcomes/objectives: Mager, Gronlund, Tyler and Eisner

The use of an outcomes/objectives approach to the planning and practice of teaching is well established in literature and a consideration of the work of two key theorists in this area provides important and helpful contextual detail regarding their use. Here the focus will be on four key writers: Mager, Gronlund, Tyler and Eisner.

In his seminal work *Preparing Instructional Objectives* (1962, 1984), Mager, a pioneer in the field of the construction of objectives, argued that if instruction is to be successful the teacher must decide (metaphorically) where she wants to go. Then she must create and administer the means of getting there and arrange to find out whether she has arrived. *Specific objectives* (as Mager termed them) of instruction must then be written on the following basis:

1 describe what students will be *doing* when demonstrating their achievement and indicate how the instructor will recognize what they are doing

2 identify and name the desired behavioural acts of the students, define the conditions under which the behaviour is to occur and state the criteria for acceptable performance

3 construct a separate objective for each learning performance.

In *How to Write and Use Instructional Objectives* (1981), Gronlund argued that Mager's 'specific objectives' are most useful where students are required to demonstrate knowledge of factual information, but that more advanced types of learning seem to require the construction and use of a different type of objective. In order to solve this problem, Gronlund advocated the use of a two-step approach to the writing of more *general* types of objective. After considering what students have to learn, through analyzing the requirements laid out in curriculum or syllabus documentation, the following process should be followed:

1 formulate *general* instructional objectives that describe the types of behaviour students ought to show so as to demonstrate that they have learned successfully

2 list, under each general objective, up to five specific *learning outcomes*, ensuring that each begins with an action verb and that each indicates specific observable responses.

Gronlund argued that there are several reasons for framing specific learning outcomes within general learning objectives. He suggested that most learning activities are probably much too complicated to be described in terms of a specific objective for each outcome. Gronlund criticized Mager's use of specific objectives on the grounds that they would encourage surface or rote learning based on simple memorization. The framing of specific outcomes within general objectives, by contrast, allows more complex learning activities to be planned for and articulated.

The selection of objectives and then outcomes needs to reflect closely the content and requirements of the syllabus or curriculum to which the teacher is working. Curriculum documents and handbooks provide a further source of general objectives. These are easily obtained and are invariably available online (indeed, the ease of access to curriculum schemes and handbooks afforded by the internet is a good example of how technology can make easier the work of the teacher), and almost always contain sufficient detail to allow the teacher to plan both individual sessions and sequences or schemes of work. By returning to the three curriculum examples already referred to in this chapter, the ways in which these documents can be used to help in the formulation of lesson plan and schemes of work can be illustrated (irrespective of whether or not the teacher or trainer chooses or is required to use Gronlund's objectives and outcomes model in their planning). Normally, it would be the responsibility of an experienced member of staff to design a scheme of work but it is important at this point to note that it is not uncommon for newly qualified FE teachers to be 'thrown in at the deep end' and have to design schemes as well as individual lessons in preparation for the new academic year.

(1) Health and Social Care
The impressive level of detail provided within the BTEC Health and Social Care documentation allows the teacher to plan both individual lessons and lesson sequences straightforwardly and thoroughly. As well as providing learning aims for each unit, the documentation also specifies the number of *guided learning hours* required for each unit (to assist in timetabling), provides details as to the *content* of each unit by breaking down each topic into a number of different elements, and provides guidance as to how each learning aim might be *assessed*.

(2) Electrical Installation
The City and Guilds curriculum documentation is equally detailed. This is perhaps not surprising when it is remembered that this curriculum – like many others that are delivered in FE colleges – is mapped onto a wider set of standards – in this case, British Standard BS7671 *Requirements for Electrical Installations*. Each unit lists not only the recommended guided learning hours and learning outcomes, but also details of both the *practical activities* that candidates will be expected to perform and the *test rig and inspection and testing equipment* that will be expected to be employed.

(3) Counselling Skills
The curriculum documentation for this NCFE award is not as extensive as the two documents that have already been discussed, but this is simply a reflection of the nature of this curriculum rather than of a different approach by the awarding body to the

provision of curricular documentation. Within each unit, individual learning outcomes are broken down into distinct elements that specify the topics or themes that will need to be covered.

All three of these curriculum documents, therefore, provide outline information regarding the topics or themes to be covered. Taking into account the overall number of guided learning hours that are recommended, recommendations for resources and assessment guidance, it becomes a relatively straightforward task to plan a sequence of lessons for each of these programmes of study. It is also a straightforward task for the teacher to map core or transferable skills onto these schemes of work: opportunities for developing the literacy or Information and Communications Technology (ICT) skills (for example) of students are foregrounded in the majority of curricular documents that are currently in use.

In his now classic work *Basic Principles of Curriculum and Instruction* (1949) Tyler advocated a concentration on the design and use of *general objectives* and rejected the use of specific outcomes/objectives entirely. The most useful way of defining an objective is, according to Tyler, to consider three key issues – *behaviour*, *content* and *context*. 'Behaviour' was described by Tyler as the kind of behaviour to be developed in the student. 'Content' meant the content or area of life in which the behaviour is to operate. Context was a third area of concern. What, asked Tyler, is the precise significance of a behavioural objective requiring a student to think critically? About *what* ought he or she to be thinking? What is the value of content devoid of context? What is the learner supposed to *do* with the law of diminishing returns or the calculus?

The use of specific outcomes/objectives was also criticised by Eisner in his work *Curriculum Evaluation* (1970). Eisner positioned Mager-type objectives (that is, objectives which specify unambiguously the particular behaviour (a practical skill or a body of knowledge, for example) the student is to acquire after having completed one or more learning activities) as having a limited value. Eisner argued that the outcomes of teaching are too complex and numerous to be encompassed by Mager-style objectives: the quality of learning that stems from student-teacher interaction is very difficult to predict. Therefore, the teacher cannot specify, with any accuracy, behavioural goals in advance of instruction. Moreover, there are some subject areas in which the specification of learning objectives is impossible, even if it were desirable (which, he would argue, it would not be). How can one state criteria and objectives in arts-based subjects? And what of those teaching episodes which yield unpredictable, yet desirable, behaviour which comes as a surprise to both teacher and student? Most of the outcomes of instruction, Eisner argued, need not be specified in advance. The teacher ought not to ask: 'What am I trying to accomplish?' Rather the teacher ought to ask: 'What am I going to *do*?'

Eisner therefore proposed an approach to planning that would focus on the behaviours of the teacher – of teaching – as distinct from the behaviours of the student – of learning. He suggested the use of what he termed *expressive objectives*. An expressive objective describes an educational encounter: it does not specify the behaviour a student is expected to demonstrate after having participated in learning activities. It is evocative rather than prescriptive; it serves as a theme around which a student's earlier-acquired skills can be extended and elaborated, rather than as a simplistic behaviourist criterion that needs to be 'ticked off' at the end of the lesson. Or, to put it another way, the use of expressive objectives, as opposed to learning outcomes/objectives, puts teaching rather than learning at the centre of the lesson planning process. And this is appropriate because learning is a difficult – if not impossible – process to plan and account for because it is so difficult to predict.

Criticism and problems relating to learning outcomes/objectives

The prevalence of outcomes/objectives models in the FE sector – in curriculum documents, in lesson plan templates, would seem to suggest that a behaviourist model of planning and assessing learning occupies a dominant position within learning and teaching cultures in the FE sector. But there are counter-arguments, well established within educational research and literature. To suggest that overt behaviour is the sole criterion of a learner's cognitive attainment is to miss, it can be argued, the 'real point' of education. Further, it is claimed that the learning outcome, by its very nature, defies the precise, quantitative analysis upon which the theory and use of learning outcomes/objectives rest. To attempt to formulate learning outcomes in exact terms is, it can be claimed, to trivialize other more important goals of instruction. How does one measure, for example, emotional development or personal enrichment, the learning that allows people to contribute to the cultures and conversations of society at large? There is a fear, too, that the minimum requirements of a learning outcome/objective may become the maximum level of attainment, so that innovation and exploration could be discouraged.

Hogben (1972), in an article that has over time been shown to be predictive of current audit cultures in FE, drew attention to the practical problems of drawing up objectives (to use his terminology). He wrote about the sheer number of statements and the considerable expenditure of time which would be involved in translating a curriculum into behavioural terms and at the same time emphaszed that the type and quality of much classroom learning is largely unpredictable, so that objectives cannot always be stated realistically in advance of the lesson. There is more to education, he urged, than objectives and minutiae that can be stated unambiguously in terms of student behaviour. In particular, what he termed 'responsive diversity' must be encouraged. He made five suggestions in relation to the formulation of objectives.

The formulation of objectives (Hogben, 1972)

1   some course objectives can be stated, but they need not be framed in specific, behavioural terms
2   long-term objectives (which may not become apparent to students until long after the end of a course) ought to be stated
3   unexpected and unintended outcomes of learning ought not to be ignored
4   objectives in their totality ought to mirror the goals which generated them
5   objectives which cannot be easily assessed ought not to be ignored in the building of a curriculum.

Popham (1970) similarly articulated a series of arguments against the validity of behavioural outcomes/objectives. Because trivial learner behaviour is the easiest to cast in the form of objectives, he argued, the really important outcomes of education may not receive appropriate emphasis. The stating of explicit goals prevents advantage being taken of those opportunities unexpectedly occurring during a lesson. Further, in some subject areas (the fine arts, for example) it is very difficult to identify measurable student behaviour. Finally, measurability generally implies accountability, and teachers might be judged on ability to change behaviour alone. In this last argument, Popham has, like Hogben, been proved right over time to a significant degree.

Macdonald-Ross (1973) maintained that most of the claims advanced in favour of the use of instructional objectives are false. If the meaning of the word education is to be taken seriously, he suggested, then the mere observation of a student's actions cannot be used in order to prescribe objectives of an educational nature. There are no well-defined prescriptions for the derivation of objectives. Indeed, defining objectives before the event often conflicts with 'the spirit of exploration' which should characterize the learning process. Unpredicted classroom events cannot be utilised fully in the context of pre-specified goals; indeed, in some disciplines appropriate criteria can be considered only after the instructional events. And finally, he argued that lists of objectives do not constitute an adequate reflection of the real structure of knowledge: knowledge, and understanding, involve a coherence of ideas, an articulated set of concepts which form a unified whole. Lists of behavioural objectives can make no contribution to understanding structures.

Conclusion: The use of learning outcomes/objectives – some critical perspectives

There are, therefore, several complex issues that arise when considering the use of learning outcome/objectives – a practice that is not made any the clearer to the teacher or trainee teacher (and perhaps even the teacher educator as well) by the variations in terminology used by awarding bodies in their curriculum documentation. It cannot be contested that for a lesson (whether this will be a theory-based lesson in a classroom, or a practical lesson in a workshop) to be successful, it needs to be carefully planned. It is absolutely the case that if time is spent thinking carefully about what is going to go into a session (what topics will be covered and in what sequence, how these topics might be assessed, how this session fits in to the broader curriculum being followed, what resources are needed, what strategies or resources will be employed by the teacher, and so forth), then that session is more likely to be successful.

The complexities arise when what 'successful' means starts to be considered or defined. What makes a session successful? Simply saying that a successful session is one where the learning outcomes/objectives have been met is not a sufficient answer because this assumes that the actual practice of setting learning outcomes/objectives and using them as a yardstick for a successful session is unproblematic. In fact, the opposite is the case. There are two aspects to this problematization of outcomes/objectives. The first is theoretical and the second is practical. These shall be explored in turn.

The theoretical turn against outcomes/objectives, as has been expressed above, centres on the ways in which they risk trivializing the learning process or marginalizing some forms of learning over others. If it is accepted that outcomes/objectives always have to be assessed (which in turn is another complex issue), does it therefore follow that teachers and trainers will only set outcomes/objectives that they know can be straightforwardly assessed, rather than outcomes/objectives that meaningfully capture significant learning within the context of the curriculum being followed? The outcomes/objectives model also makes assumptions of the students. Does learning always happen within predetermined periods of time? Do students always learn something after a 45–minute session, or a two-hour session, and so forth? What happens if a student needs longer, needs time to think over or to practice something before she or he can be said to have properly learned something? Outcomes/objectives need, so it is said, to be SMART (**s**pecific, **m**easurable, **a**chievable, **r**ealistic, **t**ime-bound). What if some kinds of learning are not – are never – measurable? What if the time boundaries that are needed by some of the students in a group are quite different to those imposed by a timetable and a scheme of work? Attempts to answer these questions will depend on the broader theoretical and professional position occupied by the teacher or trainer and may be complex and nuanced.

The practical aspect to the problematization of outcomes/objectives rests in the practice of writing up lesson plans and schemes of work. Or, more correctly, it rests in how such documents are first written and then used or referred to. Reference has already been made to the research done by one of the authors of this book relating to the writing of lesson plans. One of the conclusions of this research was that although teachers do not necessarily write a lesson plan for every session that they taught, they did plan their lessons with a great amount of care. Writing lesson plans using institutional templates was seen as a distraction from the 'real work' of teaching, and the lesson plans that they were asked to use were not seen as being helpful documents. the teacher of fine art, to provide one example, planned their lessons quite differently to the teacher of bricklaying. As such the 'official' paperwork of lesson planning – including the formulation of outcomes/objectives – was seen as an irrelevant, bureaucratic task and not as a relevant, professional one.

With such theoretical and practical difficulties to consider, how is the teacher and trainee teacher to make sense of the outcomes/objectives planning process? The following is intended as a series of guidelines that, it is hoped, capture the importance of careful planning for learning but resist the worst excesses of bureaucratization within the FE sector.

1   The use of learning outcomes/objectives in the classroom necessitates a highly structured and carefully planned instructional activity in which the teacher plays a clearly defined role. The nature of this role can vary, however, and can be defined, for example, in didactic terms (that is, where the teacher occupies a dominant role in the lesson, leading the activities or actions that have been planned for) or in facilitative terms (that is, where the teacher plans for activities that are student-centred during which she or he acts to facilitate more hands-on learning activities). 'Teaching' need not – does not – have to involve constant talking by the teacher or constant bustle and activity. Teachers need to learn when to talk and when to listen, when to act and when to stand back and observe.

2   Planning a scheme of outcomes/objectives is important. The outcomes/objectives, which must never be of a trivial nature or focus narrowly on data or neglect the higher levels of cognitive learning (this theme is returned to in the following chapter), must be planned and listed in schematic, sequential form. To have as few outcomes/objectives as possible, given the specific demands of the module or unit being followed, is a useful practice. Curricular documents should be referred to when formulating these.

3   The use of time must be planned carefully. Teaching periods of at least 45 minutes seem to be needed where outcomes/objectives are in use.

4   The designer of a pattern of outcomes/objectives must take decisions on whether the *purpose* of the lesson has been kept in mind, whether the planned lesson displays an appropriate *balance* of expected outcomes, and whether the types of outcomes/objective are *matched* correctly to the selected approach to instruction.

5   Students should be informed carefully of the purpose of this type of instruction, and should be made aware of the relationship of outcomes/objectives to the subject

or curriculum *as a whole*. Where it is possible to issue lists of learning outcomes/objectives at the beginning of a session, motivation can be heightened and concentration can be focussed; the outcomes/objectives can act as a useful reference point, checklist and self-assessment material for students. Many FE colleges have whiteboards in classroom that are specifically used to display the planned outcomes/objectives for a session.

6 Failure to attain an outcome/objective is not to be viewed by teacher or students as being problematic. The aphorism suggesting that 'an unattained objective is an incorrectly drawn objective' is unhelpful: it does not take into account, for example, the phenomenon of unexpected and uncontrollable 'noise' in communication channels. Instead, it should be remembered that learning is a complex process that cannot be straightforwardly timetabled in the way that teaching activities can. Therefore, consideration should be given to the concept of behavioural outcomes/objectives as providing indicators of progress along roads rather than as terminal points of travel. (One of the authors of this work invariably uses the prefix 'working towards' when discussing session objectives/outcomes with his students, in order to circumvent the problems of having objectives/outcomes that are too rigidly time-bound).

7 Complete records of student achievement in relation to assessments (formative and summative) involving the use of outcomes/objectives ought to be kept.

Successful teaching will always involve careful planning. But the planning process has, arguably, been distorted by the quality assurance and paperwork systems of the audit and inspection cultures that are dominant within the FE sector (indeed, in education as a whole). Too often, conversations with teachers in FE revolve around the excessive demands of form filling. It needs to be remembered that writing a lesson plan is not the same as lesson planning.

Further reading

Aims, objectives and outcomes can be a rather dry subject, and are probably best approached in the first instance through more general teacher-training literature. The following general texts are recommended here for their accessible approach to the subject:

Gould, J. (2012), *Learning theory and classroom practice in the lifelong learning sector*. 2nd edition. Exeter: Learning Matters.

Hillier, Y. (2011), *Reflective Teaching in Further and Adult Education*. London: Continuum.

Scales, P. (2013), *Teaching in the Lifelong Learning Sector*. 2nd edition. Maidenhead: McGraw Hill.

A more critical approach can be found in:

Fairclough, M. (2008), *Supporting learners in the lifelong learning sector*. Maidenhead: Open University Press. Chapter eight.

Tummons, J. (2010), Are lesson plans important? In Wallace, S. (ed.) *The Lifelong Learning Sector reflective reader*. Exeter: Learning Matters.

16 Taxonomies of Learning

In the biological sciences, organisms are grouped and classified on the basis of class, order, genus, species, and so forth. There is always a hierarchy implicit in such classifications. Lower classes of organism are subordinated to higher until, finally, the most inclusive category with which the science is concerned, is reached. The overarching structure into which organisms are placed in this way is referred to as a *taxonomy*, a term which refers to a formal classification (a word derived from ancient Greek – *taxis* means arrangement, and *nomia* means distribution) based on perceived relationships.

Classifying things into categories according to a pre-established taxonomy is not only to be found within the biological sciences, however: it is also found within educational theory. This is in part a reflection of the attempts of educationalists in the first half of the twentieth century to establish the study of education as being based on 'scientific methods', in much the same way as the social sciences did (which is why they are called social *sciences* and not, for example, social *arts*). The 'scientific' basis of academic disciplines such as education and teacher-training or sociology is, at the present time, widely disputed. It is argued that the attempt to use 'scientific methods' in disciplines such as these is inappropriate, not least as these disciplines are incapable of being researched within controlled laboratory settings. Whilst early attempts to ensure that these subjects were taken seriously by academic communities, by using 'scientific methods' to research them, were entirely understandable, a more modern, critical perspective would instead argue that to apply so-called objective scientific methods to education, as a discipline, is erroneous at best. Nonetheless, the traces of this 'scientific method' continue to be visible to the present day, not least in the behaviourist theories of learning that continue to appear within teacher-training curricula. The use of taxonomies in order to classify learning is another such example.

Perhaps the most widely known and influential taxonomy of learning objectives is that associated with the American educational psychologist Benjamin Bloom (1913–99), of the University of Chicago. It was first set out in 1951 at a symposium of the American Psychological Association at Chicago, entitled 'The Development of a Taxonomy of Educational Objectives'. 'Bloom's taxonomy' (as it has come to be known, although it has since been revised) was first presented in published form in 1956, and it continues to be widely used in the FE sector. Consequently, it frequently appears in teacher-training textbooks such as this one. Its influence can easily be seen in areas such as curriculum or syllabus and assessment task construction, the use of outcomes/objectives, schemes of marking and evaluation, and the identification of training needs in industrial and commercial contexts.

At this point, it is important to recognize that caution is necessary when considering Bloom's use of the term 'taxonomy'. In most areas of science it refers to a *strictly ordered classification* of objects and phenomena. The categories that Bloom classifies (such as 'knowledge' or 'synthesis' – these will be discussed more fully below, as will classifications proposed by other educational theorists) are neither objects nor phenomena in the usual scientific sense. That is to say, they cannot be identified, inspected and argued over as can, say, botanical specimens. Furthermore, it must be remembered that classification schemes such as those discussed here are, in common with many of the other theoretical frameworks used in education, essentially the result of human processes of thought which in this case are being used to define properties of sets or classes before naming them. The foundations upon which any classification or taxonomy rest do not necessarily reflect anything other than personal attitudes and values, concepts and perspectives. They are not necessarily aspects of objective reality.

The background to Bloom's taxonomy

Curriculum theory, as an aspect of educational research and theory, has long been established in the USA in a manner that the UK educational community has never quite managed to match. Curriculum theorists in America have long been concerned with the search for 'reliable' educational objectives: that is to say, they have been concerned with discovering or codifying educational objectives that can be scientifically planned, organized and evaluated. Thus, John Franklin Bobbitt, a pioneer in curriculum theory, argued in *The Curriculum* (1918), that because human life always consists of specific activities, then an education that could adequately prepare someone for life should by extension be aligned to these specific activities. The task of the educator, therefore, would be to study life so as to ascertain the abilities, habits, appreciations and forms of knowledge that people needed. These would in turn form the objectives of a curriculum that would be based on the skills needed for their attainment. In *How to Make a Curriculum* (1924) he enumerated 160 educational objectives classified in nine areas. For Bobbitt, an effective curriculum necessitated the clear formulation of specific instructional objectives (Eisner, 1967).

Following a meeting of American college examiners at Boston in 1948, it was decided to mount a series of discussions on the formulation of a theoretical framework to be used to facilitate communication among examiners. Out of these discussions emerged the goal of *a systematized classification of educational objectives*. The classification was to be derived from three sets of principles: educational, logical and psychological. Value judgements concerning objectives and behaviour were to be avoided. The use of a taxonomy might assist teachers in labelling their objectives in terms of properties and in obtaining ideas as to the most appropriate sequences in which objectives should be placed.

Three important questions were raised early in the discussions. First, was it in fact possible to classify educational objectives? Secondly, would the availability and use of an educational taxonomy result in restricting the thinking and planning of class teachers in matters concerning the content of the curriculum? And thirdly, might not the use of a taxonomy lead to an undesirable fragmentation of educational purposes, which ought to be considered as integrated wholes? (It should be noted that these questions remain as themes for discussion and debate today).

The first problem was met by the assertion that educational objectives could be expressed adequately in behavioural terms (refer also to the previous chapter for a more extensive discussion of this point). The second was answered by an expression of hope that the very consideration of a taxonomy would help teachers in their work in the wide field of relating curriculum objectives and teaching procedures. The third question was recognized as embodying a real and very deep fear and was countered by the assertion that, if the taxonomy were to be stated in *general* terms, educational purpose should not be affected too seriously.

The essence of Bloom's taxonomy

At the outset, it is important to remember that the original work that led to this threefold taxonomy of learning was a collaborative enterprise, which is commonly referred to as 'Bloom's' taxonomy. In fact, the categorization of the affective domain (see below) more properly belongs to one of Bloom's colleagues, David Krathwohl. Moreover, the categorization of the psychomotor domain was never undertaken by Bloom and his colleagues, but by other scholars at a later date (as discussed below). With this in mind, the term 'Bloom's taxonomy' is used here simply as a reflection of its commonplace status.

Bloom's taxonomy comprises of both general and specific categories, which embrace intended goal behaviours, that is, the likely outcomes of instruction. What was being classified, Bloom insisted, was the intended behaviour of students – the ways in which they are to act, think or feel as the result of participating in some form of instruction – of education. The taxonomy would assist in explicit formulations of the ways in which students would be expected to be changed by the process of education.

Bloom's taxonomy proposes three major divisions, or *domains*, of learning. The *cognitive* domain is concerned largely with factual information and knowledge. A typical example of learning within the cognitive domain would be the study of a subject based on factual information and the evaluation and synthesis of these facts, such as sociology AS level. The *affective* domain relates to attitudes, emotions and values. A typical example of learning within the affective domain would be the study of a subject based on values and ethics, such as those elements of a course in health and social care that focus on areas such as confidentiality or child protection. The *psychomotor* domain involves muscular and motor skills. A typical example of learning within the psycho-motor domain would be the study of bricklaying, requiring increasingly finely-honed motor skills as the course progresses. The structure of each domain of learning will now be briefly explored.

The cognitive domain is based on a sliding scale or continuum, beginning with 'mere' knowledge of facts and ascending to the intellectual process of evaluation. Each category within the domain is assumed automatically to include the behaviour of the lower levels. There are six major categories within this domain. They comprise a hierarchy based on a growth in the level of quality of learning and intellectual work at each stage, and the higher levels are assumed to be founded on the skills of the lower levels.

1 *Knowledge*. This is based on recall and methods of dealing with recalled information. It consists of:

(a) knowledge of specifics (such as subject specialist terminology and specific facts)

(b) knowledge of ways and means of dealing with specifics (such as conventions, trends and sequences, classifications and categories, criteria and methods)

(c) knowledge of the universals and abstractions in a field (such as principles and generalizations, or theories and structures).

2 *Comprehension*. This is the ability to grasp and utilize the meaning of material. It embraces translation or transfer from one form to another (for example, from words to numbers), interpretation (for example, explaining or summarizing), and extrapolation (such as predicting effects or consequences).

3 *Application*. This involves the ability to utilize learned material in new situations or contexts. It requires the application of the already-acquired principles, theories and rules, together with any relevant recourse to already-acquired factual knowledge.

4 *Analysis*. This involves the ability to break down already-learned material into component parts so that the underpinning structure or framework of the material is made clear. The analysis of relationships and the identification of the parts of a whole are vital.

5 *Synthesis*. This refers to the ability to combine separate elements so as to form 'a new whole'. Deduction, comparison and other aspects of logical thought are involved.

6 *Evaluation*. This concerns the ability to judge the value, worth or utility of learned material, with such judgments to be based on the relevant criteria or standards that have been established within the subject under consideration.

The affective domain

This domain revolves around feelings and attitudes towards the object or topic that is being learned. It is attitudinal in concept and ranges very widely, from heeding the simple reception of stimuli to the complex ability to characterize by the use of value concepts. There are five major categories within the domain. As with the cognitive domain, each category is seen as cumulative and the learning from one category is understood as supporting or reinforcing the learning that comes from the next. As previously discussed, it is worth noting that this domain should properly be referred to as *Krathwohl's* domain of affective learning.

1   *receiving* – this involves 'attending', that is, heeding messages or other stimuli. Awareness, willingness to attend and controlled attention are subsumed under this heading

2   *responding* –.this involves the arousal of curiosity and the acceptance of responsibility in relation to response.

3   *valuing* – this involves recognition of the intrinsic worth of a situation so that motivation is heightened and beliefs emerge.

4   *organizing and conceptualizing* – this involves the patterning of responses on the basis of investigation of attitudes and values, and the beginning of the building of an internally consistent value system.

5   *characterizing by value or value concept* – this involves the ability to see as a coherent whole matters involving ideas, attitudes and beliefs.

The psychomotor domain

The psychomotor domain involves practical or motor skills, such as bending copper piping (a common feature of plumbing courses) or installing a lightning conductor (a common task on electrical installation courses). In his 1956 work *The Taxonomy of Educational Objectives*, Bloom spent relatively little time discussing the psychomotor domain, arguing that as it had only a very small role in schooling, it did not require significant consideration. Only later did other researchers and writers explore this domain and provide a series of categories for it.

A research group led by Elizabeth Simpson at the University of Illinois proposed a classification of objectives in the psychomotor domain, based on seven categories (1966):

1   *perception* – this involves the use of the learner's eyes, ears and sense of touch in order to obtain those cues essential for the guidance of motor activity, such as sensory stimulation, cue selection, and the translation of sensory cases into a motor activity

2   *set* – this refers to the state of readiness for the performance of a certain action. These are divided into mental, physical and emotional sets

3 *guided response* – this necessitates performance under the general guidance of an optimal performance model (which might typically be provided by a teacher through a demonstration) and involves imitation, trial and error

4 *mechanism* – this refers to the ability to perform a task repeatedly with an acceptable degree of proficiency

5 *complex, overt response* – this refers to the performance of a task with a high degree of proficiency or fluency

6 a*daptation* –this requires the use of previously acquired skills so as to perform tasks that have not been tried or encountered before

7 *origination* – this refers to the creation of a new style performance of a task – a new way of doing something – after the development of skills.

Anita Harrow, who taught at Florida State University, proposed an alternative taxonomy of psychomotor learning, (1972), which is organized as follows:

1 *reflex movements* – these are the involuntary motor responses to stimuli. They are the basis for all types of behaviour involving bodily movement

2 *basic fundamental movements* – these are inherent movement patterns built upon simple reflex movements

3 *perceptual abilities* – these assist learners to interpret stimuli so that they can adjust to the environment. Responding to things that might be seen or heard is an example

4 *physical abilities* – these abilities are the essential foundations for skilled movement. Speed, exertion, suppleness and flexibility are examples

5 *skilled movements* – these are the components of any efficiently performed, complex movement. They cannot be acquired without learning, and therefore necessitate practice

6 *non-discursive communication* – this comprises the advanced behaviours involved in the type of communication relating to movement, such as ballet. Movement becomes aesthetic and creative at this level of the domain.

Alternative approaches to classifying and categorizing learning

Although Bloom's taxonomy (here understood to include the theoretical contributions of Krathwohl, Simpson et al.) is the best known and most widely applied model, a number of other educational researchers and theorists have proposed taxonomies of learning.

Norman Gronlund (1965), who has written extensively about assessment and educational objectives, provided a hierarchy comprising nine *learning outcomes*, which he uses to delineate the principal areas in which instructional outcomes/objectives could be classified.

1 knowledge

2 understanding

3 application

4 thinking skills (critical and scientific)

5 general skills (e.g. communication, social, computational)

6 attitudes (social, scientific)

7 interests (personal, educational, vocational)

8 appreciations (literature, music and so forth)

9 adjustments (social, emotional).

Although Gronlund's model is by no means as commonly referred to as Bloom's, aspects of his model has proven to be highly influential. Specifically, the division of outcomes/objectives into categories – 'knowledge and understanding', 'application', 'transferable skills' (which include what he termed 'thinking' and 'general' skills) – remains a common feature of awarding body specifications.

Robert Ebel is one of several educationists to have put forward taxonomies which claim to be *simpler* than Bloom's classification (1979). His taxonomy is based on the following seven elements:

1 understanding terms

2 understanding facts and generalizations

3 ability to explain or illustrate

4 ability to calculate

5 ability to predict

6 ability to recommend an appropriate course of action

7 ability to evaluate.

Robert Gagné (1988) proposed a five-category taxonomy of learned capabilities from which instructional objectives may be constructed.

1 intellectual skills (discrimination, identification, classification, demonstration, problem solving)

2 cognitive strategies (encoding, retrieval of complex material, i.e. 'the internally directed control processes that regulate and moderate other learning processes')

3 verbal information (i.e. 'knowledge consisting of propositions that are semantically meaningful')

4 motor skills (i.e. execution of coordinated movements)

5 attitudes (i.e. choice of personal actions that a learner is expected to exhibit).

Problematizing taxonomies

Criticism of Bloom's taxonomy is, at the time of writing this book, somewhat muted, and certainly does not enjoy a foregrounded position within education and teacher-training curricula. The extensive array of teaching and learning materials produced by the Standards Unit (established by what was then the Department for Education and Skills (DfES) under Tony Blair's New Labour government) and which can now be found online as part of the Excellence Gateway, epitomized what might be termed the 'normalization' of Bloom's taxonomy – a theory (for this is all that it is – Bloom's taxonomy is not based on meaningful empirical research, which perhaps constitutes the single most significant reason for rejecting it as an element of professional practice) that had become so completely established, it became an 'official' theory within pedagogic literature produced by the then government.

Nonetheless, a number of objections to Bloom's approach can and should be made. These criticisms have tended to be based on three grounds. First, there is the complaint that it is derived from the 'fallacious view' of learning that is proposed by the behaviourist school. The second complaint is that it is derived from a naïve and, therefore, inadequate theory of human knowledge. And thirdly, there is the complaint that the divisions between the cognitive, the affective and the psychomotor cognitive/ affective dichotomy are unreal and, therefore, do not provide the teacher with a safe or reliable framework for planning instruction.

The fallacious nature of behaviourist theories of learning
Bloom's taxonomy clearly accepts learning as a response to stimuli, the desired response being the behavioural outcome or objective. Consequently, the armoury of anti-behaviourist arguments has been drawn on heavily for an attack on the implicit assertions of the taxonomy. In general, advocates of Bloom's taxonomy have been reminded that educational outcomes/objectives should not be merely behavioural, and that outcome ought not to be equated necessarily with learning. It is perfectly possible for someone to have learned something without being able to convey to another person any evidence of having learned. Assessed behaviour, it is argued, ought not to be accepted as the only reliable indicator of the attainment of those goals set by a teacher or trainer. The taxonomy is condemned, therefore, as simplistic and inadequate as a guide for the class teacher.

Criticisms based on the inadequacies of behaviourist outcomes/objectives in turn inform a more fundamental critique of Bloom's approach: that it is based on theories of learning that are inadequate at best. Criticisms of behaviourist and neobehaviourist theories (refer to Chapters 3 and 4 for a more extensive discussion) can therefore be extended to include Bloom's taxonomy. At the same time, theories of learning as social practice (as discussed in Part 3 of this book) offer teachers and trainers ways of thinking about how people learn and what people know (a topic that shall be returned to below) that cannot so easily be reduced to simple categories.

Michael Oakeshott condemned the entire system of thinking underpinning the concept of the taxonomy from a philosophical perspective (Fuller, 1989). Learning, he argued, is an activity which is possible only for an individual who is capable of choice and self-direction in relation to his or her impulses and environment. Learning allows one to know oneself and one's surroundings: it is interminable and relates to conduct, not behaviour. The world which surrounds an individual consists not of abstractions, but beliefs. A person may enter and possess his or her world only through those disciplined activities which constitute learning, and this involves the active processes of teaching and being taught. It is only through the transactions which emerge from the process of learning that one's world becomes comprehensible. This view of education is an implicit rejection of a mode of teaching which appears to concentrate on encouraging the accumulation of facts and which lacks an overall sense of the humanizing influence of traditional patterns of culture and human growth.

Inadequate and naïve theories of knowledge

A further fundamental criticism of the taxonomy arises in response to its view of human knowledge. Bloom, it has been argued, has ignored much of the contemporary analysis of the cognitive processes associated with *epistemology*. Epistemology is the study of the nature, methods and validity of human knowledge, which seeks to answer fundamental questions such as: 'What does it mean to say that "one knows"?' or 'By what means can knowledge be acquired?' or 'What distinguishes belief from knowledge?' or 'Can anything be known with certainty?' (Eraut, 1994; Nespor, 1994; Scheffler, 1961).

There are a number of elements to this argument. First, there is the exclusive nature of the categories in the taxonomy itself. Consider the first three categories in the cognitive domain – knowledge, comprehension and application. Has 'knowledge' any real significance in isolation from 'comprehension' and 'application'? Can a student have know something without also having some level of understanding – of comprehension – of it? Can a student on a teacher-training course be said to have *knowledge* of Donald Schön's theories of *reflection-in-action* and *reflection-on-action* (these are discussed in Chapter 32) if he or she is able to quote the wording of the theories in an assignment, but is unable to *apply* these theories in writing up his or her reflections on sessions that they have taught? In part, it may indeed be the case that there is nothing wrong with the taxonomy as such: it is simply the case that some of the categories need to be given new classifications. But this is hardly a satisfactory response to the criticism that the first three categories of the taxonomy rest on divisions that can be seen as being artificial if not mistaken. How can something be known without being understood or applied? Surely it is in the application that this knowledge and understanding can be appropriately demonstrated and assessed?

Dividing learning into domains

Bloom's separation of learning into the three domains of cognitive, affective and psycho-motor has been criticized for its reliance on a false dichotomy. James Gribble, philosopher of education at the University of Melbourne, argued that the drawing of a distinction between 'cognitive' and 'affective' objectives in education was logically incoherent, and that it was unintelligible to propound 'the education of the emotions' as an aim independent of cognitive development (1983). Bloom failed to see, he argued, that the cognitive activity of 'judging' or 'evaluating' is the crucial factor in determining the adequacy of an affective response. Indeed, every emotional response involves a judgement, an appraisal of a situation, and a perception of some feature of the situation. Or, to put it another way, every emotional response involves some kind of cognition. Therefore, the attainment of educational objectives in the affective domain must necessarily be related to the cognitive core of the affective responses and to the appropriateness of the way the object of the affective response is perceived. Related to this, other educationists have long advocated the doctrine of 'confluence in education' based on the interrelationship and 'flowing together' of the cognitive and affective dimensions of learning; the doctrine stresses the difficulties of isolating intellectual from emotional experiences and calls for recognition of their common factors when lessons are planned (Brown, 1975). Such arguments in many ways have prefigured the more broadly prominent role of the attitudinal or affective in education and training more generally (culminating in the widespread – though to a significant degree troublesome – concept of 'emotional intelligence' in education practice and policy (Ecclestone, 2007; Sharp, 2001)).

Even at an anecdotal rather than academic level of discussion, these domains of learning are shown to be problematic. Consider the relatively familiar experience of learning to drive a car. Upon approaching a roundabout, the learner driver has to engage in a multitude of tasks: changing gear, indicating, observing. At the same time, the learner driver has to accomplish fluently a number of 'psychomotor' tasks, but these are also driven by 'cognitive' concerns (such as knowing when and how to indicate, or those elements of the highway code that relate to roundabouts), and 'affective' concerns as well (such as knowing when would be a 'safe' time to manoeuvre). Can these actions, which all need to happen at the same time, really be separated into different kinds of learning? Indeed, is it useful to do so?

Defending the use of Bloom's taxonomy

Advocates of Bloom's taxonomy retort that, in spite of a perceived lack of empirical validation of the hierarchical structure and its domains, it provides, nevertheless, an organized framework within which objectives can be stated and classified with some precision. If the defining of goals is accepted as sound educational practice (or at the very least, recognized as being positioned as such by successive governments as well as by Ofsted inspectors), a taxonomy such as Bloom's is needed in an attempt to translate those goals into more specific forms. The taxonomy has given, it might therefore be argued, an intensive stimulus to the search for a means of stating syllabus content in a balanced way and, by grouping together outcomes/objectives of a similar nature, has made the formulation of teaching and learning strategies easier. Such groupings have assisted in the arranging of sequential units of instruction. The taxonomy obliges teachers, trainers and assessors to keep in mind that most searching question: 'What precisely are we testing?' It has acted as a warning against ambiguity in the definition of learning outcomes/objectives and has assisted in the construction of statements of goals which enable teachers to evaluate attainment by reference to a yardstick (albeit a yardstick that is my no means perfect). Its comprehensive analysis of the outcomes of instruction provides a new vantage point from which the content of the curriculum or syllabus and the examiner's scheme might be surveyed and scrutinized in detail.

Bloom's taxonomy, therefore, can assist the teacher in answering the fundamental questions: 'In what ways should my students have changed as the result of my teaching, and what evidence can I accept as proof of that change?' The very posing and consideration of these questions may constitute a step towards the provision of some of the essential conditions for effective learning.

Classifying learning and knowledge: Other approaches

If it is accepted that through thinking about how learning might be classified or categorized, the planning and delivery of successful episodes of learning can be facilitated, then the use of some form of classificatory system becomes desirable. The difficulty for the teacher, then, comes in finding a schema that is aligned to the theories/frameworks of learning that she or he adheres to. Put simply, if a teacher rejects behaviourist theories of learning, then Bloom's taxonomy becomes redundant because it is based on this very same theory. If, however, other theoretical models could be considered that – unlike Bloom's taxonomy – are based on meaningful empirical research, then they might be used in a more theoretically satisfactory manner. Here, two approaches will be considered: first, the skill acquisition model of Dreyfus and Dreyfus; secondly, the insights offered by social practice views of learning.

The Dreyfus and Dreyfus Skill Acquisition Model

A quite different approach to Bloom's classification of learning was proposed by Stuart and Hubert Dreyfus, based initially on their research into artificial intelligence (1986). (Interestingly, this model has been extensively applied to professional learning, including the learning of trainee teachers (Eraut, 1994; Gossman, 2008).) Their approach is of interest not least as neither of them are educational researchers: Stuart Dreyfus is professor emeritus of Industrial Engineering and Operational Research and Hubert Dreyfus is professor of Philosophy, both at the University of California, Berkeley. Dreyfus and Dreyfus proposed a five-stage model of learning in order to analyze the transition of the learner from 'novice' to 'expert' status:

1 Novice. At this stage, the learner adheres rigidly to rules or schemes that have been taught.

2 Advanced beginner. At this stage the learner starts to build an understanding of the context in which s/he is learning ('situational perception'). Tasks are treated separately and with equal importance (that is, with no sense of hierarchy or classification).

3 Competent. At this stage the learner can manage multiple activities at the same time, and can also manage and make sense of accumulated information. Tasks can become routinized and actions can be linked to goals.

4 Proficient. At this stage the learner can take a holistic view of a situation, prioritizing what is important and what is not, and correctly assessing deviations from standard practice. The learner also begins at this stage to draw on professional knowledge and theory, although at a relatively simplistic level, to illustrate and inform rather than to analyze.

5 Expert. At this stage the learner has the capacity to work beyond existing rules and guidelines and to critique rather than follow professional knowledge. Problems and new situations are responded to from an analytical perspective rather than trial and error.

Finally, it is worth noting that at a later stage and in response to critiques from other researchers, Hubert Dreyfus proposed a sixth stage ('innovation') and a seventh stage ('practical wisdom').

Social Practice Views of Learning

At first look, it might seem counter-intuitive to draw on social practice theories of learning (as discussed in Part 3 of this book) in order to think about how learning might be categorized or classified so that the sequential planning of a curriculum can be facilitated. However, this body of theories offers the teacher, and the trainee-teacher, a useful array of frameworks and metaphors for thinking about the learning process. Vygotsky's concept of the zone of proximal development (as discussed in Chapter 9) leads the educator to consider the extent to which her or his students can work with or without guidance, to think about which resources, tools or other scaffolding objects may – or may not – be required. Lave and Wenger's concept of the community of practice (as discussed in Chapter 10), borrowing language from other apprenticeship models of learning, provides the teacher with the concept of the novice and the expert, but goes beyond this to think about how, as the novice travels through a community of practice and is given opportunities to learn, the tools and ideas of that community become available to her or him.

Social practice theories such as these turn around the focus of the lesson planning and sequencing process, because they are focussed on people – on learners – and not on knowledge. Instead of planning lessons on the basis of which bits of information will be parcelled up and assessed, they help the teacher to think about the learners themselves: where they are, the distance they have travelled and where they need to go next, how they need to be spoken to and when they might need guidance or help. Approaches such as these put 'the learner' at the centre of the planning process in a way that Bloom's taxonomy can never do. And yet, ironically, it is Bloom's approach that remains dominant in an educational culture that purports to 'put the learner at the heart of what we do'.

Summary

The taxonomies of learning proposed by Bloom et al. continue to occupy a dominant place within and across educational sectors. FE colleges and adult education centres sometimes *require* teachers to produce their lesson plans and schemes of work according to Bloom's taxonomy. This book argues instead that if the lesson planning process is going to rest on any kind of theoretical position, then it should be a position that the teacher has critically explored and reflected on. If teachers in FE are to be taken seriously as professionals, it follows that they need to draw on a body of knowledge relating to pedagogy that has been carefully considered, and not simply accepted because it means that a lesson plan template becomes more easily completed or an essay on a teacher-training course can be more straightforwardly completed. This book is *not* arguing that teachers should reject Bloom's taxonomy: but what is being argued is that if it is to be accepted, then it should be accepted properly and critically, mindful of the theory of learning on which it rests. And if after such a critical exploration it is found wanting, then different approaches can and must be considered when planning lessons.

Further reading

For those readers who would value practical examples of how an approach to learning based on taxonomies (such as those described here), the resources originally created by the DfES Standards Unit and later managed by LSIS (and one, assumes, to be managed in future by the FE Guild), are available at:

http://www.excellencegateway.org.uk/node/18239 [accessed 15 May 2013].

PART 5

Managing the Teaching–Learning Process

17 The Teacher as Manager and Leader

There is much more to being a teacher in a FE college than simply 'teaching'. It is by no means uncommon for new teachers in an institution, and newly qualified teachers as well, to be asked to serve as admissions tutors or as module or course leaders, as liaisons with external examiners or verifiers, or to take part in internally or externally-driven quality assurance processes such as course validation by a professional body, or inspection by Ofsted. These roles – at the very centre of teaching processes and yet at the same time apart from the actual process of teaching – are but aspects of a wider responsibility, which tend to be referred to as course management. Not all teachers relish taking on management roles such as these, although they are sometimes difficult to avoid.

However, it is important to recognize the distinction between these management roles, which are not in essence teaching, and the ways in which the teacher has to manage the broader learning and teaching processes that form the centre of her or his professional practice in the classroom or workshop. In this latter sense, therefore, the teacher can be considered as the manager of a situation in which effective teaching is expected to produce a desired standard of learning. This requires from the teacher the exercise of certain functions broadly associated with management, in the formal sense of that term, so that the desired environment for teaching and learning can be established. Here, 'management' is understood to refer to the process of getting people to work to accomplish a number of desired objectives or actions using those resources that are available.

So, here the focus of discussion is not on those aspects of the teacher's workload that more properly are referred to as management roles (Clow, 2005; Lumby, 2001; Shain and Gleeson, 1999). Nor is this chapter concerned with a discussion of college administration, that is to say, those aspects of management or control that are associated in a typical FE college with the duties of the director, departmental heads and registrar. Instead, the focus here is on examining the professional role and responsibilities of the individual tutor in the light of management theory and classroom practice. Specifically, this section of the book – starting with the present chapter – will explore the teacher-manager's tasks in relation to the teaching–learning environment, curriculum, syllabus and course design, the retention and retrieval of knowledge and transfer of learning, the tasks necessary in order to teach students how to study ('study skills'), the maintenance of discipline, and the teaching of both younger (that is, 14–16) students and older (that is, adult) students. In these complex tasks, the teacher may be viewed as managing a system of which he or she is a part. The role of the teacher is in directing an organization, viewed as a unified set of interacting parts.

Theoretical approaches to the organization

In the past, some educational writers and researchers have found it useful to perceive an educational organization (which here is understood to be a FE college or adult education centre, acknowledging that the latter tend to be significantly smaller than the former) in terms of a 'machine' which will carry out its tasks satisfactorily if all the parts behave exactly according to their design and purpose (Smith, 1982; Tilles, 1963). This metaphor suggests that, within a successful college, input is transformed into output, deviations from plans are noted and corrected, patterns of power and control assure a stable environment. The appropriate organizational form that might be applied here is that of the *bureau-cracy*, based on a hierarchy in which everyone knows her or his place and works for the attainment of organizational goals (although these can sometimes be quite abstract as can be quickly ascertained by looking at the 'mission statement' of a FE college). In practice, however, this approach to organization invariably creates its own problems: adaptation to changed circumstances often becomes difficult; bureaucracies tend to work in an unquestioning fashion in which predetermined goals rather than innovation dominate; a narrow interpretation of efficiency often becomes more important than flexibility and creative actions. The very term 'bureaucracy' has acquired pejorative overtones, for reasons that are easily understood by college tutors as they struggle to comply with the always-increasing numbers of forms and documents that characterize their working lives. As such, it is – perhaps unsurprisingly – not an entirely helpful model.

An alternative though similarly well-established metaphor for management, under the influence of biological research and advances in cybernetics (that is, the study of organization and communication in human beings and machines), is the concept of the *system* (Hanna, 1988; Scott, 1987). This concept refers both to a complex of interdependencies between parts, components, and processes that involve discernible regularities of relationship, and to a similar type of interdependency of such a complex and its surrounding environment (Parsons, 1960). An organization, such as a group of students and their tutor, may be viewed as a unified, purposeful system composed of interrelated parts, and the activity of any part of the organization will affect in some way the activity of every other part. The conduct of a student in class or, perhaps more obviously, the performance of a tutor, will affect class performance as a whole. A system is 'open' if, as in the case of a college, it interacts with its environment; it is 'closed' if there is no such interaction.

The systems model emphasises three distinct elements. First, there is the significance of the *environment* in which the organization exists. A FE college has goals and aims related specifically to the demands of the local community; of local, regional and national employers; of local and national policy makers; and of funding agencies and auditing bodies. Each single class of students within the college operates in the context of those goals and aims, irrespective of the size of the student group, the age of the students, or the curriculum being followed. Sensitivity to occurrences in the wider world of which one is a part is necessary for effective management, even when focussing attention down to classroom level. Secondly, the model stresses the *coherence* of the organization. The organization – the college – should be perceived by its staff and students as having purpose, as taking the form of a meaningful entity. Conflict and clash of interests may often be not far from the surface, but systematic, purposeful integration of resources is generally accepted as one of the goals of the college and its staff, notwithstanding differences regarding how exactly the aims of the college should be achieved. Thirdly, there should be a *structure,* which is clear and recognizable. The 'structure' of a college, or of a single class, is a description of the interrelations among components, the arrangement of its parts, and the potential influence they may have upon one another. This can be easily seen in a college organizational chart, which will usually reveal some general aspects of the structure of the institution.

System components

Notwithstanding the extent of the body of literature that expounds and discusses organizational theory, a number of key themes can be identified as common, as constituting a number of key basic propositions regarding organizations. There are four key issues to be considered here:

1   Members. Members can be paid, can be volunteers, can be part-time or full-time and can occupy different roles or positions, but they are necessary: without members, an organization cannot exist. Membership can provide benefits to members, but can also impose obligations or demands, which may be more or less formal. Thus, both tutors and students are members of a college – but each have very different obligations and responsibilities.

2   Purpose. The purpose of an organization relates to its coherence (as described above). These may be financial (as has indeed at one level been the case with FE colleges since incorporation in 1993) but may also be linked to broader societal themes (such as the desire for an educated population). External agencies or stakeholders may be involved in defining the purpose of organizations. In the case of FE, such external stakeholders are both numerous and ever changing (Edward et al., 2007).

3   Resources. Resources here are understood to refer not only to financial resources, but also to include all of the elements that contribute to the work of the organization. Thus, the expertise of members becomes a resource, as do the members themselves. As with finances, other resources must be used efficiently, managed carefully and 'spent wisely'. Unfortunately, though mindful of the fact that the management and organization of the FE sector is relatively under-researched, there are indications that teaching staff are not always used 'wisely' (Mather et al., 2009).

4   Tasks and structures. Organizations have tasks to accomplish. In the case of a FE college, such tasks include the teaching of lessons and the organization of a curriculum. At the level of the individual lecturer in her or his classroom, such tasks might include facilitating student presentations or conducting formative assessment. In order for these tasks to be completed in the right way and at the right time, overall structures are created. Some of these will be created by management teams, and others by individual lecturers. Typical examples include timetables, lesson plans, and meeting schedules.

The following key concepts of systems theory can also be used to generate reflection and discussion in relation to the classroom and management tasks of the college tutor (Meister, 1991):

1 Subsystems. These are the parts making up the whole. Systems, too, will probably be the subsystems of a larger whole. The student is a subsystem of a larger system- that is, her or his tutor or seminar group, which in turn functions as a subsystem within the college. Subsystems are interrelated, and it is the task of the teacher-manager, in planning and carrying out the processes of instruction, to be aware of the dynamic nature of the relationships. Students are not single, isolated persons: they are parts of a wider framework within which their personalities, backgrounds, motives and reactions have to be considered.

2 Synergy. The whole is greater than, and distinct from, the sum of its parts. Students within classes, tutors and departments within a college, can usually achieve more where they act together than where they operate in isolation. The task of the teacher-manager is to create the links, formal and informal, making this possible.

3 Feedback. Information concerning the effect of instruction is essential for the functioning of the teaching system. It is important to remember that the use of the term 'feedback' here is distinct from the use of the term in relation to student assessment.

4 Objectives. A system implies some purpose, such as survival or growth. The objectives of the college will affect the nature and work of subsystems, such as classes or instructional groups.

The essence of management and management skills

We now extend the provisional definition of management given above, and now define it as comprising 'those processes by which persons plan, direct and operate organizations so as to meet their objectives and goals'. In general, it involves the planning, direction and coordination of human activities through the medium of organizational structures. Specifically, the manager is concerned with the setting of objectives, the formulation of plans, the organization of activities and the direction and control of operations. In more formal terms, the manager may be considered as engaged in directing the transformation of inputs into outputs.

The essence of management, whether in the context of bank, office or FE classroom, is to be discovered in its nature, purpose and chosen modes of operation. Its nature is that of a 'process' – a continuous and systematic series of activities. Its purpose is related, invariably, to the achievement of synergy involving organizational aims and objectives. Its modes of operation are based on the techniques of coordination – the assembling of resources and the planning and synchronization of procedures necessary for the attainment of desired ends.

The functions of management have been described as universal, in that they may be discerned, in one form or another, in any type of management process. Outwardly, the planning of a production schedule may have very little in common with a college lecturer's formulation of lesson outcomes and choice of learning and teaching activities. Fundamentally, however, both types of activity may be perceived as reflecting the essence of planning: the process of thinking before doing, the devising of a line of action to be followed, the stages to go through and methods to be used. The lecturer's overall function in the workshop or classroom, in relation to the process of instruction, may be viewed as a facilitating activity that allocates and utilizes resources, influences human action and plans change in order to accomplish rationally-conceived goals (Haimann and Scott, 1978).

Three basic skill sets – technical, altruistic and conceptual – have been identified by some researchers as essential for all types of manager. Technical skill implies the ability to use specialized techniques: the teacher must be able to utilize appropriate instructional procedures. Altruistic skill – which is of considerable significance in teaching and training – involves the capacity to understand, motivate and work with other people, individually or in groups, such as when teaching seminar groups, running a demonstration or holding a one-to-one tutorial in instructional classes. Conceptual skill is the mental capacity to coordinate the interests and activities of those people who make up the system: that is, the students for whose learning and development the lecturer is responsible.

Styles of management: Classroom/workshop perspectives

It will quickly become obvious to trainee teachers that there is no 'one best way' of organizing instruction, not least through a consideration of the differing styles or approaches of teacher education lecturers. The *form* which is considered appropriate (and which will create synergy) will depend on the specific task and the environment with which one is dealing in the classroom or workshop. Methods which are very effective in one situation may prove unworkable in another, and there are a number of variable factors to consider in this regard, such as the age of the students, the nature of the curriculum, or the resources that are available.

It is the task of the 'teacher-as-manager' to identify the particular technique which he or she considers as appropriate to the instructional situation and which will best contribute to the attainment of instructional goals. The teacher's work must be concerned with achieving an appropriate fit between the organization of instruction, its environment and goals. He or she may adopt the so-called 'contingency approach' to management tasks in the classroom, based on the principle that no universal rules or approaches will, in reality, fit all situations. However, approaching the management of learning and teaching from such an improvizational perspective will seldom be able to generate an environment that is conducive to learning on any kind of regular, systematic basis. Instead, a more appropriate management style will depend on the reactions of the teacher – or trainee teacher – to specific problems at the very time they present themselves.

The teacher-as-manager must, therefore, consider an approach to this aspect of the professional role which reflects an ability to make decisions under different, perhaps unexpected conditions, such as when a student group react negatively to a style of activity that in the past has been both popular and effective. One long-established approach in terms of how such a situation might be managed, although at first look it might appear to be a far from advisable course of action, is to 'muddle through' (Lindblom, 1959). Lindblom suggested that, all too often, when managers have to deal with problems of an ambiguous or novel nature, mere theory might be restrictive and inappropriate. The manager should, in such circumstances, put aside any possible search for a 'best solution' to the problem, and instead make step-by-step, marginal and incremental comparisons among policies and solutions until a 'better solution' is found and the system returns to equilibrium (that is, the flow and direction of the classroom or workshop has been restored).

An alternative conception of the characteristics of the manager was provided by Mintzberg, based on a systematic review of other available theories and models of management (1990, 1997). He argued that there were ten distinct roles that managers had to perform at different times, according to context: figurehead; leader; liaison; monitor; disseminator; spokesperson; entrepreneur; disturbance handler; resource allocator; and negotiator. He went on to expand his approach to management through the concept of 'framing'. Drawing on her or his own values, experiences and knowledge, a manager creates a frame for a task that needs to be accomplished: a typical task example from a FE context might include the delivery of an entirely new curriculum. The frame consists of three elements (Mintzberg, 1997: 132):

1 What the manager views as the purpose of the task (in this example, the purpose of moving to a new curriculum might internally-driven and related to curriculum content, or externally driven and related to changes in funding).

2 The manager's perspective on what needs to be done (which will require the involvement of other people – lecturers, finance officers, accreditation bodies – as well as other subsidiary tasks such as the preparation of documents or course validation and approval events).

3 What the manager sees as a specific set of strategic positions for doing (which will involve specific tasks to be carried out in an appropriate order and the use of relevant resources: here, the focus is equally on both the institutional requirements of the curriculum, and the ways through which the curriculum will be delivered to students).

Management and leadership

A third well-established body of literature rests on the concept of the *leadership* role of the teacher-as-manager. In this sense, the teacher is seen as 'leading' his students, by motivating and assisting them, to a pre-determined point (typically, the successful completion of a module or programme of study) which is characteristic of 'effective teaching'. For some writers and researchers, management *is* leadership: the concepts are conterminous. In other published works of research and scholarship, however, the concepts rarely emerge as synonymous. Instead, leadership is positioned as an interpersonal process, which in turn is an aspect of the organizational process, which we term management. Successful management involves elements of effective leadership, but an effective leader is not necessarily an effective manager. Thus, leadership is a part of management, but not all of it. A manager is required to plan and organize. Leadership is the ability to persuade others to seek defined objectives enthusiastically. It is the human factor which binds a group together and motivates it toward goals. Management activities such as planning, organizing, and decision-making are dormant until the leader triggers the power of motivation in people and guides them toward goals (Davis, 1967).

A convenient analysis of leadership was proposed by Grint (1999), who argued that there are in essence four types of or approaches to leadership:

1 Trait approaches. In this approach to leadership, it is the traits or characteristics of the individual leader that are of most importance. Irrespective of the context or situation, the 'right person with the right traits' will be the best leader.

2 Contingency approaches. In this approach to leadership, the relationship between the leader and the context is explored. It is argued that leaders need to be aware of and to reflect on their own characteristics or abilities, and that these need to be aligned to the situation or context that they are working in. thus, different situations will call for different leaders, depending on their traits.

3 Situational approaches. In this approach to leadership, the notion that certain contexts demand certain kinds of leadership is sustained. But in this approach it is assumed that leaders can be flexible and that instead of characterizing a single approach to leadership, are instead able to draw on a repertoire of leadership styles, according to the situation in which they find themselves.

4 Constitutive approaches. In this approach to leadership, the details or challenges of the environment are interpreted by leaders who will then go on to propose whatever actions are necessary in order to manage the current situation. Leaders respond to the culture in which they operate, but also work to influence that culture.

The concept of leadership has undergone further investigation, often by theoreticians who are interested specifically in the problems of teachers. Acting on the basis of a general definition of leadership as 'actions intended to influence the behaviour of individuals or groups', the following points have emerged (which translate with ease into a FE college context):

1 'Leader behaviour' will be acceptable and satisfying to a group of 'followers' to the extent that the group interprets the behaviour as 'an immediate source of satisfaction or as instrumental to future satisfaction'.

2 'Leader behaviour' will motivate 'followers' to the extent that it makes satisfaction of their needs contingent on effective performance, and effectively enhances the environment of the 'followers' 'by providing the coaching, guidance, support, and rewards necessary for effective performance'.

3 'Leader behaviour' will be acceptable where it is perceived as helping members of a group to clarify their expectations.

4 'Leader behaviour' will be widely acceptable where the leader chooses a 'participative' style of operation: this involves total trust in his subordinates, and a rejection of the autocratic style in favour of joint decision-making. Teacher and students are seen as joint participants in a venture aimed at the good of all. Effective leadership of this nature in the classroom 'will focus on results, with a balanced emphasis on organizational objectives and personal goals'.

If the metaphor fits, why not wear it?

In 1990, a landmark special number of the journal *Theory into Practice* was published that focussed on the use of metaphor in the research and analysis of educational processes across different context. Several of the papers in this journal are of specific interest to the present discussion. The first of these, by Elizabeth Cohen and Rachel Lotan and titled 'teacher as supervisor of complex technology' (1990: 78–84), draws on organizational theory in order to accomplish the task of analysing teaching and learning in the classroom setting. Cohen and Lotan argued that the technology of the classroom might be viewed as varying from that involving simple systems (where all the students are carrying out similar routine tasks) to highly differentiated systems (where, for example, small groups of students are engaged on different tasks). For example, a teacher might be working with a class that contained two groups of students who were following two distinct curricula, but who had been grouped into a single teaching group for timetabling purposes or due to a shortage of staff. Or, to put it another way, a teacher might be working in a class where a number of different subsystems are operating simultaneously in the main system. Essentially, the teacher, faced with classroom situations characterized by uncertainty and differentiation, can enhance class effectiveness by adapting some fundamental management techniques, such as assessing, organizing and controlling in accordance with pre-set requirements. Teachers, therefore, have to learn how to delegate authority, but still maintain control. They need to avoid 'hovering' over their students unnecessarily, whilst still engaging them in appropriate tasks or activities. Moreover, students should get used to working collaboratively in groups and performing their assigned roles within those groups (such as when producing a group presentation, for example). Management theory (as it relates to planning and control) can be used, Cohen and Lotan argued, to train not only teachers but also students in these tasks.

The second article to be discussed here, written by David Berliner and titled 'If the metaphor fits, why not wear it? The teacher as executive' (1990: 85–93) suggests that the literature of the last few decades, describing the role and functions of management demonstrates a significant overlap with contemporaneous descriptions of the role of teachers and the functions that they perform. He notes that one can say of managers and teachers that their job is not to tell people what to do, but rather to enable them to perform well. Both managers and leaders have a responsibility to contribute to the goals of the organization in which they practice. In this sense, according to Berliner, the classroom can be understood simply to be a 'workplace' in which the planned output is to be seen in terms of human development, a task that requires the formal techniques of management.

Six functions of teacher

Six functions of the teacher in his or her role as manager are included in Berliner's analysis:

1   Planning. Choosing the content of a lesson, scheduling time for different activities, forming groups of learners and choosing appropriate activity structures are analogous to the tasks of a manager. The necessary decision-making which accompanies planning involves complex tasks for both manager and teacher.

2   Communicating goals. It is the task of the teacher to communicate expectations of performance (for example, the outcomes of a learning session or the requirements of an assessment task), a similar job to that undertaken by the manager who has to convey to her or his staff goals and the necessary work arrangements which are involved.

3   Regulating activities. The pace of production within a workplace is analogous to the pace of instruction in a classroom: both require the exercise of the management function. The sequencing of events and timing require from both managers and teachers the abilities to handle information and make decisions swiftly and accurately, so that the required work is done in the time available.

4   Creating an appropriate work environment. This is an important task for both the manager and the teacher. In terms of systems analysis, the subsystems which comprise the total system require suitable settings (that is, an appropriate atmosphere) if they are to function in accordance with plans. The establishment of an environment that is conducive to learning might rely on something relatively simple such as the way in which the furniture is arranged (so that open sight lines are established amongst everyone in the room). Or it might be more complex, involving the provision of appropriate quantities of specialist resources.

5   Motivating work group members. Where a workforce or members of an seminar or workshop group lack motivation, output is unlikely to be satisfactory. The task of motivation (that is to say, arousal and maintenance of interest, creation and reinforcement of expectancy, provision of incentive) often falls to manager and teacher.

6   Evaluating performance. No system will function in accordance with plans in the absence of regular evaluation of performance. Both manager and teacher are expected to measure and assess the results of those activities for which they have responsibility, as a prelude to corrective action.

Hermine Marshall's article, titled 'Beyond the workplace metaphor: the classroom as a learning setting' is the final work to be considered here (1990: 94–101). In her article, Marshall argues against uncritical acceptance of the classroom as workplace. Rather, it is essential, she contends, to conceptualize the classroom so that 'learning' rather than 'work' is emphasized. The workplace model tends to stress the end product of academic work. Such an approach ignores the significance of those theoretical perspectives on learning in which the learner is playing an active role in the process of constructing knowledge rather than reacting to external forces (1990: 97). Marshall draws on cognitivist approaches to learning in her analysis (as discussed in Chapter 6 of this present text), although it is worth noting that other perspectives that similarly foreground the activities of the learner might equally apply (such as social constructivist theory (as discussed in Chapter 9) or communities of practice theory (as discussed in Chapter 10)). She furthermore contends that it is not easy to make a worthwhile comparison of the tasks of the teacher with the 'mechanical' tasks of the manager. Learning, Marshall contends, is often an unintended consequence of the teaching process and therefore demands goals that centre on process rather than product (echoing debates over process and product models of curriculum – these are explored in the following chapter). The teacher's tasks are much more complex than those envisaged in the phrase 'enabling students to learn'.

Marshall notes that authority relationships in the classroom are less hierarchical than those that exist in the workplace. The teacher's authority relationship cannot be compared validly with that of the manager. It is necessary, Marshall concludes, to move *beyond* the workplace metaphor so that the unique qualities of the teaching function might be recognized and understood.

Teachers, managers and leaders: Critical perspectives

The very term 'leadership' is not always popular within educational circles. For some staff, particularly those by whom a humanist approach to learning and teaching is preferred, it will have unpleasant overtones relating to authority. For others, the very idea of 'a leader' is perceived as incompatible with the view of the functions of the teacher as including the encouragement of autonomy (together with both its privileges and its duties) among students. Indeed, in an educational culture within which the 'student voice' is not only encouraged but also, arguably, privileged, such notions of leadership can seem antiquated at best and antithetical at worst.

As such, it is for the individual teacher, or trainee teacher, to decide on the basis of her or his experiences whether or not to accept as valid the analogy which suggests the existence of important similarities between teaching and management, as have been outlined above. Some teachers will reject systems theory in its entirety as being a theoretical perspective that seeks to over-simplify and which can never apply to the classroom, with its innumerable, rich complexities, its shifting structures, its intensely individual actions and its often unpredictable nature (save in some few, trivial matters). Educational activity is unique and its organization cannot be understood by reference to a frame of events from which it is qualitatively dissimilar. It is, say critics of the teacher-as-manager concept, an absurdity to bracket the teacher with the industrial manager. Each is engaged in totally different types of activity and each has different ends. Neither would recognize the other as sharing any communality of activity. The teaching-managing analogy is, it is argued, meaningless, save in a very insignificant sense.

In favour of the analogy is the perception of the teacher as one who is objectively carrying out the functions of a manager when he or she accepts responsibility for the deployment of resources, the planning of instruction and its administration in the interests of efficient learning. Specifically, the teacher has a management responsibility within the college system for each of the following activities:

1 the creation and maintenance of a classroom environment in which learning can take place effectively
2 the interpretation and enactment of the syllabus or curriculum that is being followed
3 the selection and enunciation of teaching outcomes/objectives
4 the selection of appropriate activities and resources in accordance with an overall approach to teaching (which will be more or less explicitly based on a particular theoretical perspective)
5 class motivation and control
6 the delivery of instruction
7 the assessment of student learning
8 the provision of informative, constructive and timely feedback to students.

In management terms, these and related activities may be classified under four headings: planning, organization, directing and controlling. As a *planner*, the teacher has to define the necessary instructional outcomes/objectives based on his or her appreciation of what ought to be achieved, and what can be achieved, allowing for the kinds of constraints that are typically found within the FE sector (which range from changes in teaching accommodation to having to teach mixed groups who are following different curricula). As an *organizer*, the teacher has to determine a teaching strategy based on his or her outcomes/objectives and resources. As *director*, the teacher has to carry out an operational task which involves the highly important functions of motivating and encouraging students. As *controller*, the teacher has to monitor and assess the students' progress and adjust his or her teaching so that the planned outcomes/objectives (which might relate to a specific session, to a unit/module, or to a programme of study) can be attained.

In more precise terms, the purpose of management of the teaching-learning situation may be seen as the modification of the learner's behaviour in accordance with predetermined outcomes/objectives, the attainment of which should enrich and advance personal growth. The teacher-manager's functions should have significance only as a contribution to that end.

Further reading

The study of management and leadership in education really requires a book – or several – in it's own right. The approach taken here proposes that an understanding of broader educational management approaches can be as useful at the level of the individual classroom as at department or faculty level. With this in mind, the following are recommended for the reader who wishes to explore further:

Marsden, F. and Youde, A. (2010), Administration and course management. In Avis, J., Fisher, R. and Thompson, R. (eds.) *Teaching in Lifelong Learning: a guide to theory and practice.* Maidenhead: McGraw Hill.

Tummons, J. (2010), *Becoming a professional tutor in the lifelong learning sector.* 2nd edition. Exeter: Learning Matters. Chapters 1 and 2.

Wallace, S. and Gravells, J. (2007), *Leadership and Leading Teams in the Lifelong Learning Sector.* Exeter: Learning Matters.

18 Course and Curriculum Design and Content

This chapter aims to introduce and explore the role of the FE teacher in relation to the planning of teaching methods and learning activities and the use of relevant resources. The teacher is seen here in the role of controller, as far as circumstances might allow, of the instructional setting (that is to say, the workshop, tutorial room or seminar room) and organizer of a teaching and learning strategy appropriate to not only students' aspirations and needs but also the demands of the curriculum that is being followed. He or she is bringing together the components of a learning architecture – students, teacher, learning environment and instructional materials – in order to achieve a desired objective.

The immediate teaching environment – the physical features of the classroom or workshop that is being used, such as layout, furniture and so forth – ought to be accepted by the teacher as one of the factors constraining the learning and teaching process, which he or she can manipulate only in limited fashion. There is only so much that can be achieved through moving furniture around (although it is nonetheless an effective step to take in preparing for a lesson). However, modifications in the use of space may be made, and the teacher may view the instructional setting as an important aspect of the learning and teaching process which can contribute to the establishment of an environment that is conducive to learning.

Curriculum and course design and implementation will be shaped by the teacher's interpretation, normally in consultation with other subject group colleagues, of the wider goals of the curriculum for which the college as a whole is responsible. Curriculum is in itself a disputed term and can carry several distinct meanings (Tummons, 2012). Further explorations of the term will be considered below. For the present, two definitions are offered. The first, by Eisner (1979) positions the curriculum as a series of planned events that are intended to have educational consequences for students. A second, by Taba (1962), defines curriculum as containing a statement of aims and of specific objectives; as indicating some selection and organization of content; as either implying or manifesting certain patterns of learning and teaching, whether because the objectives demand them or because the content organization requires them; and as including a programme of evaluation of the outcomes.

Any FE college, through its various committees will have decided on appropriate curriculum goals at an institutional level within the broader setting of demands made by government funding agencies, trade and professional bodies, and local and regional needs. The FE teacher will translate these goals into instructional programmes, reflecting availability of resources, chosen modes of instruction and the sequencing of teaching.

The instructional setting: Preparing an environment for learning and teaching

It is not always the case that the teacher is able to exercise much control over the wider, physical environment in which he or she works. The shape of a classroom, its situation in relation to other rooms, its general facilities, cannot often be altered. But the important details which have a direct effect on the process of instruction – the layout of the room, the relative positions of teacher and students, seating arrangements, the position of teaching aids, temperature, illumination, ventilation – that is, the accommodation arrangements, require careful consideration and organization. Problems of accommodation can often play a disproportionate role in the outcome of the lesson. Classroom temperature, illumination and background noise which are outside an acceptable range may distract students from the work that the teacher has prepared. Where such conditions can be controlled, the teacher ought to experiment so as to achieve the most satisfactory environment for the class. All of the factors which shape activity within the classroom are related to the overall learning process; as far as possible, therefore, they all should be controlled.

The layout of the classroom is usually under the direct control of the teacher and it is desirable that it be arranged in accordance with the specific requirements of the modes of instruction which are being employed. A discussion group demands a layout of furniture which allows open sight lines between participants. The use of a data projector necessitates a class arrangement which will ensure that everyone has a clear view of the screen on which the presentation is being displayed. The teacher in a FE college ought not to accept as immutable the traditional arrangement whereby a class is seated in rows, all facing a whiteboard which is placed exactly in the centre of the front of the room. Some alternative arrangements have proved successful and experimentation by individual class teachers is essential. The first thing for the teacher to do, therefore, is to move the furniture.

Prints and photographs of schools taken a hundred years ago reveal an obsession with symmetry, presumably derived from the belief that order and symmetry were equivalent. School buildings laid out with geometrical regularity were paralleled by precise rows of fixed desks in each classroom. The teacher's place was usually slightly below the middle of the front row, or on a raised platform in that position. This arrangement is still followed by some teachers, under the impression that 'you can be seen and heard from there by all the class'. This is often not the case; the best position from which to speak, from which to manage the class, has to be discovered by individual experiment.

Seating arrangements in a class should be determined, where possible, by the precise instructional strategy favoured by the teacher. Thus, precise spacing and arrangement of chairs and desks might be considered appropriate for a formal lesson, presentation or lecture. Informal spacing and arrangement might suit a discussion session, with chairs arranged in clusters, with or without tables. The question to be answered by the tutor is: in what ways can class seating arrangements facilitate the process of learning, given the particular form of instruction I intend to use? Of course, it may not always be possible to move classroom furniture between sessions. In such cases, a 'best fit' design that affords clear sight lines to the teacher and to the whiteboard (for formal input) and at the same time allows for interaction amongst the students (for group work, for example) is to be encouraged. Relatively consistent findings have emerged from research into spatial classroom arrangements. Among these findings, which are of much interest to the practising teacher, are the following:

1 There seems to be a direct increase in student participation in the teaching-learning process with a decrease in distance between teacher and student.

2 A high rate of student participation appears to emerge where the class is based on a U-shaped arrangement and the teacher sits in the centre of the U-gap (see Figure 18.1), or where students are arranged in small groups around clusters of tables (see Figure 18.2).

3 By contrast, students at college level appear actively to dislike the traditional, standard seating arrangements that are characteristic of formal schooling (that is, rows of desks faced by the teacher's desk). There appears to be a general preference for less rigid arrangements.

4 Students prefer, where places in the classroom have been allocated, to keep their own places: there is a general reluctance to be moved from one part of the classroom to another. Nonetheless, there are educational benefits to be had from varying peer group composition within classes, and teachers are to be encouraged to move student groups around from time to time, for example in order to facilitate a specific activity.

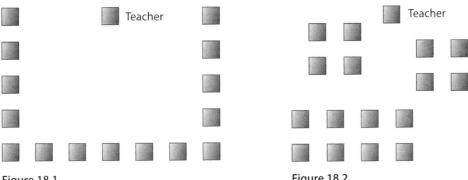

Figure 18.1   **Figure 18.2**

The arrangement of furniture, equipment and resources within workshop settings (which might be used for motor vehicle courses, for pottery courses or for furniture design courses) necessitates a rather different approach on the part of the teacher. For example, in a design and technology workshop, students tend to sit at high workbenches that are often bolted to the floor: in rooms such as these, moving the furniture is impossible. Large items of equipment such as extractor fans as well as smaller items such as sewing machines require the layout of the workshop to remain as fixed in place, much as the furniture in a computer suite might be. Similarly, in larger spaces such as motor vehicle or plumbing workshops, workstations will be installed at fixed points. In environments such as these, the teacher will need to think carefully about how and where to stand and how and when to direct her or his students. When demonstrating how a specific tool might be used or a specific process might be carried out, the teacher will need to ensure that all of the student group can see.

But there are some problems that the teacher will need to manage that are common across all areas of the FE college curriculum. A shortage of resources or a lack of space in the room would equally affect the teaching-learning process in an ESOL class and a bricklaying class. Such conditions are not uncommon and whilst there is no ideal solution, techniques such as pairing students together to work at a single workstation or splitting a group into two and allocating different activities to each can alleviate such pressures (refer generally to the chapters in Part 6 of this book).

Curriculum and syllabus: Interpretation and compilation

It is not uncommon for even a newly qualified teacher in a FE college to be involved in the preparation of not just single lessons, but sequences of lessons. Typically, this would entail the planning of a sequence of sessions to cover a specific module or unit as part of a larger programme of study. The teacher would need to ensure that the correct course specifications, in terms of course content and course assessment (this topic is discussed in Chapters 30 and 31) were being followed. A level two NVQ in brickwork, for example, would need to meet relevant occupational criteria. It would also be required by relevant funding agencies that the course being offered met nationally agreed benchmarks (although issues concerning funding are, quite properly, beyond the remit of most classroom or workshop teachers in FE). Put simply, the teacher or trainer will be expected to work to a syllabus, provided within the – often extensive – documentation distributed by awarding bodies such as City and Guilds or NCFE (examples of such documents are provided in Chapter 15).

A syllabus generally lists a series of topics which should be covered during the course or unit and which will then in turn form the basis of the relevant assessment process. It may be drawn up in wide terms, which makes the teacher's interpretative task very important; it may, on the other hand, be presented with a wealth of detail which allows for little in the way of individual interpretation on the part of the teacher. However, even if there is an absence of detail, the teacher responsible for drawing up the sequence of lessons or scheme of work need not be at a disadvantage. Through drawing on conversations with other more experienced colleagues, feedback from past students, reports from and conversations with external examines or verifiers and her or his own specialist expertise, the teacher will be able to plan and organize the programme of study on the basis of the detail he or she considers necessary.

Similarly, a syllabus will not always indicate the relative importance of its topics or the order in which they are to be studied. In some cases, those who compile a syllabus tend to follow the traditional textbook order of contents, or a pattern prescribed by a logical approach to the subject, or – consciously or unconsciously – the shape of a university or college course in which they may have participated as students. Often, however, the teacher will feel that the subject demands a different approach. For example, where the teaching of the syllabus for one unit or module can be planned so that it coincides with teaching of related areas in other modules, the probability of meaningful learning occurring is increased.

The interpretation of the syllabus presents the teacher with the necessity of making decisions based on answers to the following questions; his or her decisions will result in a scheme of work that will provide an outline of which topics are to be covered and when, how resources are to be appropriately allocated, how and when assessments are to be completed, and so forth. Many FE colleges, adult education centres and private training companies provide staff with an institutional template for a scheme of work. Nonetheless, whether the teacher is completing a template that has been provided for them or designing a scheme of work from scratch, the same questions ought to be considered:

1 what ought to be the content of the scheme of work?

2 what ought to be the shape of the scheme? How should it be organized?

3 what should the precise outcomes or objectives be for each session so that the syllabus is completely covered?'

4 what teaching and learning methods are necessitated by the topic and by the outcomes/objectives?

5 what forms of assessment are appropriate for encouraging learning? What forms of assessment are required by the syllabus, and at what time?

6 what allocation of course time is to be made for each topic or element of the syllabus?

It is important to remember that students attending their first session are often not – or only partially – aware of the published syllabus. Some may not know of its existence at all. Therefore, the preliminaries of the course – the induction period – ought to include a discussion of the syllabus with the class: its overall purpose, its value, its general contents, its relation to the students' development, order of topics to be followed and allocation of time. Similarly, the teacher ought to provide guidance to the class at the beginning of the course regarding assignment deadlines, requirements for private study time outside of the workshop or classroom, any materials or resources that students might be expected to obtain, and so forth.

Selecting modes of instruction

- 'I understand the content and overall requirements of the syllabus and I am able to identify my appropriate objectives. What must my students *do* to learn?'
- 'What type of learning do I expect? Surface learning (reflecting extrinsic motivation only) or deep learning (reflecting intrinsic interest in the subject matter) and how do I ensure the one rather than the other?'
- 'How much time should I allocate for demonstration before allowing students to practice for themselves? And how will I accommodate the students who I know will take much longer to complete the tasks?'
- 'How may I best facilitate learning? Should I deliver more formal lecture-style elements within my sessions? Would such a formal lesson be appropriate or should I use a workshop format? Are there any materials that have been produced by a relevant professional body that might be useful?'
- 'Should I show my students a clip from youtube, which has been produced by other teachers working on this type of course? How will the requirements for private study be responded to?'

These and similar questions must be posed and answered by the teacher, who has the responsibility of designing and implementing a range of teaching and learning strategies across the unit or programme of study in question. (The most commonly used modes of instruction are explored in depth in Part 6 of this book).

There may, of course, be a very restricted range of choices facing the teacher. She may lack resources in terms of accommodation, audio-visual aids, ICT and so forth. She may have a much larger – or much smaller – student group than anticipated. She may have a student with specific needs or learning disabilities who will require additional resources, extra time or additional staff support. But whatever the specific conditions that she may have to manage, her first question must be: 'given my specific teaching aims, how best do I attain them?'.

The subject matter itself will to some extent dictate the mode of teaching. Students on a counselling course are more likely to be taught through role-play than are students on an electrical installation course. Lessons based on demonstrations and observed practice are likely to be the chosen mode for the teacher working, for example, with engineering students on the techniques of lathe operations. The case study and the discussion group are likely to be selected by the management studies tutor who is instructing an intermediate management course in the principles of industrial wage negotiations. A formal lecture might be selected as appropriate by a teacher seeking to outline the structure of the English courts to students who work as legal executives. A seminar followed by a short video, to act as a revision tool, may be selected for the introduction of childcare students to some of the principles of learning through play.

The use of taxonomies of learning (refer to the discussion in Chapter 16) provides a more rigorous approach to planning and designing teaching and learning activities. Indeed, the scheme of work and/or lesson plan templates used within FE colleges often draw on frameworks such as Bloom's taxonomy. A useful approach for the newer teacher to consider when planning lessons, therefore, is to consider the domain of learning in which the topic is situated. In very general terms it may be suggested that:

1 Where the instruction is linked to outcomes/objectives in the cognitive domain, (for example, knowledge, comprehension, analysis and so forth), most methods of instruction may be acceptable. In the planning of instruction relating to those parts of the syllabus which involve relatively simple cognitive objectives (such as knowledge of specifics, terminology, conventions or translation from one level of abstraction to another) formally-structured lessons and the use of appropriate texts (textbooks, magazine articles, websites and so forth) can be considered.

2 Where the instruction is related to outcomes/objectives in the affective domain, (for example, valuing, organizing, conceptualizing and so forth), most methods of instruction may be utilized successfully. Where the outcomes/objectives are relatively advanced, such as those that require more complex ethical and value statements to be explored and applied (when discussing complex issues such as safeguarding the welfare of children or vulnerable adults within a health and social care curriculum, for example), the tutor may find that case studies, group discussions, student-centred group tasks and tutorials are most productive.

3 Where the instruction has outcomes/objectives in the psychomotor domain, hands-on approaches such as guided demonstration, the employment of relevant visual aids, the use of models, machines and check lists, will all be valuable. In particular, verbal instruction, based on demonstrations of skills, followed by periods of concentrated practice will be essential if mastery or fluency of a particular operation or procedure is to be achieved. This might apply to examples as diverse as decreasing the period of time in which a fractured gas pipe can be repaired in a workshop, a canvas can be prepared in an art studio, or a series of new steps can be performed in a dance studio. At the same time, it is important to remember that the pace of instruction will vary according to not only the type of skills being practiced, but also the aptitude and prior experience of the student group.

A note on outcomes and objectives

Course design requires that attention be paid to the precise sequencing of the topics that are to be covered (that is, the outcomes/objectives that have been planned). The acquisition of simple skills must precede the learning of complex skills: for example. The varying uses of the term 'objectives' are noted by Gagné (1988; see also the discussion in chapter 4), who differentiated their significance carefully. Lifelong objectives involve the expectation that acquired skills will continue to be used after the course has ended. End-of-course objectives set out the performance expected from the student immediately on termination of the course. Specific performance objectives state the precise outcomes expected from a student following completion of a unit of instruction. Curriculum documentation invariably specifies the exact type of outcome/objective being planned for when setting out desired levels of attainment.

Sequencing course content

The term 'sequencing' is used here to refer to the process of arranging the order of topics or themes to be covered within a module or programme of study according to some defined pattern or principle. The resulting sequences should be those intended to promote effective learning. Essentially this is a management task carried out by the teacher in his or her role as planner. The teacher will have in mind the purpose and content of a particular unit of instruction, the outcomes/objectives, the existing state of knowledge of the class, the resources and his or her previous experiences in arranging the conditions of learning at this particular level (or, for newer teachers, the experiences of longer standing colleagues or of external validators and examiners). The importance of sequencing for learning was emphasized by Ausubel (discussed in Chapter 6) who argued that learners' 'stability of cognitive structures' and their long-term retention will be influenced directly by the sequences in which learning occurs.

A common-sense approach is the basis of much sequencing in practice, although curriculum theory can also contribute to this process (this is discussed below). For example, it seems self-evident that simple skills have to be taught as prerequisites for the accomplishment of complex skills. Concepts with a relatively low degree of meaning are learned before the student moves to more advanced concepts. Generalities may be taught before specific examples are given: thus an overview will precede a detailed study. Much will depend on the subject matter to be taught: subject areas may have their own distinctive patterns, structures, relationships and inner logic, demanding the learning of one concept prior to the study of another. And such patterns are frequently found within the curriculum documentation that is provided by awarding bodies. In many ways, the approach that the teacher takes to the sequencing of a curriculum will rest on not only her or his professional knowledge and experience of the curriculum, but also her or his own experiences, as a student, of an earlier iteration of the same curriculum.

So, for example: an apprentice car mechanic will learn the correct use of different spanners before learning how to use a torque wrench. A student on a sports and exercise BTEC programme will learn about anatomy and physiology before learning about the impact of injuries on different parts of the human body. And a student in a hair and beauty salon will learn cutting and finishing before learning about hair extensions.

Historic approaches to curriculum sequencing

At this point, it is worth noting that such discussions are by no means a recent phenomenon. The German philosopher Johann Friedrich Herbart (1776–1841), one of the founders of the academic discipline of pedagogy, advocated a sequencing scheme over a century ago, based on the following structure, which can still be considered in course design today. It is based upon the notion of the 'reception of new ideas'.

1   Preparation. The teacher should arouse the students' interest in a manner which will lead to their being prepared to understand the new material which is to be presented. Their existing knowledge in relation to the subject matter to be taught should be called upon.

2   Presentation. The teacher should then present the essential new information by means of illustrations, examples, and so forth.

3   Association. The teacher should assist students to assimilate the new ideas through comparison with previously acquired ideas by a consideration of similarities and differences. The new and the old should be connected.

4   Generalization. The teacher should seek to derive general principles relating to the new material and designed to move comprehension beyond the immediate level of perception.

5   Application. The teacher should assign tasks involving the application of the newly-perceived general principles so that they are integrated with existing patterns of understanding. The solving of problems will be advantageous in this final part of the lesson.

Davies (1981) argued that, when a teacher has surveyed the material which is to constitute a unit of instruction, a general theme will emerge which will act as a link between sections of the intended lesson. The sequence will be a reflection of the general theme and aim of the lesson and will take into account the sets of relationships which constitute the structure of what is to be taught.

Gagné's (1988) prescription for the design of instructional sequences was based on decisions which must be taken by the teacher, concerning topics, lessons and lesson components. The general rule is to define aims by constructing a programme based on wide goals down to outcoms of an increasingly specific nature. These are then translated into the sequences necessary for their attainment. New skills demand the recall of subordinate skill components, which must at first be revised before being extended by the presentation of new topic.

Tummons (2012) argued that there are three different approaches to curriculum sequencing:

1 Linear sequencing. In a linear curriculum sequence, the different areas or topics that make up the curriculum are arranged one at a time according to the requirements of the programme. Typically, that might involve arranging curriculum units according to levels of difficulty. Once the module or unit has been run – that is to say, once the module has been taught, assessed and the results of the assessment recorded – then it is completed and there is no formal need to return to it. In a linear sequence, modules are treated on a standalone basis with no formal integration.

2 Spiral sequencing. In a spiral curriculum sequence, the different areas or topics that make up the curriculum are studied more than once. At first, they are covered at a relatively brief level, and then they are returned to so that they can be explored more critically, usually over a longer period of time. A spiral sequence therefore allows students to more quickly gain an overall sense or picture of the course being undertaken, thereby allowing students to learn in a more holistic manner, although there is a consequent risk that a spiral sequence can be seen as repetitive.

3 Thematic sequencing. In a thematic sequence, some of the different units that made up the curriculum would include core or key themes that would be returned to throughout the course as a whole. These central themes would be seen as underpinning all of the work that students do whilst studying the curriculum. Other themes or topics would be introduced, practiced or studied and then progressed from as the course ran.

In summary, the sequencing of instruction will reflect both the long- and short-term aims and objectives of the course, the nature of the subject area, the perceptions of the teacher as to the most appropriate learning pathway for the students, and the teacher's managerial decisions as to the most effective utilization of the time and resources that are at her or his disposal.

Theories and models of curriculum

The study of curriculum theory is a complex subject and lies beyond the cope of a general teaching text such as this one. Curriculum theory encompasses a wide range of models and approaches to theory and consider not only straightforwardly educational issues, but broader social and philosophical issues as well (Tummons, 2012). In the context of the current discussion, there are two theoretical approaches to curriculum that are of relevance to the teacher who is responsible for course sequencing: process models of curriculum, and product models of curriculum: these will be discussed in turn.

The process model of curriculum is associated with the work of Lawrence Stenhouse (1926–82), a British educationalist and researcher. In his landmark work *an Introduction to Curriculum Research and Development* (1975), he proposed a model of curriculum that:

1 contains principles for planning a curriculum, in terms of content, teaching strategies and sequencing

2 contains principles for researching a curriculum, in terms of researching and evaluating the experiences of both teachers and students, and the context within which the curriculum is delivered

3 contains a justification of the curriculum which stands up to external, critical scrutiny.

Stenhouse argued that curriculum planning should focus on the gradual development of the individual student and should be shaped in large part by the teacher. Curricula should not be overly prescriptive, and should allow for interpretation by the teacher in terms of both teaching and assessment strategies. Such an approach places a great deal of emphasis on the professional qualities of the teachers, therefore, who need to have sufficient expertise in their subject so that they can both act and react to the needs of their students. Aims and outcomes are seen as being overtly prescriptive and lacking in genuine educational value. Instead, students should be allowed to discover and explore the subjects being studied at their own pace. The process model draws on cognitivist psychology (as discussed in Chapter 6), which stresses that learning should be seen as a process whereby students learn how to think and how to make sense of things for themselves.

The product model of curriculum is associated with the work of Ralph Tyler (refer also to the discussion in Chapter 15), and his influential work *Basic Principles of Curriculum and Instruction* (1949). He proposed a four-part model of curriculum that addressed the following key points:

1 what are the education purposes of the curriculum? What are its aims and objectives?

2 which learning experiences will help these aims and objectives to be attained?

3 how should these experiences be best organized so that the curriculum is as effective as it can be?

4 how should the curriculum be evaluated? Which parts of it were not effective?

Tyler argued that a curriculum should contain a concise statement of aims and outcomes, which should be unambiguous and specific. As a result of the careful specification of curriculum aims, it follows that learning activities, assessment, sequencing and evaluation will be similarly precise in scope, and capable of being evaluated in a thorough and scientific manner. The behaviourist/neobehaviourist psychologies upon which Tyler's model rests (as discussed in Chapters 3 and 4) allow this approach to curriculum planning and sequencing to be aligned to taxonomies of learning (as discussed in Chapter 16).

Evaluating the course

In discussing the evaluation of a course or programme of study, we refer here to the evaluation of short courses, including those planned and mounted in response to requests from organizations within the area served by the college, special 'one-off' courses intended to meet a specific demand, and to the evaluation of entire programmes or pathways of study. The evaluation of specific sessions or lessons, of the assessment of students through formal examinations and of teaching staff through inspection processes, are considered elsewhere in the text at appropriate points.

The term 'course evaluation' is used here as relating to the programme of activities intended to produce an informed judgment as to the *overall effectiveness* of the course. An evaluation of this nature is not an optional extra: it is a key management function, designed to monitor aspects of college output, and to be viewed, therefore, as an important response to queries concerning the real cost, nature and quality of teacher performance.

The elements upon which such an evaluation typically include: the results of examinations and assessments (in order to ascertain the progress made by students during the course), and interviews with students and, where possible, their employers and representatives.

Evaluation of courses

Evaluation should take into account answers by teaching staff to the following questions:

- was the course content valid in the circumstances? Did the course content meet the needs of students, employers and other stakeholders?

- could there have been significant improvements in the range and quality of instruction, such as pace, style, sequencing, delivery or assessment method?
- was the utilization of teaching aids well-planned and generally adequate?
- were mechanisms for generating feedback designed adequately, and how was feedback used by staff? Was the overall rate of student progress monitored appropriately?
- did the level of class attendance (including finishing and retention rates) throw any light on attitudes of students to the course?
- would the college be justified in offering the course again, given modifications suggested by assessment and feedback?

The common sense notion that the ways in which teachers might plan to deliver a syllabus might not in reality be met, have a more rigorous expression in a further element of curriculum theory: the concepts of planned curricula and received curricula. The planned curriculum is understood to refer to the ways in which awarding bodies, colleges and teachers intend a course or module to be delivered. The received curriculm is understood to refer to the actual experiences of the students – and the teacher – as the course or module is delivered. Examples of the variables that might lead to a disjunction between the planned and the received curriculum include the avaialblility of particular resources, the time given over to the study of the content, the particular expertise or interest of the teacher and the ease with which the students are able to acquire the skills or knowledge being presented. These and other factors can affect the ways in which a course is delivered and, therefore, how it is received.

Summary: Planning and sequencing the curriculum

In carrying out the operations mentioned in this chapter – modifications to the instructional setting, planning, organizing and operating courses, selecting instructional strategies – the teacher is fulfilling a management role (as discussed in the preceding chapter). But this is not to say that such a role is not somehow concerned with learning and teaching. Indeed, he or she has concentrated on a number of essential tasks, has created structures which reflect teaching strategies and theories, and has taken decisions that will impact on the future delivery of programmes of study in the workshop or classroom – the very essence of managing the broader teaching-learning process.

Further reading

For the reader who is new to the study of curriculum theory and practice, there is an excellent essay at the *Encyclopedia of Informal Education*:

Smith, M.K. (1996, 2000), 'Curriculum theory and practice' *the encyclopaedia of informal education,* www.infed.org/biblio/b-curric.htm [accessed 15 May 2013].

Two well-established textbooks on the subject that relates specifically to the FE sector are:

Neary, M. (2002), *Curriculum Studies in Post-Compulsory and Adult Education.* Cheltenham: Nelson Thornes.

Tummons, J. (2012), *Curriculum Studies in the Lifelong Learning Sector.* 2nd edition. London: Sage/Learning Matters.

For those who wish to focus on theory, the following is recommended:

Scott, D. (2007), *Critical essays on major curriculum theorists.* London: Routledge.

19 Theoretical and Practical Approaches to Learning and Knowing

The cumulative effects of students' past learning experiences will invariably have a greater or lesser influence on their learning journeys within a FE college. The capacity to understand the present so as to plan for the future demands from students some ability to draw on past experiences; they can bridge the present and the future by utilizing their memories of the past. Whether memory exists as an active process or a 'filing cabinet' constitutes a rich subject of research. The controversy has stimulated investigation into what is inferred as happening when a student finds one topic easy to remember, but has much difficulty in recalling another. Increasingly, research has suggested that too many laboratory-based experiments into memory are proving less productive than research based on naturalistic study: the place to investigate student learning should be in the classroom, not the laboratory (Freeman, 1982; Lave, 1998). Researchers have preferred to investigate 'everyday memory', believing that the 'ordinary experiences' of individuals within their normal situations provide material for an intensive study of memory of events (Koriat and Goldsmith, 1996). Attention has also been drawn to the 'fuzzy' nature of the phenomenon of remembering, often rendering precise investigation difficult.

Analogies and metaphors are common in memory research, as in other areas of educational inquiry. Memory has been considered in terms of 'clay tablets' on which impressions and traces are made, and it has been considered in terms of information processing. Recent examples of educational research that draw on neuroscience use terms such as 'brain plasticity' to summon up an image of the brain as being flexible and mouldable (Goswami, 2004). Whilst considering such theories, teachers should keep in mind their own experiences concerning students who seem to remember easily, and those who quickly forget the simplest data. The theories presented below (as is the case with the other theoretical positions explored in this book) should be considered alongside those experiences.

Retention and recall of knowledge: The problem

'I revized the work with them only last week and today they can't answer a single question about it!' Statements of this nature must have been made in most college staffrooms at one time or another. They express the bewilderment of the teacher confronted by a class unable to recall the content of a recent lesson. For students, too, there is dismay in discovering that, although they can recall effortlessly the words and tune of a song heard (and never consciously 'learned') five years ago, they cannot recall lesson material committed to memory five days ago. It is a responsibility of the teache to arrange instruction so that knowledge *is* retained by the learner.

Three important questions are of relevance:

1 what is the basis of 'memory'

2 why do we forget?

3 how can the process of instruction be structured so as to aid retention and recall?

Memory

Memory refers to the ability to bring to mind past events whose characters, locations, happenings or materials are no longer present to our senses (Doyle, 1987). By 'memory' we refer to those structures and processes essential for most intelligent behaviour, including learning, by which a person is able to recall past experiences to his present consciousness. Memory has been described as an organized and integrative process combining both perceptual and motor activities (Smith, 1966), as a property, shared by a large number of living organisms, of storing information about past experiences so that these can be acted on later to improve the animal's chances of surviving (Evans, 1978), as the habit state of a subject that gives the capacity for correct recurrences of a criterion response (Adams, 1969) and as a term used to characterize instances in which an organism's current behaviour is determined by some aspect of its previous experience (Domjan, 1998).

There can be no learning without remembering; but learning and remembering are not equivalents, they are different aspects of the same phenomenon. To remember is to retain the effects of experience over a time; to learn is to retain information over a period of time. Hence, memory is implicit in all types of learning. In order to demonstrate that a student has *learned*, it is necessary to show that he or she has *remembered*, that the student is able to retain and retrieve information learned on a previous occasion.

Information-processing models of memory: Different theoretical apporaches

During recent years several models of memory have been constructed and discussed by educational researchers and writers, some of whom will be discussed below. A number of these models reflect an information-processing or computational approach (Bredo, 1994), which views the memory system as involving three sequential processes: registration, retention, and retrieval of information.

1 *Registration* comprises the perception, encoding, and neural representation of stimuli at the time of a learning experience. Perception involves the set of events following stimulation that occur in the brain's input part. Encoding involves the selectivity of registration: perceived stimuli are transformed into an organized, conceptual, and meaningful mode. Encoding processes may emerge as diagrams, images, patterns and so forth. The teacher should note that a student's motivation, attention, previously acquired knowledge, will affect the selection of stimuli for registration.

2 *Retention* allows the neurological representation of the student's experiences to be stored over a period of time for later use. (Hence, to forget may be considered as failure to retain that which has been registered.) Tulving (1983) therefore suggested that 'learning' is merely an improvement in the student's power of retention. By contrast, Domjan (1998) emphasized that retention necessitates rehearsal, a process whereby information is kept in an active state, so that it is readily available for use in the influencing of behaviour or the processing of other information.

3 *Retrieval* allows the student to have access to information previously registered and retained. It may be that the mechanism of retrieval is distinct from that which places information in the memory. Popper and Eccles (1984) suggested that 'databank' memory is stored in the brain, especially in the cerebral cortex, and is retrieved by a mental act. 'Recognition' memory then allows critical scrutiny of the retrieval; that scrutiny continues until the retrieval is judged to be correct, or is abandoned. Domjan (1998) suggested that retrieval cues or *reminders* trigger the processes of retrieval. These cues act so as to remind one of a past experience because they are associated with the memory of that last experience. Further, stimuli which were present while a previous memory was acquired (such as sounds or tastes) *may* become retrieval cues for that memory.

Memory, learning and forgetting: Different theoretical approaches

A number of different theoretical models have been proposed that seek to align theories of memory with theories of learning. The research that is described here is by no means exhaustive, but attempts to provide an account of a much broader body of scholarship that is of immediate practical interest to teachers in FE.

Waugh and Norman (1965)

According to this model, the memory cycle begins with environmental stimuli impinging on a sense receptor. Typical examples would be the reading of a webpage or textbook page, where the eyes would be the sense receptor, or listening to a teacher speaking, where the ears would be the sense receptor. These neural impulses are available for a very short time: no more than one second after the force of the stimulus ends. The sensory memory relating to the visual sense is 'the iconic store'; that relating to the auditory sense is known as 'the echoic store'. In the absence of immediate rehearsal or repetition, for example through the use of a classroom exercise designed to reinforce what has been demonstrated or explained, the effect of the stimulus will remain in the short-term memory for about 15 seconds. Where there is rehearsal, information is likely to be transferred into the long-term memory (known also as 'the secondary memory') where it may remain indefinitely.

This model has been used to underline a view of learning as 'structuring': the trans-formation of stored information into patterns which we use so as to interpret new experiences. New information is processed by reference to similar ideas stored in the long-term memory, and patterns of equivalence are established; the new units of infor-mation are examined for their content and qualities, and, where they seem to resemble in fundamental fashion aspects of existing structures in the memory, they are embedded into existing structures.

Atkinson and Shiffrin (1968)

The Atkinson and Shiffrin model involves three components: a sensory memory or store, a short-term store (STS), and a long-term store (LTS). The stores differ in their duration and storage capacities. The information in one's sensory memory (resulting from a simple sensory stimulus, as with the Waugh and Norman model, above) lasts only a fraction of a second. Such information will decay rapidly unless processed into one of the other two stores. IF attention can be maintained, then some of the information in the sensory memory is transferred to the STS. However, information may then be lost from the STS in about 15–20 seconds by a process of displacement or lack of rehearsal. If rehearsal does take place, however, it is then transferred to the LTS. Information in the LTS may remain there permanently, although it is subject to interference and a process of decay. It is the LTS which is of the greatest interest to the teacher, therefore; it represents the permanent

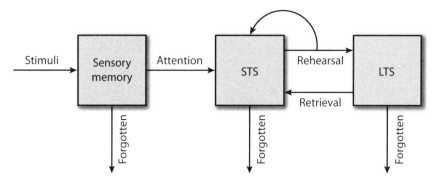

Figure 19.1

part of the learner's memory system reserved for information of high future use. A much-simplified diagram, illustrating the basic features of this model is given in Figure 19.1.

Baddeley and Hitch (1982)

The Baddeley and Hitch model of working memory was formulated as a response to the perceived over-simplifications of the 'short-term store, long-term store' model. The working memory is considered as short-term retention of information that is needed for successful responding to the task on hand but not for subsequent (or previous) similar tasks. It seems to operate where it is necessary to retain information only for the required period of time needed to complete a particular task. This may be exemplified by our retaining *recently-acquired* information, but for a limited duration. There are three components of working memory:

1 *Central executive.* This comprises a short-term memory store and an executive processor, storing information briefly. It is assisted by the buffer stores named below.

2 *Phonological loop.* This subsystem holds information through the aid of 'inner speech', such as when we silently articulate words or numbers that 'hang in the air' for some few seconds and are capable of being sensed by the mind's ear. Repeating a name or number while we search for a pen so as to write it down provides an example. Thus, the loop has been said to act as a slave system, serving the central executive.

3 *Visuospatial sketchpad.* This subsystem functions as a buffer store for visually- or spatially-coded information, acting as a useful form of mental representation.

Why we forget

Inability to recall or recognize may range in intensity from a momentary slip of memory (such as referring to a friend by the wrong name) to the functional disturbances of the memory such as amnesia, as a result of which the sufferer cannot recall immediate personal history. A variety of reasons for the phenomenon of forgetting have been proposed, and these can be briefly summarized as follows:

1 *Trace decay.* Trace decay is inferred from the phenomenon which is known as the curve of forgetting: simply put, over time, people forget more if the material learned is not practised. The amount which the student tends to forget does *not* vary in direct proportion to the passing of time – there is a gradual levelling out after an initial steep decline. According to Thorndike (discussed in Chapter 3), if actions fall into disuse and are not practised, they weaken and disappear from the memory. Teachers should, therefore, plan activities that allow students to rehearse and practice new knowledge and skills in order to aid remembering.

2 *Cue-dependent forgetting* refers to a failure of retrieval because the cues which were present at the time of learning are not present at the moment of attempted recall. There is a trace in memory, but the lack of appropriate cues prevents the learner's access to that trace. Provision by the teacher of *contextual cues* is useful in such situations, such as referring to a video shown in class as a 'trigger' for a conversation about a specific topic.

3 *Interference* refers to the inhibition of one piece of learning by another. Where the learner forgets something because of something else he or she learns *afterwards*, the effect is known as *retroactive inhibition*. Where s/he forgets something because of something else s/he has learned before, the effect is known as *proactive inhibition*. Most cases of proactive inhibition do not result from memory failure, but rather from persons remembering too much and responding on the basis of irrelevant information. In the case of retroactive inhibition, which appears to result from memory loss rather than mere confusion, disruption of practice or rehearsal plays an important part. The more similar the subject matter learned, the greater is the possibility of interference, resulting in forgetting. The importance of this finding for the planning of the teaching process needs to be stressed. Timetables should be arranged so as to separate as widely as is practicable subjects with a similar content. Further, in relation to teaching, since interference seems very powerful over short periods of time, the importance in verbal communication of leaving a short gap after a significant statement is based not on any practice of the art of rhetoric but on the need to allow time for some fact to sink in so that its chances of being retained by the learner are increased (Gregory, 1984). There is also evidence that trying to learn too much may result in forgetting, since the short-term memory may have a finite capacity (Miller, 1956; Schimmell, 1993). This, too, has significance for the planning of instruction, in particular for the timing and spacing of lesson content. Failure of recall may be the result of the teacher's understandable wish to impart as much information as time will allow, without taking into account the possible overburdening of the students' short-term memory. 'Mental indigestion' may be an imprecise metaphor; it draws

attention, however, to the difficulties for the student who is required to assimilate a large mass of material in a short period.

The teacher's role in aiding retention and recall

The practical experience of teachers, underpinned by some of the theory discussed earlier in this chapter, combine to indicate that the learner can be aided in tasks of memorization, consolidation and recall if lesson preparation and presentation take into account certain matters. These are considered under the following headings: timetabling, content, preparedness, presentation, and revision and practice.

1 *Timetabling*
The timetabling of a course ought to take into consideration the difficulties that might arise for the learner as the result of proactive and retroactive inhibition. Timetabling should space out similar subjects, should allow for breaks, and should not overload the student with long, unvaried sessions so charged with material that acquisition and retention become impossible.

2 *Content*
The content of the lesson ought to be presented not as an isolated unit but, essentially, as a continuation of that which has been learned previously. It ought to be associated clearly with the learner's existing stock of knowledge. As noted above, the provision of *cues* for the recall of relevant information is also an important contribution the teacher can make to the process of assisting retention and recall. Perhaps above all, the content of the lesson must be *meaningful* to the learner if it is to lead to firm retention and swift recall. Meaningful material is usually remembered more clearly and for longer periods of time than that which has little or no relation to the student's interests and level of learning at the time of the lesson. The statement couched in simple terms, introducing new concepts in terms of those which are already known or by establishing links or points of comparison with other ideas or concepts which are familiar to the student, has a higher chance of acquisition than that which goes outside the student's conceptual framework, thus making comprehension and retention very difficult.

3 *Preparedness*
Preparedness involves the teacher's explanation, in carefully contrived terms, of the significance and usefulness of the learning in relation to the learner's life style. Seligman has suggested that memory may be related directly to the learner's preparedness. It is for the teacher to *motivate* the learner in a manner which will arouse and maintain personal involvement with the topic which is to be remembered (this topic is discussed in the following chapter).

4 Presentation

Presentation of the lesson, if it is to aid retention, demands a logical, clearly connected and organized sequence. The short-term memory seems to be associated with the organization of information. Therefore, adequate rehearsal is important if information is to be retained more or less permanently. Where the parts of the lesson are organized coherently, comprehension, acquisition and retention of the whole ought to be facilitated since patterns are usually more acceptable to the learner than disjointed fragments. A 'warm-up period', particularly before relearning, is usually beneficial to the student's recall processes. Further, the student should be stimulated by the presentation so that attention (that is, her or his surface memory) remains focused on the lesson material, thus assisting assimilation and retention. Wherever possible, the presentation ought to avoid an outcome which is no more than rote learning. The teacher should aim, rather, at the achievement of insight and the understanding of principles which will facilitate retention. Principles are generally retained much more effectively than a mass of material which has been committed to memory without understanding. Note, also, suggestions that the teacher can assist memorization by making ideas stand out, such as through verbal exaggeration, or through underlining and the use of bold print and colour in a text.

5 Revision and practice

Assimilation, consolidation and retention of lesson content require recapitulation, rehearsal, periodic revision and review. The teacher's recapitulation at regular intervals of the lesson headings may help in their assimilation. Rehearsal – by which is meant an activity in which the students goes over the lesson material *by themselves* after its initial presentation (which may be equivalent to a repetition of the lesson's stimuli) – can take the form of reading a handout which contains a summary of the lesson's main points, working independently to complete a practical task that has been demonstrated to them, or studying and reciting one's own notes. Such activities are examples of the 'deep' processing which is said to improve the memory, in that it contributes to the durable encoding of lesson content in the long-term memory. Revision – which involves re-studying the lesson – should take place as soon as possible after the lesson has ended. It should be repeated at intervals and, preferably, be linked with assessments which examine recall. The final revision ought to be planned by the class teacher and could be the occasion for a full examination which will assess the level of comprehension and recall. Davies (1976) suggested that recall tends to rise to its maximum point about ten minutes after the conclusion of a lesson, and that this may be the result of the mind's 'putting material into focus'. A very steep decline in remembering then takes place and, by the next day, approximately 75 per cent of the lesson may have failed to move into the long-term memory. Frequent and spaced reviews of lesson content are therefore essential if learning is to be effective.

The assimilation of material presented in class and the building and maintenance of memory may be assisted by the process of its being applied in *practice situations*. In particular, where psychomotor skills (as discussed in Chapter 16) are being taught, practice ought to walk hand in hand with theory rather than follow on its heels. For example, the theory of the use of the navigational compass is of no real benefit or purpose to the student – and, therefore, of no real meaning – unless the student has the opportunity actually to use a compass in an orienteering, or similar, exercise. Therefore, the knowledge of how to use a compass will be best assimilated by the student who is able to participate in planned projects involving the practical use of the instrument. A course on animal care and management will not be able to provide meaningful opportunities for learning if the students do not in fact have the opportunity to work with animals in real life as opposed to watching videos or working with models.

Helping students to remember

Drawing on the preceding theoretical discussion, it is both natural and logical for teachers in FE to think about ways in which memory and recall amongst student groups can be improved. But it is important not to conflate this with simple rote learning. Through helping students to remember what they have been taught and shown or have had demonstrated to them, teachers can encourage deeper, more profound learning and levels of mastery and expertise. Slavin (1998) suggested the following positive methods: use of mental imagery (involving the visualization of 'vivid key words'); use of mnemonics; massed practice (learning facts by repeating them on many random occasions during a time period); distributed practice (repeating items at fixed intervals during a time period); part learning (learning and seeking to memorize the material, one segment at a time); and overlearning (involving practising newly acquired knowledge after the achievement of mastery). Fontana (1995) advised the following routines so as to assist consolidation and improvement of the efficiency of the long-term memory: repeating processes or explana-tions and questioning the learner about them; making instruction relevant, understandable and interesting; introducing practice into the learning process; and practising recognition and recall. Davies (1976) recommended employment of the following instructional tactics: concentration on the sequencing of instruction; attempting to stress key points by empha-sizing essential facts; organization of teaching material into patterns by the use of diagrams and charts; and stressing relationships between newly learned material to that which is already known.

Transfer of learning: Its essence

The importance of ensuring that students remember what they have studied – that is, that they learn – is not simply restricted to the accumulation of certificates and diplomas. If students do not remember what they have practiced and studied beyond periods of formal examination and accreditation, then the broader educational processes in which they had been enrolled would be called into question. Learning in colleges of FE, as in other educational institutions, may in some ways be considered to have meaning, significance and value only if it is related to the personal development of the student as a member of society. An important justification of the teacher's role in providing the conditions for effective learning must be, ultimately, *the value of that learning to the student in the world outside the classroom*. Training in the ability to transfer knowledge, to generalize from learned basic principles, to utilize stored experience in the facilitation of new learning, constitutes therefore, an essential factor in the education of the student. The driver for this can be most straightforwardly seen in calls from employers to ensure that upon leaving a period of education and training, young people are equipped with 'employability skills' and 'core' or 'generic' transferable skills, in addition to the specific skills, aptitudes and bodies of knowledge that they have acquired from their studies. An important task of the teacher, therefore, is the planning of instruction so that a high degree of positive transfer shall result wherever appropriate.

Transfer of learning

Transfer of learning has been defined as the extent to which the learning of an instructional event contributes to or detracts from the subsequent problem solving or the learning of subsequent instructional events (Royer, 1979). According to this definition, transfer of learning can exhibit a number of variations:

1   Positive transfer. Examples of positive transfer include the use of basic arithmetical processes applied successfully to a new mathematical problem, or dexterity in the use of a tenon saw applied to the use of a coping saw. Subordinate capabilities have been mastered (an essential factor in transfer situations) and applied successfully to more advanced and demanding tasks.

2   Negative transfer. The concept of *interference* (as discussed above) can explain the phenomenon of negative transfer. *Proactive* interference can be used to describe a type of negative transfer in which the memory of previous learning experiences slows down, or even inhibits, new learning. *Retroactive* interference occurs when the learning of new information disrupts the retention of previously held information; it is as if the learning of a new response extinguishes the old learned response. Teachers soon become aware, for example, of the phenomenon of failure in one area creating inhibitions preventing future learning in a similar area (unhappy memories of a failure in mathematics creating difficulties in the learning of some aspects of physics), or the learning of idiom in a foreign language driving out acquired formal rules of grammar in that language.

3   Lateral transfer. Examples of lateral transfer (prior learning affecting new learning at approximately the same level) are seen in the use of mathematics in the solution of problems in engineering, the use of underpinning theory in biology to diagnose and treat sports injuries, and the use of scientific method in the solution of a question in applied economics.

4   Vertical transfer. Vertical transfer (defined here as an instance when prior learning affects new learning of a 'higher' or 'more difficult' quality) is exemplified by the progress of the learner from the elements of arithmetic to the use of the calculus, from the use of simple tools to dismantle a bicycle to the use of more complex tools to build a bicycle wheel, or from knowledge of health and safety and safeguarding to the planning of learning through play amongst preschool children.

Critical perspectives on the transfer of learning

Formal educational provision, within not only the FE sector but other sectors as well, rests more or less implicitly on the notion of transfer of learning, which tends to remain under-criticized and under-explored. This notion can be seen at work in many different settings: in the assumption that a student with good GCSE grades will 'automatically' do better in their National Diploma programme than a student with lower grades; or in the assumption that if a student is a fluent and confident user of facebook or itunes, they will be able quickly to learn how to use a virtual learning environment. Sometimes, such predictions are borne out. But on many other occasions, such transfer is by no means straightforward.

One of the earliest modern critiques of learning transfer came from the American educational psychologist William James, in the early twentieth century. James (who taught Dewey and Thorndike, amongst others) undertook to measure the time he spent in learning 158 lines of a poem by Victor Hugo before spending one month memorizing a longer poem by John Milton. He then memorized a further 158 lines of Hugo's poem but found that it took him longer than on the previous occasion. Memory did not seem to be an independent faculty capable of being trained in this way. Similarly, Thorndike (discussed in Chapter 3) showed by experiment that practice in verbal learning did not by itself improve general learning ability. Together with Robert Woodworth, Thorndike went on to propose that the transfer of learning could be understood as being based on the theory of 'identical elements'. Transfer occurred, they claimed, if the two or more tasks being explored had common elements. The amount of transfer would depend on the number of those elements.

To a greater or lesser degree, the Thorndike-Woodworth model of learning transfer remains dominant today, not least as it is reinforced by theories of learning that assume learning to be an individual, mental process as discussed in Part 2 of this book. However, social practice theories of learning, as discussed in Part 3 of this book, raise a number of challenges to the idea that learning can be straightforwardly transferred. Research by Jean Lave (1988) into mathematics learning showed that adults who were capable of using particular arithmetic operations in their everyday lives (for example, when calculating costs and quantities during supermarket shopping) were incapable of reproducing them in formal examination conditions. Research by David Barton and Mary Hamilton (1998) into literacy learning showed that people who were fluent users of language and literacy in their everyday lives (for example, when reading about hobbies or writing and printing newsletters) were similarly incapable of demonstrating an equivalent level of literacy in formal settings. Research such as this has helped to foreground the importance of the setting or context within which learning happens and across which learning might transfer.

Summary: The transfer of learning in the classroom

Transfer of learning rarely occurs spontaneously in the classroom; almost always it is the result of a teaching strategy aimed specifically at transfer and emphasizing underlying principles. Such a strategy will generally involve direct methods of teaching and will include the practice of skills and the application of principles in realistic situations. Where the instructional objective is concerned with lateral or vertical transfer, the mastery of subordinate tasks is an essential prerequisite for success. Revision and recapitulation so as to ensure this mastery must have a place, therefore, in a transfer strategy. In particular, the identical elements of the transfer situations must be analyzed and presented to students in detail.

Several key studies in transfer have offered the conclusion that successful retention and transfer may depend on the ability of the learner to generalize by obtaining insight into the basic principles underlying her or his work (the findings of the Gestalt psychologists discussed in Chapter 6 are of particular relevance to these studies). Discovery by the learner of common patterns of content or technique has been said to facilitate the application of principles to novel situations. The necessity for instructional outcomes/objectives to be concerned with discovery and understanding if transfer is to be achieved, implies the need for careful consideration to be given to those modes of instruction which tend to encourage the comprehension of principles which will be applicable to new learning. Practice in a large and varied number of stimulus situations may be essential if generalization and transfer of knowledge are to result. The classroom teacher should remember two points: that generalization involves an understanding concerning relationships; and that training in when and how to generalize is of high significance as an aim of instructional activity.

Harlow's (1949) work on transfer suggests a further principle of direct importance for the classroom that is still of great relevance today. Whenever the positive transfer of learning takes place, then, according to Harlow, students are 'learning to learn' and acquiring 'learning sets' which facilitate their performance in the situations that they encounter in the future. To teach students how best to learn is to help in ensuring a degree of success in their task of generalization of learned principles. Thus, when considering the students who have finished their programmes in a FE college, it is not just what they already know and can do relating to their specialism that is of importance, but also their broader aptitude or ability to take what they have already learned and add to this when they encounter new problems or move to new environments. In this sense, it is indeed the responsibility of colleges to help young people learn how to learn. But it is also the responsibility of employers to accept that learning will need to continue once these young people are in employment.

Further reading

Knowledge and memory are fascinating subjects, and it is perhaps to be regretted that they do not enjoy a more prominent role within the FE teacher-training curriculum. For those who wish to read further, the following are recommended:

Duckworth, V. and Tummons, J. (2010), *Contemporary Issues in Lifelong Learning.* Chapter 7.

Gould, J. (2012), *Learning theory and classroom practice in the lifelong learning sector.* 2nd edition. Exeter: Learning Matters. Chapter 10.

Tummons, J. (2012), *Curriculum Studies in the Lifelong Learning Sector.* 2nd edition. London: Sage/Learning Matters. Chapter 6.

Wallace, S. (2011), *Teaching, Tutoring and Training in the Lifelong Learning Sector.* 4th edition. Exeter: Learning Matters. Chapter 7.

20 Motivating Students to Learn

The wide variety of student behaviours in FE colleges is generally taken for granted by new as well as experienced college lecturers. One student might work hard throughout her programme of study; a second may drift in and out, producing work of variable quality; and a third may view her course as of no value in her plans for the future and therefore disengage from her studies. The attitudes of these three students may be explained in terms of *motivation*, and different theoretical explorations of motivation are considered in this chapter. Practical suggestions will also be made for the establishment and enhancement of a learner's initial motivation in the classroom. The central argument made in this chapter, therefore, is that responsibility of the FE lecturer for promoting conditions for effective learning can be understood, in part, as being based around motivating students to engage in their specific programmes of study.

Motivation: A general introduction

Motivation has been broadly defined by psychologists as the phenomena involved in a person's drives and goal-seeking behaviour, and the internal state or condition that results in behaviour directed towards a specific goal. In the discussion that follows – and by extension in this book as a whole – the term is used in a general sense to refer to a person's aroused desire for participation in a learning process. *Intrinsic* motivation comes from within the individual. *Extrinsic* motivation comes from outside and is imposed on the individual by her or his environment. The initial encouragement and sustaining of the student's enthusiasm for learning (that is, the utilization of his or her power of motivation in the service of the learning process) constitute important tasks for the teacher. The harnessing of the learner's drive is to be seen as of paramount importance in learning, for drive is the basis of intrinsic motivation in the workshop or classroom.

The presence of motivation is considered by most teachers to be essential to effective communication and learning. Its absence creates conditions in which learning may be adversely affected or even come to an abrupt stop. Motivation arouses, sustains and energises students; it assists the teacher in the direction of tasks; it is selective, in that it helps to determine students' priorities; it assists in organizing students' activities. Teachers and trainers in FE are aware of the relative ease of teaching intrinsically motivated students and of the frustrations and difficulties that arise from sessions with students who, for example, see no link between their aspirations and the content of the curriculum that they are following.

The need for the teacher to recognize signs of declining motivation at an early stage is, therefore, of obvious importance. Low motivation can act as a stimulus to behaviour that takes the form of disruptive behaviour or even overt hostility, which may threaten class discipline as a whole. Signs of failing motivation may be perceived in any one or more of the following patterns of behaviour: poor attendance in class; a consistent lack of punctuality; arriving at a lesson without appropriate equipment, files or books; failure to participate in question and answer session; refusal to play an active role in class discussions; reluctance to take part in a practical demonstration; missing assignment deadlines; and open indifference to the accepted social norms of participation in formal education and training such as by interrupting a lesson with loud conversation or using a mobile phone whilst the teacher is talking. These are some examples of the kinds of behaviours or episodes which indicate a decline in student motivation, and which therefore require interpretation within that context.

Motivation: Theoretical approaches from psychology

Psychologists tend to speak of the concept of motive in terms of that which accounts for a learner's energy, direction and persistence of behaviour. As such it becomes possible to infer a learner's motives from observation of her or his use of learned behaviour, from the direction of that behaviour and from its persistence in pursuing and attaining a goal. A person's motives include those related to his or her physiological needs (such as hunger) and those related to self-esteem and ability to deal with his or her environment.

In addition to the well-known work by Abraham Maslow (as discussed in depth in Chapter 7), a number of other psychologists, from different theoretical traditions, have put forward other accounts of motivation that have been used to explore learning processes. Clayton Alderfer (b. 1940) reformulated Maslow's hierarchy into a new model (commonly referred to as his ERG theory) of needs based on three levels (1972):

1 *existence needs*, such as physiological and safety needs
2 *relatedness needs*, such as needs involving social and interpersonal relationships
3 *growth needs*, such as those needs relating to the development of human potential.

In addition to Alderfer's hierarchy being based on a need–satisfaction process it also incorporates a need-frustration-regression process. For example, where students experience repeated frustration in their efforts to satisfy some higher-order needs, they will place greater importance on the preceding lower-level needs.

Frederick Herzberg (1923–2000) conducted empirical research (to a much greater degree than Maslow) that was more directly concerned with peoples' working lives and job satisfaction (1959). He argued that motivation was affected by two factors, which he described as motivator factors and hygiene factors (thus giving rise to the description of his work as *Two-Factor Theory*):

1   *Motivator factors* are the factors directly associated with the content of an activity, and examples include positive recognition for the work being done, a sense of responsibility, and feelings of accomplishment. By extension, if these factors are present in the workshop or classroom, motivation will be enhanced, having a positive effect on learning.

2   *Hygiene factors* are the factors directly associated with the context of an activity. As applied to a workshop or classroom setting, examples of such factors are the style of instruction adopted by the teacher, the extent to which the learner feels welcome and comfortable, and interpersonal relationships in the classroom. When met, hygiene factors such as these prevent dissatisfaction, but do not necessarily lead to satisfaction

A different approach, from the Gestalt school of psychology (as discussed in Chapter 5), was proposed by Fritz Heider (1896–1988), professor of psychology at the University of Kansas. Heider, originally from Austria, was a pioneer of *attribution theory*, a theory concerned with the reasons why people explain events in the ways that they do. *Internal* attribution involves explaining a person's behaviour through reference to internal factors such as attitude or effort. *External* attribution involves explaining behaviour through reference to external factors such as environmental conditions. According to Heider's theory, motivation to learn can be explained through recourse to attribution theory. Students who are highly motivated equate success with their own effort (internal attribution), and equate difficulties with external factors that are beyond their control such as 'a difficult question' or 'bad luck' (external attribution). Students with lower motivation equate success with 'good luck' (external attribution) rather than their own effort or ability, which they perceive as lacking, leading to disengagement from study (internal attribution).

John Bowlby (1907–90) was a psychologist and psychiatrist at the World Health Organization. He conducted pioneering work into *attachment theory*, a theory which initially focussed on relationships between parents and young children but which since has been extended to explore wider relations between adults and young people. According to Bowlby's theory, the relationship that students have with their teacher is central to how the students behave in the workshop or classroom environment. Students with positive and secure relations with their teacher are more likely to feel motivated to explore and work in this environment with confidence, and be willing to take risks and make mistakes. Students with insecure relations with their teacher will lack the motivation to engage, and will withdraw from workshop or classroom practices.

Daniel Berlyne (1924–76) was professor of Psychology at the University of Toronto. His contribution to the understanding of motivation and learning (which continues to be significant to this day) came through an exploration of the role of *curiosity* (1960). He explored why people display curiosity, why they explore their environments, and why they seek out information and knowledge. He theorized that if people encountered situations that led to discrepancies between what the current situation might mean and what people already knew and could do, then a particular form of motivation would result, so long as the new situation was not so challenging that it might become overwhelming. In the workshop and classroom, Berlyne's theory is best seen at work when students are given challenges to work through or tasks to accomplish that are not too simple (otherwise not much can be learned) and also not too difficult (because they will be off-putting) – a concept that is easily recognizable to the practising lecturer.

Peter Jarvis (currently Professor of Continuing Education at the University of Surrey) has offered a related view of motivation to learn through his exploration of the concept of *disjuncture* (2006). He argues that when people encounter something about which they have no prior experience, knowledge or understanding (whether it is something that they have heard, something they have read or something they have touched), they experience a disjuncture which in turn becomes the starting point for a new possible episode of learning. He proposes that there are three possible learning responses to such a new situation or stimulus:

1 non-learning – for example, when people choose not to learn something new or rely (perhaps mistakenly) on something they already know in order to make sense of the new situation

2 non-reflective learning – for example, when people memorize or practice something by rote

3 reflective learning – for example, when people think about what they have learned, experiment with what they learn and problematize it.

Motivation: Theoretical approaches from physiology

The physiological mechanisms behind behaviour directed to the fulfillment of goals remain obscure, although research continues. Some theories, which have direct implications for teachers, are nonetheless worth mentioning here (an account of physiological research relating to learning more generally is given in Chapter 33). The concept of *homeostasis* (the tendency for bodily biological processes to neutralize change and maintain a stable equilibrium state) is associated with Walter Cannon (1871–1945), who was professor of physiology at Harvard Medical School. In his 1932 book *The Wisdom of the Body* he suggested that human beings sought to maintain themselves at an optimum level of functioning. Any imbalance (that is, any indication of the body deviating significantly from that optimum level) would result in a drive to correct the imbalance. Motivation would be the result of drive which arose from disequilibrium in the body's homeostatic process.

Clifford Morgan (1915–76) was professor of psychology at the University of Texas. In his 1943 book *Physiological Psychology*, he introduced the construct of a *central motive state* (CMS), a construct that has since been refined by other researchers. The CMS, Morgan suggested, was a function of neural activity, which is generated by stimuli, internal and external, and the presence of chemical substances in the blood. Eliot Stellar (1919–93), who was professor of physiological psychology at the University of Pennsylvania, suggested the hypothalamus (a group of nuclei in the forebrain) as the brain area which coordinated the stimuli producing the CMS (1954). The hypothalamus is of considerable importance in the control of the pituitary gland, the autonomic nervous system, and behaviour. Motivated behaviour, he argued, was a direct function of the amount of activity in certain excitatory centres of the hypothalamus. Activity of this nature leads directly to 'drive arousal'.

Donald Lindsley (1907–2003) was professor of psychology, physiology and psychiatry at the University of California. He suggested that the brain's reticular formation (RF) (a bundle of axons running along the brainstem, and responsible for controlling heartbeat, blood pressure, sleeping and waking) alerts and arouses a human being to specific stimuli (1957). It is involved, therefore, in activating and maintaining those behaviours assumed to be necessary for drive satisfaction. Control exercised by the RF over motor neurones, its influence on the cerebral cortex (responsible for motor functions), its control over sensory input are, according to Lindsley, at the basis of the involvement of the RF in the translation of motivation into appropriate behaviours.

Donald Hebb (1904–85), professor of psychology at McGill University in Canada, put forward a theory of arousal functions (1958, 1980). According to Hebb's theory, the 'cue' (the message associated with a stimulus) is transmitted directly to the brain's sensory areas along neural pathways. The resulting stimulation also activates areas of the brain through the reticular activity system (RAS). The RAS comprises the ascending fibres of the RF (see above), and stimulates activity and attentiveness throughout the entire cortex. Activation of the RAS defines the arousal function of a stimulus. For any specific activity there is an appropriate level of arousal at which the learner's performance will be optimal. At any given time the learner will behave so as to maintain the level of arousal which is near-optimal for his or her activities. Hebb suggested also that the search for excitement was a significant factor in human motivation: he argued that up to a certain point, threat and puzzle have positive motivating value; beyond that point, negative value.

Categories of motivation

Those psychologists who have been concerned with understanding learning have put forward a number of categories of motivation, or groupings of students' motives for learning. Four such categories are easily identified in current and recent literature: instrumental motivation; social motivation; achievement motivation; and intrinsic motivation. When considering these, it is important to remember that they are not mutually exclusive. That is to say, more than one category may be seen as influencing learner motivation at any given time (Biggs and Telfer, 1987).

1   *Instrumental motivation.* This type of motivation, which is purely *extrinsic*, is in evidence where students perform tasks solely because of the consequences likely to ensue, for example, the chance of obtaining some tangible reward or avoiding a reprimand. It is in total contrast to intrinsic motivation (see below). In the face of motivation of this nature, the teacher should ensure that the task to be performed is placed in a context perceived as constructive.

2   *Social motivation.* Students influenced by this type of motivation tend to perform tasks so as to please those they respect, admire, or whose opinions are of some importance to them. Rewards are of limited significance even if tangible; the reward here is non-material and is related in direct measure to the perceived relationship between the student and the person whose reinforcement activity (praise or approval, for example) is considered important.

3   *Achievement motivation.* This is involved where students learn 'in the hope of success'. David Ausubel (discussed in depth in Chapter 6) suggested that there are three elements in motivation of this type (1968): *cognitive drive* – the learner is attempting to satisfy a perceived need to know'; *self enhancement* – the learner is satisfying the need for self-esteem; *affiliation* – the learner is seeking the approval of others.

4   *Intrinsic motivation.* In this case there are no external rewards; the task is undertaken for the pleasure and satisfaction it brings to the student. It seems to be central to high quality involvement in a task and to be self-maintaining and self-terminating. Curiosity and a desire to meet challenges may characterize the attitude and approach to learning of students motivated in this style.

Motivation and the problem of perception of irrelevance

When course content is regarded by students as irrelevant and lacking meaningfulness (that is, when a topic under discussion or a practical task being demonstrated is understood as being outside the students' self-constructed boundaries marking out and separating the useful from the non-useful) there will be little motive to participate in the learning and teaching process. Teachers in the FE sector often equate the desire of the individual student to stay in education beyond the age of compulsory schooling with a full engagement with the programme that she or he has decided to follow. However, student attitudes (and, sometimes, the attitudes of lecturers as well) towards their studies are rarely so simplistic. Students working towards a level 2 Certificate in Basic Plumbing Studies may not at first understand why they have to learn how to work with sheet lead, but as it is a component of the syllabus, it is required that they do so. Students working towards a level 3 Certificate in Child Care and Education may not at first understand why one of the compulsory units of their programme requires them to have to learn some of the outline details of five pieces of current legislation that have to be adhered to in settings such as nurseries. And students who are working towards a level 6 teacher-training qualification for the learning and skills sector may not appreciate the importance of studying the theories and principles that underpin classroom practice.

Teachers and trainers cannot simply ignore attitudes such as these. Instead, some form of action is required, aimed at the creation or restoration of need, drive and incentive. Analysis of the situation in terms of the theoretical construct of motivation, and an interpretation of the problem from the student's standpoint, are essential.

To begin, there must be a full explanation to students of the *significance* of those subject areas that are perceived to be redundant, meaningless or otherwise unacceptable, in terms of content, its links with the curriculum subject as a whole, and its contribution to comprehension of that subject. At the same time, short-term goals such as the successful completion of assessments, the acquisition of professional skills and the award of a certificate and (if applicable) license to practice, must not be deprecated by the teacher in any way whatsoever. For the student they are, quite correctly, matters of much consequence. And remonstration based on appeals to 'broaden one's outlook' or 'the importance of extending cultural horizons' is likely to be resented and to go unheeded. It is not sufficient simply to state that students 'need to know' something: they need to be told *why* they need to know.

Therefore, a more positive approach is needed, and the role of the lecturer in such contexts is to establish links between the short-term and long-term goals of the student. This can involve both broader abstract notions as well as subject-specific issues. For example, the need to acquire professional competence and corresponding levels of knowledge may be of importance not only in order to complete the programme of study currently being followed, but also in order to maintain a license to practice after initial quali-fication, through continuing professional development (CPD) for example. It is important, therefore, to plan teaching and learning activities that will relate these 'unacceptable' areas to the students' existing levels of understanding, ability or knowledge. Thus, an explanation of the use of lead flashing on boiler flues would be of benefit in the case of the plumbing apprentices who question why they have to learn how to work with lead. The childcare students who do not understand why they have to learn about government legislation could be helped to make sense of what might be seen as an abstract theoretical subject through a discussion of the impact of the Early Years Foundation Stage on the day to day working lives of nursery staff. And the trainee teachers who resist the study of the theories and principles that underpin learning, teaching and assessment practice will hopefully (perhaps through reading books such as this one) come to understand that theoretical knowledge can help them to plan, design and evaluate a variety of activities and assess-ments for their own students. Teachers and trainers need to establish the relevance and authenticity of all aspects of curriculum content. In this way, the engagement of the students – and, consequently, a *deep* approach to their learning (discussed below) – can be encouraged.

Motivation in the classroom

An important task for the teacher or trainer, therefore, is to create a learning environment that relates the learners' activities to their needs and aspirations, so that competence is developed and strengthened and a sense of self-improvement is heightened. The teacher has to identify the motives of students and channel them into activities that accomplish the requisite educational goals. This will almost certainly require a combination of teaching techniques which will deliberately keep alive, utilize and strengthen the learner's initial motivation. These techniques need to take into account the following factors:

1 The individual learner's motivations and goals should be understood and the aims of the course should be clearly and repeatedly defined and explained to him or her. An expectancy of the performance to be achieved as a result of learning should be established.

2 Goals that are too hard or too easy to attain are neither motivating nor reinforcing when attained. Objectives that are challenging but attainable seem to be a useful motivator. Performance is probably most efficient when some challenge is essential.

3 Short-term goals should be explained to students in relation to long-term achievement. An excessive focus on unit or programme assessment should be avoided in favour of a broader explanation of the aims and aspirations of the curriculum being followed.

4 Lessons should be planned by the teacher and perceived by the student as part of a sequence eventually leading to the attainment of the desired ends.

5 Tasks set by the teacher should be appropriate to the student's level of abilities. Opportunities for success must always be provided. These should where necessary be carefully differentiated to take account of the levels of progress of individual students.

6 Attainment of a required level of competence ought to be explained and accepted, not as an end in itself, but as a key which opens the door to higher levels of ability, technical accomplishment, understanding and achievement.

7 Lesson material and communication ought to be relevant, meaningful and presented with enthusiasm, ought to arouse curiosity and ought to involve students actively and personally.

8 The level of communication (for example, in the use of specialist terminology) during a lesson ought to be pitched carefully so that there is no comprehension gap between teacher and student.

9 The fatigue which accompanies boredom and which destroys motivation ought to be avoided by a planned variety of teaching and learning activities.

10 A variety of motivating techniques should be used: variation of activities; encouragement of intrinsic motivation such as curiosity as often as possible; employ extrinsic incentives if considered necessary; and be aware of, and willing to acknowledge, differing levels of aspiration among students.

11 Understanding of topics discussed in class or demonstrated in the workshop ought to be assessed regularly. It is important to note that assessment can be informal as well as formal (as discussed in Chapters 30 and 31).

12 Feedback from assessments ought to be conveyed to students as swiftly as possible and ought to be interpreted in the context of immediate and long-term aims. Students should be aware of assessment criteria. Feedback should always be constructive and should provide guidance to aid future performance as well as judgement on past performance. (These issues are discussed more fully in Chapter 30).

13 Competence, mastery and progress ought to be recognized and reinforced by prise from the teacher or trainer. This can be done through both verbal (a simple "well done" or "good effort" can be surprisingly effective) and non-verbal means (such as a smile or nod of recognition, a thumbs-up sign, or similar). Satisfaction derived from the learning process is a powerful motivator.

14 Temporary failure ought to be considered by both the student and the teacher as an occasion for a fresh attempt to overcome difficulties. The teacher should keep in mind, however, that although the concept of 'learning from one's failures' may have positive features, some difficulties, including the disintegration of motivation, might result when a student learns from failure merely that he or she has failed. There is a high probability of a student who has experienced specific failure generalizing to the conclusion that he or she is a total failure. Careful handling of the process of assisting a student to learn from failure is essential. Positive assistance, intended to demonstrate that the causes of the failure can be discovered and overcome, is vital if motivation is not to crumble.

Linking motivation to learning

A student's attitude to learning is often dictated by her or his motivation, and this tends to determine the style, nature and direction of her or his approach. This is not to equate motivation with learning, however, or to consider motivation as an element of learning theory. Rather, it is assumed that motivation is a background factor in the promotion and encouragement of students' engagement in the kinds of activities that afford opportunities for learning.

The general direction of learning will require a strategy intended to produce the student's desired learning output. Researchers and writers in educational theory and practice have delineated two important attitudes or approaches to learning, often mutually exclusive, which feature extensively in the study behaviour of college students: the surface approach to learning, and the deep approach to learning.

1 The *surface* learning approach reflects extrinsic motivation. The student adopts a strategy of learning based upon her analysis of the syllabus so as to discover what she believes to be the key topics in her area of study. These are studied through the use of rehearsal techniques so that basic material can be reproduced with literal accuracy. Rote learning is often favoured. The learning task is not viewed as a whole and is generally perceived as comprising discrete units of study, associated in arbitrary fashion. Students using this approach tend to rely on reproducing memorized information to the exclusion of a comprehension of principles, and demonstrate a lack of interest in the background, and purpose, of their subject matter. Ideas are accepted passively, with little reflection on their implications.

2 The *deep* learning approach suggests intrinsic motivation. Student learning of this nature generally produces study strategies aimed at investigating the subject area in detail so as to obtain an overview of its significance and underlying principles. Hypotheses may be constructed and tested, the relationships of concepts are examined so that the student is able to perceive the logic underlying the subject matter. Learning of this type is accepted as resting upon previous knowledge, which is consciously reviewed so as to link it to what is emerging from current study, and the relationship of theory and practice is kept in mind. The context of the subject area is

explored. Above all, the student displays a positive approach to understanding what she is learning. The deep approach can be fostered and encouraged in significant measure by teacher guidance on the awareness of the matters noted below.

The metaphors of deep and surface learning are immediately recognizable to many teachers and trainers in FE, but in themselves do not satisfactorily explain the not uncommon phenomenon of the student who performs at an accomplished level in one area of their studies, and at a much less motivated level in another even though they are perfectly capable, all things being equal, of a greater level of engagement. The *strategic* learning approach is a term used to describe the ways in which students might move between surface and deep approaches. It is not understood as being an approach to learning in its own right: rather, it is intended to describe the ways in which a student might choose to vary the intensity of their work and their learning, according to their particular level of motivation towards the subject or programme of study in question. As a concept, it also helps remind teachers that those students who adopt a surface approach do not necessarily do so because of a lack of competence or understanding, as they may at the same time be engaging at a deeper level in another aspect of their studies.

In addition to the concepts of deep and surface learning, a further attempt to create links between motivation and learning can be found in *learning styles* theory. Learning styles theories offer – at first look – a more 'personalized' way of understanding student learning. According to learning styles theories (of which there are many – an issue that will be returned to shortly), each individual student in a workshop or classroom will have particular preferences regarding how they learn. Some may prefer practical learning activities, and others may prefer the theoretical; some may exhibit a preference for learning by seeing, and others for learning through listening, and so forth. Students can ascertain their learning styles preferences, it is argued, through completing a learning styles questionnaire or audit – a form of self-assessment that allows the student to identify how they like to learn best. Put simply, the motivation of students can be raised if the ways in which their teachers prepare and deliver their sessions in such a way that they can be matched onto their learning styles.

Learning styles theories purport to offer students and teachers a powerful way of exploring, and hence maximizing, student learning. They have at times been widely used across the FE sector, and students are asked to complete learning styles inventories as part of their programme of studies. However, the fundamental weakness of this approach is not difficult to ascertain, not least as there are so many different versions of learning styles theories in circulation (over 70). Only a minority of these theories rest on any serious educational research, and only a minority of them suggest that what the student should do is work to enhance those areas of learning that the inventory informs them constitute an area of weakness. At the same time, it would appear that the vast majority of learning styles approaches are not sufficiently valid or reliable as forms of diagnostic assessment, make unsubstantiated claims regarding their efficacy in classroom practice, and fail to take account of *what* is being learned (Coffield et al., 2004; Curry, 1990; Hargreaves, 2009). Consequently, this book rejects the use of learning styles models, questionnaires and inventories as tools for encouraging student motivation and engagement, understanding student learning and for planning lessons.

Summary: Learning and motivation in further education

The FE sector has historically been seen as the 'cinderella' sector or the 'second chance' sector – labels that invariably reflect the attitudes of people outside the sector who fail to appreciate it's importance and the contribution that it makes to the lives of the students who pass through it. One of the things that the FE sector does well is to take in diverse student populations and encourage high levels of participation and achievement. Motivating students to learn is not a straightforward task, but through careful planning and the application of an enthusiastic and positive approach to not only the student group but also the broader curriculum, and through taking the time to allow students to explore and understand why their programmes of study are meaningful and relevant to them, motivation – and hence learning – can be encouraged.

Further reading

For discussion relating to student motivation that contains a mixture of theoretical argument and practical advice, the following are recommended:

Kidd, W. and Czerniawski, G. (2010), *Successful teaching 14-19: theory, practice and reflection*. London: Sage. Chapter 14.

Wallace, S. (2007), *Getting the buggers motivated in FE*. London: Continuum.

For a more critical, but entirely rewarding, stance, the following chapter is also highly recommended:

Hayes, P. (2007), What's motivating students? In Hayes, D., Marshall, T. and Turner, A. (eds.) *A lecturer's guide to further education*. Maidenhead: Open University Press.

21 Managing Behaviour

One of the (many) responsibilities that teachers in FE have to consider is the establishment and management of workshop or classroom behaviour, in order to create appropriate environments for learning and teaching. The management of behaviour between teachers and students, or amongst students themselves, is – it is argued here – a necessary prerequisite for learning. The teacher's role in managing behaviour may range from relatively simple matters such as punctuality to more disruptive matters such as excessive and inappropriate use of mobile phones. However, there are no universally applicable rules: some students will be more talkative than others; some students will have genuine reasons for being late for class; for some students, disruptive behaviour may be a consequence of an undiagnosed learning difficulty; and some students will exhibit disruptive behaviours in the workshop or classroom as a consequence of experiencing more profound difficulties outside their college lives. Teachers and trainers in FE are not expected to be able to manage all such situations, but they do need to be sufficiently aware of them so that they can establish and maintain appropriate behaviour amongst their student groups.

The appearance in a textbook dealing with FE of a chapter devoted largely to behaviour management and discipline may elicit surprised comment (but not from experienced teachers in the colleges). Discipline is held by some to be a matter for concern only in the school context, not for the post-compulsory sector. A highly motivated student population in the colleges of FE, eager to participate in the courses that they have chosen, should not create the type of problem associated with a breakdown of classroom behaviour and discipline. Further, it is suggested, there is little point in discussing the problem of behaviour management and discipline with teachers in training: they will quickly learn from experience, and if they do not, they will not survive as teachers. Knowledge of how to control a class will emerge quickly enough from contact with reality in the workshop or classroom.

The first point suggests a naïve and idealized picture of colleges, which does not in fact stand up to close scrutiny. In fact, a relatively small proportion of students in FE experience behavioural and other problems which can and often does result in difficulties for the teacher attempting to exercise class control. Furthermore, approaches to behaviour management are made more complex due to the increasingly diverse age-range of students who attend college: the slow growth of the 14–16 age group in FE (which at the time of writing is set to expand in the near future) brings with it particular issues surrounding classroom management that are distinct from those that relate to the mainstream student body. The second point is based on the false assumption that one learns a technique best from 'on-the-job' experience. In fact, the opposite may be the case, not least as colleges of FE offer such different experiences to both trainees on placement and to newly qualified teachers (Avis et al., 2009).

Theoretical and practical instruction in the understanding and handling of behavioural and disciplinary problems in the college environment ought to feature in the work of all institutes involved in the training of teachers. Too often, however, requests for practical advice and assistance in comprehending and dealing with problems of class discipline (a matter of concern for many inexperienced teachers) are ignored or turned aside by the use of semantic quibbles seeking to equate 'behaviour management' with 'authoritarianism', by dogmatic pronouncements suggesting, incorrectly and unhelpfully, that the misbehaviour of students invariably reflects inappropriate teaching methods, and by erroneous assumptions that students who do exhibit disruptive patters of behaviour are so fragile that any attempts to correct such behaviours would cause irreparable damage to their self-esteem (Ecclestone and Hayes, 2008).

The view taken in this chapter implies that discipline and behaviour management have to be seen in terms of the relationship of factors in and outside the workshop or classroom, and that their maintenance is an essential element of teaching, without which effective learning is impossible. Procedures concerning the establishment of positive behaviour should be based on an analysis of a variety of problems, which can almost always be solved. This is not to deny that in some situations, disruptive or challenging behaviour does indeed indicate more significant behavioural, emotional or social difficulties. But it remains the case that for the vast majority of teachers and trainers in FE, the behaviour of their students will almost always be positive and if not, will be straightforwardly managed.

The nature of discipline

This chapter rests on the assumption that if student behaviour is managed appropriately, environments that are conducive to learning can be encouraged. Such environments require the establishment of *discipline*. In the context of FE, discipline can be taken to apply to group conduct held to be essential in the teaching situation and in relation to the personal development of individual students who comprise the learning group.

Discipline as a universally cultural phenomenon is considered as serving a number of specific functions in the growth process of young people: it assists them in developing those standards of conduct acceptable within society; it helps them to acquire characteristics of a positive nature, such as self-control and persistence; it assists in securing stability of the social order within which the young may achieve personal security and maturity.

It is important not to confuse 'discipline' with 'order'. Order is not always a reliable indicator of the presence of discipline. The informality and bustle of students in a motor vehicle workshop, with its apparent lack of order but based nevertheless on a disciplined approach to the task in hand, may be contrasted with the feigned attention of a group of ill-motivated students, apparently in a well-ordered class but, in reality, withdrawn from the positive teacher–student relationship which characterizes discipline in its fundamental sense. The trappings of a superficial discipline – silent students, instant obedience to a command – have little connection with the core of the controlled and disciplined instructional process based on a voluntary and active partnership of teacher and class.

The breakdown of discipline

A variety of reasons for the breakdown of class discipline can be enumerated. Their common factor is the provision of explanations of circumstances in which the management of behaviour proves ineffective, so that learning for the class as a whole becomes difficult if not impossible. In one way or another, lack of intrinsic and extrinsic motivation (as discussed in the previous chapter) may be discerned as being at the root of the problem. Where a student has no real desire to participate in the process of instruction, he or she will rarely enter the class in the sense of involvement in the lesson; he or she may withdraw, which can be expressed by silent non-participation or by active opposition to the teacher's demands. The student who does not contribute to the work being done in the workshop or classroom may in turn provide a role model which elicits a like response from other students. It is in a situation of this nature that discipline begins to break down.

It is important to differentiate those factors in and outside the classroom, which can be discerned in an analysis of disciplinary problems. Thus, a student's personal background and home conditions, parental models (perhaps adopted unconsciously), and educational history before entering FE are factors for which the individual teacher or trainer has no responsibility because they reflect an environment outside the classroom. Nonetheless, they may have an impact on behaviour and as such, teachers need to be aware of them as possible factors or barriers to learning. Similarly, membership of a social peer group with attitudes at variance with the ethos and proclaimed aims of a college may create behaviour problems involving students. Issues such as these have their roots outside the workshop or classroom, perhaps outside the college as a whole, but still have to be accounted for.

Some of the more important reasons for the breakdown of discipline and consequent manifestation of undesirable patterns of behaviour associated more specifically with the situation in the classroom are set out below:

1 *Compulsory attendance.* A popular assumption regarding students in FE is that because they have *chosen* to attend, any disruptive behaviour is likely to be minimized. In fact, the opposite is often the case. Moreover, this issue seems set to accelerate as new regulations regarding the age until which young people have to stay in compulsory education come into force. In fact, students may be in attendance at college through no real desire of their own. They may work in an industry that insists on attendance at college, or they may be sent to college by an enlightened employer, but against their will. They may be attending college in response to parental pressure, perhaps in response to the threat of being made to leave the parental home. This can result not only in those passive attitudes indicative of lack of motivation but also in active resentment of, and hostility to, the college, its staff, standards and work. This is not to suggest in any sense that the 'compulsory student' is invariably a source of discontent, for this is, demonstrably, not the case. It is to emphasize, however, the specific disciplinary difficulties, which can often stem from compulsory participation in an undesired activity.

2 *The college seen as an extension of employment.* Young employees may dislike their daily work, so that any activity thought to be associated with it (such as a class held to improve work skills) is also disliked. In such cases participation in college work, with its accompanying demands, may be resented and resisted.

3 *The college seen as a symbol of failure.* Attendance at a college course may reflect, for some students, their inability to obtain full-time employment which they want, which is interpreted as an attack on self-esteem. Resentment directed generally at society's failure to provide the kind of work in which students wish to engage is channelled towards the college and its classes. Alternatively, attendance at college and specifically enrolment onto particular programmes of study, may represent a 'second best' option for students who did not obtain the GCSE grades that would have allowed them to progress to their 'first choice' option upon leaving compulsory schooling (this is an attitude that is sometimes shared by parents, further diminishing the intrinsic motivation of the student).

4 *Frustration.* The organization, structure, demands and external trappings of the colleges of FE may serve to fan the spark of frustration latent in some students. Frustration may emerge because they see themselves 'back at school' in an atmosphere which may be heavy with unpleasant memories and because their expectation of being treated as adults is perceived as having been destroyed by a return to what appears to be the status of 'school pupil'. For some, the course content may be a mere repetition of work attempted unsuccessfully at school, with a consequent blow to motivation and self-esteem; for others, the course may necessitate work at an inappropriately high level and may be linked with standards and long-term goals beyond their comprehension and ability. Some may not see their programme of study as having any significance for their personal development; others may see it as forcing them

into a pattern of activity which has no relevance to their preferred life style. For some the course will appear unrelated to everyday work; for others the lack of a career structure or general opportunities in their employment can reduce the significance of their efforts in college. Frustration and boredom constitute a fertile breeding ground for uncooperative and aggressive attitudes in the classroom, as elsewhere; the withholding of cooperation from the teacher may be viewed as an escape route from an unacceptable situation.

5 *Distracting personal problems*. A student's anxiety induced by health, family, emotional or financial problems can result in both resentment towards and rejection of the demands of a course of study. In cases of this nature, the individual teacher should always help students to make use of the specialist counselling and advice services that colleges provide. Although teachers and trainers often act as a first point of contact when dealing with difficult situations such as these, it is important to refer to specialist advisers.

6 *Lack of confidence in the teacher*. Students' confidence has to be earned; it is not there for the asking. It will vanish, understandably, where, under the critical gaze of a class, a teacher or trainer is shown to be unprofessional, incompetent, ill-informed or otherwise ill-prepared for her or his role. A teacher's lack of interest in a subject, poor lesson preparation, or obvious discontinuity and muddle in a sequential programme of instruction, will not remain hidden for long. Their emergence often coincides with a decline of confidence in the teacher, which results in a weakening of class discipline.

7 *Resentment of the teacher as catalyst*. Often, but, fortunately, not always, the teacher whose attitudes and probing questions challenge accepted lifestyles may be viewed by some students as someone who challenges and then disturbs their understanding, opinion or world view in a manner that the students in question can find uncomfortable or disconcerting. Far from the teacher's questions and attitudes arousing an enthusiastic response in the class, they may be resented and may result directly in a withdrawal of cooperation. Such students may employ defensive tactics including the deliberate avoidance or rejection of the new information so that their inner stability is restored. Defences against learning such as these can range from rejection (where the student ignores the new knowledge and learning does not take place) to distortion (where the new knowledge is distorted into something acceptable) (Illeris, 2007).

8 *Breakdown of communication*. Where communication breaks down, control becomes impossible. An analysis of poor discipline will often reveal poor communication channels (as discussed in Chapter 13) that teacher and students are rarely in meaningful contact. Badly structured lesson material, inappropriate modes of instruction, or failure to monitor the results of teaching, can destroy communication and, with it, class discipline and control.

Principles and strategies for managing behaviour

Quite correctly, formal punishments of the kind found in school have no place in college life. A partial solution to the problems caused by disruptive behaviour lies in two processes: first, there is the critical appraisal of the situation; secondly there is swift and effective action in accordance with that appraisal. It is essential for the teacher to try to see the circumstances surrounding an episode of disruptive behaviour through the eyes of the student or student who are involved. Why should a talented student suddenly disengage with her or his studies? Why should a student of promise unexpectedly adopt a hostile, uncooperative posture? No answer will easily be found unless an attempt is made to consider the class situation as the student might be viewing it. Personal discussions outside formal class contact time with the student may assist in discovering the roots of non-cooperation. It is important, too, that the teacher views, as dispassionately as possible, his or her own contribution, if any, to the breakdown of discipline in the case of individual students.

Inappropriate behaviour or lack of discipline arising from frustration ought to be dealt with, where possible, at source. The student's suitability for a particular course should be reassessed and a detailed explanation of the objectives of the course and its relation to her or his career development ought to be given. Contact with the student's personal tutor or employer, as appropriate, may be valuable on occasions such as these.

Where college rules designed to help in the maintenance of class control and discipline are published they should be unambiguous, comprehensible and capable of enforcement. An important breach ought to result in prompt action. Rules which cannot always be enforced, so that a blind eye has to be turned to their being broken (such as 'a lack of punctuality can lead to exclusion from classes'), ought to be redrafted in precise terms or withdrawn. It can be helpful to draw up a set of class rules, negotiated between the teacher and the students, at the start of the new academic year or programme of study. Agree on what each looks for from the behaviour and actions of the other, and if possible, display it in the workshop or classroom.

It is extremely important, in relation to the maintenance of positive behaviour and discipline, that the teacher should seek to understand the class as a group with its own internal, informal organization. A class is more than the mere sum of its individual students: it is a dynamic group, often with its own unofficial leaders, its internal tensions, conflicts and crises, which must be acknowledged and understood by the teacher. The teacher who is able to view the class in these organizational terms and accept the inevitability of tension and occasional conflict (a task which becomes easier as comprehension of class structure becomes deeper) will find that the resolution of class management problems is made easier.

The maintenance of class control and discipline within a college as a whole is, of course, the collective responsibility of the entire teaching staff, supported by both curriculum managers and members of the senior management team. Lecturers who, in disciplinary matters, find themselves at odds with their seniors, and who are unable to count on their full support, are unlikely to be able to teach effectively. In the college context, behaviour management and discipline are social problems, demanding unity of purpose from all staff.

Reinforcing positive behaviour and managing students: Practical steps

There are no universal, golden rules for the maintenance of positive behaviour and discipline in class: if there were, there would be few unresolved disciplinary problems. Each problem requires a separate analysis and set of responses as it occurs. The following suggestions should be found useful, always provided that they are interpreted, not in a mechanical way, but in accordance with the exigencies of specific classroom situations. The strategies involved in class control must always match context, and must be in line with the principles embodied in statements of college policy.

1 Ensure, as far as possible, that the classroom conditions appropriate to your lesson requirements have been prepared. Seating arrangements are important: to seat students where they are unable to see or hear important parts of the lesson is to create an atmosphere in which order can break down quickly. Start and finish on time, and ensure that the aims of the session are clearly stated.

2 Prepare your lesson thoroughly (which is not the same as writing a thorough lesson plan). Pitch it at a suitable level so that an appropriate climate of participation is established. Make sure that you do not lower class motivation by demanding impossible standards. Ensure, similarly, that students do not feel degraded by being asked to participate in trivial activities which obviously require minimum standards only, or embarrassing activities that will only serve to make students feel uncomfortable and lead to their disengagement. Students who believe that their time is being wasted – no matter what the pretext – are unlikely to approach their tasks in disciplined fashion. Provide opportunities for success in class.

3 Where the aim or relevance of a task is not immediately obvious, be prepared to explain its meaning or significance. Discipline rarely flourishes where students are asked to engage in activities for incomprehensible ends.

4 Know your class. The tutor who has taken the trouble to learn the names of the students – and to use them – and to study their occupational backgrounds and prior academic attainments is demonstrating an interest in those for whose education and training he or she is responsible. Cooperation between students and their teacher can be intensified in this way, with a corresponding, positive effect on patterns of behaviour in class.

5 Adopt an appropriate professional style in the classroom, and keep to it. Students are rarely impressed, and often embarrassed, by those teachers who seek to identify with them by affecting an exaggerated or inauthentic style of behaviour which, they believe, will bridge the tutor-student gap or eradicate the distinctions between teacher and learner. Similarly, an austere, autocratic style may have little appeal. The general rule is – as in most matters relating to class control – aim at moderation. To be either too friendly or too remote is, almost always, to forfeit some respect, with marked effects on class discipline. To be oneself is probably the best guide.

6 Watch very carefully for early signs of trouble. Try to pre-empt difficulties. The teacher must learn to watch for those events which come before a more significant episode of disruptive behaviour or loss of class control. The loud conversations which continue after the tutor has complained of their interference with the lesson, the hostile silence which follows a request for cooperation, the continued failure to complete assignments, the record of unexplained absence or lack of punctuality – these are early-warning signals which tutors ignore at their peril. They demand swift assessment and action.

7 Establish learning momentum at an early stage in each session that you teach. Avoid over-long introductions to sessions and focus attention swiftly on the day's work. Keep up a reasonable pace of class activity and involvement. Periods of inactivity can produce the boredom which spills over easily into indiscipline: ensure that additional extension tasks are available for those students who finish their required work quickly. Check progress regularly.

8 Do not confuse the trivial and the important. Over-reaction to a minor breach of a rule can be counter-productive. (Consider carefully the implications of a policy of 'zero tolerance'.) Learn to assess swiftly the real significance of events in class. Studiously ignoring what is, in effect, a deliberate challenge to one's authority may be perceived by students as an admission of defeat; reacting intemperately to an unimportant attempt at provocation may be perceived as evidence of unreasonableness. Neither type of response from the tutor is calculated to maintain that respect for him or her which is essential for class discipline and, hence, for learning.

9 Take great care to ensure that you are seen as fair-minded and impartial. Favouritism of any kind, conscious or unconscious, bias and prejudice, will be interpreted by a class as an indication that fair treatment cannot always be expected. Demonstrably unfair treatment can lead to the withdrawal of cooperation.

10 When you have to issue orders, do so firmly and unambiguously. Ensure that your choice of words is appropriate and that you are only asking for something that can in fact be achieved.

11 The reprimand is the most common (often the only available) form of primary reaction to misbehaviour in the college classroom. The teacher must know *when* and *how* to reprimand. Reprimands are based on overt responses to unacceptable behaviour; they may be verbal or non-verbal (a gesture or frown), formal or informal. The precise form should be dictated by the situation, the nature of the behaviour, college policy, and the effect desired by the teacher. Useful rules are: do not over-react; use the reprimand sparingly; avoid expressions of hostility and idle threats; do not injure a student's self-esteem; consider the effect of the reprimand in the short-term and long-term on the student in question and on the rest of the class as a whole; learn when to ignore a minor, isolated manifestation of disruptive behaviour, but watch for a build-up of potentially disruptive activities; and reprimand firmly any important infraction of previously published rules.

12 If you feel that you have to impose a form of punishment that is approved within the college, ensure that the situation really demands it and that the consequences will be worthwhile. You must decide what constitutes misbehaviour and when it requires a firm response; your judgment as to the necessity for sanctions may vary from group to group, or student to student, but it must be based consistently on principle. The decision to impose a sanction (for example, in the form of a severe reprimand or a formal warning) is in no sense an admission of failure. On the contrary, it may be a perfectly appropriate response to behaviour which critically threatens the maintenance of a positive environment for learning class control.

13 Consider without hesitation the sanction (where it is available) of exclusion from class where the continued presence of a disruptive student threatens the wider environment in the workshop or classroom and consequently impacts on the learning of the rest of the group. Exclusion can be followed by discussions with the student and, where appropriate, a college counsellor. However, it should be noted that exclusion has been shown to be of only very limited value in changing student behaviour, and that students perceive exclusion as being used according to reputation – that is to say, those students who are perceived as being 'difficult' are more likely to be excluded (McCluskey, 2008).

14 Follow up all important disciplinary matters. Analyze what initiated and precipitated the breakdown of discipline. Do not confuse symptom and underlying cause. In the future, apply whatever positive lessons you have learned from a successful solution of disciplinary problems.

15 Know your subject. At first look, it may seem out of place to discuss the subject specialist knowledge of the teacher or trainer in the course of a wider conversation regarding the maintenance of positive behaviour amongst students. However, a teacher who is knowledgeable and confident in her or his subject is more likely to enthuse and engage her students than a teacher who is only 'one chapter ahead' of her class.

Behaviour contracts, classroom management and theories of learning

The ways in which a teacher or trainer will reflect on and respond to patterns of disruptive behaviour in the workshop or classroom will to some degree rest on the broader theoretical approach to learning that she or he subscribes to. For example: the use of a simple positive reinforcement strategy such as a reward chart rests on an acceptance of neobehaviourist approaches to learning and teaching (as discussed in Chapter 4). It will also rest on how the teacher understands student motivation and engagement (as discussed in the preceding chapter). If ways of managing behaviour can be found that also serve to support the motivation of the student, then behaviour can be seen as an aspect of the wider learning process. Indeed, social practice theories of learning (as discussed in Chapter 3) explicitly position the behaviour of the student as an important aspect of student *identity*, which is shaped by the student's participation in episodes of learning.

With these perspectives in mind, it is worth revisiting in more depth the concept of the behaviour contract, drawn up between a teacher or trainer and the students with whom he or she is working. Such approaches to behaviour management which seek to include students as partners, and thereby engage them more profoundly with the process, rest on a number of rights and responsibilities for both teachers and students.

Rights and responsibilities – teachers and students

1 Teachers must insist on decent responsible behaviour from their students: the wider community expects it, the college expects it, students need it in order to engage with their studies, and its absence will impair the process of education.
2 Teachers must accept that firm class control, maintained in a balanced form in order to establish positive behaviour, is both humane and liberating.
3 Teachers must be aware of their educational rights and responsibilities within the workshops and classrooms for which they are responsible, and these include: the right to establish environments that are conducive to learning; to determine, request and expect appropriate behaviour from students; and to receive help from other members of staff in the college when it is needed.

The rights and responsibilities of students are as follows:
1 students have the right to be taught by teachers who will help them to learn to manage their behaviour
2 students have the right to have teachers who will provide positive support for appropriate behaviour
3 students have the right to choose how to behave with full understanding of the consequences that automatically follow their choice (for example, knowing that if they choose to behave in a disruptive fashion, then they are in effect choosing to remove themselves from their studies).

Working with younger learners: 14–16s in further education

At the time of writing, groups of younger students have been attending FE colleges, in different parts of the country, for about a decade. Over the last ten years, and particularly since the change of government in 2010, the policy background to 14–16 and 14–19 provision has changed drastically and at the present time, it is anticipated that the number of 14–16 students who attend FE colleges is expected to increase. This poses particular problems for teachers and trainers in FE, not least as many of them have chosen to work in colleges, as post-compulsory institutions, specifically in order to engage with a body of students who they perceive as attending on a voluntary basis and therefore as being more engaged with their studies.

Over time, it has been shown that for those students aged 14–16 who have attended a FE college, the experience is a positive one (although up to now, this has predominantly been on a part-time basis). But whilst the students responded positively to an environment that treated them as 'adults' rather than as 'children', college staff did not feel adequately prepared to manage any behavioural problems that might occur (Harkin, 2006). Nonetheless, there are a number of factors that can be identified as potentially impacting on the learning of 14–16s in FE colleges, with consequences for engagement, motivation and, therefore, behaviour (Atkins, 2009; Tummons, 2010a):

- Nervousness. Starting a new course or programme of study is never easy. Starting in a new institution, which is quite different from a school, may be an additional pressure.

- Apathy. Some 14–16s have found their way onto the vocational curriculum as a consequence of disengagement with the National Curriculum. That is to say, attending college may not have been a positive or meaningful choice, but one which has been imposed on them.

- A feeling of failure. For some students (including 16–19s as well as 14–16s) enrolment onto a college course might reinforce those wider societal attitudes regarding the vocational curriculum as being 'second best' in comparison to the academic curriculum.

- Hostility. Some 14–16s may have negative attitudes towards learning. This might relate to their own self-esteem and belief about their own abilities, or their attitudes towards teaching staff. These attitudes may be the consequence of disengagement at school.

- Specific learning needs. A surprising number of learners, upon entering FE, go on to receive diagnostic assessments (these are discussed in Chapter 30) for specific learning needs such as dyslexia or dyspraxia which have been previously undiagnosed but which have contributed to previous disengagement from education.

In many ways, therefore, the behaviour of 14–16s in FE can be seen as being shaped by similar external pressures as the behaviour of 16–19s. For these younger students, however, their relative physiological immaturity and state of development may also be a factor in influencing their behaviour. For example, young people continue their neurological development during their teenage years and as such their decision-making faculties are not yet fully matured leading to – at times – erratic behaviour and confusion (Duckworth et al., 2012). This relative immaturity needs to be borne in mind by the teacher, as does the different status of younger learners, as opposed to mainstream FE students, when considering how to manage behaviour. For 14–16s, obligations of care are quite different and these students cannot, for example, be straightforwardly excluded from class because they need to be under adult supervision at all times.

Summary: managing behaviour in further education

The central assumption of this book is that the majority of students in FE colleges will be a joy to work with and to teach. This book also assumes that from time to time the teacher or trainer may encounter patterns of disruptive behaviour that need to be managed in order to establish the discipline that is required for successful learning. What counts as acceptable behaviour may vary somewhat between departments, for example, in whether or not students should be allowed to listen to music as they work. But more widely applicable expectations – of effort, of courtesy, of punctuality and mutual respect for both fellow students and for teachers, and of a willingness to take responsibility for one's own behaviour and progress – are to be encouraged in the FE sector as an essential element of wider preparation for life, future study, or future employment.

Further reading

The following are all recommended for further study:

Duckworth, V., Flanagan, K., McCormack, K. and Tummons, J. (2012), *Understanding Behaviour 14+*. Maidenhead: McGraw Hill.

Kidd, W. and Czerniawski, G. (2010), *Successful teaching 14-19: theory, practice and reflection*. London: Sage. Chapter 11.

Peart, S. and Atkins, L. (2011), *Teaching 14-19 learners in the lifelong learning sector*. Exeter: Learning Matters. Chapter 5.

Vizard, D. (2012), *How to manage behaviour in further education*. London: Sage.

22 Working with Adult Learners

The term 'adult learner' is a commonly recognized one, although changing political and social fashions have led to a proliferation of terms to describe those students in formal education or training who are adults. "Adult learners", "mature students", "non-traditional students", and "adult returners" are all terms that have slightly different meanings and are in current use. Clearly it is very difficult to find a single, satisfactory descriptor for such a diffuse group of students. Full-time students aged 16–19 are clearly not 'adult learners': but in what ways does a 21-year-old count as an 'adult learner' that would not be equally applied to a 20-year-old? Some courses and funding bodies stipulate that 24 is the age at which a student is classified as a 'mature student'. Adult learning theories (these will be returned to shortly) glibly refer to the adult learner as distinct from the child learner, but with little unity amongst the theorists concerned over when this state of adulthood is reached, let alone whether or not 'adulthood' is itself a single, unchanging stage of the lifespan (notions of 'third age' learning being the most well-known example (Illeris, 2007)). Perhaps the most acceptable thing to do in the current social milieu of self-advocacy and ownership is to assume that any adult who is in either part-time or full-time education and who wishes to refer to himself or herself as an adult learner is one. Or perhaps it is simply safer to acknowledge that it is indeed a nebulous term, yet one which for the majority of teachers and trainers in FE colleges there is a great deal of shared recognition and understanding of. Many practitioners recognize the different pedagogic approaches that are required when working with adult learners: the aim of this chapter, therefore, is to not only explore some of the ways in which such approaches can be critically understood, but also to analyze some of the myths and stereotypes that persist in regard to adult learners, as well as proposing learning and teaching strategies.

Over the last two decades, the profile and presence of adult learners have changed considerably not only in FE colleges, but across wider adult education provision as well. As a consequence of subsequent reforms to the funding of part-time provision, the evolving nature of the FE curriculum and different patterns of employment, both the kinds of courses offered as well as the profiles of the adult learners who might enrol on them, has changed. The simple divisions between daytime provision for 16–19 full-time students and evening provision for adults, or between accredited vocational and technical courses and recreational or leisure courses, no longer apply. Indeed, even what is left of what used to be called recreational adult education or community education, often accommodated within FE colleges, is now formally assessed – a process that is, arguably, in opposition to broader traditions in adult education (Jarvis, 2004; Wallis, 1996). Nonetheless, there are clearly identifiable areas of the curriculum that are designed to address the education and training needs of people who are retraining, seeking a new career or updating their professional skills. Students on such courses (which can range from professional courses for book keepers and accountants to courses that are less obviously linked to employment, such as millinery) tend to be adult learners.

Teaching the adult learner often presents a variety of unique problems. The 30–year-old engineering supervisor attending a college-based short management course requires a learning and teaching environment and programme specification which will differ from what is considered appropriate for the 17–year-old BTEC level student; the professional workers who may form the majority of enrolments for an evening course on political affairs, will present problems and opportunities for their tutor which differ from those related to the day-class students, whose average age is 18. In this chapter we comment on some important matters concerning the adult learner – the use of theory to explore aspects of adult learning (including theories that purport to focus specifically on the learning of adults), instructional strategies and the management of the learning process.

In considering the contribution which can be made by the colleges of FE to the life of adult learners, it is worth keeping in mind the work of Basil Yeaxlee who worked alongside other important adult educators such as Albert Mansbridge (founder of the Workers' Educational Association) and the economic historian Richard Henry Tawney in the middle of the twentieth century. Yeaxlee, who finished his career at Mansfield College Oxford, argued that the *social* reasons for fostering the concept of lifelong education are as powerful as the personal (1929). To that notion, a further sentiment might also be added: namely, that these social reasons are as powerful as the economic.

Defining the 'adult learner': Approaches from Lifespan Psychology

The age at which a student is classified as belonging to the 'older' age group seems to be quite arbitrary. Terms such as 'young person' and 'adult' have a variety of meanings when used in the different literatures of educational administration, research and policy. Simply defining an adult learner as being beyond the 16–19 demographic seems to be rather unsatisfactory; not least as it is patently not the case that the behaviours and practices of learners suddenly undergo a qualitative change upon their twentieth birthdays. Therefore, if research or policy discourses cannot agree on a single age at which a student becomes an 'adult student', it seems appropriate to consider a theoretical model that might allow a meaningful categorization or distinction to be made.

Lifespan Psychology constitutes a body of research that focuses on the identification and demarcation of different stages of life, and demonstrates that people at different stages of life have different motivations and contexts for their actions and – consequently – different reasons for engaging in education and training (Sugarman, 2001). According to lifespan psychology, the phase of life which is called *adulthood* is characterized by the following (although these are not necessary conditions – an individual does not necessarily need to have 'achieved' all of these states in order to be considered an adult):

1 The individual has moved out from their childhood home and has taken responsibility for their own life project (that is, establishing a home of their own, engaging in independent, self-directed social activities and so forth).

2 The individual has established or looks to establish a long-term relationship with a partner and perhaps also with children.

3 The individual has completed their basic, compulsory, stage of education or training, which might include having gained qualifications relating to a specific occupation or profession.

4 The individual is aspiring to a more or less permanent position of employment (depending on the nature of the qualifications already achieved).

5 Both family and work conditions are subject to change (for example, family conditions might change if the individual has to take on the role of primary carer for an elderly or infirm relative; work conditions might change due to fluctuations in both regional and national economic conditions).

Mindful of the fact that any set of pre-established criteria that attempt to define a person or group of people is always imperfect and should be treated as such (for example, an adult may have a secure career route but still live in their parents' home), it is this definition of adulthood that is used to define the 'adult learner' in the present discussion.

Understanding the adult learner: Approaches from Perceptual Theory

Perceptual Theory is built on the concept of our perceptions as the only reality we can know, and the main purpose of our activities as control of the state of our perceived world (Coombs and Snygg, 1959). Thus, according to perceptual theory, human behaviour is characterized as 'the control of perception'. Therefore, how people view their environment – the people, things and events with whom and with which they are involved – will affect their behaviour to a significant degree. The older person's perception of his or her world must differ, in general, from that of the younger person. In particular, the adult's past experiences, which are represented in the totality of his or her past and present perceptions, will be of a different quality from those of the younger person. Adults' previous experiences in other groups will influence the way in which they engage in learning and that the most important single factor influencing new adult learning is what has been already learned and organized in conceptual structures (Jarvis, 2004; Lovell, 1984).

The determinants of older people's perceptions include their values, beliefs, attitudes, needs and self-experiences. Their feelings concerning their preferred way of life and what they consider to be of lasting value, will affect their perception of their present environment. In the same way, their view of reality will be coloured by their beliefs in the worth of others and of themselves. For the adult, there may be two limits to educational growth: the real practical limit of one's maximum ability or potential capacity and the no less real psychological limit which each person places on themselves. Consequently, it is often the case that adult learners tend to underestimate their abilities and may often experience difficulties with tasks requiring the interpretation of complex instructions, where such instructions are perceived as a barrier (Kidd, 1975; Lovell, 1984; Rogers 2002; Rogers 2007).

Perceptions of threat or discomfiture from the outside world are understood as having particular relevance for an understanding of the educational difficulties that can impact on the engagement and learning of adult learners (Rogers 2002; Verduin, 1978). Threat is defined in this context as the perception of an imposed force requiring a change in behaviour, values or beliefs. One of the greatest threats to people is the requirement to change behaviour when beliefs, values or needs remain unchanged. Adult learners may often feel threatened when forced to alter the ways in which they attempt to maintain their self-organization: a typical example would be the requirement to retrain in order to maintain employment as a consequence of changes to working conditions. The teacher of the adult learner ought to consider, first, the removal of any perceptions of threat from the teaching environment. Feelings of safety and security should not be attacked and destroyed; a mere perception of external threat to wellbeing will put adult learners on the defensive. The self-image of the older person is peculiarly susceptible to perceived dangers stemming from suggestions of the need for fundamental change; hence the somewhat autocratic, highly defensive attitude towards younger students (and teachers) often adopted by the adult learner. The teacher should attempt where necessary to modify the interpretation of past experiences; those experiences remain the same, but the way in which students interpret them can be changed. Clarification of the environment, of needs, attitudes, values and their interrelationships is an important task for the teacher, who has to assist the adult learners to perceive their goals and their significance, and to perceive their experiences as a potential asset for learning. They will learn in response to their own needs and perceptions, not those of their teachers.

Understanding the adult learner: Approaches from learning theory

Malcolm Knowles (who popularized the term 'andragogy' as meaning the art and science of assisting adults to learn) argued that adult learners are affected by changes in self-concepts, and, as they have matured, they have become generally more self-directed, that they have built up valuable stores of mental resources as a result of experience, that they have a high degree of readiness to pursue learning in areas which they perceive as relevant to their lives, that they have developed their own learning styles, based upon their having become increasingly problem-centred, and that they are oriented to general learning, resulting in a high degree of intrinsic motivation. Knowles' work can be summed up according to the following six key concepts:

Knowles' six concepts

1. adults need to know why they are need to learn something before the learning process can begin
2. because adults are responsible for their own lives, this self-concept of autonomy is extended to learning. As such, adults show a preference for *self-directed learning*
3. adults come to learning and education with a wealth of life experience which can – and should – form a basis or foundation for their future learning
4. for adults to learn, the relevance of what is being learned needs to be clear and unambiguous. The motivation of adult learners rests on the real-world application of what is being learned
5. adult learners are more engaged with learning that is centred around problem-solving, rather than around bodies of knowledge or content
6. adults are motivated to learn more by intrinsic rather than extrinsic factors.

Challenges to Knowles

There are also a number of challenges to Knowles' theory (Davenport 1993; Jarvis, 2010):

1. Knowles' work is based on assumptions, not empirical research. Knowles did not engage in any serious educational research in formulating his conception of andragogy, which rests predominantly on a philosophical rather than empirical position.

2   Andragogy is therefore not a theory. The lack of any systematic inquiry based on empirical research prevents andragogy from being taken seriously as theory. At best, it represents a framework or, perhaps, an ideology, concerning the ways in which adults ought to be taught.

3   Claims regarding andragogy rest on an inadequate understanding of pedagogy. The positioning by Knowles of andragogy as an 'opposite' to pedagogy rests on a narrow, and arguably incorrect, understanding of pedagogy that does not take into account contemporaneous constructivist and social constructivist approaches to the learning of children.

Even at an anecdotal level the problems with andragogy as a concept quickly emerge. Knowles does not define the moment when a learner stops being a child and start being an adult. How should contemporary practitioners in the lifelong learning sector define 14–16 learners in FE colleges – as children, or as adults? Are all adult learners 'the same', equally capable of self-directed learning that rests on their own experience? There are some areas of education research that have more or less intentionally challenged the kinds of ideas about adult learning that have been listed above. To take one example: the adult as a self-directed learner who can learn how to learn. Research about the ways in which young people learn how to play multi-player video games, involving complex game architectures, rules and discourses, would suggest that these processes of learning are indeed self-directed and involve learning how to learn (Gee, 2004). And yet, many such game players (though by no means all) would not, in a formal educational setting, be classified as adult learners.

Although andragogy continues to be widely referred to in some circles, the argument presented here is that as a theory, it lacks sufficient empirical scholarship and authority to be taken seriously (Thomas, 2007). At the same time, there are other, more robust theoretical models and concepts in current use, and there are a number of common themes that can be drawn out from related literature (Morgan-Klein and Osborne, 2007; Osborne et al., 2007; Tusting and Barton, 2003):

Adult learning: theoretical assumptions

1   adults can learn how to learn: tutors can facilitate this process in order to make learning more effective and meaningful

2   adult learning is self-directed: that is, adults are or have the potential to be autonomous learners

3   adult learning is purposeful: adults choose to learn for reasons to do with their lives outside the classroom or workshop

Problems of learning experienced by the adult learner

The process of ageing brings problems and opportunities for the student. In the case of adult learners, their experiences have multiplied, have been interpreted and reinterpreted and their perceptions of the world may have changed radically. Their rate of learning – but not their efficiency of learning – may have slowed down. Their intensity of motivation – but not necessarily the requisite skills and abilities – may have been heightened. They may experience some difficulty in recalling isolated facts, but they have often acquired the technique of perceiving conceptual wholes. In sum, the adult learner brings to the process of learning a variety of abilities and previously acquired skills, together with some handicaps, none of which is of an insuperable nature.

The adult learner will probably have experienced some deterioration in physical agility, in the acuity of his or her senses, in certain intellectual abilities, and in short-term memory. Where learning tasks involve speed, the adult learner may be at a disadvantage; time may have acquired a particular significance for him or her, so that he or she will be more concerned with accuracy and precision and will tend to work more slowly. Problems in retrieving stored information, arising largely because of lack of rehearsal, may make tasks of memorization increasingly difficult. (It often becomes necessary for the tutor to convince the adult learner by demonstration that one's long-term memory does not undergo inevitable, swift and irreversible decline as one grows older.) His or her patterns of coordination, rhythm and fluidity, acquired during a process of skills training, may have deteriorated; creativity and flexibility of mind, associated with discovering solutions to problems, may have apparently diminished.

The adult learner's awareness of a decline in some abilities and associated skills can be mirrored in a lack of confidence and a growth in anxieties. Therefore, the teacher or trainer will need to establish a learning environment which will minimize anxieties and improve confidence. As his or her level of achievement moves to a plateau which can presage swift decline, the older learner, conscious of self-image, becomes much more cautious, and can be easily disheartened by temporary failures; hence the need for appropriately-designed courses which will help adult learners to compensate for perceived deficiencies. Often, older learners tend to resist change, are initially suspicious of novelty and do not always welcome innovation. They may be highly critical of teachers, who may be perceived as lacking the 'practical experience' which the older learner sometimes considers as the root of all worthwhile knowledge.

Specific anxieties related to particular subject areas (such as mathematics or information and learning technology) and situations (such as formal examinations and other activities involving negative comparisons with one's peers) may affect the performance of adult students. One result may be a pronounced reluctance to engage in discussion in the seminar room or workshop; another may be continuous distraction from the learning task. Some educational theorists have suggested that this may stem from a 'mobilization of personal defences' and a resulting strain on the learning faculties. The teacher's reaction should take the form of choosing a mode of instruction which will ensure that the adult learner is provided with the competence needed for the programme of study; special introductory classes based on revision of fundamental techniques will be advantageous. In addition, the adult learner should be made aware of the nature of the learning process; this ought to figure prominently in the early stages of the course. To be aware of one's learning processes is understood by many practitioners as well as researchers as being a prerequisite for learning to learn.

It has to be remembered that adult learners are frequently highly – and diversely – motivated learners. Often they will be attending a course of study simply because of a desire to study, or because of a perception that their own advancement is dependent on the acquisition of further knowledge, or because of a particular interest in the subject matter of that course, with no thought of career advancement – they have simply developed a need to know. The adult learner may have long-range goals which have become internalized, allowing him or her to perceive the college course in terms of a direct contribution to the attainment of those goals.

Experience of the outside world may result in the adult learner having acquired a capacity to make decisions accurately and under conditions of stress. When carried over into formal educational conditions, this quality of thought can be advantageous in the processes of learning. A heightened capacity for analytical thought has been noted by tutors of adult learners, who have been guided through earlier courses involving the exercise of powers of discrimination and investigation. Further, adult learners, who have undergone and assimilated the lessons of events in the wider world outside the classroom, may have acquired a mental set of much value in the analysis of apparently complex situations. The contrast between a discussion on, for example, trade unionism, involving, on the one hand, young A level students and, on the other, industrial workers, will illustrate well the significance of experience, which comes only with involvement and age, in a deep understanding of social and industrial problems, and their wider implications. Adult learners move through successive transformations towards analysing things from a perspective increasingly removed from personal or local perspectives (Mezirow, 1979).

Working with adult learners: Instructional strategies

The essence of a relevant strategy for teaching the adult learner is the provision of a 'positive supportive-learning' climate in which self-direction will predominate. Verduin's

(1979) investigation of appropriate strategies culminated in his advocating the techniques of explanation and demonstration which he argued were of particular significance for (though by no means limited to) adult learning, particularly where adults experience difficulties of 'unlearning', of rejecting errors and their consequences after they have once occurred.

Explanation, as the central component of instruction for the adult learner, was described by Verduin as description, interpretation, analysis, direction giving, and clarification in an informal and conversational manner. The technique has certain advantages for adult learners. First, it emphasises and reinforces what they have been taught previously; additionally, it provides a review of what they have read. Secondly, it summarizes and synthesizes information presented to them. Explanation acts, in this sense, to underline the significance of acquired information. Next, it clarifies particular points which might not have been clear to the student initially. It repeats, stresses and reinforces matter presented in outline. Finally, explanation assists the learner in adapting what he or she has learned to new situations and to other content areas. Problem-based learning situations will assist in developing transfer of knowledge; in particular, synthesis and evaluation, rather than mere conscious memorization, have been found to be useful learning strategies for adult learners concerned with independent learning leading to transfer.

Demonstration was described by Verduin as showing adults how something works and the procedures to be followed in using it. It assists in supplementing lesson content, translates pure description into actual practice and stimulates a number of senses, with the resulting intensification of learning. The demonstration acts as a focus for attention on correct procedures and applications and assists those adult learners who may experience problems in reading and comprehending directions. Time, materials and equipment may be utilized economically.

Other strategies for teaching the adult learner may be based on: providing learning tasks based on perceiving concepts as wholes, rather than in parts, taking particular care to consolidate what has been learned; ensuring correct learning as far as possible in the initial stages of instruction; utilizing self-pacing techniques; and employing practice and review in meaningful situations; demonstrating, as part of the teaching plan, the value and use of learning resources; explaining the basis of the reflective approach that is, of reflecting on one's own learning) and decision-making in the subject area.

Working with adult learners: A theory-based model for teaching adults

Fred Keller (1899–1996) was professor of psychology at Columbia University. Informed by his own adherence to the neobehaviourist research of Burrhus Skinner (as discussed in Chapter 4), he devised a system of teaching adults known as the *Personalized System of*

Instruction (PSI). He believed that adults could learn best by using techniques of self-paced instruction. The personalized system of instruction is based on the following approaches which are, it is suggested, more generally applicable to the teacher or trianer who is working with adult learners:

1 It is mastery oriented. Desired outcomes of the adult study course are specified; in particular, the most significant parts of the course are given special attention in the specification. 'Mastery' is defined in terms of an answer to the question: 'What test evidence can I, as course tutor, accept as demonstrating that the desired degree of learning has occurred?' A student will move from one module or unit to another only after demonstrating mastery of the first module. Assessment will always refer to established criteria, and students can be tested at their request.

2 It is individually paced. The adult learner moves through the course segments at a speed related to his or her ability (as well as more general demands on his or her time).

3 It involves few formal lectures. Some lectures and demonstrations intended to motivate and stimulate are offered only as options.

4 It utilizes carefully devised, printed study guides. Standard textbooks are rarely appropriate for PSI students; special material has to be written and issued in booklet form, relating to study suggestions, reading material, resource availability, and so forth.

5 It involves a mentoring – as distinct from teaching – relationship (Cunningham, 2005; Wallace and Gravells, 2007). When a student has completed an assignment, he or she reports to a mentor who may be a tutor, or even, in some cases, a student working at an advanced course level. The mentor assigns a test, the results of which are discussed with the student, who then moves on to a new segment or is given more work to do if the required level of achievement has not yet been reached.

6 Additional formal instruction is available. Lectures are available, intended to supplement the learning process, but attendance is always voluntary.

Working with adult learners: The management of instruction

The preparation of an appropriate teaching and learning environment for adult learners requires careful consideration. Nothing destroys a lesson for adult students more decisively than an inappropriate environment. Wherever possible the tutor should take pains to ensure that the environment in the workshop or classroom is appropriate to the student group. Adults generally do not care to study in a school-type environment, not least as for some adult learners, prior negative experiences in formal education constitute a significant barrier to participation. The rearrangement of classroom furniture is, therefore, important:

simply arranging tables and chairs in a horseshoe rather than in rows is usually sufficient. An introductory session before the commencement of the formal part of the lesson is also useful. During this period the tutor who knows the class can introduce the lesson in personal style and explain its significance. The objectives of the lesson should always be made clear so that students know their goals, and how to recognize their attainment. Knowing the class – knowing not only names but also something of the background, prior experience and interests of the student group – is held to be of particular importance when working with adult learners, where the establishment of a positive interpersonal relationship between teacher and student is seen as being a necessary precursor to successful teaching.

Sensitivity to the problems of the adult learner should characterize the learning and teaching activities that are used. Abstraction ought to be minimized, distraction avoided and participation encouraged. It is important to remember, however, that for some adult learners, the fact of attending class constitutes a significant act, and teachers should not be surprised if some students take time to relax and engage fully with their studies. Teachers should also remember that if a student is silent in class, it does not necessarily follow that she or he is not learning. Where instructional activities can be task-oriented, individual problem-solving should be encouraged. Group work has been found valuable for the adult learner: some educational psychologists have suggested that, as a member of the group, the adult learner is able to retain deeply held beliefs until ready for a change. Direct criticism of group members ought to be avoided, where possible. And achievement should be recognized; indeed, lessons should be so planned that learners are able to observe their achievement and evaluate its significance. In such conditions, the provision of well-designed formative assessment and feedback is essential. Adult learners may find formal, summative assessments to be problematic (again, evoking negative memories of their experiences in formal schooling) and the design of formative assessment tasks should be informal, flexible and unobtrusive.

For the adult learner (no less than for all other types of learner) the teacher's style can play a decisive role in the acquisition of knowledge. In the case of the adult learner, however, reaction to the approach and personality of the teacher is unusually important. Some teachers of adult students emphasize the vital role of the tutor in building up confidence so that self-perception is heightened. A non-authoritarian style, emphasising self-choice, is likely to win confidence. A transaction between equals, free from any suggestion of compulsion, has been suggested as an ideal pattern for adult student teaching-learning. But adult expectations must not be ignored: a class does expect the teacher to know her or his subject inside out, to display enthusiasm, to be aware of students' needs, to recognize their dignity, and to teach in a competent and professional manner. The teacher who is able to 'teach without seeming to do so' has a very good chance of winning the confidence of the adult learner who, in some cases, might prefer to reach his or her destination unaided.

In sum, the following themes are proposed as being central to the teaching and learning of adults in the FE sector:

1 Problem-based learning and teaching activities are well-suited to mature students, who are able to direct their own learning.

2 Mature students may lack confidence if they have been away from formal education and training for some time: choices of learning and teaching strategies should reflect this, and be structured in such a way that the student can benefit from more formal instruction that can be subtly withdrawn as the student progresses.

3 Mature students' histories can have a considerable impact on their learning: this can be in terms of prior personal experiences of education, or of social or familial attitudes towards education.

4 Mature students sometimes choose to take up a course of study or training for all sorts of reasons that might not be directly concerned with the actual subject or topic being taught (for example, for socialising purposes).

5 Barriers to participation by mature students may be bound up in the practicalities of their lives: arranging childcare; accessing transport; reconciling work commitments with attendance and/or private study. The possible problems caused by such practical matters should be considered to the same extent as more (arguably) profound matters such as the learners' biographies, attitudes and prior experiences.

Summary

The themes, strategies and theories that have been discussed in this chapter are all rooted in a broader body of theory, writing and research that has been specifically labelled as *adult learning theory*, drawing predominantly on humanist and constructivist theories of learning and philosophies of adult participation that reach back over one hundred years (Wallis, 1996). The critical reader will have remarked that some of the issues raised in this chapter are equally applicable to both mainstream student groups in FE (that is, 16–19s) and perhaps also to 14–16s, the other 'minority' amongst the FE population. In some ways this is not a surprise, and reflects not so much a change in the ways in which adult learning and participation are understood, but changes in the ways in which learning across the 14–19 phase is understood. The greater recognition of approaches to learning that move beyond the behaviourist (amongst practitioners and researchers, at any rate – current government policies seem to be rather more limited in their philosophy) has gradually seen 14–19 learners treated 'more like adults' (James and Biesta, 2007). It is hoped, therefore, that the perspectives presented in this chapter are not seen as narrowly applying to adults, but to the wider student body in FE.

Further reading

There is a considerable body of literature relating to both the theory and practice of adult learning and the associated themes of lifelong and lifewide learning. Any serious appreciation of this area should start with a reading of:

Jarvis, P. (2010), *Adult Education and Lifelong Learning: theory and practice*. 4th edition. London: Routledge.

The following is recommended for those readers interested in exploring issues specific to adult learners' experiences of post-compulsory education:

McGivney, B. (2003), *Staying or leaving the course: non-completion and retention of mature students in further and higher education*. Leicester: NIACE.

And for a more general commentary on adult learning:

Daines, J., Daines, C. and Graham, B. (2006), *Adult learning, adult teaching*. 4th edition. Cardiff: Welsh Academic Press.

PART 6

Strategies and Techniques for Teaching and Learning

23 Planning Lessons within Academic and Professional Contexts

In this part of the book, we consider some of the practices, techniques, strategies, rules, routines and procedures employed by teachers involved in *designed instruction*. We examine a variety of procedures commonly employed in FE, ranging from more formal teacher-led lesson structures to student-led approaches. We also explore the specificities of planning and designing for learning within both academic and professional, and technical and vocational contexts. In this chapter the focus is on academic and professional contexts, although much of the discussion will also be of interest to those teachers of vocational and technical programmes who have responsibility for the teaching of underpinning theory and knowledge.

Planning for differentiation and inclusive practice

All of the approaches to planning for learning that are outlined in this part of the book rest on the two key principles of inclusive practice and differentiation. Differentiation can be defined as an approach to teaching and learning that both recognizes the individuality of learners, and also informs ways of planning for learning and teaching that take these individualities into consideration. This is *not* to be equated with learning styles, however (as discussed in Chapter 20). Learning styles purport to allocate particular behaviours to students in terms of how they approach their learning. Differentiation is a broader notion that simply recognizes that a group of students is not a homogenous unit, but consists of a varied group of individuals who, precisely because they are individuals, need to be treated as such at the planning stage. This does not mean that each student requires a specialized learning plan: it simply means that teacher should not assume that a particular strategy or activity will always work for all of the students, all fo the time.

Inclusive practice can be defined as an approach to teaching and learning that endeavours to encourage the fullest participation of learners. It also implies a commitment to avoid the opposite; that is to say, it implies that tutors work within an ethical framework that recognizes and respects equality and diversity, and the potential for all learners to take part. Full participation is defined generously, and is seen as inclusive of, but not restricted to, students with specific learning disabilities or difficulties. In order to encourage an inclusive approach to planning, a number of key themes are to be considered as underpinning the planning process in its entirety (Powell and Tummons, 2011):

- The teacher should take time to effectively coordinate the use of time, accommodation, resources and strategies/activities.

- There should be a range of strategies such as whole class learning, paired learning and small group learning (including teacher selected small groups and random small groups) in order to allow students to engage at different levels within the group, according to their needs, confidence and prior experience/study.

- Flexible use of time is needed to respond to students' needs at any given moment. The timing of pre-planned activities should not be rigidly adhered to (this is discussed in more detail below).

- A wide variety of classroom management strategies are needed such as independent study, interest groups, learning buddies and differentiated formative assessment in order to help to target instruction to the students' needs.

- There should be clear criteria for success developed at both group and individual level to provide guidance to the students as to what would be a successful learning outcome. This should be revisited with the group and on an individual basis if necessary, during the session.

- Formative and summative assessment activities (discussed in Chapters 30 and 31) should be varied to enable the learners to demonstrate their own thoughts and learning growth. These should be adapted as necessary within acceptable guidelines, particularly with summative assessment tasks (awarding bodies invariably publish guidance relating to assessment procedures for students with specific needs).

Types of instruction

The aspects of instruction techniques presented in this part of the book include the following:

- *formal, 'teacher-led' approaches*, in which a teacher presents a learning sequence, closely involving class activity, and based upon learning intellectual and theoretical content
- *skills-based sessions*, in which the attainment of a predetermined standard of technical or practical skills emerges from demonstration and practice

- *lecture-based sessions*, in which a speaker engages in a presentation based essentially on planned, one-way communication
- *discussion groups*, in which a small number of students are encouraged to examine a problem collectively
- *seminars*, in which a class member presents a thesis or topic analysis for scrutiny by colleagues
- *tutorials*, in which tutor and learners discuss in a personal face-to-face setting, problems presented by the tutor
- *case studies*, in which a problem situation, real or simulated, is examined by a group of students
- *team teaching*, in which members of a course are taught by closely-integrated teams of teachers, working collectively as units
- *e-learning*, in which learning and teaching is supported through the use of ICTs and/or online resources.

Lesson planning

The teacher has the task of planning the lesson on the basis of available resources, and of providing a structure of direct teaching which will reflect particular demands of the subject area and the requirements of the curriculum that is being followed. Outcomes/objectives must be established and appropriate teaching and learning activities mapped out before the lesson. Lesson planning should commence with a consideration of ends and means: the topic of the lesson will define its ends; the activities necessary to accomplish the ends will suggest the instructional means.

Following the formulation of his or her outcomes/objectives, the teacher then collects the materials and resources related to the students' capabilities and achievements. Sequencing (that is, the timing and ordering of activities) and lesson structure are developed so that a series of events (for example, an oral presentation followed by a question-and-answer session, followed by a quiz) emerges, to be modified in accordance with constraints, such as the time available.

Time is invariably a constraint on lesson planning. A useful general rule employed in the FE sector is based on the '80–20' principle. Roughly 80 per cent of available time is devoted to the central section of the lesson; the remaining 20 per cent of time is divided between the introduction and the conclusion. As with all rules of thumb, time-plans may require modification in the actual lesson: thus, the opening sequence may reveal an unexpectedly high level of prior understanding, allowing immediate movement to the next sequence. Conversely, the opening sequence may indicate that the planned content will not be suitable to the student group and some content may need to be held over to another session. But some kind of overall time allocation must be planned if the lesson is to be balanced and if it is to achieve its outcomes.

Factors influencing the lesson planning process

Preparation of a formal lesson demands a consideration of three major factors: the students, the subject matter, and resources and constraints. Each factor involves a variety of problems which the teacher could examine in the following way:

1 *The students.* The kinds of questions that should be considered here include: what is their academic standard? Have they already reached the level of attainment required for an understanding of the proposed lesson material? Does my previous experience with them as a class suggest any likely problems? The answers to these questions will affect the form of the introduction to the lesson and may necessitate a re-examination of the proposed lesson outcomes/objectives.

2 *The subject matter.* How is it related to the curriculum, or scheme of work, as a whole? Do the proposed outcomes and topics demand a particular approach? What specific teaching methods might be appropriate? What kind of resources will be of assistance? How and when should I assess the students' learning?

3 *The resources and constraints.* How much time will be available? How swiftly should I be able to make progress? At what time of the day will the lesson take place? (The first hour following the lunch break often seems to demand special treatment, and Friday afternoons are rarely popular.) What kind of room will I be teaching in? Are the resources that I need straightforward to access?

The answers to these questions should be reflected in the teacher's lesson plan. Lesson plans ought to be set out so that they include: the subject heading of the lesson; the learning outcomes/objectives; the subject matter, broken down into approximate periods of time; methods to be used; audio-visual aids; and opportunities for assessment. Many FE colleges provide a template for lesson plans which staff are expected to use. These can vary quite considerably between institutions. An exemplar lesson plan template (derived from the author's own research (Tummons, 2010b)) is given in Figure 23.1, below:

East Lancashire College
Lesson/Session Plan

DATE:	COURSE:	LENGTH:
TIME:	TUTOR:	LOCATION:

EQUALITY AND DIVERSITY
All lessons should have learning materials and activities which are free from stereotyping and present positive images in terms of gender, race, age and disability.

RISK ASSESSMENT NUMBER: (Refer to Risk Assessment Form for number)

AGE COMPOSITION OF GROUP:

Number of learners under 16:   Number of learners 16–18:   Number of learners over 16:

TOPIC   Tutorial
....

LEARNING OUTCOMES – At the end of the session/lesson learners will be able to:

(NB Outcomes should always be measurable)

GROUP COMPOSITION AND ANY INDIVIDUAL LEARNING NEEDS – Consider differentiation/learning styles.

KEY/BASIC/TRANSFERABLE SKILLS LINKS:

RESOURCES REQUIRED (including ILT)

PLANNED ASSESSMENT ACTIVITIES – Please identify how learning will be checked

PLEASE INDICATE IN YOUR PLAN THE INTEGRATION OF KEY SKILLS, OPPORTUNITIES TO ASSESS
LEARNING AND DIFFERENTIATION FOR INDIVIDUAL NEEDS AND LEARNING STYLES

Figure 23.1a

TIME	LEARNER ACTIVITY	TEACHER ACTIVITY
	INTRODUCTION	
	DEVELOPMENT	
	SUMMARY	
EVALUATION AND ACTION POINTS FOR NEXT SESSION		

Figure 23.1b

Sequencing lesson content

Sequencing refers to the methodical ordering of lesson content in relation to the content to be covered, the profile of the students and the outcomes to be met. There are no immutable rules in this area. Experience may dictate that the inherent logic of a subject topic is best ignored in the early stages of instruction, or that the time-honoured principle of proceeding from the particular to the general might be reversed, or that sequences should follow the chapter patterns of the class textbooks.

A guiding principle (but *not* a rule) might be derived from the following very general suggestions. Experiment widely, in the early stages of your teaching career, with a variety of sequencing patterns which will reflect your own view of teaching theory, and which will answer the question: how do students learn? Evaluate results, modify the sequence where necessary, rejecting any aspects of the sequencing which introduce unnecessary complexity. Aim, eventually, at a simple sequence which carries the students with relative ease from one part of the lesson to another, which links one segment of knowledge to another, which avoids discontinuities, and which is perceived by students as a progression from one level of understanding to another. And finally, do not hesitate to abandon a sequence which impairs or interrupts progress.

Lesson structure

There are generally three main structural components of a formal lesson: *introduction*, *development* or *consolidation,* and *summary* or *conclusion* (terminology varies across different FE colleges). The introduction should state the object of the lesson; the development or consolidation should present, teach and assess the acquisition of the lesson material and strengthen what has been learned; the summary or conclusion should recapitulate the lesson's main themes and where necessary provide links to the next lesson or offer extension activities such as work for private study.

1 Introduction. The arousal of interest, the capturing and maintenance of attention and the setting of the scene, are essential in the first minutes of the lesson. A test on previous work should serve to focus class attention and to link the lesson with what has preceded it. Although the lesson is a self-contained unit of instruction, it must be seen as part of a wider sequence. Retention, recall and insight may be tested in these first minutes. The lesson outcomes/objectives and their relationship to the wider curriculum should then be stated clearly, so that the relevance of the subject is clear to the students.

2 Development or consolidation. The main body of the lesson may consist of the presentation in gradual fashion of a sequence of information linked with previously

acquired knowledge. The sequence ought to be logical and should be designed, whenever possible, to elicit those responses which will develop insight. Statements of facts and ideas, illustration by examples, demonstrations, discovery by the class of underlying principles, development of facts and ideas and their practical application, may feature prominently in this section. Full class participation is desirable. Question-and-answer and discussion activities will be useful. Assessments should also be included in this part of the lesson, not only as a guide for the teacher in ascertaining the extent of the students' developing understanding, but in informing students of their progress and maintaining motivation and interest.

3 Summary or conclusion. The ending of the lesson ought to be planned as carefully as the introductory and central sections. It should not comprise a few hasty words, spoken when it is obvious that time has run out and students are noisily packing their bags and looking towards the door. A conclusion provides a final opportunity of ensuring assimilation and retention and ought to include a revision exercise (perhaps in the form of question and answer), a summary of which can be presented visually as an additional form of reinforcement. A link with the next lesson should also be provided, for example, by recommending private study which should be seen as a preparation for that lesson, or by the announcement of the next lesson's title and aims.

It is important to note that even the most thorough and well thought through lesson plan may need to be changed while the lesson is actually taking place. A failure of equipment, a student's unexpected difficulty in understanding a concept, or a formative assessment which reveals a lack of comprehension of an important point, are all circumstances in which a lesson plan may have to be altered or put aside. On occasions such as these, there is no value in pressing on regardless or in going through the mere motions of completing the planned lesson. Teachers need to be responsive to the teaching environment. If students do not understand a concept, then additional worked examples should be provided. If a data projector is not available, the teacher should use a whiteboard to note down key terms and concepts that are of particular importance. If students proceed through the planned materials more quickly than anticipated, the teacher can use any additional time to introduce the next session's topic. Nor should it be difficult for the teacher to adjust the next session or two in her or his scheme of work to accommodate the changes that have been made. At all times it is important to remember that a lesson plan is not carved in stone.

Lesson teaching: Some notes on method

The teacher's aim in a lesson must be to motivate, stimulate and communicate, to hold the attention and to achieve a defined objective through class control. The following points are, therefore, of importance:

1 The lesson must be pitched correctly. The level of the class and its record of attainment must be the starting point for the teacher's preparation. This point cannot be overstressed. Information can only be incorporated in an existing scheme of thought. Arguably, the most important single factor influencing learning is what the learner already knows.

2 The lesson outcomes must be realistic and clear. They must be explained to the class and their attainment ought to be accepted as a joint teacher–class aim. The relevance of the outcomes to student development (in terms of career aspirations, for example) should be stressed. The lesson plan should be matched as closely as possible to the overall nature of the outcomes and referenced to curriculum documentation where appropriate.

3 Exposition must be ordered, simple and clear. Order and simplicity of presentation are vital if the learner is to achieve mastery of a subject. This must be reflected in the teacher's exposition of the lesson material. New concepts must be linked with previously learned material and must be shown to derive from it. New terms must be explained; it must never be assumed that the class automatically understands them. It follows that the teacher's vocabulary and language register must be intelligible to the class.

4 Development must be logical and consequential. Students usually find that continuity in the development of concepts assists in assimilation and retention. Unbridged gaps or unexplained jumps in exposition make learning difficult.

5 Presentation must be based on the essential *social* character of the lesson. The essence of a lesson is joint teacher-class activity: a lesson made up of a teacher's exposition alone is a contradiction in terms. A lesson is not a solo performance; it will include periods (often alternating) in which either the teacher's activities predominate or the students' responses are paramount. Discussions and controlled sequences of questions and answers are therefore necessary.

6 Presentation ought to involve a variety of media. The spoken word and the whiteboard are not the sole communication media. Images, key word and terms, photographs, even sounds can be embedded into presentations. Supporting handouts can provide further engagement.

7 Presentation must be related carefully to fluctuations in class attention. The decline of initial interest, and the interference produced by fatigue and diminished motivation, should be recognized by the teacher in the planning and delivery of the lesson. Varied presentation, carefully timed pauses, recapitulation and a variety of class activities may help to offset the tendency to diminishing attention. The use of the teacher's voice, often providing the central communication source in a lesson, is of great importance. Emphasis on key words, variations in pitch and tone so as to prevent monotonous delivery, and clarity at all times, aid the holding of class attention.

8 Presentation should be assisted by appropriate body language. The teacher's posture, gestures and facial expressions can emphasize, or even contradict, verbal utterances. Students respond to verbal *and* non-verbal language. Therefore the teacher has the responsibility of ensuring that the lesson presentation is assisted, and not hindered, by non-verbal communication (as discussed in Chapter 13).

9 The following procedures are of relevance to lesson presentation:

a. Proceed from the known to the unknown. Students often learn by association, so that the learning of new concepts may be facilitated by their being deliberately linked with what is already known by the class. This might be prior learning related to their studies, to their hobbies or pastimes, or to current events, for example.

b. Proceed from the simple to the complex. Consider teaching the easier topics first so that a base of knowledge is established. A gradual shift in the level of the lesson, so that the class moves from basic principles to more advanced learning, usually necessitates an ordered sequence in the presentation of concepts.

c. Proceed from the concrete to the abstract. Experiments in elementary physics and chemistry can be designed and presented with this procedure in mind.

d. Proceed from the particular to the general. A lesson might be based on the interpretation of a specific event so that its wider significance can be discussed.

e. Proceed from observation to reasoning. This is a very important principle, which draws attention to the development of the powers of reasoning and the gaining of insight as desirable lesson outcomes. To learn to reason from the 'how' to the 'why' ought to be an objective of much of the work in the colleges of FE.

f. Proceed from the whole to the parts, and then return to the whole. This principle is the basis of the lesson sequence, which presents its subject matter initially as an entity, then proceeds to an analysis of component parts, finally returning to an overall view.

Techniques for question-and-answer

Asking questions is an integral aspect of the two-way dialogue that characterizes successful lessons. It has a number of purposes. It may be used to discover the level of class knowledge so that the appropriate starting point for the presentation of new material may be determined. It can provide swift feedback, that is, it can show what progress in teaching/learning has been achieved and what revision is needed. It can be used also to gain or regain class attention, to fix and reinforce facts in the memory, to develop and check a learner's understanding and powers of reasoning and expression, to recapitulate, to prompt students to move to the next mental step, to look for progressively more precise answers, to challenge beliefs and guide consideration of values, and to develop class participation.

Good question-and-answer activities require careful preparation, timing and delivery, and should be reasonable and relevant. Direct, precise and unambiguous phrasing which elicits equally direct and precise answers is advantageous. A long, tortuous question is likely to present the class with the added problem of attempting to understand what the questioner has in mind, so that the real problem becomes secondary. The 'closed' question which demands in reply a mere 'yes' or 'no' ought not, in general, to be put, but where such a question has been asked, the reply ought to be followed by a further 'open' question that might suggest a variety of responses. Where possible, step-by-step questions and answers, each answer giving rise to the next question, should be utilized.

Questions should be put one at a time and spread over the whole class, as far as possible, and should not be confined to a small section of students who can be relied on to respond. Questions may be put to the class as a whole, to small groups or may be addressed to one student by name, depending on the nature and progress of the group. A newly established group may benefit from group work approaches to answering questions, whereas individual questions may be more suitable to a well-established group. A wait time for a response is often advisable. Prompting, or follow-up questions, can be used where a student is in difficulties. A student's answer ought to be repeated by the teacher if it is almost inaudible. Where no answer is given, the correct answer may be given by the teacher, or instructions given as to how or where it can be discovered. Incorrect or partial answers can be valuable, too, in that they provide the opportunity for further discussion: therefore they should not elicit a critical response from the teacher. Under no circumstances should a poor answer be mocked, either by the teacher or by the students: this can destroy motivation and often lead to the student's withdrawal from further participation in the lesson.

Questioning by the class ought to be encouraged as long as it does not degenerate into time-wasting or irrelevance. Where class teachers do not know the answer to a question, they ought to admit this, and promise to seek an answer, which should then be given at the earliest opportunity.

Questioning techniques in microteaching exercises

The growing awareness of the importance of effective questioning technique for the class teacher is evident in the attention given in many teacher training curricula to the use of 'microteaching' – a process in which teaching techniques are scaled down, allowing a trainee to demonstrate particular skills, such as class questioning, in a short lesson sequence of, say, five to ten minutes. Its aim is to isolate and study a small number of specific teaching skills (it is simply impractical to attempt to cover too much ground in such a short period of time). Video recordings can be utilized so as to review and analyze the trainee's performance. In this and other ways the vital technique of questioning can be taught effectively.

Extension tasks and private study: Encouraging study outside the classroom

It is common practice within academic and professional curricula for students to have to work on their studies outside class contact time. Indeed, many of the curriculum documents published by awarding bodies indicate both the guided learning hours (that is, contact time) and total learning hours (that is, the nominal period of time that the student should allocate to their studies) for the modules and programmes that they specify. Indeed, it has been argued that for any curriculum to be studied successfully, homework will be required as educational institutions simply do not have the time or resources to deliver a curriculum in full (Bernstein, 1990): private study is a necessary element of successful progress and achievement. As such, it can be said that there are four main aspects to asking students to complete work outside class:

1 to extend and amplify work already covered in class
2 to revise and reinforce work already covered in class
3 to provide opportunities for the application of content learned in class to the solution of new problems
4 to provide further opportunities for students to develop their wider study skills (such as academic writing).

Assignments or additional tasks can also be used as *extension tasks* during class: on those occasions where some students have finished the required class-based work ahead of others (as discussed above), the teacher may decide that any outstanding lesson time can be used to work towards an assignment. If a private study task has not been set or is not planned (according to the scheme of work), teachers can ask students to complete an additional task. The nature of any extension task will depend on the curriculum and the class in question, but should always be planned according to the same criteria as any other classroom activity: it should be relevant, meaningful and appropriate to the curriculum and the students. Asking students to complete a word search is generally not a constructive use of their time. Asking students to solve an additional problem or answer an additional question based on the content that has been covered that day, is more worthwhile.

Requiring students to complete work in their own time can therefore be seen as a valuable form of formative assessment. Given that the value of feedback and reinforcement tend to diminish with the passing of time, it is essential that independent work be marked and returned to students as soon as possible (the role of assessment and feedback is discussed in Chapters 30 and 31).

Giving demonstrations

It can often be helpful to give a demonstration as one aspect of a lesson. A demonstration is typically used to illustrate a particular idea, concept or theory. The teacher should stress the linking of theory and practice through the demonstration. Demonstrations require careful planning and presentation if they are to contribute clearly to the outcomes of the lesson.

A certain degree of preparation will be required if the demonstration is to achieve its optimum effect. For example, some preliminary knowledge may be essential and this ought to be covered and, where necessary, assessed in the lesson prior to the demonstration. The students ought to be informed of what the demonstration is intended to make clear, and how the principles or activities that are to be demonstrated relate to the topic currently being studied and, if appropriate, the curriculum as a whole.

The nature or function of the demonstration will vary according to the topic or curriculum being followed. For example: in a physics class, a demonstration might be used to illustrate a particular rule or phenomenon that would be difficult to teach in the abstract – such as demonstrating what happens when an electric bell is activated in a vacuum as part of a series of lessons relating to acoustic wave theory. For this demonstration, an electric bell, a bell jar and a vacuum pump would be required. In a sport and exercise class, a demonstration might be used in order to show students how to measure an individual's peak expiratory flow. For this demonstration, a peak flow meter would be required.

The physical arrangement of both the students and the demonstration equipment is important. The students should be seated as near the demonstration as is practicable, and the teacher should take care to ensure that all of the students have clear sightlines to the equipment. The demonstration ought not to be too detailed; its main points ought to emerge clearly and be underlined by the demonstrator's emphasis. It should be followed by a recapitulation of the steps or actions which the students have seen, perhaps accompanied by a series of questions or prompts to assess understanding.

Demonstrations can be made more engaging through involving students wherever possible. Mindful of the nature of the curriculum, teachers can enhance demonstrations in a number of ways:

1 A repeat of the demonstration can be conducted entirely by one or two student volunteers, it can be repeated by the teacher who will ask for prompts or reminders at key points of the demonstration, or it can be repeated by the teacher who will work in total silence whilst student volunteers explain what is happening.

2 If the equipment being used is sufficiently affordable, small groups of students can replicate what has been demonstrated as part of a reinforcement exercise. For students of acoustic wave theory, this might not be possible; for students of sport

and exercise, taking peak expiratory flow readings from each other would be relatively straightforward to plan.

3 If resources are limited, student small groups can take turns in using the equipment themselves. Whilst waiting for their turn, students can be involved in another exercise (for example, writing up notes relating to the demonstration).

Teaching concepts

The teaching of concepts – the process by which learners recognize how to sort their specific experiences into general classes and rules – presents particular problems for the teacher. Instruction in the categorization of concepts and the acquisition of associated meanings involves careful attention to lesson content and the sequencing of teaching.

A concept is an idea or symbol that brings together a group of ideas or symbols. Therefore, abstractions or generalizations in the student's mind which he or she uses to represent some group or class may constitute a concept. We may say that the functions of concepts in learning are as follows: they are essential to comprehension; they can act as short cuts to effective communication; they can assist in the transfer of learning; they can promote recall; and they allow practice in the application of principles to different contexts.

Perceptions of concepts tend to change; they develop somewhat slowly and at different rates for different students; their development is fostered where the learner becomes conscious of similarities among known concepts. Cognitivist and constructivist theorists define concepts as *conjunctive* (where all the values of the attributes of a concept are present simultaneously) or *disjunctive* (where the attributes are not present in all the examples under consideration). According to the cognitivist school, the acquisition of concepts is what makes instruction possible. Therefore, in concept teaching the performance criterion should be the successful identification of a class of things or any member of a class. For example: how do Christianity, Judaism, and Islam conform to the concept of 'religion'? Why do we classify the whale as a mammal? How does the use of a jury fit in with the idea of justice? Answers to conceptual questions in this form involve the learned ability to discriminate essential features of things or events and organize them systematically into cohesive categories. Where concept formation is the objective of a lesson, the teacher should ensure that the processes of classification, and the construction of definitions, are understood, in a very general sense, by the class.

Weil (1978) advocates the use of lessons based on the presentation of sequences of examples and non-examples, *analyzing their attributes and building hypotheses* concerning the concept in question. Empirical research into concept formation suggests that can arise from lessons in which stress is placed on the 'surrounding structure' of a concept; new concepts are taught so as to be seen emerging from those with which the student is familiar. The teacher analyzes the 'network location' of the concept he or she intends to teach, and relates it to the student's existing patterns of knowledge. The teacher then defines the concept to be taught and collects examples and non-examples (as contrasts). Matching exercises are used during the lesson to determine *'concept exemplars'*. Relationships between larger and smaller entities are emphasized. As a conclusion to the lesson, the teacher suggests new examples based on the structure of the newly learned concept (Tennyson and Park, 1980; Tennyson and Cocchiarella, 1986).

A teaching model used successfully in FE for concept formation is based on the following strategy (Curzon, 2004):

1 preliminary definition of the concept is given. A standard text is used to provide the definition

2 attributes are identified and contraries are noted

3 examples are elicited from the class and are then discussed

4 the concept is redefined

5 the structure of the concept (that is, relationships between its properties) is outlined

6 the concept is used in a variety of problem-solving exercises.

In effect, the learner has been taught in this lesson sequence to compare various aspects of an idea and then to produce an overview, which expresses important relationships between them.

The improvized lesson

Most college teachers will find that at some stage in their teaching careers they will be asked at very short notice to stand in for an absent colleague. Covering for absent colleagues is an unavoidable aspect of the FE teacher's role, not least as staffing levels in colleges are such that only very few FE teachers can manage to cover for a colleague without difficulty. The difficulties of covering for a colleague are added to when it is remembered that the session that needs covering is based on an unfamiliar programme of study. The ability to work up a lesson plan with speed and skill emerges only after much experience in teaching. The accrual over time of a wide body of professional knowledge and experience is an important aspect of the teacher's continuing professional development (Avis et al., 2009). For the inexperienced teacher faced with the necessity to plan a lesson with very little time for preparation, and a more-or-less familiar curriculum which must be followed, the following outline plan is suggested:

1 obtain a copy of the relevant curriculum documentation. If a lesson plan has been prepared in advance, so much the better. Course or curriculum leaders in colleges should be able to access such documentation easily

2 examine the title of the lesson you have to cover. Where does it fit into the curriculum?

3 what topics are suggested by the title? List them

4 what questions do these topics suggest? List them. Check that they have not been covered in previous lessons

5 use the questions as headings for sections of your lesson

6 the central section of your improvized lesson should comprise a series of key questions and answers

7 provide a short introduction and conclusion.

Summary

According to one experienced teacher-educator of the author's acquaintance, good teaching is like good gardening: it's all in the preparation. Teachers who take the time to plan their lessons properly, to source appropriate materials and to think about how, in what order and why the topics to be covered will be organized, will thrive. Teachers who meet their students in a state of ill preparedness will not. Students can quickly tell if their teacher is properly prepared and sufficiently knowledgeable. And if a teacher comes to class ill-prepared, how can the teacher expect the students not to respond in kind?

Further reading

The processes involved in planning lessons within the academic and professional curricula are very well represented in the teacher-training literature. Good examples include:

Scales, P. (2013), *Teaching in the Lifelong Learning Sector*. 2nd edition. Maidenhead: McGraw Hill. Chapter 8.

Wallace, S. (2011), *Teaching, Tutoring and Training in the Lifelong Learning Sector*. 4th edition. Exeter: Learning Matters. Chapter 8.

For specific guidance relating to the planning of lessons that are both inclusive and differentiated, the following is recommended:

Powell, S. and Tummons, J. (2011), *Inclusive Practice in the Lifelong Learning Sector*. Exeter: Learning Matter.

24 Planning Lessons within Vocational and Technical Contexts

The wider principles of teaching formal lessons within academic or professional curricula that were discussed in the preceding chapter also apply to teaching vocational and technical courses. This is itself should not be seen as surprising. If the overall aim of the teacher is to provide a series of activities and opportunities for learning, accompanied by a carefully chosen selection of relevant materials and resources, then it follows that whether the aim of the lesson is an exploration of attachment theory or the principles of building bicycle wheels, the planning process is the same. Time, accommodation and resources all need to be accounted for, the prior experience of the students needs to be considered, opportunities for feedback need to be identified, and so forth. Put simply, the general principles related to the teaching of a formal lesson apply also to the teaching of motor skills (or psychomotor skills, if the teacher is drawing on learning taxonomies theories, as discussed in Chapter 16), that is, those series of learned acts requiring simultaneous or sequential coordination. The principles of instructional technique are basically the same whether the subject matter is arc welding or economic geography, database management or algebra. However, 'learning by doing' tends to feature more prominently in lessons aimed at motor skill acquisition. The encouragement of fine motor skills, or good hand-eye coordination, or the fluent and confident use of specialist tools, usually requires a type of lesson content and an appropriate lesson structure, based on the learning of sequences of physical actions or steps, that is distinctive within vocational and technical curricula.

Defining skills

A brief survey of everyday usages of the word 'skill' within the FE sector quickly indicates a variety of meanings, depending on context. Common usage of the work implies some expertise in an activity developed as the result of training and/or experience enabling the learner to perform particular tasks. Consequently, the word 'skill' has been variously defined as:

- choosing and carrying out strategies which are efficient (Welford, 1968)

- an ability to produce consistently an intended effect with accuracy, speed and economy of action (Mace, 1973)

- the ability to execute useful tasks to publicly agreed standards of performance (MacDonald-Ross, 1973)

- any ability, generally assumed to have been learned, to perform a complex task involving psychomotor coordination with ease, speed and accuracy (Evans, 1978)

- a set of strategic adaptations to the mechanical limitations of the brain and of the body, which enable human purposes to be achieved, built up gradually in the course of repeated training or other experience (Howarth, 1981).

However, over recent years the meanings of 'skill' (and the associated term of 'competence') has moved. This is indicated by the usage of expressions such as 'transferable skills' and 'employability skills'. These concepts remove the word 'skill' from a specific, contextualized meaning – that is, when skills are attached to or associated with specific crafts or trades, for example – and instead move it to a more general discussion about the learning that takes place in FE colleges. This more general discussion, informed by changes in political and economic pressures over time, rests on definitions of skills such as:

- functional skills – practical skills in English, Information and Communication Technology ICT) and Mathematics, that allow individuals to work confidently, effectively and independently in life

- transferable skills – any skills acquired from a variety of contexts (education, employment, hobbies, volunteering) that can be seen as being transferable to other contexts

- employability skills – those transferable skills that are positioned, by employers, as necessary attributes for successful employment (such as problem solving skills, team working skills or time management).

These meanings of 'skill' are quite different to the 'common usage' definitions already provided. The 'common usage' definition positions 'a skill' as a specific attribute or competence that, once practiced and acquired, would allow the student to perform a particular action or procedure as part of a programme of learning within a specific area (for example, carpentry, jewellery making or hairdressing). But the definition of 'skills' that is proposed by notions such as 'employability skills' is more generic, seeing skills as something that can be acquired in a variety of ways and applied to different employment or educational contexts. At the same time, 'skills' become part of academic and professional curricula as well as technical or practical curricula. For the purposes of this discussion, however, it is the 'common usage' definition that will be followed.

Skilled performance and motor skills

Sensorimotor activity, which is at the basis of all skilled activity or performance, is defined as motor (physical) activity initiated and controlled by sensory input (sight, sound, touch) from the student's environment (the workshop) and from the student him or herself. The systematic motor skills, which make up those activities taught in the skills lessons in FE colleges, are based generally on a series of coordinated movements, the execution of which requires both repeated practice and correct timing. Students must learn to be attentive to their environment, to respond to, or ignore, certain types of cue from that environment and to mark their responses by selecting immediately an appropriate and accurately timed movement from the repertoire they have acquired as the result of previous learning and practice. The kinds of stimulus or prompt, which the student should be attentive to, might include the movement of a needle on a dial, an alarm sounding on a timer, a reading on a digital meter or a measurement using a vernier calliper. Stimuli such as these ought to result in swift, precise responses characterized by complete coordination of mind and muscle.

Among the distinguishing features of a skilled activity (installing copper piping, cutting hair, painting a sash window) are dexterity (in which speed and precision are essential), coordination (in which abilities to grasp and manipulate may be vital), the ability to respond quickly, spatial ability (that is, the capacity to deal with relationships involving more than one dimension), the capacity to share attention among a number of more or less simultaneous demands, accuracy in timing, anticipation of movement and a fluency or smooth flow of movement. The student, in exhibiting such behaviours, is able to make sense of what she or he perceives and to translate her or his perceptions into organized activity. It is one of the main tasks of the skills teacher to assist the learner in the acquisition of powers of activity organization and learning, and to enable her or him to obtain the maximum information out of the minimum number of cues.

The concept of 'fluency' or 'flow' is particularly important in teaching and learning skills. The practical significance of this concept for the teacher is mirrored in the theory that motor skills are seen as multi-dimensional behaviour patterns rather than discrete responses over a period of time (Smith, 1966), or that the learning of skilled behaviour culminates in unconscious competence, that moment when a skill has been practiced so often and learned so well, that it becomes 'second nature' (Baume and Kahn, 2004).

The creation and growth of skills

There are a number of theoretical perspectives relating to the teaching and development of skills. One of these, the Dreyfus and Dreyfus model of skill acquisition, has already been discussed (refer to Chapter 16). A further selection of theories is discussed below:

1 Robert Gagné: stimulus-response chaining theory

Gagné (1985) argued that skills result from the connections of a set of individual associations, or stimulus-response sequences. Part-skills should be taught first, followed by instruction in how and when these part-skills should correctly be used. Stimulus-response associations are fixed and reinstated as the result of guided practice. The chains which result are reinforced by further practice. The chains represent mastery of units of activity and result in the appearance of a skill.

The conditions for mastering these units of activity were described by Gagné in terms which continue to be of particular relevance for instruction in the college classroom and workshop:

- Previously learned, relevant stimulus-response associations must be thoroughly revised and tested. Reinstatement in correct sequence is essential and this can be assisted by the use of prompting, involving external cues.

- Separate links (part-skills) in the chain should be practiced in a continuous series.

- Repetition of the chained sequence is valuable; this necessitates guided practice.

- The final link in the chain must act to reinforce the learning of the skill as a whole. For example, the repaired electrical socket must function correctly, or the overhauled thermostat must provide the required service. The absence of immediate reinforcement by the final link can lead to the disappearance of the entire chain of learning acquired by the student.

2 Paul Fitts: three-phase theory of skill learning

Fitts (1967) argued that the acquisition of a complex skill necessitates the learner passing through three overlapping phases. The transition from phase to phase may take the form of a continuous rather than a sudden change. He viewed complex skill learning in terms of the acquisition of a number of semi-independent subroutines which may go on concurrently or successively. The role of the teacher is to all identify correctly the appropriate subroutines that make up the skill. The three phases are as follows:

- The cognitive, early phase. The beginner seeks to understand what has to be done and attempts to comprehend the background to the tasks he or she has to master. The teacher guides the learner towards the required sequence of actions and builds on previously acquired part-skills (that is, the subroutines). Frequently, recurring errors are pointed out to the learner. As a result of this phase he or she acquires a subroutine – the required procedure.

- The associative, intermediate phase. Correct patterns of response are established in the learner's repertoire as the result of demonstrations, imitation and practice. Part-skills are smoothed by the elimination of inadequate movements, and sub-skills are integrated into required total skills.

- The autonomous, final phase. Skilled acts are now performed automatically, without the learner having to stop to think about what comes next. Errors have been eliminated, speed of performance has been increased, resistance to the effects of stress is built up and improvements in skill continue (although at a decreasing rate).

3 Herbert Klausmeier: internal programme theory

Klausmeier (1975) defined a skill in operational terms as the level of proficiency attained in carrying out sequences of action in a consistent way. He sets out the following characteristics of a skilled performance.

- the learner acquires a central motor programme (CMP) by practice, as a result of which his or her performance no longer depends on voluntary control or upon continuous attention to feedback; the CMP has attained 'automaticity'
- there is increased freedom from reliance on external cues – they have been internalized into the learner's CMP
- coordinated movement patterns emerge under the control of the CMP
- the ability emerges to perform the skill well under different types of changing conditions.

4 Donald Norman: chaos to automaticity theory

Norman (1982) highlighted the significance of learning and continued practice for any consideration of skilled performance. He argued that the distinction between a skilled performer and an amateur could be discerned in five areas:

- skilled performance reveals ease and smoothness in execution of a task
- skill brings with it a decrease in mental effort and a lessening of fatigue in performance
- stress tends to decrease where the performance is executed with skill
- skilled performance involves a wide variety of activities which have coalesced into a unitary skill
- skilled execution of a task involves a degree of automaticity.

Norman argued that the acquisition of a skill required a sequence of experiences, necessitating moving from whole to part and back to whole again. Initially, the requisite performance will appear to the learner as chaotic and lacking in organization. Systematic analysis, under the supervision of an instructor, will reveal the component parts of the task. It then becomes possible to learn the sub-skills separately and then in combination. A synthesis of the sub-skills emerges and task structure appears. Practice and tuning will in turn produce a performance which is automatic.

Preparing for the psychomotor skills lesson

There are very few short cuts to the permanent acquisition of procedural sequences of motor skills. Lesson preparation must, therefore, take into account the necessity for careful, planned and methodical teaching and learning of the routines of sub-skills out of which mastery emerges. The appropriate entry behaviour of students must be stated and checked and their possession of any necessary pre-requisite skills *must* be ensured.

In order to prepare for a skills-based session, the teacher should first analyze the task that is to be practiced and learned, before then analyzing the skills that will be required in order to perform the task at an acceptable level. It is important to note that these analyzes should be carried out by all teachers, irrespective of their own level of relevant trade or occupational competence or length of relevant workplace experience.

The task analysis should include the following steps:

1 a description and analysis of the operational system within which the task is carried out should be made so that the task is seen in context. It is important in teaching a skill that its context be explained to the learner

2 the relevant task is isolated and analyzed in relation to its objectives

3 cues and signals involved in the job (for example, required equipment, instrument readings, arrangement of materials) are identified and recorded

4 task elements associated with mastery of the job are identified and classified as either procedural tasks (such as checking that the locknut on a bicycle wheel is correctly tightened) or problem-solving tasks (such as the detection and identification of a puncture in a bicycle wheel)

5 the analysis is checked in a variety of operational conditions.

After the task in question has been identified, the skills required can be analyzed according to the following steps:

1 what are the precise actions performed by an experienced worker during the various stages of the task? How are the actions sequenced and do they involve any inherent difficulties of execution?

2 what information from each of his or her senses does the worker receive during the stages of the task?

3 how does the experienced worker utilize sensory information in deciding how to select and control the physical movements needed for a skilled performance?

Planning skills-based lessons

Lesson planning in relation to the acquisition of skills can benefit from a study of the significant functions that characterize a skill-based process (Miller, 1960). There are seven factors which ought to be taken into account when skills techniques are to be taught:

1 the ability to recognize objects (for example, components, parts, tools, equipment) and symbols (for example, abbreviations or standard units of measurement) used in the skilled task by name and appearance

2 the viewing, search and detection of cues or indicators relevant to the task (for example, a bolt that could not be tightened might indicate that the thread has been stripped from it)

3 the identification and interpretation of cue-patterns (for example, identifying common situations in which the thread might be stripped from a bolt)

4 the temporary retention or short-term recall of information needed to complete particular sequences

5 the long-term recall of procedures

6 decision-making

7 appropriate response, using appropriate motor skills and/or tools.

Based on the theoretical principles outlined above, the following principles should therefore be considered by teachers and trainers in the planning and execution of lessons aimed at the acquisition of skills, and based on defined learning outcomes/objectives that relate to those psychomotor skills:

Initial demonstration of the skill
The skill ought to be demonstrated initially in its entirely as a fully integrated set and cycle of operations and it should be stressed from the very beginning that mastery can be acquired by those who are willing to learn. There must be no suggestion that competence can be attained only by a chosen few. The demonstration ought to be accompanied by a clear, non-technical commentary. (Technical vocabulary and expressions can be introduced later if required, either during a follow-up demonstration or in a separate, classroom-based session). Above all, it must be a demonstration of mastery which can be emulated. The correct movements which go to make up the skill must be in evidence from the outset. The demonstrator must not forget that what is second nature to him or her – posture, the holding of a piece of equipment, the guiding of a tool – must not be taken for granted. It must be seen as part of the skill to be acquired and must be analyzed and taught accordingly

Breakdown of the skill

The skill must then be broken down into its component, subordinate activities. Each action should be demonstrated, explained, analyzed and demonstrated again so as to emphasize its particular importance and its significance for the skill as a whole. The relation of separate activities one to the other and their integration into a hierarchy of complete routines, which make up the skill, must be stressed. Order, sequence, pattern and rhythm must be emphasized.

1 The learning of skills should be based initially on units of tasks which can be practised with some assurance of success. The reinforcing value of a correctly performed action in the early days of skill acquisition cannot be overstressed. The importance of careful and sympathetic guidance will be obvious. Positive feedback, given neither undeservedly nor indiscriminately, is a valuable reinforcing agent. The first successful actions of the engineering apprentice working at the bench, the hairdressing apprentice working with a client (as opposed to a block) at the college training salon, or the carpentry apprentice cutting a dovetail joint, ought all to be acknowledged and praised.

2 There are advantages in dividing complex tasks into naturally-occurring units, rather than unnecessarily small units which have to be combined at a later stage if they are to be meaningful to students.

3 The sequencing of the component parts that make up the new skill area must be emphasized.

The importance of practice

Skills acquisition lessons require supervised, reinforced, and carefully spaced practice by students. Technique and understanding must be linked so that the learner attains the objective of an autonomous, overall competence built from those separate activities of which the total skill is composed. Where the skill is linked closely with speed, practice must be arranged so that this feature is stressed. When planning for practice, the following issues should be taken into account:

1 Distributed practice based on activity followed by intervals of rest (in which consolidation can take place) appears to produce better results than those emanating from one long, unbroken period. Two separated 30-minute periods of practice are often more productive than one hour's continuous practice. In this way, those periods when practice seems to produce no improvement in performance may be avoided.

2 Supervision and, where appropriate, physical guidance of all aspects of practice will be vital if errors are to be noted, analyzed and eliminated. The teacher or trainer will need clear sight lines and space to walk around so that the students can be observed whilst they practice.

3 The importance of accurate timing must emerge from practice. Timing is not always a matter of the swift response to a stimulus; it must involve an anticipation of what is coming next and a linked ability to select swiftly from one's repertoire of responses. Supervized practice should stress the significance of this concept.

4 The continuous flow of separate actions combined into a skilled performance has to emerge from practice. This requires that the teacher shall point out the importance of acquiring a natural rhythm in the performance of a task.

5 There is evidence to suggest the importance of maintaining a minimal rate of information input in practice if the learner is to acquire efficiency in the skill. Students can be overloaded if they are asked do too much too soon. Conversely, if they are asked to do too little, then boredom and disengagement may occur.

6 The pattern of skill factors making up a task appears to change progressively with practice; hence the content of a practice session must be altered regularly as that pattern is seen to change.

Feedback
Continuous, swift and accurate feedback must be provided for learners and they must be taught to interpret the feedback correctly (this topic is discussed in more detail in Chapter 31). Learners must be reminded of the benchmarks or criteria that they are working towards, and must be informed of any gap between their current level of achievement and the required standard. Then, they must be shown how to close that gap. The feedback process must become second nature for both teacher and student: that is, the teacher must take the time to become adept at giving feedback accurately, and in a constructive and timely manner, and the student must take the time to become used to responding to it quickly and positively. However, feedback should look beyond the specific task being practiced, and take account of the skills required to extrapolate from present activities and to apply knowledge to new situations with immediate and accurate activity.

Authentic assessment
Assessments ought to be administered regularly, and always in authentic work-based or work-related settings (this topic is discussed in more detail in Chapter 30). Insight and retention ought to be assessed, along with the capacity to transfer acquired skills to novel and demanding situations.

The structure of the psychomotor skills lesson

The three-part lesson model that was introduced in the preceding chapter also applies to the planning of skills-based lessons. This model (introduction, development/consolidation, summary/conclusion) can be revisited for the specific demands of technical and vocational curricula (Davies, 1981). A skills session planned according to this model would consist of:

1 Introduction.
   The teacher should tell the students what to do, how it is to be done and what are the appropriate procedures (including health and safety issues, correct use of equipment and resources and so forth). Any necessary signals or cues should be explained. Short periods of teacher-led activities should be used at first, with occasional pauses to allow for questions or clarification.

2 Development/consolidation.
   The teacher should gradually move away from any cognitive or perceptual processes that have been outlined (the 'underpinning theory') and move on to emphasize the physical skills that are required. Intensive practice on routines should be allowed. As they are practiced, different routines or small tasks should be chained together so as to allow practice of the entire skill. Longer teaching periods can then be introduced, with a consequent concentration on coordination, judgement and planning. The complete skill should be practiced until it is learned and can be assessed (if required by either the curriculum or the scheme of work).

3 Summary/conclusion.
   The teacher should establish links to wider sequences of skills within the curriculum as appropriate. Links to occupational competences should also be emphasized. The correct ways of clearing up after the task has been finished (appropriate cleaning and storage of tools and equipment) should also be explained and demonstrated where necessary.

As with lessons in academic or professional contexts, a number of other variables will impact on the ways in which this three-part model might be used:

1 The position of the lesson within the curriculum.
   If a new skill or procedure is to be introduced for the first time, the introduction and development sections may require more teacher-led input. An initial demonstration will need to be conducted more slowly than a repeat demonstration, with more time for questions and comments. A repeat demonstration by the teacher working on his or her own will be faster than a demonstration which is facilitated by the teacher but carried out by one or more students – a lengthier activity, but one that is more likely to encourage deeper learning (as discussed in the preceding chapter). A lesson in which students are continuing to practice a series of processes that have already been demonstrated and rehearsed may, on the other hand, require only a very perfunctory introduction.

2 The availability of resources.

In an ideal world, the workshops and training rooms in FE colleges would be sufficiently spacious and well-equipped to allow each student to work individually on the process or activity that is being practiced. However, this is not always the case. Fluctuations in student numbers may lead to group sizes being increased, and students having to share workstations and/or tools and equipment. Inadequate teaching accommodation may mean that there is insufficient space for the number of workbenches that might optimally be required. In these situations, the teacher has to plan so that all students are able to spend time engaged in practice, taking turns in pair groups or alternating between two activities.

3 Assessment and examination arrangements

If the curriculum indicates that a practical under test conditions is imminent, or that the submission of a completed portfolio is due, teachers may – subject to the availability of resources and accommodation – opt to offer additional 'open' or 'drop-in' sessions which are only loosely structured and which aim, in the first instance, to provide opportunities for further practice and feedback.

The use of questions in the psychomotor skills lesson

As with the teaching of academic and professional courses, the teaching of vocational and technical courses rests on open lines of communication between the teacher and the students, reflecting the essentially social aspect of the teaching and learning process more generally.

From the point of view of the teacher, questions directed at the students encourage participation, initiative, and keep the group alert as to what is going on. Understanding can be checked and mistakes in comprehension or application can be revealed. Specific questions accompanying a demonstration of the tasks or skills being taught must be pitched at an appropriate level: that is to say, they must always be aligned to those tasks that have already been demonstrated. Questions can be used to check understanding, but also to ascertain the extent to which prior learning might be applied to the new situation. They can also be used whilst students are engaged in individual or grouped practice.

Questions from the learner should also be encouraged during a skills lesson. Questions raised by students during a demonstration or explanation may provide a useful measure of feedback and may indicate the level of understanding of the class as a whole, prompting – if necessary – the repetition of a particular task or an additional explanation as to why something has been done. On other occasions, a student's question might best be answered through a practical demonstration, which should always be accompanied by further commentary and opportunities for checking learning. Skills concern doing, and answers to question relating to skills, will therefore involve an activity utilizing the mechanism or other object involved in the exercise of the skill.

Effective skills instruction: a checklist

Fleck and Law put forward the following rules as basic to effective instruction in the skills (1988), which provides a useful checklist for the teacher when writing schemes of work and lesson plans:

1   long-term and short-term outcomes/objectives must be worked out and enunciated clearly at the beginning of instruction
2   different types of learning should be encouraged and appropriate instructional methods must be selected carefully
3   individual differences among members of the class must be taken into account; hence small groups and alternative instructional strategies are essential if individual learning problems are to be identified and resolved
4   demonstrate rather than talk. Avoid verbosity and use speech to reinforce what is being seen by the learner
5   invite class participation by specific rather than general questions, and allow time for learners to reflect on what they have observed
6   encourage learners to perform tasks unaided and to ask for help only when it is obviously needed
7   provide objective appraisals and employ comprehensible strategies for error correction
8   check the effectiveness of instruction by methodical questioning and close inspection of learners' work.

Psychomotor skills teaching and the liberalization of education

Historically, the work of colleges of FE has been seen as assisting in dispelling the myth which suggests that the acquisition of manual skills is incompatible with the aims of a broad, liberal education: the encouragement of the power of judgement, the ability to think swiftly and accurately, and the capacity to discriminate and perceive relationships. All of these are characteristics of the trained mind that is central to the liberal education tradition. The challenge that the liberal tradition poses to teachers in FE can be seen as asking them to impart specific skills whilst at the same time making a deliberate attempt to extend horizons and to develop insight.

However, notwithstanding the efforts of those educationalists who sought to extend the liberal ethos (for example, through the expansion of adult and community education in the latter half of the twentieth century (Wallis, 1996)), the divide between the academic and vocational curricula has persisted. The vocational curriculum continues to occupy a second-best status and even though employers consistently complain that too many college leavers lack the right employability skills, they continue to give more jobs to people with academic qualifications than vocational ones (Allen and Ainley, 2007). At the same time, the number of people completing vocational or technical qualifications has increased, as the number of available qualifications grew (until the 2011 Review of Vocational Education led by Professor Alison Wolf).

There is no reason why the vocational and technical curricula cannot stretch the capacities and minds of students in FE. The second-class status of the vocational curriculum is a consequence of social attitudes and government policies: a comparison with Germany, where more younger people are now going to university because they cannot find an apprenticeship, exemplifies this point. Therefore, whilst teachers of car maintenance, hair and beauty therapy or electrical installation have to spend their working lives persuading employers that their leavers have the 'right skills' (even if there are no jobs other than unpaid 'placements' or volunteering posts to go to), these same teachers need to remember that they are also able to effect broader changes in the outlook and ethic of their students.

Summary: Practical courses for practical people?

It is particularly common within the vocational and technical curriculum – as distinct from the academic and professional curriculum – for teachers to continue to identify themselves in terms of their occupational background and qualifications, a phenomenon referred to as dual professionalism (Orr and Simmons, 2009). As such, adopting a new professional role – that of a teacher – can cause some difficulties. Being a teacher – irrespective of contractual status or the subject matter that is being taught – needs to be placed at the forefront of the individual's mind. Of course it is important that a teacher is current and has up-to-date knowledge of the trade or vocational that she or he is preparing students to enter, but upon entering the FE college, the carpenter is no longer only a carpenter, but a teacher of carpentry, and the beauty therapist is no longer only a beauty therapist, but a teacher of beauty therapy. Not everybody who studies sociology A-level will become a sociologist. Similarly, not everyone who studies painting and decorating will work as a painter and decorator. But both students of sociology and students of painting and decorating will – if they take part in formal instruction that has been appropriately planned, resourced and sequenced – learn much from their teachers even if, in the long run, they choose an entirely unrelated occupation.

Further reading

The additional reading recommended at the end of the preceding chapter is also of relevance to this chapter.

25 Giving Lectures and Presentations

In a culture of student-centred learning, differentiation, e-learning and widening access, the thought of delivering a lecture might seem to be wilfully out-of-date. But whilst the stereotypical image of the lecturer mumbling into his notes whilst the students in a large lecture hall alternate between taking notes and sending each other text messages may have some small degree of truth, the reality is that from time to time, the provision through a teacher-led talk, presentation or lecture (they are all variations on the same theme) is a useful and important pedagogic activity, as just one of a number of strategies that will be employed by the teacher, especially if working with large student groups. It is in this context that the arguments presented in this chapter regarding the use of lectures should be understood. The 'lecture' is here understood to refer to any formal presentation or talk made by the teacher, which might last anywhere from ten minutes to an hour, although the latter is uncommon in the FE sector.

A lecture involves a continuous oral and formal exposition of, or discourse on, a particular topic or theme (Bligh, 1998; Race, 2002). By definition, a lecture is teacher-led and rests on a one-way pattern of communication and, as such, has often been criticized. And yet the lecture persists as a common mode of instruction in colleges of FE and elsewhere. Indeed, the continued use of lectures in the higher education sector can be used to argue that lectures should be used in colleges as well in order to provide students with the study skills that they might need upon progressing to higher study. Typically, it is used to introduce course material, to give groups of students specialized information such as the results of research, or to present a final recap of a programme or module. Its weaknesses and strengths and its peculiar difficulties for the lecturer will emerge in the consideration of lecture structure, planning and delivery.

The demands on the lecturer are almost always considerable, particularly in the presentation and transmission of values and attitudes inherent in affective objectives. Effective lecturing has little to do with the lecturer's ability to write and read from his or her lecture notes; it calls for a variety of skills, particularly the ability to attract and hold one's audience. Some of the more important skills are considered below. The management tasks of the lecturer resemble, fundamentally, those of the class teacher involved in the broader process of lesson planning: lecture outcomes must be planned; resources and constraints must be taken into account; the existing level of knowledge of the audience must be considered; and particular attention must be given to the organization of material such as PowerPoint slides and handouts.

Formal lecturing: Pros and cons

Criticisms of the lecture are often uncompromising: lecturing is said to be a negation of the teaching process; its autocratic form and style necessarily work against the establishment of the partnership between students and teachers considered essential to facilitative approaches to learning. The passive role of the listeners and the lack of discussion are said to be a contradiction of the process of free flow and exchange of ideas which the learning process demands. The lack of feedback impairs the learning process. The lecture is said to leave much to be desired as a mode of creating the conditions for effective learning. And long-standing research has argued that students apparently learned as much from reading passages from a book as from hearing the same matter delivered in a lecture,that lectures are not generally effective in teaching students to think, and that students attending lectures do not always recognize important points rather than unimportant details. Indeed, jokes and other types of humorous remarks made by lecturers are often remembered by students more clearly than lecturers' major statements.

Other research suggests a different point of view. It has been argued that the experience of listening to a lecture differs markedly from reading a printed version of the same text. The content may be the same, but the processes involved in reading and listening – reception, coding, interpretation and storage– are different. Some researchers suggest that acuity of thought is best heightened through the auditory channels. Further, a lecturer can be more flexible than a written presentation: no author is able to modify presentation on the basis of readers' reactions, whereas a lecturer who is able to obtain clues from the audience's reception of the material is able to change presentation swiftly. The lecture provides a live model of a person thinking: an enthusiastic lecturer, posing a problem and moving to its solution step by step, provides an experience for students which it is difficult to duplicate in any other way. A poor lecturer might induce mind-numbing weariness in the audience, but a lecturer who provides a well-delivered challenge based upon fact and argument can have a positive effect on the mental activity of listeners (Brown and Race, 2002; Saunders, 1990).

Underlying this chapter is the belief that a well-constructed lecture, which takes into account broader principles of effective instruction, can, and very often does, succeed in capturing students' attention and communicating patterns of information.

Types of lecture

There are different types or styles of lecture or formal presentation, which are commonly delivered in FE colleges. The main features of these are briefly discussed here:

1 The oral essay

This is a highly structured lecture, which presents information related to a body of systematized knowledge which is central to a course of instruction. Owing to the formal nature of this type of 'one-way' presentation, a lecture in this mode may lack the dimension of 'interpersonal communication' which is often held necessary for student motivation. It should be possible, however, where the lecturer is aware of this problem, for time to be found for a short question-and-answer session after the lecture has ended. This type of lecture can be supported by the production of a short handout, listing a number of key facts or definitions, as well as through expecting students to take their own notes. A lecture can be accompanied by key facts, quotations, images or photographs, arranged as a PowerPoint or Prezi file and viewed via a data projector.

2 The expository lecture

This type of lecture moves beyond the oral essay, by being less rigidly structured and by addressing points of debate and discussion rather than established bodies of knowledge. Such a lecture might include a number of short question-and-answer sessions at planned points within the structure. Lectures of this nature are commonly used in colleges. A lecture of this type might take the form of the presentation of an argument, presented in formal style, with careful use of visual aids to present data upon which the lecturer commented. A number of points for argument might be provided and then countered, and breaks in the presentation for small group discussions can encourage student participation.

3 The problem-centred lecture

In this type of lecture students are led through the steps necessary to solve a problem, which is stated with appropriate emphasis during the lecturer's opening comments. A successful lecture presented in this style demands a high degree of concentration from the audience and a carefully linked presentation if the threads of exposition and comprehension are not to snap.

4 The lecture-discussion

A short lecture is followed by a discussion around a key point in the lecturer's opening statement. Careful timing is essential. This type of lecture might last for 15 minutes, supported by material in a structured-notes handout. It might then be followed by a discussion split into equally timed segments, analyzing the principal points outlined in the lecture. The lecturer can then collect comments and feedback from the group as a whole before providing a short recapitulation to end the session.

5 The lecture-demonstration

A lecture can also be used to introduce a demonstration, typically so that the teacher can introduce or revise any underpinning knowledge that the students will need to keep in mind as the demonstration proceeds. It is a straightforward task for the teacher to use diagrams and/or photographs of the process or experiment to be demonstrated in her or his presentation. These diagrams can in turn be provided in handout form for students to annotate during the lecture or the demonstration itself, or as part of a follow-up exercise designed to reinforce what has been demonstrated.

As in the case of the lesson more widely, content will play a large part in the determination of lecture structure. The purpose of the lecture must be reflected in the way it is constructed. A lecture on the implications of the Data Protection Act for the management of databases is likely to demand a structure somewhat different from that used in a lecture on observing children learning through play. The structure of the former lecture is likely to be based on a verbal presentation illustrated by quotations from relevant legislation and annotated screenshots from a desktop computer, while the structure of the latter will probably be based on verbal exposition, accompanied by photographs or diagrams. The major determinant of structure should emerge from the lecturer's broader approach to teaching and learning, and built around answers to the questions: what is the purpose of this lecture? What do I hope to achieve? What are the specific outcomes/objectives that are being worked towards? Does the subject matter demand the use of any additional resources? Does the subject matter necessitate a particular approach?

Physical environment of the lecture

When a purpose-built lecture theatre is available much can usually be done to improve arrangements so that communication between teacher and students is as effective as possible. Sight lines should be clear, due to the tiered seating that is characteristic of the lecture theatre, but audio-visual resources must still be set out with care so that their use is not an interruption to the even flow of the lecture. The positioning of screens, flipcharts and data projectors also requires attention prior to the delivery of the lecture, as do more practical matters such as font sizes on PowerPoint slides, lighting, the tabling of handouts and so forth.

Where the lecturer is obliged to use a standard classroom, the seating must be prepared so that notes can be taken without difficulty. In some of the rather cramped teaching accommodation of the 'new-build' colleges of the early 2000s, this is not always straightforward and rooms should be inspected prior to the lecture (or any other kind of classroom-based session, in fact) if possible. The positioning of the lecturer's desk should be determined by experiment, and lecturers should be willing to spend some time walking around the room to ascertain the best available sight lines.

Planning the lecture

The lesson plan for a lecture will be determined most appropriately – as is the case for other styles of session more generally – by a consideration of three major areas: the students, the subject matter, and the resources and constraints. The problem of pitching the lecture at an appropriate level is particularly difficult to resolve where the audience is likely to be large in number. As such, many different levels of learning are almost certain to be represented. The students' profiles (prior experience of study, prior achievements, specific needs, and so forth) must be kept in mind, and this necessitates making allowance in the lecture plan for time to define terms, to give a number of specific and authentic examples, to illustrate and to recapitulate.

The introduction to the lecture, including a clear statement of its position within the curriculum and the outcome/objective that it helps work towards (reinforced, perhaps, by a visual display), requires careful treatment: it should aim deliberately at stimulating interest and gaining and holding attention, and should attempt to create an appropriate relationship with the audience. The conclusion of the lecture also requires detailed consideration. It provides an important opportunity to reinforce what has been said and to establish links with the next session or activity that the students will be engaged in.

The amount of material to be presented in the lecture must be planned with care. Lecturers must not fail to take into account the limits of the short-term memory. A lecture based on relatively few concepts may have a greater chance of success in attaining its objective, therefore, than one which requires the assimilation of a large volume of information.

The lecture plan will reflect the necessity to arouse and keep attention, which may require the carefully planned use of visual material (photographs, diagrams, video clips, sound files) so as to break the monotony of speech, to present appropriate stimuli and to reinforce responses by correctly timed recapitulation and restatement. The sequence of statement, elaboration, review and recapitulation is worth considering in the planning of a lecture.

Some writers suggest that a lecture plan can be based around the identification and use of key points in the topic which is to form the subject of the lecture. Key points should be expressed as simply as possible, should be illustrated by examples, qualified or elaborated and, finally, restated in the form of a conclusion. This is a valuable mode of planning which can be used where there is little time to prepare a lecture fully.

The lecturer's own notes, referred to during the course of the lecture, may take the form of a detailed, sentence-by-sentence account (useful for those teachers who have little lecturing experience), or an elaborated plan based on the framework of what is to be said. Note, however, that the fact that detailed lecture notes have been prepared must not result in the lecturer giving the impression of merely reading a prepared statement in mechanical fashion. It is difficult for the lecturer to establish eye contact or to use non-verbal as well as verbal cues if she or he spends the entire lecture, head bowed, reading from a series of notes. Some spontaneity of expression and delivery ought to emerge even in the most carefully planned lecture.

How long ought a lecture to last and at what stage does it cease to have any impact? There is no golden rule, because the threshold of assimilation will vary from student to student. One may be unable to concentrate or retain data after ten minutes' unbroken speech, while another will assimilate with ease the contents of a 20-minute talk. In general, pauses ought to be made in the interests of concentration and assimilation after each 10-15 minutes of continuous speaking. After that period of time there may be a decline in audience attention. The pause may be used to recapitulate what has been said up to this point, perhaps with a chart which illustrates or recapitulates a key point, to introduce a question and answer session or to deal with any ambiguities or misunderstandings. Many lecturers' experiences suggest that the entire lecture session ought to last not longer than 50 minutes. After that period attention tends to diminish very rapidly and assimilation becomes difficult.

Planning lectures and presentations – notes for new teachers

It is often a trying experience for lecturers in FE to plan their first lectures or presentations. There is always a difference between delivering a 20-minute microteach to fellow teacher-training students, and a 20-minute presentation to a group of second-year BTEC students. Lecturers tend to be judged on their first appearances before audiences which are swift to pronounce on sub-standard performances and not always ready to express satisfaction with the carefully-planned and well-executed lecture. Newly appointed lecturers are often advised to discuss their first lecture plans with established and experienced members of staff (a mentor or subject learning coach, for example).

Here, it is recommended that lecturers (both newly appointed and longer established) take into account the following general planning principles:

1   plan around central points or general themes that bring together a number of topics
2   find a place in your plan for matters which will be of high interest to students
3   do not hesitate to include in your plan matters which are difficult and which will demand effort of thought – a lecture should not be viewed by students as a soft option that does not require work and attention
4   do not plan for the inclusion of material which is not linked in any way with students' attainment and progress within the curriculum
5   plan, if possible, for an opening 'attention grabber' and seek to produce an expectation that the lecture will be of significance in the overall course programme
6   plan so that thinking is promoted by what you will say, and keep in mind those factors which will stimulate the processes of deep as opposed to surface learning.

Delivering lectures and presentations

A teacher's lesson style, mannerisms, speech, gestures, eye-to-eye contact with students, clarity of expression, appearance – so-called 'personality' – can have a considerable impact on the class; positive, where it aids communication, but negative, where it acts to interfere with the transmission and reception of information. Impact of this kind is even more marked in the case of the lecture. It can be said with some truth that, for a lecture audience, the medium is the message. A lecture is dependent for its success – to a marked degree – on the personality and communication skills of the lecturer. That person is the sole focus of attention for most of the lecture period; his or her style of delivery can result in acceptance and assimilation, or rejection, of the lecture content. The lecturer's expressiveness, that is, an obvious enthusiasm for the subject, a perceived desire to communicate, and an ability to generate student interest, can make or break the lecture.

Lecturing technique involves an ability to speak clearly, to modulate voice, tone and pitch, to use gestures sparingly, but effectively, and to speak at a pace which does not prevent assimilation and understanding. When considering lecture delivery style, therefore, the following general points should be considered:

1 The style of delivery ought to be neither casual, nor in the pattern of grand oratory. A natural mode of delivery requires, paradoxically, much practice. It ought to be characterized by clarity, simplicity of expression and planned timing (which may require rehearsal).

2 The emphasis of key points may require variations in the pattern and intensity of speech, a gesture, a pause, or a visual illustration. In a lecture, a carefully positioned pause can serve as a signal for a key statement, or as a kind of emphasis.

3 Flamboyant, exaggerated gestures rapidly become meaningless, divert attention from the words which they accompany and may snap the thread of communication.

4 Some mannerisms may amuse initially, but in a short time may irritate, even offend and alienate, eventually creating a barrier to effective communication. Walking rapidly around the lecture room while one is lecturing, for example, rarely assists communication. As soon as lecturers become aware of these mannerisms, they ought to work towards removing them from their repertoire. Unconscious mannerisms (constantly removing and replacing a pen lid, or the use of particular expressions for example) can be identified through lesson observations.

5 Avoid excessive humour in a presentation: the role of 'lecturer-as-entertainer' palls swiftly. The lecturer who has discovered that she or he has a talent to amuse should exercise that capability only occasionally, such as when it might underline a particular point. Its repeated use tends to be interpreted swiftly as a downgrading of the subject matter and a demeaning of the audience.

6 Dictate very sparingly indeed. Consider confining this activity, say, to short definitions and explanations of new technical words and phrases.

7 It is vital that the lecturer should convey genuine enthusiasm and interest. Non-verbal cues – facial expressions, eye contact (the absence of which is often interpreted by an audience as nervousness, fear or lack of interest), use of the hands – are rapidly communicated to students, who are swift in interpretation. Students expect their lecturers to be knowledgeable and enthusiastic.

8 Where the lecture involves the use of visual aids, they ought to be prepared and ready to hand, so that continuity in presentation is maintained. Images, pictures, charts, maps, photographs or film clips can be easily integrated into a presentation, and it is rare that a lecture will need to be given in a teaching room that does not contain a data projector and a PC. It is important that the lecturer quickly runs through her or his presentation before the lecture/class, so that any problems caused by viewing the presentation on a different PC to the one that was used in preparing the slides, can be resolved.

9 A message conveyed by the lecturer is stored temporarily in the student's short-term memory; it is then forgotten unless it is noted or transferred to the long-term memory. Links between lecture content and existing facts in the student's memory are essential; messages that are incompatible with already acquired knowledge tend to disappear rapidly unless reinforced.

10 Students' attention during a lecture must be maintained at a high level. A variety of methods of keeping an audience attentive should be employed: spacing one's delivery, using the buzz group occasionally or utilizing a very short question and answer period, may have positive effects on concentration. Some experienced lecturers plan so as to introduce change in the form and nature of the demands made upon students. So, for example, after every period of 20 minutes during the lecture period, listening is expected to give way to listening plus viewing of charts and other visual aids.

In sum, lecturers should remember that, because they are the focal point of attention, they are communicating along a variety of channels, some of which are noted by implication in the preceding paragraphs. The linguistic channel is, by its very nature, of great importance: choice of words and clarity in speech are essential features of an effective lecture. The paralinguistic channel, involving the lecturer's vocal tone and quality of expression, provides a vital, individual contribution to overall lecture content and delivery. The visual channel involves not only the use of visual aids, but refers to the lecturer's personal appearance, which can introduce unwanted interference into the communication process. The kinetic channel, along which the lecturer's body movements are transformed into messages and interpreted by the audience, must not be overlooked.

Establishing feedback during lectures and presentations

When delivering a formal lecture or presentation, teachers suffer from the disadvantage of not knowing at any given time the nature of the reactions of the audience, since they cannot generally assess, save in an imprecise manner, the effectiveness of their efforts to communicate. Lecturers cannot periodically halt the flow of the lecture in order to provide for a formal formative assessment so that progress in understanding can be checked. To rely on the facial expressions of one's audience is of relatively little value when attempting to assess learning (other than recognizing unambiguous states such as confusion or lack of engagement), and a discussion or test after the lecture has finished obviously comes too late to assist assessment and control of the lecture itself, although it will be of help as part of a wider evaluation of the teacher's lecturing style. In effect, the lecturer is deprived of the means of measuring *immediate* class reaction and this may account for the learning difficulties of some students whose instruction is based almost entirely on lectures. But where the lecturer perceives in his audience signs that attention *is* breaking up – conversation replacing silence, inordinate fidgeting with mobile phones, a cessation of note-taking – an immediate modification of the plan for the remainder of the lecture is called for. Research into aspects of non-verbal communication in relation to lecture-audience feedback has been interpreted as suggesting that a slight, but potentially useful, element of feedback is available to the lecturer who is able to read and interpret the body language of the audience swiftly and accurately.

Some lecturers have used the buzz group technique to provide feedback as well as to break up the continuous exposition which characterizes the formal lecture. At carefully selected points in the course of the lecture the audience is asked to split into small prearranged groups of 4–6 students, each with a reporter and perhaps a note-taker as well (these roles can be rotated throughout the programme of study), to discuss their responses to a direct question. The groups can be formed by those sitting together in various sections of the room. The lecture is resumed after some of the group comments are reported and discussed.

The insertion into a lecture plan of a short question-and-answer segment, so as to provide the lecturer with a slight element of feedback, is potentially valuable, but also potentially problematic. For some lecturers the process of asking for questions, which characterizes the formal lesson, is unacceptable in the lecture situation because it can breach continuity, or can throw a lecture totally off course. It is one thing to call for (and welcome) questions at the end of a lecture (thus giving the lecturer some indication of learning outcome), but quite another to encourage the asking of questions during the lecturer's narrative. How can one deal with a very important question which requires a complex answer likely to take up the remainder of the lecturer's time? Many lecturers, accepting the 'feedback value' of question and answer, encourage questions during specified periods only, but insist that such questions be short and confined to topics that are relevant only to the topic of the presentation, while pointing out to students that other types of question will be welcomed during future specially-programmed question-and-answer sessions. Questions that are not directly related to the lecture can be written down (perhaps on a whiteboard or flipchart, depending on availability) and followed up at the end of the session if time permits, or at the next available opportunity.

Taking notes and providing handouts

What is the best way for a student to record the sessions that she or he attends? This is an issue which must be considered by every college lecturer. Should the lecturer distribute a printed version of the entire slideshow, provide outline notes, or rely on students making their own notes during the lecture? Should the handouts or notes be distributed (either on paper or by uploading a file to the college virtual learning environment) well in advance of the lecture, or a few minutes before or at the end of the lecture?

There are several reasons why notetaking by students should be encouraged, not the least of which is that any activity that supports the development of students' literacy skills ought to be promoted. The very process of listening and recording by writing forms an important response to the stimuli presented by the lecturer, enabling new impressions to be fixed and assisting assimilation. Notetaking is the student's own work and, it is represents a degree of active participation in an otherwise passive instructional process. It helps to overcome the limitations of short-term memory, thereby assisting revision, long-term retention and recall.

But some students do find notetaking to be difficult. Some are simply unable to write both quickly and legibly. Others may be unable to discriminate so that they fail to note an important point made by the lecturer, instead paying attention to less central themes. And some may have difficulty in concentrating simultaneously on listening and writing. The lecturer should not, therefore, take for granted the ability of the audience to make notes. For many in the audience it may be a relatively new experience. As such, it would be advantageous to provide guidance on the technique of notetaking, rather than assuming that students are already accomplished notetakers. Such guidance might include advice and practice relating to the construction and numbering of paragraphs, sections and sub-headings, and to ways of giving emphasis to key topics or themes by spacing, underlining or highlighting. It can also assist students if they are told by the lecturer of those vital points that are to be noted down. Students must also be shown how to use their notes, how to expand them so that they can be added to and how to use them for revision.

The lecturer should also ensure that the environment and the style of delivery allow notes to be taken. If the lighting has been dimmed to allow the use of a data projector, it may later have to be increased so that students can see their notes. Short pauses during the lecture (which can be timed so as to coincide with divisions in the subject matter) are of great assistance to the note writer who is trying to catch up. And the writing of the main headings of the lecture on a whiteboard, flipchart or PowerPoint slide may help in the taking of notes and may provide a useful summary of the lecture, which can be used for recapitulation and revision.

Some lecturers, recognizing the difficulties that surround notetaking, prefer to distribute their own handouts –on the grounds that the advantage of student participation by writing is outweighed by the students possessing an authentic record of the lecture content. Handouts may list lecture outcomes/objectives, suggest reading, give appropriate references, diagrams, key points, outline the body of the lecture in précis form and draw attention to difficult points. The handouts can be distributed in advance of the lecture, allowing for the checking of references for preliminary reading and the consideration of problems likely to emerge, *or* they can be given out (as is usually the case) at the point in the lecture when a final recapitulation is about to be made, or when the lecture has ended. Handouts may be used to trail the next lecture by indicating its title, and by statements, such as: 'the next lecture has been designed on the assumption that students will have read carefully the following pages in the course text book'.

A note on recording lectures and presentations

It is not uncommon for one or more students to ask that they might record a lecture or presentation. Such requests have become increasingly common in part due to the prevalence of readily affordable technologies that allow such recordings to be easily made (using a smart phone or tablet PC) and then downloaded to a desktop computer if necessary. Such technologies are of particular value to students with specific learning difficulties or disabilities. Departmental rules should always be referred to when such a request is made. Normally, permission should be given unless there is a good reason for the lecturer to refuse, but such circumstances are rare. Indeed, the refusal of a request from a student with a disability might be interpreted as discriminatory behaviour. It is quite another matter when a request is made to record a seminar however: in these situations, all of the students will need to agree, as they may appear on the final recording.

Summary: The lecture in further education

In spite of the alleged weaknesses of the lecture as a mode of instruction and of its general unsuitability for the teaching of skills, it continues to be employed, often with great success, in the colleges of FE. Its advantages ought not to be forgotten and they are summarized here:

1 younger students may learn more readily when they listen than when they read.

2 the lecture can be of particular value in introducing a subject

3 the lecture is valuable where knowledge is advancing rapidly and up-to-date textbooks are not available

4 the lecture can awaken critical skills in a student

5 the lecture can provide aesthetic pleasure

6 the lecture is highly economic of staff time, can cover more ground than a tutorial or seminar and can reach large numbers of students.

Course content covered entirely by lectures is rare in the colleges of FE, whereas courses, which include lectures combined with other modes of instruction, are more common. Thus, lectures might be used to begin a course, to provide a final recapitulation and revision, or in combination with seminars and tutorials. They also figure prominently in some types of team teaching (as discussed in Chapter 27). But in conclusion, it is worth noting that if it is carefully prepared, well-timed and skilfully delivered, the lecture can be a powerful and stimulating mode of communication and instruction.

Further reading

Hints and strategies for giving lectures and presentations are not difficult to find. Alongside the generic teacher-training literature there are some other books that offer a fresh and creative angle. The obvious first port of call is:

Haynes, A. and Haynes, K. (2012), *53 Interesting things to do in your lectures*. London: Professional and Higher Partnership.

And other useful advice can be found in:

Bligh, J. (2000), *What's the use of lectures?* San Francisco: Jossey-Bass.

Exley, K. and Dennick, R. (2009), *Giving a lecture: from presenting to teaching*. London: Routledge.

26 Planning for Student-Centred Learning and Teaching

Formal lessons and lectures, as discussed in the previous chapter, differ quite markedly from the discussion group, the seminar, the tutorial and the case study, which are discussed in this chapter. The former are *teacher-led* strategies; the latter are *student-centred* strategies, directed at facilitating learning within an environment in which the teacher plays a mediating role and interactive participation from the students is the norm. The former generally depend for their success, in large measure, on the teacher's performance; the latter achieve success only from the continuing collective activity and interrelationship of teacher and class.

Planning seminar groups or preparing case studies is, in its own way, as demanding as the planning and writing of a formal presentation and shold never be seen as easy options. Student-centred activities require considerable skill to be exercised by the directing tutor who should have some understanding of the rationale of discussion and its techniques, and an appreciation of general group dynamics. The tutor should understand the concept and basic form of a 'group' and its nature, the ways in which group members might be expected to interact, the effect of individual differences in status, abilities and expectations on the group as a whole, and the structure of a group. He or she needs to understand the nature of participation in discussion, the value of reciprocal influence among students in the facilitation of learning, the differences between facilitating, controlling and dominating a discussion, and the types of instructional process which can be served by discussion periods. The decision to enhance learning through supervised discussion will require, for its successful implementation, spontaneity, creativity, and tolerance for the unknown as well as diligent preparation.

It is important to remember that terms such as 'discussion group', 'seminar' and 'tutorial' have not acquired standardized meanings. A tutor who is asked to include 'seminars' in his or her scheme of work should make sure that there is a common understanding by departmental heads and staff as to the precise meaning of the word.

Discussion groups: Charateristics, advantages and disadvantages

A discussion group is constituted by a tutor and class seeking to examine a matter by means of the free flow of argument. Essentially, the members pool knowledge and ideas in the cooperative task of endeavouring to understand a problem by learning from one another. Speaking, listening and observing are essential attributes of the discussion method. The discussion group, allowing two-way talk, is free from the relative formality of a seminar. Its freedom, however, necessitates careful preparation and control by the tutor, who must be a good listener, if the benefits of discussion as a mode of instruction are to be realized in full.

The purpose of a discussion group is usually the collective exploration and evaluation of ideas. Discussion heightens student interest, builds participants' understanding of the topic in question by supplementing each participant's information with information possessed by other members of the group, by stimulating different perspectives on the topic, by allowing conjectures on the subject matter and providing opportunities for criticism and refutation, by encouraging mutual adjustment of opinions. Participants also learn the social and procedural conventions surrounding such debates, such as courtesy for the person speaking, respect for the comments made by fellow students even if they are disagreed with, and so forth. Two important points should always be borne in mind by the tutor when planning a discussion group. First, the discussion must have a clear aim/objective. Secondly, prerequisite knowledge of the elements of the topic to be discussed should be considered in the preparation of the group session.

1 Establishing a clear aim/objective.
   The discussion group is a learning event which must be an integral part of the teaching programme, and ought to be accepted by students as such, and not seen as an optional extra or somehow less important to their progress as a formal presentation. The discussion group might serve as a follow-up session to a lecture, as a mid-course exploration of ideas or as a recapitulation session. In any of these roles, students will be required to talk through aspects of their study, to answer questions and then justify their answers. In this way, it can facilitate deep, as distinct from surface, learning of concepts through the encouragement of meaningful participation by all the members of the student group.

2 Prerequisite knowledge.
   Discussion groups can only be effective if the student group already possesses prerequisite knowledge of the topic under discussion. If the group has this knowledge, the discussion can serve to reinforce, to challenge and to extend students' understanding. Without this, there can be no effective participation and the result is likely to be little more than a ritual exchange of platitudes, preconceptions and vague generalities.

There are several problems associated with running discussion groups. Unless the topic is carefully chosen and the session structured and controlled, there will be a marked tendency for the discussion to degenerate into an informal debate from which a dominant hierarchy of speakers emerges. A pecking order of participants soon forms, so that the more forceful members hold the floor, while a significant proportion of the group, increasingly hesitant and unwilling to risk public contradiction, become silent observers. Because some groups can be readily dominated, false conclusions, presented in a facile, persuasive manner by a member on whom the group has become over-dependent, may be accepted all too easily. In addition, it may provoke anxiety in those students who find structured teaching and learning strategies to be more conducive to their progress and thereby interfere with their learning.

The advantages of the discussion group are said to emerge, largely, from its democratic and collaborative nature (as contrasted with the autocratic character of the presentation or the lecture). Group experience assists social facilitation, so that people tend to work more intensely when in a group. Group judgements may sometimes be more accurate than those resulting from an individual examination of problems and membership of a group might benefit those whose thoughts can be clarified by discussion with others. Further, the conflict and disagreement, which emerge in any lively discussion group, may become the starting point for critical thinking and new exploration, resulting in the group's increased tolerance of varying points of view. Group discussion also enables a class and teacher to get to know one another's thoughts, opinions and attitudes. And it provides for the teacher a useful element of feedback where the discussion has centred on the content of previous lessons and lectures.

Preparing for the discussion

The first issue for the teacher to consider when planning a discussion group is whether or not the course has reached a stage where a group discussion of a key of a problem is useful, and the extent to which a discussion group can provide particular opportunities for learning that cannot be provided in another way. To approach the discussion group method merely as a break in routine or as a substitute for some other type of instruction is to weaken its chances of success. Next, the aim of the discussion must be clear. This is not to suggest that the discussion must be so planned and manipulated that it will reach a particular, desirable conclusion. Rather, the aim must be to hold a reasonable examination of a specific topic.

The group should be told why members will be participating in the discussion, what they are expected to accomplish and what resources will be made available to them. Group members could be asked to prepare at least one short item to be used as a contribution to the discussion. Reading lists containing suggested approaches to the discussion topic ought to be distributed and announced in advance of the date of discussion. Boundaries relating to which subjects can be covered and which cannot, should also be considered by the tutor. Visual material might be needed so that basic data, images, maps or statistics can be presented.

Seating arrangements should be made so that the flow of conversation, which typifies the good discussion group, is facilitated. Small groups allow for more participation from each member. Face-to-face interaction, enabling all members to communicate, is helpful. A circle of chairs, a U-shaped arrangement of tables and chairs (since communication tends to flow across, rather than around, a group), a whiteboard or flip chart on which key points can be noted by the teacher and data displayed may require some rearrangement of the furniture.

Where a class is too large for the type of discussion envisaged here (around 15 is a good number for a discussion group), other discussion techniques may be used. The fishbowl method allows a small group discussion, with the remainder of the class listening and viewing beyond the discussion group. Students from the fringe who act as viewers can contribute ideas after the formal discussion has ended. The jigsaw method allows a topic to be broken down into segments. Different groups meet separately, discuss their segment, and meet later in plenary session to fit together their findings.

Managing the discussion

In order to prevent the kinds of problems, mentioned above, that can arise in discussion groups, the tutor will need actively to manage the student group. He or she must ensure that all members feel free to contribute to the discussion and must be prepared to relinquish some of his or her general, overt authority and control in pursuit of this goal. Members' participation should not be constrained by over-rigid rules, but an accepted framework of conduct is necessary if informality is not to result in mere cross-talk and gossip. Potentially dominant personalities must not be allowed to take over the discussion and the naturally reticent must be encouraged to contribute. Many points of view ought to find expression. Language should always be temperate and never be discriminatory. Although the tutor must be careful not to take over the discussion, there will be times when an intervention is needed:

1 Setting and keeping the discussion in motion.
   Immediately the opening statement has been made or the first question has been put, it becomes the task of the group leader to initiate and encourage the expression of varying points of view, and to clarify goals. Members ought to be invited to participate at an early stage (since the first few minutes of a discussion period can be the most difficult) with encouragement to the shy, perhaps in the form of a question (based

on a common experience), which invites a direct response. The discussion ought to move around the circle of participants, briskly and pointedly. Wearing out a theme or undue concentration on minor matters ought to be politely restrained by the tutor. Faulty reasoning and circular arguments ought not to remain uncorrected, obscure statements ought to bring a request for clarification, and sweeping generalizations ought to be subjected to close examination. Interruptions, irrelevance and invective ought to elicit from the tutor a polite but firm rejoinder. Occasional summaries of arguments and matters on which there is general agreement should be given and recorded on a whiteboard or flipchart. Differences of opinion should be mediated and clarified. Respect for all group members should be encouraged. Finally, the tutor must not interpret a momentary silence as an invariable sign that discussion is flagging; it may indicate a pause for thought and may be a prelude to an improvement in the quality of the discussion. The use of silence and appropriate, expectant body language by the tutor may indeed stimulate further discussion. At the same time, a long, contrived pause may create a tension which needs to be broken by contributions from the group.

2 Using questions to encourage discussion

A single question may sometimes be enough to generate a substantial debate, but it is advisable for the tutor to prepare other questions which can be used to provoke thought and comment, to move the discussion on to a higher level or in a new direction, or to return it to the group's general line of thought. Specific questions to individual members rather than overhead questions to the group in general may serve to bring out the naturally shy and prevent one or two members monopolizing the session, or may be used to draw answers from members who have specialized knowledge.

3 Ending the discussion

Intermediate summing-up and recapitulation should occur at several stages of the discussion. A prior indication that the discussion is about to end ought to be given. The final summing-up must not be omitted; it should survey impartially the main points which have been made and should note significant areas of agreement and disagreement. It ought to link the essence of the discussion with previous lessons and should point forward to future classwork in which the discussion will be seen to have played a preparatory and reinforcing role. Notes from the discussion can, depending on how they were taken, be distributed after the class. If an interactive whiteboard has been used for notes, it is a simple task to save the notes in an appropriate format (PowerPoint or pdf, for example) and then email then to the group or post them on a virtual learning environment (VLE). If notes have been written on a flipchart then this can be photographed, or the notes can be typed up.

Seminars: Characteristics, advantages and disadvantages

The term seminar is generally used in further (and higher) education to refer to a semi-structured group discussion, which may precede or follow a formal lecture or a series of lessons and which is introduced by the presentation of a specific topic or theme, normally by one of the members of the group. In many ways, it is similar – and therefore requires similar planning – to an open discussion group. A typical seminar format, therefore, would involve an initial short presentation by a member of the group, which would then be opened up to wider discussion. The more formal provision of an opening presentation differentiate it from the discussion group. In general, the seminar appears to be appropriate as a mode of instruction only when the level of attainment of the group is relatively high and the subject matter lends itself to analytical treatment.

The main advantage of the seminar as a mode of instruction is its stimulation and testing of students' powers of comprehension and evaluation. The student who provides the initial presentation from which the seminar stems is tested, in particular, on his or her skill in arranging and formulating a sustained argument. The ability of a student to discover underlying values and assumptions in a presentation, to detect and separate principles from their context, to ponder their application and to question their relevance in certain situations, can be strengthened by a critical examination of another's thoughts. They can also assist students to think critically, as well as providing opportunities to develop presentation and communication skills.

The sequencing of seminars is an important consideration for the tutor. For a seminar – or series of seminars – to be successful, the student group will need to be sufficiently knowledgeable and well established so that volunteers can be found who are willing to present and the group as a whole are knowledgeable enough to contribute meaningfully to the follow-up discussion. The length of the seminar must also be planned carefully. Seminars planned for half an hour only may be of little value: longer time periods will be needed to ensure a meaningful discussion. Consequently, timetables will need careful arrangement.

Wherever possible, a summary of the paper to be presented ought to be made available to students. This can then act as a revision aid after the seminar has concluded. It should contain information under the following headings:

- the full title of the paper
- the outline or abstract of the argument to be presented
- the main headings or themes and sub-headings of the argument
- a list of works (books, websites and so forth) that have been referred to

And a suggested timetable for a seminar session is as follows:

- Introduction (by the tutor)
- Presentation of the paper by the student(s)
- Discussion – Part 1 (facilitated by the tutor)
- Interim review (led by the tutor)
- Discussion – Part 2 (facilitated by the tutor)
- Summary of discussion (by the tutor) and final questions or comments (from the students)
- Conclusion, including links to the next session and to future assignment/activities, as applicable.

The guidance already given (see above) relating to the preparation and use of visual aids, and the management of the students when running discussion groups applies equally for seminars, particularly in ensuring that all members of the group feel able to participate in the discussion. Similarly, the environment and arrangement of furniture should also be taken into consideration.

Tutorials: Characteristics, advantages and disadvantages

A tutorial is a meeting between a teacher and a student, or a very small group of students (two or three, for example), characterized by discussion and/or personal, face-to-face teaching, generally based on a specific topic. This might be the content of an assignment that is to be written by the student(s) or on questions raised by the tutor or the student(s). It is a mode of tuition intended to reinforce learning, and is associated historically with university teaching. A tutorial is very time-intensive, and requires a very generous staff–student ratio. Some courses in FE colleges have been able to sustain a system of regular tutorials for activities such as the following:

1 Skills teaching groups. Very small groups meet a tutor for the practice and refinement of psychomotor skills. Individual, face-to-face tuition has been found valuable in dance and gymnastics coaching, the teaching of musical and acting skills, and the practising of some machine production techniques.

2 Catch-up working groups. In some colleges individual students are encouraged to discuss with a tutor problems arising from difficulties in their studies. Where tutorial periods are used for meetings of this nature, diagnostic and catch-up work may be undertaken.

3 Supervision tutorials. In this type of tutorial meeting, student and tutor discuss some aspect of the student's work. This is the shape of the traditional tutorial and requires very careful preparation by tutor and student alike. Effectively prepared and handled, it can result in a heightening of student cognitive skills, in particular those involving analysis and judgement.

4 Pastoral tutorials. As the role of the FE professional has expanded to include pastoral as well as teaching support, some (but not all) FE teachers will find themselves responsible for the wider progress of a student group. Tutorial meetings such as these are not so much concerned with specific issues relating to the programmes of study that the student or students follow. Rather, they are concerned with the broader progress and welfare of the student.

The size of the tutorial group is a crucial factor, and it is generally agreed that a group size of between one and three students is appropriate (Davies, 1981). Because the essential feature of the tutorial is a face-to-face teaching relationship, so-called tutorial groups of, for example, 15 students are a contradiction in terms. Where a tutorial objective is the improvement of an essential motor technique or the heightening of critical skills, the tutor must insist, so far as is possible, on very small groups.

It is very easy indeed for time to be wasted during a tutorial. Lack of a clear aim/ objective, failure by the tutor or students to prepare any necessary material in advance, or failure of the tutor to understand the nature of points raised by students or to comprehend the basis of their difficulties, will lead to little progress. Adequate preparation must be made the rule, so that the tutorial is neither viewed nor used as an opportunity to evade the rigours of the learning process. Where the tutorial involves a small group rather than an individual student, the tutor must ensure the involvement of *all* members in discussions. As such, the general rules relating to discussions should be followed.

The posing of questions by the tutor during a formal tutorial session will test to the full his or her competence as a manager of teaching and learning processes. Questions will need to be carefully designed in advance, but then perhaps adjusted in content, style and presentation according to the profile of the student and the quality of the student's responses. Questions should attempt to generate answers which test capacities to comprehend, analyze and evaluate, rather than the mere capacity to recall. Responses indicating misunderstanding, or based on irrelevancies, will need to be challenged, but not in a manner which will negatively affect the student's confidence. The tutor should not expect answers immediately after questions have been asked; he or she should expect to wait for a considered response. The tutor should remember, too, that students might interpret his or her gestures and facial expressions as a non-verbal response to their statements.

Tutorials have been criticized as too demanding for students attending FE courses. The criticism misses the essence of the tutorial process. The real value of the tutorial is the intensity of tuition made possible by its very personal form. Its demanding nature is often its essential virtue. Properly planned and staffed, the tutorial should be capable of providing very valuable assistance to college students at all levels.

Case studies: Characteristics, advantages and disadvantages

The use of case studies provides opportunities for students to engage with their studies on several levels. They encourage creative problem solving. They also encourage independent, problem-based learning and peer-supported collaborative learning. As such they can be seen as an effective method of encouraging deep, rather than surface, approaches to learning.

A case study is based upon an examination, analysis and diagnosis of a real or simulated problem so that general principles might emerge in a realistic fashion. Case studies are used in colleges of FE to intensify student understanding of the complex, real world relationships embodied in, for example, childcare, business studies, catering and hospitality, or social work. The aims of the case study may be summarized as:

- the creation of an active, participatory teaching–learning situation in which the subject matter closely mirrors the outside world, thereby generating authenticity

- the improvement of the student's ability to identify underlying principles, to think swiftly and to apply his or her prior experience, knowledge and understanding to the exploration and solution of a particular problem

- the assessment of the student's current ability to translate what has ben learned in class to new situations.

A case study typically consists of a pre-prepared scenario, which is described (on no more than one side of A4 paper, or perhaps on a short video clip of a few minutes' duration) for the students. The scenario in question would usually involve one or two key topics or themes from the curriculum being followed, and would seek to explore how these themes might play out in authentic, 'real world' situations, usually by providing two or three questions or prompts that students would need to address. When planning a case study, it is important that the tutor ensures that the content of the study is broad and generalizable, so that the topics to be covered to be of value in relation to the course that is being studied as a whole. For example, a case study for students on a childcare studies course might look at the ways in which they would respond if a child were hurt whilst playing at a nursery. A case study for students on a business studies programme might look at ways in which local networking events might be used to advertize a new start-up company. It is common practice for the class to be divided up into small groups, or syndicates, when exploring case studies, and for each small group to prepare a series of answers or comments that can be fed back to the plenary after a fixed period of time. Asking students to create handouts, posters or PowerPoint presentations can facilitate the plenary session and also provide students with opportunities for developing functional skills.

Types of case study

Examples of the kinds of problems that can be explored using case studies include:

1   The critical incident study. The penultimate event in a chain of incidents is described. Students must decide on the additional data required in order to obtain a full picture of the circumstances. This can be a useful exercise in analysis and comprehension.
2   The next stage study. A case is unfolded, stage by stage. Students must suggest what is likely to happen next. The exercise usually calls for a high order of ability in analysis and synthesis.
3   The major issue study. Students are given a mass of data – much of which is deliberately irrelevant to the main issue – and are asked to identify and separate that issue and to suggest remedies for the situation which is revealed.
4   The 'role-play' case study. On the basis of an incident which is reported to them, students are required to act out (in an improvised style) the roles of the central participants. It is important that the roles be allocated with care and only after explanation; students may resent what they perceive as mere childish play-acting.

Writing and managing case study exercises

The writing of case studies is a somewhat specialized task which may be carried out best by the course tutor by drawing on authentic, real-life material and situations. The case study should be arranged so as to call for the identification of major and minor problems and the preparation of solutions with an awareness of difficulties in their implementation. The content must be appropriate to the students' background, levels of experience and comprehension.

The case study material will include all the important elements of the situation to be analyzed. Any relevant background information must be sketched in, together with an explanation of what principle is being investigated and why, the method of investigation which is to be adopted, and the level of analysis required.

Case study sessions often involve the division of the student group into small groups, or syndicates. Within each syndicate, it can be useful for the tutor to allocate particular roles and responsibilities, which should – as far as possible – be matched to the individual. For example, a student who is relatively shy when addressing the entire class may be more comfortable when working in a smaller group: this student might well be asked to summarize the syndicate's discussion on a handout, but not to present the handout to the class.

The role of the class tutor is to move among the syndicates, noting difficulties, providing additional information when it is requested and chairing the final, plenary session. Observing the syndicates working constitutes a useful opportunity for formative assessment, particularly if the content of the case studies is aligned to the summative assessments that students will be working towards (assessment is discussed in Chapter 30). In the final plenary session, each syndicate should briefly talk through their conclusions or findings, which should be justified by reference to relevant theory, principle and practice, according to the programme of study. They should also where necessary be critiqued, and any errors of interpretation should be noted.

A suggested pattern for the conduct of a case analysis is as follows (Yunker, 1984). First, the tutor should study the case carefully, obtain a general feel for the specific problem area, and note the pivotal points and key themes. He or she should then decide what concepts emerge and how each ought to be stressed. The following advice should be given to student participants:

1 take the position of each individual in the case actively and sympathetically, and try to establish why they feel or behave as they do. What fears or bias are evident?

2 isolate the major problems or issues. Examine the case closely for information relevant to those problems or issues

3 what alternative courses of action are available?

4 identify the potential risks and benefits attached to each course of action

5 select the alternative which, in all the circumstances as you perceive them, is the most satisfactory

6 decide how the alternative selected might be implemented successfully.

An alternative sequence for following case studies is as follows (Barnes, 1994; Eaton, 1982):

1 seek to understand and evaluate the information presented. Extrapolate from that information where necessary

2 diagnose what appears to be the problem area. Do not mistake symptom for cause

3 attempt to generate strategic and tactical alternative solutions to the problem which has been diagnosed

4 try to predict possible outcomes of courses of action in terms of risk and uncertainty

5 evaluate alternative courses of action and make a considered choice

6 consider contingency planning where events might take an unexpected turn

7 make a systematic presentation of your analysis and conclusions.

Case studies: Advantages and disadvantages

The case study as a mode of instruction now has a firm place in the teaching and learning cultures of many colleges. Its links with authentic professional, workplace contexts are welcomed as an aid in removing the artificial barriers of the classroom situation. Its demands on a student's powers of analysis, synthesis and general reasoning can be balanced by the high level of interest which is sustained by his or her knowledge of grappling with a live problem, rather than an arid, theoretical situation. Students are learning by doing; moreover, they may become aware of their own prejudices and bias. The sensitive use of case studies is said to improve students' skills in the detection and rejection of irrelevance, in the consideration of the possible results of a decision, in the evaluation of alternative procedures, and, perhaps above all, in the perception of the importance of facts. Case studies also accustom students to working in groups – a useful preparation for the real world of industry and commerce. Indeed, case studies can be seen as helping students develop a number of generic or transferable skills:

1 analytical skills, involving the classification, organization and evaluation of information

2 application skills, based upon practice in the use of principles, concepts and techniques

3 creative skills, which are necessary where alternative solutions to problems must be generated – an essential feature of many case studies

4 communication skills, arising in the presentation of arguments and conclusions

5 self-assessment skills, emerging from an awareness of one's attitudes to the value-judgements that arise in case discussions

6 team-working skills, necessary as a member of a group engaged in the social process of collective discussion.

At the same time, case studies also pose a number of challenges for the college lecturer. These, together with some suggested solutions, are summarized as follows:

1 Challenge: the background research, collection and interpretation all call for much preparation time. Response: outline case studies in textbooks and on the internet are readily available and adaptable to a number of situations.

2 Challenge: tutors involved in case studies presented to students who have experienced only more formal, teacher-led modes of teaching have found that the initial impact of the case method may produce difficulties in learning, because participants are often unsure as to their precise role in the case study process and are not always sure what to do. Response: as a prelude to the case study itself, time must be found for a full explanation of the process. The roles of tutor and student must be made clear; the aims of the study must be set out and some reference should be made, in general terms, to the expected outcome of case analysis.

3 Challenge: students may not be immediately aware of what they really have learned from a case study, and this may be compounded by a lack of precise feedback from the tutor from whom they have been accustomed to expect detailed information. Response: when summing up, tutors need to draw together the themes that have been discussed and illustrate, through reference to the work done by the syndicates, what has been learned and how it relates to the wider curriculum being followed.

Summary: Small group work and theories of cooperative learning

The different learning and teaching modes outlined in this chapter are all based, essentially, on the cooperative exploration of ideas and group learning. Many teachers in FE feel that this aspect of learning may be of great significance for participants in the long term. Cooperative learning constitutes an area of research in its own right, and the characteristics of it can be summarized as follows (Slavin, 1983):

- students are aware of their dependency on one another in achieving a common goal
- they are motivated to encourage one another to assist in the achievement of group success
- their positive contacts with one another in group discussion help to build understanding and tolerance
- the isolation of students is diminished when all members of the group feel that their contributions are of significance, and self-esteem is increased.

Teaching and learning strategies that encourage such social practices are clearly of obvious benefit to both students and teachers in FE. They are not straightforward to plan, particularly for newer members of the profession, but with help from mentors where appropriate teachers can over time generate a bank of resources and ideas for encouraging students to work with and learn from each other.

Further reading

The kinds of techniques and strategies discussed in this chapter, which have been grouped together under the title 'student-centered learning', can be explored in more depth in the following recommended books, alongside more general teacher-training textbooks:

Jaques, D. and Salmon, G. (2006), *Learning in Groups*. London: Routledge.

Sims, N. (2006), *How to run a great workshop*. Harlow: Pearson.

Strawson, H., Habeshaw, S., Habeshaw, T. and Gibbs, G. (2012), *53 interesting things to do in your seminars and tutorials*. London: Professional and Higher Partnership.

27 Working Alongside Other Professionals

Within a typical FE college, teachers and trainers will over time come to work with a variety of other members of staff. As well as working within curriculum teams or areas (it is highly unlikely that any individual teacher will be solely responsible for the teaching and assessment of all of the courses in one curriculum), teachers may also find themselves working, at times, with student counsellors, technicians or British Sign Language (BSL) interpreters, to name three. Learning how to work with other professionals is an important aspect of the teacher's wider professional learning in the workplace (Avis et al., 2009). Nor is this wider professional role restricted to longer-serving and more experienced staff. It is not uncommon for new teachers in a college to have to work with a range of other members of staff to, for example, meet the complex needs of an individual student. The establishment of good working relationships with colleagues is not just a focus of attention for new teachers. Longer-serving teachers often draw on the help and experience of their colleagues in a number of ways, such as:

- Teachers who have little knowledge or experience of working with learners with disabilities can seek out guidance and support.
- Teachers who lack confidence in using ICT can ask for help from technicians or other staff who can provide both practical help (for example, in switching on or setting up a data projector) and more detailed help (for example, the use of a particular IT application such as a virtual learning environment).
- Teachers who want to try something new with a group of learners can talk to other tutors who work on the same, or a similar, programme of study. A colleague could provide suggestions for a new learning or teaching strategy.

It is a matter of particular importance for both new teachers in colleges (particularly those teachers who have been recently appointed and are balancing their workloads with the need to study for their professional qualifications on a part-time basis) and for full-time trainee teachers who are on a placement in a FE college, to work to establish good relations with colleagues. Upon arriving in a new college, even a more experienced teacher may be initially overwhelmed at having to learn a new series of workplace processes (such as how absences are recorded, for example, or where students in financial difficulty should be referred to). Having colleagues who are willing to share resources, discuss difficult professional issues or set up a practical experiment is undoubtedly important. Indeed, such collaboration can be seen as a highly pragmatic and sensible way of responding to the increasingly full workload of the FE teacher. Over the last 20 years, the teacher's professional role has expanded to include such diverse responsibilities as recruitment, publicity and pastoral support. As the job of the teacher becomes more diffuse, a collaborative approach can be seen as being a necessary element of the role.

During the academic year, a teacher may well need to work with a range of other professionals: managers, administrators, learning support workers or employers. Invariably, the focus for such contact is a student or group of students, and some of the reasons why it might be necessary to work with others are as follows:

- If a teacher lacks the expertise or confidence to help plan alternative provision for a student with a seen or unseen disability, then a learning support worker can be consulted and/or employed to provide support in the classroom or workshop.

- If work placements need to be organized for a group of students on a childcare programme, a number of employers may need to be contacted in order to provide sufficient opportunities. This may necessitate site visits, to ensure that the placement provider is suitable, and compliance with health and safety and safeguarding legislative frameworks.

- Students on a construction programme may benefit from site visits of varying kinds. Good relations with local employers can help make this a straightforward process. Such visits may not be a required part of the curriculum, but they are a good opportunity for students to gain authentic experience. They also provide further links between a college and it's community.

- Many employers, such as plumbers or electrical contractors, sponsor their employees as they take part in training. In situations such as this, employees will have a strong interest in their employees' progress. This can be awkward at times. For example, if an employer wished to check on the progress of an employee, the teacher would not be entitled to release this information.

- Teachers often have to liaise with awarding bodies. This might be for a relatively straightforward procedure, such as ensuring that a student is enrolled on the correct programme. Or it might be for a more complex reason, such as organizing a form of differentiated assessment for a candidate with specific learning needs.

Establishing the professional networks that can facilitate such work is neither straightforward nor simple, not least as different colleges often have very different organizational structures and cultures. Some colleges provide thorough induction programmes for new members of staff (including trainees on placement), whereas others do not. Whether or not a college has a formal induction programme, it is more than likely that new teachers and trainers will need to find out for themselves at some point how to arrange a disability needs test, or an initial assessment for literacy, or where to refer a student to for counselling support.

Formal and informal working patterns in further education colleges

The formal structures of a FE college, as a large and complex organization, are quite straightforward to discern. The organizational charts that are distributed at induction events for new staff tend to portray the college as a multi-linear organization with specific lines of responsibility and communication between different areas, departments, or directorates (the terminology varies between colleges, and usually changes whenever a college undergoes a restructure). Named and titled members of staff are given clear areas of operational responsibility. Similarly, the procedures and paperwork that accompany the work of the teacher or trainer are grounded in the structures and hierarchies of the organization.

Awarding bodies and professional bodies also have an impact on the working life of the teacher. As well as specifying the curricula that teachers in colleges have to work towards, awarding bodies also impose at times considerable bureaucratic systems onto teachers as they seek to coordinate the activities of the sector as a whole. Once again, the requirements of external agencies such as these constitute an important aspect of the teacher's learning when starting at a new college or working within a new curriculum structure.

The pace of change within the FE sector constitutes a third aspect of the teacher's working environment that requires constant attention and revisions to working practices (Edward et al., 2007; Raffe and Spours, 2009). The recent example of the 14–19 Diploma (which was introduced in 2008) provides just one example of the speed at which a new policy initiative can, upon announcement, generate significant amounts of work that is then lost sight of as the policy is reversed. More generally, teachers in the FE sector have been characterized as being constantly challenged by a rapid pace of change that is unmatched in other educational sectors.

At the same time, within complex organizations such as FE colleges, it is apparent that there are ways of getting things done other than by following the painstaking procedures that are expounded in staff handbooks. For example: booking a laptop repair through an ICT department may mean that a few days will pass before the technical problem is solved. Knowing which person in the ICT department to ring directly, and knowing that s/he might grant a favour if time allows, may mean that the laptop in question is ready to use the following day. Failing to submit the correct paperwork on time need not mean that a college pool car will be unobtainable if the right person can be contacted and a reasonable justification given as to why procedure has not been followed. Other common tasks may cause more problems, however. Putting a large number of lengthy documents through a photocopier, instead of sending them to a reprographics department (which is significantly cheaper) will more than likely lead to some kind of reprimand. People working within colleges will often find ways to do what they are expected to do that do not necessarily always coincide with how the organization (that is, the person who designed the procedure or wrote the policy) anticipated that they would be done. Such improvized practices are common, but are unique to particular places of work. As such, even experienced teachers may need to learn new aspects of workplace etiquette when entering a new college. A mentor (this issue is discussed below) can help on such occasions. Taking time to make introductions and ask questions can also be helpful. Generally, it is through participation, trial and error and experience that the specific customs and habits of particular colleges and departments are experienced and learned.

Working with others in supporting teaching and learning

It is suggested that there are four significant professional groups that teachers in the FE sector work alongside, as part of the wider process of planning for teaching and learning in the workshop or classroom. Two of these working processes – mentoring and team teaching – are of particular relevance to trainee FE teachers on placement, and new teachers who are studying for a professional qualification on a part-time in-service basis. The other two – working with learning support workers, and working with technicians and demonstrators – are of relevance to all teachers and trainers in the sector.

Mentoring in further education

Mentoring has only relatively recently become well established as an aspect of the initial training and continuing professional development of teachers and trainers in FE. The 2004 government paper *Equipping Our Teachers for the Future* provided the impetus for a series of reforms of teacher training for the FE sector. The provision of mentoring for trainee FE teachers is also now under the purview of Ofsted. As such, it is perhaps not surprising that mentoring provision in the sector is coming under increasingly close scrutiny.

With such political pressures behind it, it might be surprising to learn that the mentoring of teachers is poorly resourced in the FE sector. There are no specific sources of funding to pay mentors; nor is there a single agreed qualification that mentors might obtain. However, an inspection of various teacher-training curricula and the Ofsted inspection framework would indicate two key elements of the mentoring role in FE. These are commonly found across teacher education programmes but, it is suggested here, are also important beyond the period of initial teacher training:

1 Providing support for subject specialist pedagogy

Initial teacher training programmes for the FE sector are generic awards (apart from specialist awards for those who are teaching numeracy and literacy – a reflection of the political importance that is, at the time of writing, being attached to functional skills). Only a very small number of teacher-training programmes for the sector contain elements of units that specifically address the subject specialism of the teacher or trainer. The role of the mentor, in this context, is to meet those development needs of the teacher that revolve around their subject specialism. There are two elements to this. The first is the pedagogy of the subject specialism – the idea that there are particular ways of teaching some subjects that are not appropriate or effective in other contexts. The second is the content of the subject specialism. Teachers and trainers in FE colleges are expected to maintain their expertise and to stay up-to-date. Teachers of technical and vocational programmes need to represent current working practice and values if their students are going to go into employment.

2 Providing feedback and guidance on workshop or classroom practice

A mentor, whilst observing a carpentry session, is highly likely to notice aspects of the teacher's performance that may not be noticed by someone who lacks a background in carpentry. The particular ways in which a specific tool should be used, the terminology used by carpenters whilst at work on site, the common problems that might be faced whilst attempting to perform a particular operation – details such as these are more likely to be constructively commented upon by a subject specialist mentor than a teacher-trainer who will be focussing on broader issues such as communication skills or the use of question-and-answer techniques. As such, an observation of teaching by a mentor is likely to generate useful feedback of a different quality to the feedback generated by a teacher trainer (which will be developmental, but more generic) or line manager or inspector (these being understood as being predominantly judgemental rather than developmental).

Although the mentor role can be said to be a formal one due to its position within the teacher-training curriculum, the ways in which mentors carry out the role are somewhat variable. This is not surprising, not least as many mentors perform their duties on a goodwill basis. Nonetheless, a number of different approaches to the mentoring role can be identified (Cunningham, 2007; Gravells, 2010). These are briefly described here (and it is argued that elements of all three of these are found in the FE sector):

1 An informal, voluntary approach to mentoring

This approach to mentoring is characterized by high levels of motivation for both the mentor and the mentee (the trainee). An informal approach will require the mentee to manage her or his own learning and take responsibility for managing the relationship with the mentor. It will be highly targeted to the self-established needs of the mentee. However, this approach can lack direction if not properly managed by the participants, does not guarantee the quality of the mentoring, and lacks resources and formal recognition.

2 A formal, structured approach to mentoring

This approach to mentoring is characterized by the provision of time and resources for mentoring, including an induction process for the mentor and the mentee. A formal approach will ensure the quality of the provision, and a more structured relationship that helps make the mentoring process more consistent within the organization. However, this approach can remove autonomy form the mentee and can restrict the kinds of learning opportunities that the mentee may wish to pursue.

3 An institutionalized, structured approach to mentoring, working to professional standards

This approach to mentoring is characterized by standardized provision that regulates the mentoring process and ensures that mentees will all be treated in the same manner. The need to reference the mentoring relationship to professional standards ensures the relevance of the learning that will take place, and provides a focus for detailed feedback from the mentor. However, this approach can generate more pressure for both the mentor and the mentee as their relationship is subject to some form of inspection or audit. The removal of all traces of voluntarism can affect motivation and, by extension, the depth of learning. Finally, the use of standards can lead to a target setting culture that is, arguably, the opposite of what a mentoring relationship should be trying to provide.

Team teaching in further education

The notion of an individual teacher controlling, in its entirety, the progress of a lesson is at the heart of much current teaching practice. The concept of a sole, dominant figure accepting direct responsibility for the planning, execution and assessment of a unit of instruction is questioned, however, by the theory and practice of *team teaching*. The claims made for this practice are wide, ranging from the assertion that it makes teaching more effective, to the more controversial declaration that the teaching team is the most appropriate instructional organization for the classrooms of a democratic society, in which cooperation at all levels and in many social activities is a worthy aim in itself. An important basic assumption made by some advocates of team teaching is that, where teachers focus their *collective attention* on an instructional problem, the solutions at which they arrive will probably be superior to those presented by each of these teachers considering the problem in isolation.

Team teaching is evident where, say, two members of staff decide to pool their efforts in pursuit of one specific teaching goal. Thus, where a teacher of design technology, wishing to see an improvement in students' standards of written work, asks a colleague who teaches English to discuss with those students matters such as elements of style, and both undertake to mark the next set of essays jointly (one with content in mind, the other with style), team teaching is being practised.

Team teaching may be said to operate where two or more teachers cooperate, deliberately and methodically, in the planning, presentation and evaluation of the teaching process. In effect, individual teachers sacrifice some of their autonomy, pool their resources and – a vital feature of team teaching – accept joint responsibility for the teaching of groups of students.

The practice of team teaching does not necessitate a uniform teaching structure, and in this country a variety of patterns has evolved. Small groups acting under a coordinator (perhaps a subject specialist or senior departmental member) typify a common form of structure. Large groups – entire departments – coordinated in their activities by a departmental head or senior lecturer, exemplify another type. A group might grow spontaneously, with a loosely knit team collaborating to deal with specific, related parts of the curriculum. Another group might be a highly organized, centrally directed unit, working to a planned timetable. In general, the structure of the teaching team will tend to reflect course and departmental objectives, strategies, and the availability of resources. Invariably, it will be based on a collective approach to the teaching situation.

Joint responsibility for the teaching of groups, appropriate team structure and student groupings are among the most important features of team teaching, but their presence in a team plan will not necessarily guarantee its success. Of vital importance is the team's conscious unity of purpose. No matter how well-organized the team or how abundant the resources and teaching aids, the chances of the team's success will depend directly on the real cooperation of its members.

A well-coordinated team will attempt to use the pooled, specialist interests of its members in the best possible way – a considerable advantage of this mode of instruction. The idea of responsibility for an instructional course being shared among a number of specialists may be novel, but ought not to be rejected on that ground alone. There seems to be a distinct possibility, in such a situation, of the members of the team learning from one another, of the widening of student horizons and the growth of a collective sense of purpose. Students may benefit from participation in a variety of teaching situations and exposure to several specialist styles of tuition and groupings of resources.

On the other hand, the demands on staff are said to be much heavier than those of the conventional teaching situation. The special arrangements of teaching space necessitated by the practice of team teaching are said to present many difficulties. The resources necessary for team teaching, it is contended, may be beyond the budgets of many colleges. (This, unhappily, may often be true but it does not weaken the case for the principle of team teaching.) It is claimed that team teaching can function efficiently only by the use of complex administrative techniques, particularly in relation to timetable construction, and this may result in the creation within the department of staffing and structural problems. (That this is an inevitable outcome may be questioned, given the experiences of teams which have functioned successfully without any radical alteration of departmental structure.) Some reports suggest that problems have arisen in teaching teams because of interpersonal strains and a general incompatibility of some members of staff. It has been suggested also that there are difficulties in bringing teachers to accept that, as part of teams, they no longer enjoy total autonomy in 'their' classrooms or workshops. Further, there is evidence to suggest that team teaching may be unproductive in some subject areas in which large groups generally show many individual differences in ability, for example in mathematics, thus making a common team approach very difficult.

Working with learning support workers

The use of learning support workers in educational contexts (primary and secondary education, as well as FE) has evolved during the last 30 years or so as a consequence of broader policies of educational inclusion. As the number of students with learning diffi- culties or disabilities (seen and unseen) who attend mainstream educational institutions has increased, so the need for additional support in workshops and classrooms has also increased. The learning support workforce is quite diverse: although specialist qualifica- tions in generic learning support do exist, other support workers will have qualifications that relate to the support of specific disabilities such as dyslexia (difficulty processing and remembering information that is seen and heard, affecting learning and the acquisition of literacy skills); dyspraxia (spatial awareness difficulties, difficulties in judging distances and heights, difficulties with the coordination of gross and fine motor skills leading to clumsy and apparent clumsiness and untidy, unintelligible handwriting); or dyscalculia (difficulties in the comprehension or production of numerical and spatial information, difficulties in conceptualizing numbers, number relationships, outcomes of numerical operations and estimation, often accompanied by difficulties with temporal and spatial awareness such as time keeping and lack of space awareness).

Learning support workers perform a variety of functions that are readily recognizable. Typical examples of learning support provision in the workshop or classroom include: the provision of British Sign Language support for students who are deaf or hearing impaired; or the provision of a note-taker (also sometimes known as an amanuensis) for a student who has limited mobility. Learning support workers are also used to provide one-to-one help for students with specific needs in a cross-curricular manner: that is to say, a learning support worker (or team of workers, depending on the needs of the student) will work to support the student in all aspects of college life, whether in the classroom, the library or the student lounge.

Defining the learning support workforce is a difficult task. In part this is because the range of activities that are classified as learning support in FE colleges is so varied. These activities have been defined as (Bailey, 2004):

- providing academic support within a single curriculum area
- providing academic support in a cross-curricula context
- providing pastoral support across college
- providing pastoral support for specific groups within the college such as 14–16s or students identified as 'at risk'.

For those teachers or trainers who are working with students with specific learning diffi-culties or disabilities, learning support workers constitute a valuable resource of ideas and techniques. They may possess specialist qualifications relating to the particular difficulties or disabilities that they help to support, and they may also have accumulated a range of experiences across the college. For both new teachers and established teachers who have rarely if ever worked with students with particular needs, therefore, the following ought to be considered when planning sessions:

1 When considering how the activities in a session ought to be timed, it will be necessary to allow for additional time so that the learning support worker can carry out her or his responsibilities/actions. If a notetaker is present, more time may be needed to allow for questions to be asked so that any ambiguities are resolved. If a BSL interpreter is present, additional time will be needed to allow for translation. If a student is using assistive technology, time will need to be allocated for setting up and operation.

2 Students with particular needs may require additional one-to-one tutorial time, for which support workers will also need to be present.

3 Some activities may not be suitable for students with particular needs. If the teacher is concerned that an activity might discriminate against a student, the support worker may be able to suggest appropriate adaptions or alternatives. For example, running a discussion group with a deaf student can be easily facilitated through implementing a careful system of turn taking (in a manner akin to a televised debate) when only the student holding the microphone (or other object – a whiteboard pen is sufficient) is permitted to talk.

To summarize, it can be said that learning support workers can be invaluable when working with learners with specific learning difficulties or disabilities, particularly in a busy workshop or classroom setting where the teacher might not always be able to provide the level of support needed (for example, in proofreading written assignments, helping to organize materials and resources, developing study skills strategies and helping with assistive technology such as voice recognition software). However, if the teacher and the support worker are to work together effectively to best support the needs of students with specific learning difficulties, it is essential for both to spend time together planning the learning that is to take place. Unfortunately, this can prove to be problematic when time is at a premium and staff are busy (as is invariably the case in colleges). As with many other aspects of college life, some element of goodwill is also required here if the students are to receive the best possible opportunities for learning.

Working with technicians and demonstrators

In many colleges of FE, some members of staff are employed on what is usually termed a paraprofessional status. Such staff, commonly referred to as technicians, demonstrators, assessors or facilitators, are not qualified teachers or trainers (that is to say, they do not have a CertEd/PGCE, or PTLLS-CTLLS-DTLLS). However to varying degrees (depending on the nature of their specific employment) they often have responsibility for particular aspects of teaching and student learning (Scott, 2005). Typical examples of the different roles that paraprofessionals hold in colleges include:

- The technician – for example, a member of staff employed as a laboratory technician who will help prepare and deliver practical demonstrations or experiments. In this situation, the class teacher would typically deliver a whole group presentation and/or demonstration (having been set up with help from the technician), before putting the students into small groups for practical work. The class teacher and the technician would then, together, facilitate the small group work and provide formative feedback. The summary of the session would be the responsibility of the teacher alone.

- The assessor – for example, a member of staff might be employed as an NVQ assessor in Brickwork. In the workshop, the teacher might open the session with a demonstration before the students moved on to their own work (building a particular arch or a chimney breast, for example). The teacher and the assessor would then be able to move around the workshop and provide formative feedback. However, if the students were working towards the completion of a particular element of their NVQ qualification, both the teacher and the assessor might be able to record formally ('sign off') the work that the student had done.

It is quite common, therefore, for teachers of vocational and technical programmes to find themselves working alongside other members of staff who are not qualified teachers as such, but who nonetheless possess relevant trade and craft qualifications and experience and often hold other professional qualifications as well (typically, NVQ assessor awards, or perhaps initial teacher-training qualifications such as PTLLS). It is important, therefore, that the teacher takes the time to establish the scope of the paraprofessional's job role, which is highly context specific (as there is no nationally agreed framework). When establishing a lesson plan or a scheme of work, therefore, the teacher (who will always be responsible for this activity) might consider the following issues in relation to planning for the work of the paraprofessional:

1 The choice of teaching and learning activities and resources. The presence of an additional member of staff who is both experienced and qualified, affords the teacher the opportunity to use activities and resources that might not otherwise be practicable. Students can be divided into different rooms according to task or qualification. For example, if a member of staff is responsible for a mixed group (a group of students working towards different qualifications but sharing accommodation, resources and timetabled hours), the supervision or formative assessment of each group can be divided between members of staff.

2 Formative and summative assessment. If the paraprofessional is a qualified assessor, then it would be reasonable for her or him to be given substantial or even complete responsibility for the assessment – as distinct from the teaching – of a group of students. This would then allow the teacher to focus her or his attention elsewhere as required. Similarly, the paraprofessional might be given responsibility for the internal verification of students' portfolios (assuming that she or he held the appropriate qualification).

The position of the paraprofessional is an ambiguous one at best (Bailey, 2004). For some, holding a technician or demonstrator position is acceptable because such a post does not carry with it particular responsibilities or requirements (such as having to complete a teaching qualification, for example, or having to be responsible for course leadership). For others, a demonstrator position might be seen as a 'stepping stone' to a full teacher role. In some colleges, however, staff are deliberately appointed as technicians or demonstrators rather than as teachers, purely as an exercise in saving money (technicians' salaries tend to be lower) and in increasing the flexibility of the workforce (technicians are usually required to have a higher number of student contact hours, and may not follow the standard college timetable). For the teacher, therefore, who is seeking to establish good working relationships with paraprofessionals, courtesy and tact will prove to be important skills to possess.

Summary: Working with others in further education

It is important for the FE teacher to consider collaborative ways of working in terms of the profession as a whole. It is worth remembering that there are also opportunities to work with staff from other institutions. It is always pleasant to meet teachers who work in different places: they might have ideas for learning and teaching that are unique to them, and their experiences, perhaps due to the size or location or specialism of the institution in which they work, may be informative and helpful. But such opportunities are unevenly distributed; in some curriculum areas, cross-college work, for example for the purposes of moderation or standardization, are a regular feature, and other curriculum areas simply do not offer the same kinds of opportunities. In these situations, it is all the more important that teachers and trainers make the most of the opportunities afforded to them by their colleagues.

Further reading

For a general commentary relating to working alongside others in further education, the following are recommended in the first instance:

Armitage, A., Evershed, J., Hayes, D., Hudson, A., Kent, J., Lawes, S., Poma, S. and Renwick, M. (2012), *Teaching and training in lifelong learning*. 4th edition. Maidenhead: McGraw Hill. Chapters 1 and 2.

Avis, J., Dalton, J., Dixon, L., Jennings, A., Orr, K. and Tummons, J. (2009), Getting to know the organisation. In Avis, J., Fisher, R. and Thompson, R. (eds.) *Teaching in Lifelong Learning: a guide to theory and practice.* Maidenhead: McGraw Hill.

Avis, J., Fisher, R. and Ollin, R. (2009), Professionalism. In Avis, J., Fisher, R. and Thompson, R. (eds.) *Teaching in Lifelong Learning: a guide to theory and practice.* Maidenhead: McGraw Hill.

Tummons, J. (2010), *Becoming a professional tutor in the lifelong learning sector.* 2nd edition. Exeter: Learning Matters.

Williams, J. (2007), A beginner's guide to lecturing. In Hayes, D., Marshall, T. and Turner, A. (eds.) *A lecturer's guide to further education.* Maidenhead: Open University Press.

28 Audio-Visual Resources for Teaching and Learning

The use of different resources in the classroom or workshop is an important element of the teaching process. If they are chosen and used carefully, audio-visual resources can multiply and widen the channels of communication between teacher and class, offering additional forms of information, stimulation and motivation. However, if they are used at random or thoughtlessly – so that they dominate or distort rather than assist the teaching process, or without careful consideration of their effect on the teaching process, –they can be an irrelevance and even a distraction. The use and selection of appropriate resources, the questions that should be asked and answered before they are selected, and some of the resources generally available for the FE teacher are considered below.

Principles of using audio-visual resources for teaching and learning

It seems obvious that a teacher or trainer would use audio-visual resources as part of their teaching. A verbal discussion of learning through play in a nursery setting might be correct, informative and eloquently delivered, but there is little doubt that it would be reinforced if accompanied by a short series of photographs of authentic nursery settings. Similarly, a verbal description of the ways by which Value Added Tax (VAT) is calculated would be strengthened if the teacher performed a small number of calculations on a whiteboard or on an Excel spreadsheet that could be projected onto a screen. Audio-visual resources can be understood as contributing to the teaching process in two ways, therefore:

1 They can be used to bring the real world into the college workshop or classroom. If the real thing (an object, a place or a process), which is the subject matter of the lesson, is unavailable, inaccessible, inconvenient or impossible to handle, resources may be employed to provide effective substitutes. For students on a childcare course who have yet to go on a work placement, photographs of nurseries provide a

valuable opportunity for learning. For students on an engineering course, a film of a CNC (computer numerical control) milling machine in operation would form a useful opportunity for learning about their characteristics before moving on to operate one in the workshop.

2 They can be used to exemplify, amplify or otherwise reinforce a topic or theme that is being discussed. Whether using a laptop computer and a data projector or just a simple whiteboard and pen, a teacher on an Association of Accounting Technicians (AAT) accountancy course can illustrate important topics such as VAT calculation or cash flow. In a motor vehicle or electrical installation workshop, photographs can be projected onto a screen to illustrate the teacher's presentation before the students move on to practice the task being discussed.

Films (on DVD or online), three-dimensional models, audio recordings or enlarged photographs, for example, can all be integrated into a teaching strategy involving the supplementation of verbal explanation, the focusing of class attention, the stimulation and maintenance of interest, and the promotion of retention of information.

The use of audio-visual resources should not be considered an 'optional extra' to a lesson. Nor should such materials be employed as the basis of a resource-led approach to learning which may render the class teacher unnecessary – in spite of claims of the most ardent champions of technology in the classroom. As mediating instruments assisting students to achieve understanding, as components of a teaching situation requiring a combination of instructional techniques, their value is beyond doubt. The use of resources such as those listed in the examples given above can result in the enrichment and intensification of student learning, improvement in perception, assimilation and retention of learned material, the promotion of transfer of learning and the widening of the boundaries of insight. But a clear analysis is needed of the overall teaching context in which they are to be used.

Criteria for the selection and use of audio-visual resources

Several models for the selection and use of audio-visual resources have been developed over time by educational researchers, each suggesting matters which the teacher should consider when presented with a choice of media. Some of these models are outlined below. It should be noted that all of the approaches outlined here are based on the fundamental principle that any choice must be made on the basis of potential for implementation of instructional objectives, and with the profile and needs of the student population firmly in mind.

- Gerlach and Ely (1980)

  The Gerlach and Ely classroom model is a prescriptive model of instructional design. It sets out the criteria to be applied to the process of selection of resources, which should take place after outcomes/objectives have been specified and the students' entry behaviour (that is, prior knowledge and/or experience) is identified. These criteria are: cognitive appropriateness (can the proposed resource provide the specific stimulus for learning required by the lesson outcome/objective?); level of sophistication (will the pattern of communication be understood by the learner to whom the resources are presented?); cost (will the result justify the real cost?); availability; and technical quality.

- Knirk and Gustafson (1986)

  Knirk and Gustafson called for the development and specification of instructional outcomes/objectives, an evaluation of available resources, the matching of outcomes/ objectives, strategies and media characteristics, following which a detailed learning system could be specified. They emphasized the importance of noting the domains of learning of the planned instructional outcomes, and argued that the cognitive, motor and affective domains would each require specific types of audio-visual resource.

- Romiszowski (1986)

  Romiszowski suggested that two types of media characteristic be investigated when media are considered for instructional purposes. Firstly, essential media characteristics, which are related directly to clarity of presentation. Thus, the choice of media for instruction in complex manual skills involves a consideration of the visual presentation of the overall skill and its sub-routines. Secondly, optimal media characteristics, which are those which concern the quality of presentation, such as attractiveness to students and links with the teacher's preferred patterns of teaching skills.

- Gagné (1987)

  Gagné noted the significance in selection of audio-visual resources of the characteristics of the learning task (for example, motor skills will demand the use of media allowing for the practising of skills and the presentation of immediate, informative feedback). The physical attributes of the media (for example, their capacity to present good visual displays) must be considered. Finally, learner variables (environment, students' entry behaviour) should be allowed for.

Questions for the use of audio-visual material

In summary, it is suggested that the class teacher who is contemplating the use of audio-visual resources should consider the following questions as a necessary part of the lesson planning process:

1   does the attainment of my lesson outcomes/objectives really require the employment of any resources?
2   what is the precise matter to be learned and how may the probability of learning be heightened by the use of resources?
3   what are the specific properties of the resource which will enable me to utilize them so as to attain the required lesson outcomes/objectives?
4   what particular responses do I require from the students following the use of the resources (such as comprehending, consolidating, or revising)?
5   what prior knowledge or experience is required from the class if they are to benefit from the resource?
6   how are the students likely to respond to the resource?
7   can the presentation of the resource be differentiated or adapted to student responses?
8   is the resource inclusive?
9   how shall I evaluate the effectiveness of the resource?

At all points, it is important to remember that the selection and use of resources should be underpinned by a concern to enhance the opportunities for learning that are being afforded to the student. Unless there is some evidence that the learning that the teacher seeks to bring about is hastened, intensified or consolidated by the use of audio-visual resources, he or she may in fact be advised not to use them.

Gagné argued that the use of resources contributes effectively to the growth of specific learning capabilities (1985). Intellectual skills are enhanced by the capacity of visual aids to stimulate the recall of prerequisite skills and to add cues or reminders for the retrieval of newly learned skills. Cognitive strategies are assisted in their growth by a variety of visual aids adding cues for the transfer of strategies to novel circumstances. Images used in instruction can broaden and add detail to context in which fresh information has been embedded. Motor skills can be improved by the presentation of images that depict processes, skills and subroutines. And attitudes can be broadened by the skilful use of human models as represented, for example, in films or photographs in which those attitudes are displayed.

Gagné's analysis led him in turn to suggest in specific terms that the exclusion of some types of media be considered in relation to specific learning outcomes:

1 Where the learning outcome is intended to be the enhancement of intellectual skills or the development of cognitive strategies, resources that lack the capacity for encouraging learner interaction and that cannot provide immediate feedback should be excluded.

2 Where the learning outcome is intended to be a heightening of verbal information, resources that cannot present such information and its elaboration should be excluded.

3 Where the learning outcome is intended to involve fine or gross motor skills, resources which do not provide for learner response and swift feedback should be excluded.

Types of audio-visual resource: Uses, advantages and disadvantages

This section is by no means comprehensive, but does attempt to discuss those audio-visual resources that are most commonly used by teachers in FE.

The whiteboard

A whiteboard can be found in just about every teaching room in the FE sector. It is one of the oldest, cheapest and probably the most used of visual aids, and continues to be a reliable stand-by for the class teacher. It is useful for building up maps, graphs and diagrams, for recording the key phrases, concepts and definitions given in a lesson or lecture, for building the scheme of a lesson as it unfolds, for recapitulating and summarizing, and for recording any other matters which occur in discussion and which the teacher perceives to be noteworthy. A word or sentence recorded on the board provides emphasis in a manner that may be lacking if the matter in question was only spoken.

Whiteboards can be used to note down key points from a presentation, and also to capture the discussions of students in small group or case study work. It is not uncommon practice for the teacher to ask one or two students to take turns in acting as a class scribe and to record discussion points during a session: this serves not only as an effective way of embedding functional skills, but also as a method of democratizing the climate of the classroom.

As the result of experiments in visual perception, strong rules regarding the use of colour are now well established. The use of a blue or black pen for writing, and a red pen for emphasis (underlining or circling key words, for example) is widely considered as best practice. The use of green pens for writing should be avoided: for some readers who are on the dyslexia spectrum, the reading of green letters on a white background causes particular difficulties. Finally, it is important to remember that whiteboards need to be kept scrupulously clean.

Whiteboards are simple technologies, but still need using with care. Writing must be large and legible, and the careful spacing of words and lines requires practice. The building up on a whiteboard of notes, or the main topics of a lesson, so that the available space is not crowded and important points are emphasized, also demands practice. And finally, the teacher must remember not to talk to the whiteboard while writing on it: a common mistake but an easy one to remedy.

Interactive whiteboards

Interactive whiteboards, either attached to a PC that is permanently positioned in the classroom or connected to a laptop installed by the teacher and calibrated to a data projector, are increasingly common in FE colleges. They have varying degrees of function-ality but are often only used as a backdrop for presentations (PowerPoint, for example – discussed below). As they run on their own software platform, the use of interactive whiteboards does require an investment of time and effort on the part of the teacher. Arguably, much of the functionality of whiteboards is more geared towards the primary, not the tertiary, curriculum. Although the most popular models contain useful pre-loaded imagery (maps, for example), much of this is readily available online. However, one simple to use feature of interactive whiteboards is strongly recommended. Teachers are able to write notes on an interactive whiteboard much as they would on a regular one. These notes can then be saved. It becomes possible therefore for the teacher to save all of the notes that are written on the whiteboard during her or his lesson. These can then be converted to a more popular format (such as pdf, for example) and uploaded to a VLE or emailed to students.

Charts and models

Charts (prepared permanent displays) may be used to illustrate, emphasize and supplement verbal exposition. They can be designed to provide examples that illustrate abstract arguments, to present factual data or comparative information in the form of graphs or pie charts or to focus attention on the characteristics of an object (such the structure of the human cuticle). Used in workshops and laboratories they can act as operational guides, stating factual data and illustrating handling methods and safety rules. Charts clamped together at the top and fixed to an easel or whiteboard can be used in a sequence to illustrate the structure of a topic or to summarize in a stage-by-stage manner.

The most useful charts are often those which are simple and clearly set out and which concentrate on a few points only. Colour contrasts are important and experimental evidence suggests that schemes combining blue and green, or blue and orange, have high attention value when used in the construction of charts.

Three-dimensional models are valuable where it is inconvenient or impossible to see or use the real thing, or where students might experience difficulty in comprehending a two-dimensional diagram, for example as where interior views of a room are required, or the shape of an object is too complex for adequate illustration on a page or chart, or much detail is needed for the complete communication of a concept, such as the working of a machine.

Podcasts, audio and other sound recordings
Over recent years, the explosion of online resources has served to provide teachers in FE with a wealth of resources. Audio recordings – whether in the form of podcasts, which can be downloaded or streaming broadcasts which can be listened to online – constitute just one such resource. The JISC (formerly the Joint Information Systems Committee) is responsible for promoting the use of technology in post-16 education and training, and has a variety of podcasts available on its website which will be of use to the teacher. There is nothing new in using audio recordings as a teaching aid and the use of audiocassettes and compact discs continues in some subject areas (modern languages being one obvious example). However, the ubiquity of ICT equipment and the availability of free audio recording software for computers makes podcasting a tool that can be easily shared with students in ways that might not have been so practicable ten years ago. Teachers can make podcasts quite easily (indeed, some teachers record their presentations and post them onto college VLEs), and can just as easily ask students to make podcasts as a formative or summative assessment exercise.

Films and videos
Video can be highly valuable to the teacher, particular in allowing her or him to show aspects of professional or technical practice that are of importance to the curriculum but that are difficult to access in real life. Film from a children's nursery can allow students on a childcare course to practice their observational skills. Film from a manufacturing plant can allow apprentices to see authentic industrial processes that they would only be able to simulate at their college. And archive film clips of experiments conducted 50 years ago can enliven and enthuse students working towards an A level in psychology.

The internet has rendered the use of video more straightforward for the teacher in FE, both in terms of playback (a youtube clip projected onto an interactive whiteboard will always give a much larger image than can be provided by anything other than a very large monitor) and in terms of access (it is a simple exercise to search for relevant clips online). At the same time, it is important to remember that DVD players and monitors can also be used, and are usually straightforward to set up if a PC with a DVD drive is not available.

Because the use of video necessitates the teacher temporarily handing over his or her active role (since, whilst the clip is being watched, the teacher 'disappears from view' and, therefore, in effect abandons class control during the showing of the film), preplanning is of particular importance. Choice of appropriate film from among the very large number now available is the first planning task. The teacher should answer the following questions in relation to the film he or she wishes to select:

Questions for the use of film material

1 what is its educational purpose?

2 what are the outcomes/objectives that watching the film will contribute towards?

3 how does it relate to the syllabus or curriculum that is being followed?

4 does it assume, and build on, the previous knowledge of the class?

5 is its content accurate, up-to-date, well-organized and well-presented?

6 is the commentary comprehensible and appropriate?

7 is it inclusive? Is it sub-titled or close captioned?

8 is the sound track clearly recorded?

9 is its length appropriate? (A length of more than 30 minutes would generally be seen as excessive and a film of this length should be shown in instalments.)

10 what instructional method does it employ?

11 will the students find it interesting?

12 might it act to generate useful discussion?

The rearrangement of the classroom is an important part of the planning. Seating and ventilation must be considered; the projector and screen positioned carefully and attention given to the placing of the loudspeaker, which should be, preferably, below or behind the screen; direct sunlight should be excluded. Equipment ought to be checked in detail before the showing.

The video ought to be introduced and its objectives noted (on the whiteboard or a flipchart) and explained by the teacher. In some cases, where time allows, the film can be shown twice, the second showing following a class discussion of its main points. During the second showing the sound commentary might be switched off, so that teachers can provide their own, emphasizing the important points of the video. Follow-up study of the film is essential, in the form of discussion, recapitulation or formative assessment (on prepared questions which can be shown on a flipchart or provided on a handout, thus acting as a guide to important points to be noticed).

The advantages of video ought not to be forgotten. Video can undoubtedly translate abstract thought into comprehensible, visual terms and, by the use of techniques such as slow motion, close up and cutting can focus class attention in a unique fashion. Above all, video brings into the classroom a variety of stimuli presented in an expert and attractive way, thus facilitating the learning process when they are integrated into an overall lesson pattern.

Disadvantages include their association with the relaxed atmosphere which tends to surround video as a mode of entertainment. The showing of a video will not automatically guarantee motivation or attention. Lack of active class participation and the loss of teacher control over the pace of presentation of information can be guarded against, to some extent, by careful planning, the use of attention-directing devices, recapitulation and testing so that the impact of video as a resource to support learning can be as effective as possible.

PowerPoint

The ubiquity of PowerPoint (the use of which is increasingly being taught in primary schools) almost renders its discussion here irrelevant, but although PowerPoint has many virtues, it can also (as is the case with any other resource) be misused and therefore be rendered a barrier to learning rather than a stimulus to learning.

PowerPoint allows the teacher to create a variety of styles of presentation which can be used to accompany a presentation or discussion. A PowerPoint presentation might consist of text, images, photographs, embedded video or sound files, and links to websites or to other PC files (such as word documents or pdf files). A PowerPoint presentation can be converted into an alternative format (such as pdf) so that it can be uploaded to a VLE and viewed on a tablet or smartphone, and it can be printed out as a handout. As such, it is a very useful software package and one that teachers should all acquaint themselves with. Indeed, the ready availability of ICT equipment in colleges means that teachers may ask students to create PowerPoint slides as part of a class-based formative exercise, for presentation to the whole group (clear instructions as to scope and timing of presentations need to be provided to students if this activity is to be used).

However, PowerPoint needs to be used as carefully and critically as any other resource. Questions about the implications of using PowerPoint extend beyond the expression 'death by PowerPoint'. Critics have argued that it leads teachers towards a didactic style and stifles, rather than stimulates, student-centred learning practices, and that although students express a preference for PowerPoint in the workshop or classroom, it's use does not lead to an increase in learning (Adams, 2006; Savoy et al., 2009). Thus, although the use of Powerpoint is generally to be recommended as a convenient and effective way of storing and managing classroom resources in one location (that is having all of the materials for a session within a PowerPoint presentation), care should be taken so that the content of the presentation is not overshadowed by the style. Bearing in mind the research cited above, the following list of recommendations for the use of PowerPoint in teaching is offered:

Recommendations for using PowerPoint

1   Ensure that dark text (black or dark blue) is always shown on a lightly coloured background (such as pale yellow or green, not white) – this will aid legibility for students with dyslexia. Light text on a dark background can cause legibility problems for some students.

2   Choose sans serif fonts, avoid italics and underlining, and use bold type to highlight key points – again to aid legibility and ensure the presentation is inclusive. Make sure the font is large enough so that the slides can be easily read from all parts of the workshop or classroom.

3   Language should be inclusive and avoid stereotyping.

4   Use relevant and good quality images to aid memorization of the content of the presentation.

5   If video or audio is embedded in the presentation, ensure that it will play correctly if the presentation is to be viewed on a different PC to the one on which it was created.

6   Do not crowd slides with too much text or too many busy images. Avoid needless animations and slide transitions: they only serve as a distraction. Animation should be used only sparingly – for example, when deliberately revealing items in sequence or when providing a model answer to a question that has first been posed to the student group.

7   Spelling and grammar should be checked carefully.

Handouts

It might seem odd to consider a handout as an audio-visual aid, but that is exactly what a handout is. Although teachers are invariably encouraged to store their materials on a VLE for students to download and print at home if they wish, the reality of teaching in FE is that handouts continue to be worthwhile resources to support learning.

Handouts are as ubiquitous as PowerPoint slides, and similarly prone to poor design and illegibility, something that must be seen as unacceptable when the prevalence of PCs, cheap and easy printing and word processing software is taken into consideration. It does not take much effort to produce a handout that is visually attractive and contains correct spelling (this latter point being of particular importance in the light of the current focus on functional skills). It is a straightforward task for the teacher to combine text and image and to select images or photographs that can be reproduced to a good standard in either black and white or colour (colour printing is expensive and reprographics departments in colleges may ration the amount of colour printing that is allowed at any one time).

Handouts can be used to provide summaries of presentations (for example, by printing PowerPoint slides – care should be taken when selecting a print option so that the slides can be read) or for class-based activities and formative assessment. Gapped handouts can be used for assessment and revision: for example, a handout could be produced consisting of a number of diagrams that have already been studied in class, but with labels/key words removed. These can then be retained by students for revision purposes.

The following guidelines for producing handouts are recommended to help ensure that they are effective and inclusive:

Recommendations for using handouts

1 fonts should always be sans serif. Italics and underlining should be avoided wherever possible and bold type should be sued to create emphasis. A font size of at least 12 point should be used. Text should be justified along the left-hand margin only. These will all help ensure a high level of readability

2 wherever possible, a paper colour other than white should be requested so that the handout is inclusive

3 images and photographs should be evaluated carefully to ensure that they are perfectly legible after reproduction. If images from websites are to be used, these should be of a high resolution so that they will not pixelate when expanded on the page

4 handouts should not be too crowded. Dense pages of text do not encourage reluctant readers

5 spelling and grammar should be checked scrupulously. Mistakes will happen, but strenuous efforts should be made to keep these to a minimum. If a mistake is found, the handout must always be corrected (the same applies for any other resource designed by the teacher)

6 language should be inclusive and avoid stereotyping.

Flipcharts

Flipcharts provide a cheap and readily available alternative to whiteboards. Their smaller size renders them inappropriate in larger classrooms or workshops, but they are very useful for capturing comments or feedback from students as part of a group work project, such as a case study (providing another opportunity for the development of literacy skills). When using flipcharts to record student group work, the following guidelines ought to be considered:

1   different coloured pens might be provided to add interest to the flipchart (whiteboard pens should not be used as the ink is less strong and hence less easily visible)

2   each small group might be asked to use a single colour for their flipchart so that the different answers provided can be easily differentiated

3   the teacher will need to remember to provide blu-tack so that the flipcharts can be easily displayed

4   flipchart paper is of a poorer quality than photocopier paper and tends to tear easily

5   completed flipcharts can easily be photographed (on a smartphone or with a digital camera), and the images uploaded to the college VLE, for future revision.

Overhead projectors

For a long time, overhead projectors were one of the most popular and versatile visual aids in use in the sector. Little technical attention is required for maintenance, and modern projectors are compact, portable machines which project excellent still images free from distortion in rooms requiring no blackout or projection screens (light-coloured walls being quite adequate). They are rarely found in new colleges, but still found in other contexts, particularly outreach centres and community education centres.

The projector may be used as a whiteboard, the teacher writing with a special pen directly on to an acetate sheet or roll, so that the script is projected in magnified form as it is being written. The roll can be cleaned and used again. Pre-drawn diagrams can be shown, blank maps can be projected and filled in as the lesson progresses, and recapitulations and prepared summaries, lecture headings (with space for detailed notes) and silhouettes, can be shown with great clarity. Techniques such as overlay (where additional transparencies are used to superimpose detail on a prepared outline) or reveal (where parts of a diagram are covered by small pieces of paper attached by tape, which are removed to build up detail as required) help in those modes of instruction based on concept analysis in particular. Transparencies, like PowerPoint slides or handouts, should be simple, their content concise and uncluttered with detail.

Daylight projection and easy control are important advantages of the overhead projector. Even more important is the fact that teacher control of the class is not lost – a fully darkened room is unnecessary and the teacher can face the class while controlling the projector. Thus the apparatus remains an aid and does not at any stage in its use take over the lesson.

A brief note on copyright

The use of audio-visual resources may attract the provisions of the law of copyright which is now an important part of intellectual property law – that part of English law which regulates the use and exploitation by one person of the fruits of another person's creative labour. The key statute is the *Copyright, Designs and Patents Act 1988*, as subsequently amended. The statute protects certain types of intangible property, such as an author's published writing, usually in the interests of the author. The author's rights may endure for 70 years after his death. Directives of the European Union have enlarged the effect of the statutes and regulations protecting copyright.

College staff must ensure that their use of published material for audio-visual resources is made with the provisions of the statute in mind. There are appropriate exceptions under the 1988 Act, such as section 35, allowing recording of broadcast and cable programmes by educational establishments for their educational purposes. The creation of 'certified licensing schemes' is allowed under section 143. College policy and local education authority regulations ought to be known by teachers using audio-visual resources.

Summary: The right tools for the right job

The careful use of audio-visual resources (which should be evaluated as rigorously as any other aspect of the teacher's practice – this issue is discussed in Chapter 32) can be considered in a similar manner to the careful use of specialist tools in a workshop: it might be possible to complete a job with an incorrect tool, but the job will be best done with the right tool. It is all too easy for teachers to get carried away with the technical possibilities of PowerPoint, or to assume that just because their students all use facebook they will be equally confident in using a VLE (research increasingly suggests that this is not the case). Teachers need to ensure that their resources work alongside their own careful preparation, their own extensive subject knowledge and their own enthusiasm and motivation. A technically accomplished presentation embedded with images and sounds is no substitute for a well-informed and enthusiastic teacher who understands how to communicate with her or his students, how to use questioning techniques to provoke thought and action, and how to give appropriate and constructive feedback. These processes can be added to – but not replaced by – audio-visual aids.

Further reading

Advice regarding the design and use of resources for learning and teaching is plentiful. Although these chapters tend all to address broadly similar themes, they often offer different examples, and sight of these can be helpful for the new trainee teacher as well as the more experienced practitioner.

Armitage, A., Evershed, J., Hayes, D., Hudson, A., Kent, J., Lawes, S., Poma, S. and Renwick, M. (2012), *Teaching and training in lifelong learning*. 4th edition. Maidenhead: McGraw Hill. Chapter 5.

Harvey, B. and Harvey, J. (2012), *Creative teaching approaches in the lifelong learning sector*. Maidenhead: McGraw Hill.

Scales, P. (2013), *Teaching in the Lifelong Learning Sector*. Second edition. Maidenhead: McGraw Hill. Chapter 7.

Wallace, S. (2011), *Teaching, Tutoring and Training in the Lifelong Learning Sector*. 4th edition. Exeter: Learning Matters. Chapter 9.

29 e-Learning and Blended Learning in Further Education

The first edition of this book contained few references to the use of the computer in colleges of FE. E-learning was not on the agenda, not even in terms of its being a possible aid to the teaching–learning process. Computers were used widely at that time in industry and commerce, but, for a variety of reasons, their large-scale adoption into educational practice was not considered feasible, largely, but not entirely, because of cost. Some few decades later, the situation has been totally transformed: e-learning is a regular feature of work in the colleges, a large proportion of staff are computer-literate, and many students entering colleges have already passed school examinations in computer studies and information technology, and expect to continue to develop their skills in college courses.

In the following pages we set out, not the technical details of computers and their programming, which are explained in a large library of specialist texts, but rather a review of the use of e-learning in the colleges, and some comments on the growth of a theory (and practice) of e-learning.

A note on terminology: E-learning and blended learning

There are several difficulties to be found in providing a simple and unambiguous definition of the term 'e-learning'. It is a term that has been around for over a decade, and has persisted even though the uses of computers, tablets and smartphones – not only in education but also in social life more generally – must be seen as having outpaced all predictions. The ubiquity of affordable, hand-held devices that can be used to surf the internet, prepare a PowerPoint presentation, download material from a virtual learning environment and access an e-book from a college library has changed the ways in which people use technology for work and for learning profoundly. Earlier editions of this book understood 'computer assisted learning' (a now defunct term) as being based in an IT suite, a dedicated computer room that teachers would need to book in advance and prepare specific lessons and activities for – assuming that such a resource were actually needed. In contrast, a cursory tour of a contemporary FE college would reveal any number of uses of technology, invariably by students who are more fluent in the issue, and have a higher level of digital literacy, than many of their teachers. Talk of a digital divide, of an underclass which is disadvantaged due to a lack of access to a high-speed internet connection and affordable technology, seems entirely inappropriate in such a setting.

The term 'e-learning' was originally used to describe the provision of education and training programmes that were entirely online and self-studied (that is, without teachers and without formal pedagogy), such as Learndirect. Proponents of these early forms of 'e-learning' argued that teaching was not needed and that self-study would be better suited to the needs of the students in question. Critics argued that such programmes only offered a very narrow, functional curriculum that failed to promote deep learning. Over time, however, and not least due to the pace of change of technology, the use of computers (including smartphones and tablets) has proliferated, permeating all aspects of the FE curriculum. Alongside this change, the 'self-study' paradigm has been sidelined and a new paradigm, of technology being simply another element of any learning episode – like a book or a pen – has become established.

The establishment of the term 'blended learning' was an attempt to capture this new approach. By stressing the blend between 'modern' technology and 'traditional' patterns of learning, the blended learning model can be seen at one level as a more realistic, if not entirely accurate, attempt to define contemporary pedagogic practice. But uncertainties still remain. The term does not offer a new theory of learning – it simply reflects the fact that learning is increasingly accompanied by new kinds of tools and resources. The actual process of learning is not different. Social constructivism is a theory of learning, as is communities of practice theory. Blended learning (like the older term e-learning) is a description of learning, not a theory. The predilections of some policy makers, government ministers, college managers and teachers to simply prefix terms with the letter 'e' does not constitute a fundamental shift in how learning, teaching and assessment are understood at the level of psychology or knowledge, but how they are changing and how they are practiced – a process that is as evident in playing video games as it is in using technology at college (Gee, 2003).

Theoretical perspectives on students' use of technology: Digital literacies

What is actually taking place when one student uses her smartphone to update her Facebook status or email her tutor a question regarding the next assignment for her programme of study, or when another student uses his tablet to download and read a pdf file in preparation for his afternoon seminar and uses comment boxes to annotate the file? Arguably, these are simply examples of students reading and interacting with texts. The texts in question are on screens as opposed to pieces of paper, and are added to or otherwise manipulated through the use of a keyboard or touchpad, but otherwise there is no meaningful difference in the learning that is taking place. Both of the students in this example are reading some things, making notes and coming up with questions – actions that could quite easily be repeated with books, notepads and pens. With this in mind, it seems logical to explore theoretical approaches to e-learning not through theories of learning, but through theories related to literacy. Here, it is suggested that theories of literacy as social practice, also known as the New Literacy Studies, provide a meaningful framework for understanding the ways in which students work on their laptops and smartphones.

The New Literacy Studies (NLS) is an approach to understanding literacy that rests on a number of key themes (Barton, 2007; Barton and Hamilton, 1998):

1 Literacy is best understood as a set of social practices; these can be inferred from events which involve and are shaped by written texts.

2 There are different kinds of literacy associated with different spheres of life; for example, workplace literacies such as writing job sheets and filling in forms in a car mechanics' workshop or completing prescriptions for medicine in a pharmacy.

3 Literacy practices are shaped by social institutions (colleges, awarding bodies, governments) and power relationships (teacher–student; assessor–candidate), and some literacies become more dominant, visible and influential than others; an example of a dominant literacy includes the ways in which students are required to write essays, as opposed to how they might compose text messages or Facebook posts.

4 Literacy practices are embedded in broader social goals and cultural practices and always have a purpose; reading and writing always 'does' something or leads to something.

5 Literacy is historically situated – it changes over time; the ways in which people spell and punctuate text messages provide an excellent example of a recent literacy practice.

6 Literacy practices change, and new ones are frequently acquired through processes of informal learning; students do not follow formal programmes of study in order to learn how to send text messages or write blog posts.

From this point of view, the ways in which students in FE use technology as part of their programme of study can be understood as being a particular kind of literacy practice. The dominant role played by digital technology in such contexts has led to these practices being referred to as digital literacies.

Differences between screen-based work and paper-based work

Meaningful differences can be found through a comparison of how student might read a book or magazine article and how they might read an e-book or an online journal. These can best be explored through a particular aspect of the NLS approach which is usually referred to as multi-modal literacy (Kress, 2003). Modality is a term used in linguistics and refers to the way in which a piece of information is presented so that it can be presented to someone to look at or read. So in this sense, a map might be one mode of presenting information, a picture would be a second mode and a body of writing would be a third.

Researchers in this field have argued that increasing and changing uses of technology have led to significant changes in the modality of what people read (Kress, 2003; Snyder, 2002). It is not the fact that there are lots of modes of information that is new, it is that there are more and more new modes in themselves that is significant. A typical web page provides a good example. The fundamental interactive and technological characteristics of a web page combine to create a modality of reading that is quite different from a printed page. Web pages can contain sound, video, multiple boxes of text of different size and different colour, and so on. And these differences change how people read things. When teachers and students (or anybody else) read a written page, the text has to be followed in a sequential manner. When the same people read a webpage, reading can go in all kinds of directions, focusing first on a text box, then on an image, or the other way around. The reader might open up a new web page by clicking on a hyperlink in the middle of a sentence. What is important is that the sequential pattern of reading has been replaced by a quite different multi-directional pattern. Put simply, reading becomes different.

It is suggested that the theoretical perspectives (drawn from the NLS tradition) discussed above relating to reading raise two key issues for the teacher that should be considered when planning for the use of (for example) web-based resources in lessons:

1 It should not be assumed that because students in FE are fluent users of digital technologies in their home and social spheres, they will be equally, or unproblematically, fluent users of applications or processes that their programme of study requires them to use. Frequent use of Facebook to talk with friends does not equate to frequent use of a discussion board in a VLE to discuss course progress.

2 It should not be assumed that students already possess the study skills needed to use online resources appropriately and effectively simply because they are confident users of laptops and tablets. Just as students might benefit from induction into how to use a physical library, so might they benefit from induction and continued guidance in using a e-library.

3 Research indicates that reading online tends to lead to a more superficial approach

to the text, as opposed to the reading of a physical book or article which promotes a deeper level of engagement (Baumann, 2010).

With these overarching matters of concern in mind, we can now turn to a consideration of the principles that underpin lesson planning when using digital technologies.

Overarching principles for planning learning with digital technologies

Only a relatively small number of robust and thorough models of teaching and learning with technology are to be found in current literature. One of the most often found is that of Salmon (2003), who proposed a five-stage model of planning for online teaching and learning which can be extended to include blended approaches and the broader use of technologies that is the focus of this chapter:

1 Access and motivation

The students are introduced to the technology in question. The teacher explains why the technology is being used, explains the tasks to be carried out and relates them to the curriculum, and provides any necessary technical support.

2 Socialization

The students become familiar with the technology. The teacher provides opportunities for students to try things out and to establish relationships with their peers regarding how the technology is used.

3 Information exchange

The students start to explore the information or facts that are available, or the different uses or options that the technology affords them. The teacher provides support and encouragement, as well group management in ensuring that students stay on task.

4 Knowledge construction

By this time, the students will be able to establish their own meanings relating to the material that they are reading, the conversations that they are having or the actions that they are performing. (Here, the essentially Vygotskian (as discussed in Chapter 9) nature of Salmon's approach becomes apparent). The teacher now takes on the role of the facilitator, overseeing discussion, debate and activity, correcting students where necessary.

5 Development

The students begin to support each other (peer learning) and to rely less on the teacher for answering questions or solving problems. The students begin to develop skills of autonomous learning and critical thinking, accompanied by a higher level of technical mastery (teachers should be mindful that for some applications of digital technology, student learning will relate to fine motor skills as well as cognitive functions).

Teaching and learning, and technology

There are a number of technologies, tools and applications that might be used by teachers in FE. This list is not intended to be exhaustive (it reflects in part the experiences and preferences of the author and of recent teacher-training students with whom the author has worked) – not least as new applications and websites appear at a bewildering speed. Nor is it intended to provide a critical account of the tools and applications listed. For more expansive coverage of technology-enhanced learning, the reader is recommended to explore some of the more recent specialist literature (Beetham and Sharpe, 2007; Hill, 2007; Ingle and Duckworth, 2013; Salmon, 2004).

Digital photography and video

Photographs and videos can hardly be described as new inventions. However, the proliferation of digital cameras (for photography and/or video) that are increasingly small and inexpensive, together with the growth of easy-to-use software applications for editing video and photographs, is noteworthy. It is a relatively straightforward task for a group of students to make a short film depicting their experiences on placement, for example, or illustrating an aspect of college life (in both cases, having ensured that relevant clearances and permissions have been granted), or for a teacher to create a storyboard using a series of photographs with captions or speech bubbles added in order to illustrate a key theme relevant to the topic being studied.

Evernote

One of the problems that accompany the use of the internet for teaching and learning is the management of the massive amount of data that can be found. Indeed, one of the causes for concern voiced in relation to the use of the internet in educational contexts is that the sheer volume of information that is available is overwhelming, hindering analysis and critical exploration, and encouraging a surface rather than deep approach to learning. Evernote is an application that helps the user to store and manage the information that she or he gathers. The teacher or student can bookmark a web page within Evernote, cut and paste documents into Evernote, make comments and add virtual post-it notes, take a screenshot and catalogue it for later, and use search functions to locate a particular piece of information later on. Bundles of saved files, photographs and webpages can be easily shared with other users as well. Work stored on Evernote can be shared across platforms as well (that is, between desktop computers, tablets and smartphones).

Facebook

Facebook is not the only social media platform that is available, but it is one of the most ubiquitous. As so many students in FE use Facebook, it is logical for teachers to consider how it might be used for teaching and learning. It is a simple task for the teacher to create a Facebook page for a student year group or module group to use. This might be for relatively simple purposes such as providing messages relating to assignment deadlines, or providing hyperlinks to useful online resources such as e-journals. Or the teacher might attempt a more complex task, and use Facebook chat as an alternative to a discussion thread on the college VLE for the discussion of class-related themes and ideas. Finally, it is important to remember that teachers and students should not friend each other on Facebook: instead, the teacher should set up a group page that the students can join, but that keeps all other information private.

Mindmeister

Mindmeister is an online tool for creating mind maps (many other programmes, such as Mind Genius, are also available, and many colleges install mind mapping software on their networked PCs). A mind map is quite simply a way of organizing notes on a page that is not in a traditional linear format. In itself, a mind map does not create or encourage new or innovative ways of thinking and more or less that any other note-taking method would, despite what some advocates of the process might declare. For those students – and teachers – who do use mind maps to organize their notes and their work, the Mindmeister application offers a number of useful functions, including the ability to embed links to other documents (which might be online or offline), and the option for a collaborative mind map to be created online, facilitated by a live chat feature (such as the one found on Facebook).

Online portfolios and document storage

A portfolio is a collection of items such as written work, witness testimonies, feedback from teachers or employers and reflections, gathered together by a student in order to demonstrate that learning has taken place in relation to a set of outcomes or criteria usually established by an awarding body (this topic is discussed in more detail in Chapter 31). An online portfolio is exactly the same, except that the documents are stored on-line, not in an A4 ring binder. A number of awarding bodies and professional bodies are already using so-called e-portfolios as formal aspects of their initial training and continuing professional development programmes (the Institute for Learning being an example of immediate relevance to teachers in the FE sector), and the Excellence Gateway contains a number of case studies relating to their use in FE settings. For teachers who wish to adopt an e-portfolio approach in an informal manner, on-line storage applications such as Dropbox readily allow the online storage and sharing of files of various formats.

Podcasting

A podcast is an audio or video recording that can be stored online or downloaded for off-line use on a laptop, tablet, smartphone or digital audio player. The variety of podcasts available to the listener is astonishing. Examples of podcast providers include: public and private sector broadcasting companies (BBC podcasts are a good place to start); colleges and universities (in the UK, the Open University offers a range of podcasts); and professional bodies (the Excellence Gateway – part of LSIS – hosts a number of podcasts that are of immediate use to FE teachers). It is also a straightforward task for teachers and trainers to record their own teaching and, for example, upload presentations as podcasts: together with the use of screencasting software, it is possible for the teacher to create a podcast that combines a presentation with an audio commentary, for example. Students might also be encouraged to create their own podcasts as a group exercise, and these could be uploaded to a college VLE or shared on a web-based platform such as soundcloud.

Prezi

Prezi is an alternative to PowerPoint, and a free version (but with limited functionality) is available. An ipad app is also available. A Prezi works in much the same way as a PowerPoint presentation (indeed, a PowerPoint can be uploaded and turned into a Prezi), but with a small number of key differences. When a Prezi is displayed (either on screen or via a data projector onto an interactive whiteboard), it is possible to zoom in and out of certain parts of the slide. This helps move away from the linear presentation-style of PowerPoint and allows the teacher to produce a presentation with a more 'holistic' feel. It is very easy to share Prezi files online (allowing teachers to bypass college VLEs if they wish), or to download them for use off-line. It is also a simple task for several people to collaborate in the creation of a Prezi online; this, it is suggested, might constitute a valuable formative assessment task for students.

Wikipedia

A wiki is a website that has been written and edited collaboratively: one user can write something in a wiki, another user can edit it, a third user can add an image, and so on. There are a number of websites that allow users to create and edit their own wikis, but Wikipedia is undoubtedly the best known such website. Wikipedia enjoys an ambiguous position amongst teachers and trainers (notwithstanding the constant concern that students will simply cut and paste Wikipedia pages when writing assignments). Wikipedia is not referenced and because it is open access, teachers are concerned as to the quality of the information and discussion that is presented. And yet because it is a source of diverse information that can be quickly and easily searched, Wikipedia can be seen as an ideal reference tool. The use of Wikipedia should not be discouraged, therefore: indeed, students can be encouraged to edit Wikipedia entries or to create their own wiki as a class project. Instead, students should be made aware that Wikipedia – like any other online resource – requires careful and critical reading and evaluation.

YouTube

YouTube needs no introduction, but a number of points relating to the use of YouTube in the classroom are worthy of rehearsal. As with any other video intended for use in the classroom, a YouTube clip should be watched in full in advance of the lesson in which it will be used, in order to ensure that it is suitable. If working with students who have impaired hearing, YouTube should not be used, as subtitles will not usually be available. It is important to ensure that the video is of good quality so that it will not be fuzzy or pixelated when viewed on a screen via a data projector. It is also important to show the video in full screen mode, to prevent intrusive advertisements or other pop-ups (which may be distracting at best and inappropriate or offensive at worst).

Benefits and advantages associated with technology-enhanced learning

The use of digital technologies (if used in an appropriate and carefully planned fashion) can be seen as having a number of generalizable benefits to teaching and learning practice. These can be summarized as follows:

1 Technology as an aid to accessibility.
   The use of digital technologies to facilitate access to mainstream education and training by students with specific learning difficulties or disabilities is a well documented aspect of FE provision more generally (Powell and Tummons, 2011). Assistive technologies (ranging from software solutions such as speech-to-text applications to adapted hardware such as trackballs and oversize keyboards), together with many of the features that are installed as standard on laptop or desktop computers (such as software that will allow a computer to read a pdf file aloud) has proven to be of particular significance in encouraging access to the FE curriculum for students with a range of needs.

2 Technology as an aid to student engagement and motivation.
   Recent research indicates that the use of technology can have a positive effect on engagement and motivation (Passey, 2004). In particular, the ability to conduct wide-ranging research, the ability to write assessed work in a variety of ways and the ability to present work in an attractive and 'professional' fashion, can all be seen to contribute to students' sense of engagement with their studies.

3 Technology as an aid to student autonomy.
   Digital technologies offer the teacher a variety of ways in which differentiated teaching and learning activities can be planned. The sheer variety of ways in which technology can be used to achieve a single task (for example, the creation of a poster or of a

presentation) allows students, working either individually or in groups, a high degree of autonomy and choice in how they work. Activities such as these are understood to help develop independent study skills and to encourage independent learning (that is to say, learning that is self-regulated and self-managed, also known as autonomous learning). The development of these aptitudes is understood, from a variety of theoretical perspectives, as encouraging deep as opposed to surface learning.

4 Technology as an authentic element of teaching practice.
Authenticity is an important element of the teacher's repertoire, and this extends to the use of digital technologies. There are two elements to this. First, it is undoubtedly the case that to varying degrees (depending on the subject matter being taught – this will be discussed shortly), students in FE simply expect teachers to use technology. Just as digital technologies have become an everyday part of the social lives of students and the working lives of parents or friends, for example, so they are also expected to be an aspect of the teaching environment, as commonplace as books. Secondly, it can be argued that certain subject areas require the use of digital technologies of various kinds if teaching is to be authentic. Examples include: the use of spreadsheets in accountancy classes; the use of a computer to interface with On-Board Diagnostics as part of a car mechanics course; the use of Photoshop in design classes; the use of Excel to teach statistics; and the use of a computer-based Salon calendar for booking appointments at a college hair and beauty salon.

Problems and disadvantages associated with technology-enhanced learning

As with any other aspect of the teaching and learning process, discernment and critical judgement need to be exercised when planning for the use of technologies in FE settings. Teachers should reflect critically on the use of ipads in the seminar room in just the same way as they should reflect on the use of case studies or question-and-answer techniques. The following themes are suggested as starting points for reflecting on the use of digital technologies as a way of encouraging learning:

1 The potential for distraction.
Teachers and trainers should not get enthused about technology at the expense of more basic, but no less important, learning and assessment strategies. A poorly designed formative assessment will not be improved on simply by including an element of computer use. Using posters made with flipcharts to report the themes of a case study can be just as effective using PowerPoint slides. There is no robust research evidence that the use of digital technologies either attracts students who

otherwise would not attend an FE college, or improves their achievement or success rates (Gorard and Smith, 2007).

2   Technology as a barrier to participation and learning.
    For many students and potential students, technology may prove to be a barrier to learning, not a conduit. This may simply be a reflection of ownership (not everyone can afford a smartphone or a laptop). It may also be a reflection of the nature of the technology: wanting students to use their smartphones in class to view online resources is all well and good, but how can the teacher ensure that students are not also engaging in off-task behaviours such as updating their Facebook statuses or browsing iTunes?

3   The misuse of technology.
    Simply loading information onto a VLE or to a college network drive is no substitute for the proper sequencing and planning of teaching and learning activities. The potential to create a collection of resources for students is undoubtedly attractive, but unless it is carefully structured and organized into appropriately sized components, students may simply get lost whilst trying to navigate their way through the material.

4   The creation of new versions of old problems for teachers.
    The ever-greater use of digital technologies has over time begun to create particular problems for teachers to cope with. These might best be understood as variations of existing problems. For example, one phenomenon that has already received much attention is 'lurking'. During a seminar or group discussion, teachers often encounter students who are unwilling or unable to participate in discussion, usually for a variety of entirely legitimate reasons. Lurking is the on-line equivalent, and refers to those students who log on to a group discussion site, but do not participate. Academic malpractice has also been encouraged through the internet, partly due to the ease by which a student can cut and paste web-based material into an assignment, and partly due to the emergence of companies who will write essays (euphemistically referred to as 'study aids') for a fixed fee.

5   Technological inequality.
    If teachers are to encourage students to make more use of digital technologies (mindful of the fact that it constitutes a functional skill), then it is important to remember that not all students will enjoy the same access to technology outside the college. When planning activities that require digital technologies, teachers will need to be mindful of the accessibility of the technology: the age of the equipment or the software application being used can affect students' ability to participate on an equal footing.

Online security, and safeguarding when using digital technologies

The welfare of students in FE should always be a matter of concern for the teacher (and particularly for those teachers working with 14–16 year old students). The ways in which young people use the internet is – quite rightly – a matter of concern for society at large. Notwithstanding the hysteria that sometimes accompanies media commentaries relating to the amount of time that young people spend online, there are particular issues surrounding the welfare of students that are particular to e-learning and blended learning environments. Ensuring the safety of students as they work online is in the first instance an institutional responsibility, but individual teachers should also contribute to this practice. Examples include ensuring that students always work on task and do not access websites that are potentially harmful, that contain explicit content, that promote inappropriate or dangerous behaviour, or promulgate undesirable attitudes. Teachers should ensure that the ways in which students talk with each other online are as mutually respectful, inclusive in language and free of discriminatory or bullying behaviour as they are when offline, and in more general terms should encourage good 'netiquette' amongst students (Scheuermann and Taylor, 1997).

Summary: Teaching, learning, and digital technologies

The possible uses of digital technologies and the Internet will undoubtedly continue to grow at a rapid rate, and as such will continue to be a changing aspect of the FE teacher's professional repertoire. At a time when the excessive evangelizing of e-learning seems to have subsided and a more sober and reflective attitude towards technology can be discerned, it is suggested that digital technologies can be seen as a necessary part of the FE landscape: digital technologies should be treated as an integral and natural part of teaching and learning cultures, not as an add-on to satisfy functional skills requirements. Students on a sociology course will almost certainly use digital technologies – as part of their learning – differently to students on a carpentry course. The teachers on these two programmes will likewise use technologies quite differently. And it is quite correct that this should be the case.

Further reading

One of the problems with e-learning is the assumption that the internet is the best resource for exploring and understanding it. This is not, on the whole, true. And so although it may seem odd to recommend books – rather than websites – as suggestions for further reading on e-learning, it is important to remember that the aim here is to foster a critical understanding of the process.

Hill, C. (2007), *Teaching with e-learning in the lifelong learning sector*. 2nd edition. Exeter: Learning Matters.

Ingle, S. and Duckworth, V. (2013), *Enhancing learning through technology in lifelong learning*. Maidenhead: McGraw Hill.

Whalley, J., Welch, T. and Williamson, L (2006), *E-learning in FE*. London: Continuum.

PART 7

Assessment and Evaluation

30 Theories and Principles of Assessment

The importance of assessment rests in the fact of its being the aspect of learning and teaching practice where the results or consequences of that practice are assumed to be able to become visible, or auditable or otherwise verifiable. Perhaps more than any other aspect of professional and academic effort within FE colleges, it is open to scrutiny from outside. Admissions tutors, future employers, funding agencies and professional bodies all look to the assessment process. More specifically, they all look to the certificates, records of achievement and statements of competence that are produced. Employers need to be confident that the students who leave FE colleges do indeed possess those skills, attributes or competences that they require. Admissions tutors – in higher education institutions or in other colleges – need to be confident that students who are applying for new programmes of study are equipped with the prior experience, ability or knowledge that these new programmes will require. Ofsted inspectors scrutinize achievement statistics, as do funding agencies. Assessment is, arguably, the single most important aspect of the work of a teacher or trainer within a FE college.

With so much scrutiny attached to it, it is hardly surprising that assessment is such a widely discussed, written about and researched activity. At the same time, however, it is important to remember that assessment is, in essence, another aspect of a wider learning and teaching process. Consequently, interpretations of assessment – what it is, how it is done and what it means – are unavoidably bound up in broader assumptions about learning and teaching. The teacher who subscribes to a model of learning that is based on neobehaviourist theories and to a model of classroom practice that draws on behavioural objectives, will respond quite differently to the teacher who draws on social constructivist theories when planning for and reflecting on learning. For the most part, such discussions are outside the scope of this chapter, which focuses more specifically on assessment theories and principles, although some reference to those broader frameworks discussed in Parts 2 and 3 of this book will be made. In the following chapter, the focus of the discussion will be on practical matters relating to assessment in the FE sector. In this chapter, the discussion will focus on the key principles that underpin this practice.

Phases of assessment

Assessment is a process that is inextricably bound up in those broader processes that tend to be described as 'learning and teaching'. It is difficult, if not impossible, to imagine a session in a pottery studio or a motor vehicle workshop, a lesson in a health and social care seminar room or a basic skills tutorial that does not, at some point, involve the teacher or trainer making a decision regarding how much the students have learned, whether or not they have demonstrated competence in performing a specified task or whether they have shown that they understand the topics being discussed. All of these are forms of assessment of one kind or another, in just the same way as completing written assignments, adding to a portfolio or completing a number of tasks in a certain amount of time or in a correct sequence are all forms of assessment. In order to help make the process of assessment more understandable, it is possible to identify a number of distinct types of assessment according to the stage or moment at which they tend to occur and the purposes for which they are practiced. This is not to say that these types of assessment are stand-alone or discrete: there is often some blurring at the edges. Nonetheless, such a typology allows for a meaningful as well as convenient method of analysing assessment processes.

Diagnostic assessment

Many of the programmes of study that are offered in FE colleges – apprenticeships, short block-release courses, part-time programmes – operate processes of selection. It is not uncommon for students to have to go through some kind of formal selection process prior to enrolment, to ensure that they have, for example, any necessary prior qualifications or experience. Often, such *entry requirements* are specified within curriculum documentation. For example a Level 3 BTEC National in health and Social Care specifies that for entry to the programme, applicants should already possess at least one of: a BTEC First qualification in a related vocational area; four GCSE passes at grade 'c' or equivalent; other related level 2 qualifications; and other related work experience. By contrast, to access a level 2 BTEC First Certificate in Health and Social Care, no other qualifications have to be achieved beforehand, and no prior knowledge and skills are necessary. In all such circumstances, the teacher will be required to take part, to varying degrees, in the application and enrolment process. She or he might be asked to provide advice and guidance to applicants, to check prior qualifications, to ascertain the extent to which the applicant demonstrates an enthusiasm towards as well as understanding of the required programme of study, and so on. The function of these processes is to ensure that the programme that has been chosen is appropriate to the needs and capacities of the new student. If a student has been allowed to enrol on a programme for which she or he is not suited (either through interest, capability, or prior qualifications or experience), the student is said to be *set up to fail*. There is little point in enrolling a student who will never be able to engage with the curriculum. Features of the application and enrolment process such as interviews, the checking of certificates and so forth all constitute a form of diagnostic assessment. And finally, it should be noted that this is not necessarily a role given only to experienced members of staff: it is not uncommon for newer members of staff to perform this role.

Other forms of diagnostic assessment occur after the students have begun their programmes of study. Sometimes, these diagnostic assessments are formally embedded into the curriculum: examples include the assessment of students' *learning styles* (discussed in Chapter 20), or the assessment of a student's literacy or numeracy levels (if the student does not have a GCSE or other equivalent Level 2 qualification). Normally the results from diagnostic assessments such as these will be recorded in the student's individual learning plan or record of progress (or similar).

A final form of diagnostic assessment can be identified in the assessment of specific learning needs or disabilities. This is a complex and highly specialized form of assessment that will only usually be carried out by suitably qualified professionals: a proper needs assessment for a student with a disability (this might be a seen disability, such as impaired mobility, or an unseen disability such as a mental health issue) would be beyond the professional competence of the vast majority of teachers and trainers in FE. Where the FE teacher might find herself involved, however, is in noticing that such an assessment might be needed. It continues to be the case that for some young people, it is only upon entering the FE sector that previously undiagnosed learning difficulties or disabilities (such as dyslexia and dyscalculia) are noticed and then properly diagnosed for the first time. Therefore, although FE teachers do not need also to be experts in issues such as these (separate qualifications exist for those professionals who have an interest in becoming dyslexia specialists, for example), it is important for all those who teach in FE to be aware of the issues and to be able to refer students to appropriate colleagues in learning support departments.

Ipsative assessment

The development of autonomous, self-directing students can be seen as an integral aspect of the broader educational philosophies of those teachers who subscribe to cognitivist, constructivist or social practice theories of learning. Consequently, these same teachers then need to be able to help their students improve their own learning and performance, partly through encouraging them to think about their own progress, to consider for themselves how they think they are doing and to become responsible for thinking about their own approach to learning or studying: a process referred to as *learning how to learn* or *metacognition*. An important part of this is a form of assessment, which is known as self or ipsative assessment. Ipsative assessment can be understood as an individual process of assessment, which allows the student to achieve three main tasks:

1 The identification of the student's own initial entry behaviours relating to prior knowledge, experience and qualifications, thereby allowing the student to consider and then identify any specific areas that require development or particular attention.

2 The establishment of targets against which future progress can be assessed. These targets will need to refer to curriculum requirements and/or professional or occupational standards, as appropriate to the programme of study being followed.

3 The assessment of needs independently of the student's teacher or trainer.

Invariably, this process is captured in writing, generally on paper, although web-based e-portfolios are becoming more widespread. Such documentation can take varying forms, and can range from a substantial document such as an Individual Learning Plan (ILP) which would be updated by the student throughout their programme of study and which may as a whole form an assessment object in itself, to a smaller document such as a tutorial record. In this sense, ipsative assessment takes on a formative function (this is discussed below) because the process is intended as an activity that can encourage learning. However, it is the central role of the student in directing the process gives such assessment activities their ipsative character. A tutorial process that was tutor-led, as opposed to student-led, would not be an ipsative one.

Ipsative assessment can also have a diagnostic aspect (as discussed above), for example in the assessment of specific aptitudes such as basic or key skills, or specific learning difficulties or disabilities. In such contexts the assessment method in question is not led by the student, but the student may have an active role in the interpretation of the assessment results and in any subsequent action.

For the process to be a meaningful one for the student, however, she or he will need a very clear understanding of the direction or purpose of the learning programme that is being undertaken. This is in fact a far from straightforward process, as curriculum documents, ILPs and the like can be bulky or awkward documents that demand much of the student. To put it another way, the use of ILPs can often seem to be a barrier to learning and participation because of the complexity of their construction. At another level, ILPs can be responded to in an instrumental manner, as an exercise in form filling and nothing more. Assumptions relating to the encouragement of autonomous learning are similarly problematic. ILPs allow students to think about how they might arrive at particular outcomes, but the desirability or utility of those outcomes is never questioned. At the same time, the very notion of an 'individual' learning plan might be seen to be at odds with a paper-based or screen-based exercise that requires all the students on the programme to go through the same process, filling in the same boxes and reflecting on their learning using the same written prompts or questions.

Ipsative assessment, therefore, is a form of assessment practice that can be characterized as being fraught with difficulty. But the goal is a laudable one, and if it is done well, ipsative assessment strategies can allow students an immediate and relevant engagement with their learning, thereby encouraging motivation.

Formative assessment

Formative assessment, or assessment for learning (AfL), is invariably discussed in terms of the influential research of Paul Black (emeritus professor of Science Education at King's College, London) and Dylan Wiliam (professor of Educational Assessment at the Institute of Education, University of London). Their work, although not focused on the FE sector, has been widely used across educational contexts and can be seen as contributing to a theory of assessment practice (1998; 2009).

Formative assessment has been defined in various ways by different authors and there is, arguably, no single uncontested definition (Ecclestone et al., 2010). Perhaps one of the most comprehensive definitions – and which, it is argued in this text, constitutes a workable starting point for teachers and trainers – was published by the Assessment Reform Group at the University of Cambridge. This group argued that there are ten aspects to formative assessment or assessment for learning (2002):

Ten aspects to formative assessment

1 AfL should be part of the planning process, including feedback, with a focus on the progress being made towards the goals set by the course or programme of study
2 AfL should focus on how students learn as well as what they learn
3 AfL should be seen as central to all pedagogic practice, such as demonstrations, question-and-answer sessions, observing learners and so on
4 AfL should be seen as a professional skill, requiring training
5 AfL should encourage motivation through positive reinforcement (for example, emphasizing achievements) rather than negative reinforcement (for example, emphasizing failure)
6 Students should be encouraged to work with assessment criteria ad part of AfL in order to plan their own learning
7 Constructive feedback that focuses on how students can improve should always be part of AfL
8 AfL should encourage students to reflect on their own learning
9 AfL should recognize that learners will achieve a differential levels
10 AfL should embody an ethic of care to the student as a whole person and not simply focus on results.

Formative assessment, therefore, is the assessment that takes place during a course or programme of study, as an integral part of the learning process, and as such it is down to the teacher or trainer to Implement and perhaps design it. The fundamental aspect of formative assessment is that it is a kind of assessment practice that is part of the learning process. It is a practice that seeks to encourage and facilitate learning, as well as acting as an assessment tool for the tutor, who can thereby gauge how much learning has already taken place. As such, it can be a vehicle for formative feedback (discussed more fully in the following chapter), which in turn contributes to the learning process.

Formative assessment is invariably based within a teaching session, in the widest meaning of the term. That is to say, any activities in one-to-one or whole group sessions, in a workshop or a classroom or over the internet, have the potential to be formative. And the kinds of activities that might be employed are similarly varied: case studies; quizzes; presentations; short-answer tests; multiple choice tests; practical tasks; simulations. These may be designed solely by the tutor, or adapted from resources supplied by a colleague, or other open sources. Viewed from this perspective, it is clear that many if not all of the learning and teaching strategies employed by teachers and trainers within an FE setting have a formative assessment aspect to them. It is in the methodical manner of their employment within a classroom or workshop that the key characteristics of formative assessment are found (Tummons, 2011a):

1 to facilitate learning

2 to see whether learning has taken place

3 to provide feedback to teachers and trainers on how students are progressing

4 to provide feedback to students concerning their own progress

5 to diagnose students' needs or barriers to learning.

Formative assessment is sometimes confused with continuous assessment. These terms in fact need to be carefully distinguished. Formative assessment refers to assessment for learning. It may be a process that is continuous throughout a programme of study, but it is not continuous assessment. In it's correct sense, continuous assessment is a form of summative assessment (see below) that is conducted in instalments over a predetermined period of time.

Summative assessment

Summative assessment is the term used to describe those modes of assessment that seek to establish and then record what has been learned during a course or programme of study. It is always a formal process, and it is used to see if students have acquired the skills, knowledge, aptitude, behaviour or understanding that the curriculum that they have been following set out to provide them with. Historically, the majority of summative assessments were performed at the end of a programme of study, but over time patterns of curriculum delivery have changed and summative elements can be positioned during a programme of study. Some programmes of study require students to submit small elements of summative work on an ongoing basis; this is referred to as continuous assessment. The completion of an assessment portfolio (which might contain written work, photographs, testimonies, evidence of work-based learning or engagement and so forth) provides a common example of continuous assessment.

Sometimes teachers design and mark the summative assessment tasks, with responsibility both for making sure that the assessment activities that they design are compatible with the curriculum documents received from the awarding body, and for making sure that work is marked according to the criteria that the awarding body provides. It is common practice in these circumstances for an internal verifier, who will have to have received specialized training for the role, to evaluate both the assessment tasks that have been written, and the marking process. On other occasions, the awarding body provides very specific guidance as to how the summative assessment is to be carried out. On these occasions, the responsibility of the tutor is to implement these assessments correctly, in accordance with the established procedure.

The current (2012) specifications for the BTEC First Certificate in Health and Social Care provide examples of assessment practices that require teachers to design and implement assessments on an internal (that is, college) basis, whilst also implementing other assessments that are set and marked externally (that is, by Edexcel, the awarding body). For internal assessments, guidance is provided within the curriculum documentation regarding a range of issues, including:

- establishing the validity and sufficiency of the assessment task (discussed below)
- ensuring that instructions, resources, timings and so forth are clearly set out
- ensuring that the content of the tasks is current, local (that is, representing local employment contexts) and consistent with national standards.

The BTEC curriculum also specifies a small number of external assessments. For two of the modules within the curriculum, a one-hour, paper-based examination is specified. When managing these examinations, the responsibilities of the college, and by extension the teacher, include:

- preparing a suitable location for the assessment that meets required examination conditions (for example, ensuring a quiet location, arranging furniture appropriately and so forth)

- ensuring that the students are fully prepared to sit the external examination (that is, that the syllabus has been delivered to the appropriate standard;
- ensuring that students are entered for assessment at the correct time
- informing students of opportunities for resitting an examination if necessary.

Summative assessment invariably leads to the award of qualifications: grades, diplomas and certificates. For some students, a qualification will lead to new employment or changes to existing employment. For others, a qualification may be needed in order to progress to a higher level of educational provision. Other stakeholders have an interest in summative assessment as well. Employers rely on qualifications and records of achievement to ascertain the skills and abilities of their new employees. Award bodies need to make sure that their qualifications and assessments are being uniformly carried out across the country. Funding agencies want to know that they are receiving value for money. As such, summative assessment can be described as high stakes assessment, with several stake-holders relying on the reliability and validity of the results that are produced (Knight and Yorke, 2003). Summative assessment, therefore, has four key characteristics (Tummons, 2011a):

1 to record achievement, through the award of certificates and diplomas
2 to anticipate future achievement
3 to allow students to progress to higher level study
4 to allow students to enter or progress within the workplace.

Self-assessment and peer assessment

It is becoming increasingly common for teachers to involve students in the assessment process. Students are encouraged to think about the tasks that then are completing and the criteria that they are working towards, or the ways in which their work can improve and go from being a 'pass' to a 'merit', or from a 'merit' to a 'distinction'. In tutorials and in whole group sessions, the merits of involving students in their own assessment – that is to say, engaging students in *self-assessment* – can be summarized as follows:

Self-assessment

1 Ownership of the assessment process. Through involving students as active participants in, as opposed to passive recipients of, the assessment process, teachers can encourage a higher level of both intrinsic and achievement motivation (as

discussed in Chapter 20). Self-assessment strategies allow the wider assessment process to be explored and understood as being as relevant and meaningful to the students, as is the curriculum as a whole.

2   Autonomy of learning. If it is accepted that self-assessment can stimulate higher levels of motivation and engagement amongst students, it follows that a deep as opposed to surface approach to learning will be encouraged, with consequent benefits for the learner (and, by extension, the teacher). For those teachers who subscribe to cognitivist, constructivist or social practice theories of learning, such a deep approach will be understood as being a necessary requisite of meaningful learning.

Self-assessment – literally, encouraging or requiring students to assess their own learning and progress against the criteria or outcomes established by the programme of study being followed – can therefore be a powerful tool but is, arguably, best suited to one-to-one work or private study. In order to generate a similarly student-centred approach to assessment in whole group situations, *peer assessment* can be used. Typical examples of peer assessment activities include:

Peer-assessment

1   small group presentations that receive feedback (following already agreed criteria) from one or two other members of the class
2   peer-led demonstrations of practical or technical operations
3   reading and assessing peers' assignments, in reference to relevant course criteria.

When running peer assessment activities, teachers may be concerned that the feedback that will be given is at risk of being biased or otherwise partial, perhaps as a consequence of group dynamics, friendship groups, or a broader lack of understanding of the assessment process. In fact, current and recent research indicates that if properly planned and managed, peer assessment and feedback is on the whole both valid and reliable (Falchikov, 2005; Jessen and Elander, 2009).

Blurring the boundaries between assessment modes

It is important to remember that the different functions or modes of assessment that have been explored here (diagnostic, ipsative, formative, summative) are not mutually exclusive. That is to say, depending on the ways in which the curriculum being studied has been structured, summative assessment tasks can have a formative function, and formative tasks can be diagnostic. In these matters, the role of *feedback* (discussed more fully in the following chapter) is crucial.

For example, when studying the BTEC First Certificate in Health and Social Care, students take four compulsory units (two of which are externally assessed, and two of which are internally assessed, as described above) and four optional units (all of which are internally assessed). Upon completion of the *Social Influences on Health and Wellbeing* option module, students may then move on to the *Impact of Nutrition on Health and wellbeing* module. The feedback that the student might receive relating to the first of these modules will not only relate to how well she or he has performed in relation to the assessment task, but will also offer more general advice regarding assesses work, the presentation of written work, study skills and so forth. In this way, the feedback – which can be understood more correctly as *feedforward* – can have a formative function, by providing the student with advice and guidance that can contribute to her or his learning and progress more generally, in line with the definition of AfL that has already been discussed (see above). In just the same way that a single piece of evidence in a portfolio can be mapped against more than one assessment criterion, so an assessment task can have more than one function.

Formal and informal assessment

There is one final aspect to assessment sequencing to be considered: the extent to which it is a formal or informal process. *Formal formative assessment* is the term used here to refer to those assessment strategies that have been designed and delivered as a carefully considered and delivered aspect of classroom or workshop practice: for example, a short answer written test followed by peer marking and feedback. Formal formative assessments such as these will be a conspicuous element of the planning process and need to be identified in schemes of work and lesson plans. *Informal formative assessment* is the term used here to describe those aspects of teaching practice that may be a more spontaneous, small-scale or even unconscious part of the teacher or trainer's repertoire, that can nonetheless have a formative aspect to them: for example, asking questions, listening to answers to assess student understanding, and looking at student posture and body language to ascertain understanding or even motivation.

Validity and reliability

Having established the modes by which assessment is commonly practiced, attention can now be drawn to two key concepts that inform all forms of assessment. Whether ipsative, diagnostic, formative, or summative, all assessment practices need to be trustworthy and rigorous. Everyone involved in the process – students, teachers, employers, funding agencies and government departments – need to know that the certificates and credentials that are increasingly necessary for work and for further study, are worthwhile. That is to say, these stakeholders need to know that assessment is valid and reliable.

A *valid* assessment is an assessment that covers the course as a whole, uses appropriate real-life methods, is most suitable to the subject or vocational area and helps predict how the student will perform in the future. A summative assessment that relies on content or understanding or other performance that the course or programme of study did not cover would lack validity. Similarly, a formative assessment relying on content that had not yet been covered in a class or workshop-based session, would lack validity. Validity can be seen as constituting a number of different aspects. First, the assessment must assess the actual body of knowledge of skill that the course or programme of study set out to deliver and assess in the first place; secondly, there must be adequate coverage of the content of the course; thirdly, the assessment methods should be appropriate to the subjects being studied and assessed; fourthly, the assessment needs to be able to predict the future performance of the student.

For teachers working within assessment structures that are tightly defined and controlled by an awarding body, responsibility for the validity of summative assessment is to some extent lessened. That said, it is worth noting that awarding bodies are not perfect, and errors can creep in that vigilant tutors will pick up on and report back to an external verifies or examiner. For those teachers who design their own summative assessments, and for tutors who design their own formative assessments, validity can be encouraged through a number of strategies (Tummons, 2011a):

1 wording the question, explaining the task or defining the activity correctly, to prevent students performing activities that do not correctly match up to the course outcomes
2 setting assessments that do not miss out one or more of the outcomes or content areas of the course
3 taking care not to unintentionally includes something that was not part of the course content
4 ensuring sufficient resources to allow for authentic assessment.

Reliability of assessment is all about consistency, about ensuring that personal or environmental factors do not affect the assessment process. In an educational environment where assessment systems are imposed on a national basis across many hundreds of sites, which employ many thousands of teachers and trainers, the need to prevent local or personal factors from affecting assessment practice is self-evident. In the context of summative assessment, therefore reliability relates to consistency in a number of ways (Tummons, 2011a):

1 assessors or examiners will agree on the mark or grade to be awarded to a given piece of work
2 there will be consistency between the students' work and the markers' or examiners' grades
3 there will be consistency between students' grades or marks irrespective of where or when they completed the examination or test
4 the language used during the assessment process is clear, unambiguous and inclusive
5 the environment in which the assessment will be carried out will not affect the process
6 students or candidates will not have been coached.

Formative assessment draws on the concept of reliability in a rather different fashion, however. It goes without saying that teachers always have to ensure fairness and consistency in the assessment decisions that they make. Even an informal formative assessment such as a quiz needs to be worded and structured in such a way that it can provide reliable results. However, the potential for formative assessment to be used to encourage as well as measure learning means that in order to account for the differing levels of ability or progression or understanding that may be exhibited by a group of students, a teacher may quite legitimately decide to concentrate more attention on one student or group of students rather than another. This is a form of bias, admittedly, but it is an entirely well intentioned and correct approach. If formative assessment is assessment for learning, then it follows that some students may find themselves under closer scrutiny, or spending more time with their teacher discussing the outcomes of the assessment, compared to others.

Validity and reliability: Critical perspectives

Both validity and reliability can be seen to be key concepts when contemplating the objectivity of any assessment process. To some extent they intertwine with each other and also with ipsative assessment. The quality assurance procedures that surround assessment are considerable, and the maintenance of validity and reliability can be seen as being the responsibility of external verifiers and examiners, and awarding bodies, as well as a responsibility of those tutors who design and administer summative assessment. A variety of procedures and tools are used to maintain validity and reliability, therefore, including:

1 the creation of detailed written criteria for assessment activities

2 the use of marking and/or feedback proforma

3 the establishment of internal verification, second marking, and external verification and examination procedures

4 the positioning of assessment as a focus for quality assurance and inspection, most conspicuously by Ofsted.

And yet despite the proliferation of systems and procedures to regulate and order assessment, and to ensure that assessment decisions are always impartial and objective, the fact remains that subjectivity can and does find its way into the process. This might be at the level of individual or idiosyncratic interpretation of assessment criteria, or of differences of opinion relating to the extent to which students may or may not have met the learning outcomes of a particular course or programme of study. Another factor that has to be considered is the extent to which an assessor might take a holistic view of the progress made by a student that might lead to an assessment decision based on a conflation of criteria rather than based on scrupulous examination of each criterion in turn (Colley and Jarvis, 2007). This is not to say that such subjectivities are to be ignored; rather, they should be discussed in an open and frank manner, at standardization events and moderation meetings, so that a shared understanding between teachers and trainers can be established.

Summary

Within the contemporary culture of FE that focuses on performance and achievement statistics, it is all too easy to reduce assessment to a benchmark, to distort broader learning and teaching processes so that a focus on assessment takes centre stage – a process referred to as *curriculum creep*. However, it is important to remember that assessment is just one integral element of the learning and teaching culture of FE, a means to an end and not an end in itself. It is undeniably important, not least as upon leaving FE the opportunities and life chances that open up to students depend to a significant degree on the certificates and transcripts that the assessment process awards them. But it should not be allowed to distort the wider learning cultures that the teacher seeks to establish in her or his workshop or classroom, which should be based upon affording all students opportunities to engage, learn and grow.

Further reading

Theories of assessment are covered in most of the generic textbooks that have already been listed in these suggestions for further reading. For a more critical analysis, the following are recommended:

Ecclestone, K. (2010), *Transforming formative assessment in lifelong learning*. Maidenhead: McGraw Hill.

Isaacs, T., Zara, C., Herbert, G., Coombs, S. and Smith, C. (2012), *Key concepts in educational assessment*. London: Sage.

31 Designing, Administering and Evaluating Assessment Tasks

The valid and reliable summative assessment of students' learning (as discussed in the preceding chapter) represents the *sine qua non* of teaching and learning practice in FE (indeed, in formal education provision across all sectors). For students, the certificates that they receive provide passports for employment or higher education. For government departments, the achievement of students in FE colleges represents a validation of policy as well as value for money. For college managers and principals, good achievement rates represent financial security as well as curricular achievement. And for teachers, the assessment process represents a form of professional validation: the summing up of all of the work that they have been doing with and for their students during the academic year or programme of study.

Assessment is, in many ways, a high stakes process. Consequently, it falls on all of those professionals who are involved to ensure the quality of all stages of the process, from the moment when a summative assessment is designed and/or implemented (the extent to which a teacher will design a summative assessment task will depend on the curriculum specifications being followed), to the moment when the student received their final feedback and/or grade.

In this chapter, common methods of summatively assessing students in FE are described and evaluated, and an outline of the principles and practice of feedback is also provided. Key themes relating to the quality assurance of assessment in FE are also discussed. The applicability of these themes to formative assessment practice is also discussed as appropriate.

Assessment in further education: Themes, methods, advantages and disadvantages

Assessment practice in the FE sector can be characterized as consisting of a fairly small repertoire of practices or formats that can be seen across academic, professional, technical and vocational curricula. The most common are discussed below.

Portfolio-based assessment

A portfolio is, at its simplest, a collection of documents, materials or other work produced by an individual student during her/his time spent studying on any programme or course. For an art and design course, a portfolio might include technical drawings, sketches, notes made whilst researching particular artists or artistic techniques or photographs. For a brick-laying course, a portfolio would include all the evidence that the student has collected to demonstrate that the different competences outlined in the curriculum have been learned or acquired. Such evidence may include reports from workplace observations, notes from interviews, witness testimonies, short-answer written assignments (to demonstrate underpinning knowledge) or other artefacts generated in and/or for the workplace by the student (such as photographs of arches or fireplaces that the student has constructed). In general, therefore, a portfolio would consist of a variety of different types of evidence to demonstrate those areas of knowledge, skill and understanding that are relevant for the qualification in question.

The creation of a portfolio is positioned as being the responsibility of the student, and as such this method of assessment is seen as being valuable in encouraging interest, enthusiasm and ownership in the student, thereby encouraging self-assessment, reflection and autonomous approaches to learning. Through analysing and reviewing the material collected, the student can revisit their experiences. Portfolios can be valuable tools to encourage learning, therefore. And assuming that the different components of the portfolio are carefully linked to specific objectives or outcomes, assessment validity is high. For work-based or work-related qualifications, the generation of materials for the portfolio is very often drawn directly from, or modelled on, workplace practice, thereby ensuring authenticity (a key component of assessment validity).

Portfolio-based assessment is normally defined as continuous, summative assessment: continuous because they are collected over a period of time, summative because they assess learning on a programme or module against outcomes or criteria that lead to certification. However, portfolios can also have a formative function: as tasks are completed, feedback from the teacher (discussed more fully below) can be designed so as to not only report on the learning that the student has just completed and demonstrated, but also offer developmental, forward-looking comments designed to improve future performance.

Portfolio compilation and assessment can be time-consuming and bureaucratic, however. For some qualifications, the sheer volume of evidence required and the time taken to physically (or virtually, if using an e-portfolio) arrange it in a file can be off-putting. There is in addition a danger that the search for sufficient evidence can lead to a rather mechanistic approach to portfolio building where the physical collection of evidence takes precedence over learning and reflection on practice.

Simulations and other work-based or work-related tasks
Within programmes of study where the aims and outcomes are predominantly concerned with the practical application of skills, knowledge or understanding, then realistic, authentic practical tasks need to be arranged. A trainee plumber could complete a VLE-based multiple choice assessment in order to demonstrate underpinning knowledge, but would also need to be observed – more than once – carrying out practical tasks such as bending copper piping or installing a sink. A trainee childcare assistant could be assessed through an essay-based examination, but he or she would be better able to demonstrate her knowledge and practical ability whilst on placement in a workplace setting, where he or she could be observed. Many FE colleges provide real-world environments where students can learn and work: common examples include motor vehicle workshops, hair and beauty salons, stonemasonry yards, restaurants and travel agencies. The majority of these are open to the public and as such provide authentic work-based opportunities for learning. It might sometimes be necessary for students in a hairdressing salon – for example – to work on each other if there are no paying clients, but the fact remains that such environments are highly effective learning environments.

Working environments relating to other areas of the curriculum are not so straightfor-wardly recreated within the college environment, however. Students on counselling courses or hospitality, catering and tourism courses, for example, might not be able to access authentic working environments. In these cases, the teacher might choose to establish a simulation, normally based around a specified theme, in order to allow students to generate evidence for a portfolio. A typical example would be a role-play (for example, relating to managing customer complaints and expectations) that can be recorded and written up. For some programmes of study, however, simulation is not permitted and authentic working practices have to be assessed (curriculum documentation should therefore be checked carefully by the teacher), reflecting the distinction between work-based programmes (courses that require the student to be in employment) and work-related programmes (courses that do not require the student to be in employment). However, simulations can be awkward, even embarrassing, and should be negotiated carefully with the students in order to ensure a good level of engagement and motivation: a poorly prepared simulation, or one which encourages only reluctant or restricted participation, will lack assessment validity (Solomon, 2007).

Practical tasks and activities can find their way into many other subject areas: technical, art or craft-based programmes, and science and technology programmes are the more obvious candidates, but it is also worth remembering that practical tasks can be usefully employed within other curriculum areas as well. Activities such as putting together poster displays, creating business plans, designing websites, making films or podcasts, organizing participating in artistic ventures such as theatre performances all have the potential to be engaging, authentic (that is, aligned to the vocation or profession that the qualification covers) and relevant both to the curriculum and to the students.

Essays, short-answer tests and multiple-choice questionnaires

Essays are commonly found in academic courses (Psychology or History, for example), in some professional courses (such as childcare or nursing courses), and in access to higher education courses (essay-based assessment being a common feature of HE). Essays are often used in examination settings for summative assessment, as well as during a programme of study for both formative and summative assessment. Indeed, for those curricula that are summatively assessed through essays (whether completed in examination conditions or over a longer period of time as project work), the use of essays as formative assessment, set by the teacher, provides useful practice and developmental feedback prior to the final examination.

Having set an essay as a formative assessment, the teacher will also need to design a framework for how it is to be marked: guidelines from the awarding body in question should always be used on such occasions so that students are receiving formative grades and feedback that will be aligned to their final examinations.

Essays can be difficult for some people. Students who are nervous or lack self-esteem, who have left school with unpleasant memories of written assignments, or who are returning to formal education, can find the process of writing an essay (as distinct from the topic being covered) difficult, which may affect reliability. Essay practice during term-time can help alleviate such worries. For those students who do find essay writing difficult, mindful of the impact on assessment reliability, alternative forms of written assignment include short-answer tests and multiple-choice questionnaires.

Setting short-answer tests can solve some of the problems raised by essays. Rather than being faced by a single essay question, a series of short-answer questions provides a more structured framework for the student to follow. This can help build students' confidence in attempting written work and reduce the risk of misunderstanding the task, therefore increasing reliability. Marking is also more reliable. Shorter, specific questions can be marked with the aid of a model answer sheet, and marks can be awarded for each component. Careful choice of question can also be used to ensure wide coverage of the syllabus, which further enhances validity, in contrast to the narrower focus of the essay format. The drawback of short-answer exercises compared to an essay is in the level of analysis and detail: it is much easier to encourage detailed, critical work in a longer essay-style format rather than in a short-answer assessment.

A multiple-choice questionnaire allows the teacher to cover a large body of knowledge or understanding quickly and thoroughly, simply by setting at least one question for each topic covered in the curriculum. The questions can be structured in a number of ways (true or false, or giving four possible answers and asking the candidate to select the correct one).

It is easy to pitch questionnaires at different levels simply by making the questions more demanding. They are easy and quick to mark, irrespective of the difficulty of the questions. Multiple-choice questionnaires can be both valid and reliable, therefore.

The disadvantages of multiple-choice questionnaires are the time they take to prepare and that it is easy to produce a questionnaire that is trivial and lacks rigour. If done properly, constructing the test and checking all the answers is a lengthy process. The possibility of guessing answers reduces validity, and the lack of meaningful developmental feedback further limits their suitability, particularly for academic subjects.

Presentations

Asking students to prepare and deliver a short presentation can provide a valuable alternative to written work such as essays or short-answer tests. As well as assessing the knowledge and understanding of the topic being covered, presentations also afford teachers the opportunity to assess a variety of functional skills (ICT, literacy, communication). The mode of the presentation can vary, and be differentiated if required according to the needs of the students. Students might be asked to deliver a presentation accompanied by a PowerPoint or Prezi presentation, to create a poster or series of posters (which may be accompanied by a presentation or may form part of a more unstructured exhibition), or to create a resource such as a handout, which might accompany the presentation. The teacher should carefully consider the structure of the presentation. The time that will be available for the presentations should be carefully managed so that presentations do not overrun. Ten minutes to deliver a presentation is usually sufficient, if the time is properly managed: teachers need to be willing to cut short presentations if they are exceeding their time limit, not least as this impacts on other presenters who may feel rushed.

For some students who are reluctant writers or are nervous about their essay-writing skills, presentations offer a useful alternative format. A presentation will still require research, and will also require writing, but this will be in a different genre to the traditional essay, which for some students may be helpful. Other students may be nervous about any form of public speaking however, and this might impact on the reliability of the assessment. Other drawbacks to using presentations for assessment are the time involved (as well as the actual presentations, the amount of time needed for setting up slides and posters, for handing out supporting materials, for giving feedback and even for agreeing who will do their presentation first) can be considerable. The potential for repetition is a more significant drawback: the prospect of sitting and listening to several presentations on the same subject matter can be daunting to the highly motivated teacher. Students may not discern any benefit to having to sit through several iterations of the same content (in fact, it is doubtful if sitting through such series of presentations would have any benefit). To reduce the risk of boredom and repletion, therefore, presentations should be planned so that they cover a variety of relevant topics.

Self-, peer and group assessment

It has become quite commonplace over recent years actively to involve students in their own assessment processes. In part, this is a reflection of conversations about teaching and learning moving from being focussed on teacher-led approaches to student-centred approaches. And in part this is a reflection of associated theories of deep learning and student motivation and engagement: if students are seen as active participants in assessment – as opposed merely to having assessment imposed on them – they will be more willing to engage. Self, peer and group assessment is also understood to contribute to the development of generic study skills, helping students to learn how to learn (Scales, 2013).

Activities such as presentations and poster displays lend themselves to group assessment – whether formative or summative – for a number of pedagogical reasons. The essentially collaborative nature of group assessment provides opportunities for students to learn from each other, to manage their own learning and to develop independent study skills, all student-centred teaching and learning activities that are characteristic of constructivist and social practice theories of learning that support high levels of motivation and engagement and, therefore, deep approaches to learning.

However, there is a danger that if the teacher is entirely absent from the process, the students will question the validity of what they are being asked to do: there is always a danger that student-led activities will be perceived as an 'easy option' for the teacher. In order to ensure that peer or group assessment activities such as these are valid and reliable, and are seen as such by the students, it is important that the teacher maintains an active management role throughout, observing and using question-and-answer to check ongoing progress, making sure that all of the groups are regularly checked and actively managing the final display or presentation. If students are going to formatively assess or provide feedback on the work done by their peers, clear feedback criteria will need to be agreed by the group in advance. This process will need to be facilitated by the teacher, who will also need to ensure that the feedback given is constructive and relevant. It may also be helpful for the students if the teacher devotes some time to a thorough explanation of the assessment criteria that are used on the programme of study in question. This can help ensure the validity and reliability of the peer and group feedback process (by ensuring that all of the students work to the course criteria). It can also help students develop skills of self-assessment: by explaining how they will be assessed on their programme, students can begin to apply the relevant criteria to their own, individual assignments. For students who are completing individual learning plans as part of a portfolio, an understanding of the course assessment criteria will be particularly important.

Observation

The simple act of watching a student or group of students at work is, arguably, one of the most effective forms of assessment in FE. Observations in workplaces (when students are on placement, for example), in seminar rooms (whilst students are preparing responses to a case study) or workshop (whilst students are rehearsing a series of procedures that have just been demonstrated to them).are commonly found across a number of different curriculum areas. If the observation is part of a summative assessment, the use of an observation pro-forma where specific criteria or competences are listed can ensure validity. However, in order to ensure reliability, it is vital that the observer is properly qualified in the subject matter that is being assessed through observation: that is to say, the teacher (the assessor) and the student (the assessee) have to both be part of the same subject specialism (this is referred to as assessor–assessee intersubjectivity).

In informal, formative assessment contexts, observations can still be useful. Careful attention to students' tone of voice, posture, body language or action can be as fruitful a form of informal formative assessment as an impromptu question-and-answer session.

Interviews and oral assessments

Talking with students, in more or less formally structured contexts, is used in a number of different curriculum areas within the FE sector. Obvious examples include the use of oral examinations in language classes, but interviews can also be used to summatively assess underpinning knowledge in work-based and work-related programmes. Informal, formative assessment can also be based on talking with and listening to students: teachers and trainers can often assess knowledge and understanding in this way. Examples include: dialogue during a classroom based session, or a question-and-answer session during a practical activity (in order to assess the underpinning knowledge that accompanies a practical task). The use of a standard list of questions or pro-forma can ensure consistency between oral assessments and ensure broad curriculum coverage, and the recording of an oral assessment (on audiotape or videotape) can allow for second marking and moderation (discussed below).

Interviews can also be effective as a form of initial or diagnostic assessment. Prior to the commencement of a programme of study, interviews can be used to ensure that students possess relevant entry qualifications and have met any other course requirements (such as access to a work placement). In addition, teachers can use interviews to follow up any questions regarding specific learning difficulties or disabilities and begin to coordinate responses from relevant departments in the college.

General rules for designing assessment tasks

When specifying an assignment, the teacher requires a thorough grasp of the subject, clarity in envisaging and defining desired learning outcomes, an understanding of the students to be tested, an element of creativity, and skill in the application of the relevant writing rules. Several of these rules are present in the literature on assessment, and these are briefly summarized here:

Feedback in further education: Principles and methods

Feedback can be understood as a dialogue between two people: the teacher or trainer, and the student. During this dialogue, the teacher has several questions that she or he will wish to have answered: how much has the student has actually learned? What new skills have been acquired? What new knowledge has been understood? The feedback dialogue has two main features, therefore: first, to tell the student that they have mastered a new skill to the required standard, or demonstrated knowledge and understanding to the required level; secondly, to provide advice and support for those students who have not yet reached the required level of competence or who have not yet understood fully the body of knowledge being studied (Armitage and Renwick, 2008; Ecclestone, 2010; Tummons, 2011a). There are, it is suggested, six key features of good feedback, described as follows:

1 Feedback should be clear and unambiguous.
      The language that is used when giving feedback should be clear, concise and easy to follow, straightforward and written in everyday language. If more specialized language is needed then it is important for the teacher to ensure firstly that the student understands what the words used actually mean. Finally, it is important

that the student understands what actions are needed to develop or improve their performance both in relation to future assignments and also (if required) if the current assignment has not been passed.

2 Feedback should be specific.
Offering specific comments allows the teacher or trainer a good way to open the feedback dialogue. Specific comments relating exactly to the task that the student has completed or accomplished are effective in reinforcing existing good progress and encouraging further achievement. Similarly, corrective feedback needs to be unambiguous. The student needs to know exactly in what way the task that they have completed is inadequate or incorrect. Here, reference to learning outcomes/objectives can be helpful (normally relating to summative assessment) in maintaining the specificity of the feedback. Good feedback should therefore refer explicitly to the criteria or learning outcomes that are at hand.

3 Feedback should be supportive, formative and developmental.
Good feedback should allow the student to build on her/his past successes and at the same time move away from errors in understanding or mistakes in technical execution. Feedback should always include an element of feedforward and highlight where appropriate aspects of the completed task that relate to future assessment tasks within the programme of study.

4 Feedback should be timely.
The exact timing of feedback will depend on several factors: the time it takes for the tutor to mark written work or organize practical demonstrations; the availability of tutor and student to meet; whether or not an assessment needs to graded internally or externally; and the nature of the assessment itself (informal formative assessment of a class-based activity can be instantaneous). Allowing for differences as a consequence of the exact type of assessment in question, feedback that is as immediate as practicable will be the most useful to the student. It is worth noting that colleges and awarding bodies set guidelines as to the time by which students can expect to receive feedback for summative assessments.

5 Feedback should be understood.
Having read or listened to feedback, the student should be able to understand how they have performed in reference to the objectives/outcomes and/or criteria for the assessment and the course; he or she should be able to describe and then perform those steps necessary for further development either for the current assessment (if competence has yet to be achieved) or for the next assessment or course; and above all, the student should be able to make sense of the assessment, and the feedback from it, as a learning episode within the course or programme of study. Teachers should use open-ended question-and-answer techniques if there is any doubt as to the student's understanding of any feedback that has been given.

6 Feedback should be delivered in an appropriate environment.

In some assessment contexts, particular consideration should be given to the environment in which the feedback is given, allowing for the nature of the curriculum and the needs of the student. Giving marked work back to a group of students is of course appropriate, but if one of the students either needs or asks for more detailed support, a follow-up meeting on a one-to-one basis may be necessary. If one-to-one feedback is not achievable (for example, when giving feedback relating to a practical task whilst in the workshop), the teacher should be sensitive to volume and tone of voice and should if required find a quiet corner or space in the workshop away from the main business of the session.

In brief, if feedback is clear, specific, supportive, timely, understood and appropriate, then it should encourage learning, help students make sense of what they need to do next and motivate students to further engage with their programme of studies.

Assessment and feedback in further education: Evaluation and quality assurance

Summative assessment within FE colleges is subject to a rigorous system of checks designed to assure the quality of the process. For all of the stakeholders involved (students, employers, funding agencies, professional bodies and awarding bodies) to have confidence in assessment, a number of processes have over time been established, which are of immediate relevance and importance to both the newly appointed teacher as well as the more experienced teacher (however, it is unlikely that a trainee teacher on placement would be asked to be involved in these processes). There are four main processes by which summative assessment is quality assured, and these are described below. It is important to note that the ways in which these quality assurance procedures are used varies according to the specifications of the awarding body in question:

1 Second marking

The simplest process by which the reliability of an assessment decision can be assured is through second marking. This can be done either 'sighted' (when the second marker sees the comments, feedback and grade – as appropriate – of the first marker) or 'blind' (when the second marker does not see any of the comments of the first marker). If a dispute arises between a first and second marker (for example, if one argues that the student has met the required competence but the other agues that she or he has not), then a third marker will be asked to assess the work involved. If two of the three markers agree, this will be recorded as the final assessment decision.

2 Internal moderation

Internal moderation is a process by which assessment decisions made within the college are scrutinized by another member of staff (who may need to hold specialist qualifications if assessing NVQs). The purpose of internal moderation is not to mark work again but to examine the process by which the work has already been marked. For example, after a set of assignments has been first and second marked, the entire set would then go forward for internal moderation. The role of the internal moderator would be to ensure that the first and the second marker have both followed the correct assessment procedures that have specified by the awarding body involved.

3 External examination or validation

As well as ensuring the quality of assessment decisions within teaching teams in colleges, awarding bodies and funding agencies also need to be confident that assessment decisions are reliable and valid across the sector as a whole. The function of external examination or validation (different awarding bodies tend to use different terms, but the function is the same) is to scrutinize assessment practices across a number of different colleges. This is commonly performed on a regional basis. The role of the external examiner/validator varies somewhat according to the specifications of the awarding body in question. Some externals monitor assessment processes and then provide feedback as to their efficacy. Other externals may have the authority to overturn assessment decisions that have been made at one of the colleges under their purview (although this is a rare occurrence).

4 Inspection

Coverage of the ways in which Ofsted inspects FE colleges falls outside the remit of this text. However it is worth mentioning that assessment constitutes a significant aspect of learning and teaching activity and as such comes under the purview of Ofsted inspectors.

Evaluating formative assessment and feedback processes

The formative assessment tasks that teachers design, as part of their lesson planning, should also be evaluated. A more general discussion of the ways in which teachers might reflect on and evaluate their teaching can be found in the following chapter. Here, the focus is specifically on the ways in which the teacher can establish the extent to which formative assessment and feedback practice is contributing to student learning. Thee are two elements to this evaluation process. First, the teacher should evaluate the assessment tasks that she or he has designed. Secondly, the teacher should evaluate the work that the students have completed when engaging in these tasks.

When evaluating formative assessment tasks, the teacher should consider the following:

1 Was the assessment valid and reliable? Has the assessment covered the range of competences or topics planned for, and have all of the students been able to participate equally?

2 Was the assessment authentic and sufficient? Was the assessment properly rooted in the curriculum subject area and were the planned tasks sufficient in depth and scope?

3 Was the assessment marked or graded fairly (if applicable)? If grades were used, was the marking scheme correctly aligned to the marking scheme used within the unit or programme of study as a whole?

4 Was the assessment understood correctly by the students? Did the students understand what they were asked to do and respond accordingly?

5 Were the results of the assessment recorded appropriately? Have any relevant notes or details about the students' progress been noted down in a course file or in an individual learning plan (as appropriate)?

6 Were appropriate opportunities for feedback included in the assessment? Has the teacher planned opportunities for two-way dialogue during and after the assessment task?

And when evaluating the work that students have completed, the teacher should consider the following:

1 What does the work done tell the teacher about what has been learned and what has not been learned? Have some topics been covered thoroughly but others omitted? Have a number of the students all made the same mistake?

2 What does the work done tell the teacher about how they have been taught? Have subjects that were covered in student-led sessions been learned as thoroughly as those that were covered in tutor-led sessions?

3 To what extent does the work provide feedback regarding the student's predicted progress in relation to the summative assessment of the module or programme being followed? Has the formative assessment provided meaningful opportunities for the student to practice or rehearse key topics or procedures?

Summary: Assessment practice in further education

The assessment roles occupied by teachers and trainers in FE can vary quite considerably. Whilst some curricula require teachers to design, implement and grade formative and summative assignments, others provide very tightly specified assignment tasks that will be marked externally. Teachers in FE often teach on more than one course at once, and as such can expect to encounter a variety of assessment processes, irrespective of the length of time that they have been teaching: it is not uncommon for a new teacher to have to acquaint her or himself with several different assessment models at the start of the academic year. Whatever the requirements of the curriculum, however, it is important for all teachers in the sector to be aware of the principles underpinning assessment practice – arguably the single aspect of the teacher's role that has the most direct impact on the future lives and careers of students.

Further reading

More extensive discussions of assessment that focus on the practitioner, and that offer a range of examples, case studies and suggestions for practice, can be found in:

Armitage, A. and Renwick, M. (2008), *Assessment in FE: a practical guide for lecturers*. London: Continuum.

Ollin, R. and Tucker, J. (2012), *The vocational assessor handbook*. 5th edition. London: Kogan Page.

Tummons, J. (2011), *Assessing learning in the lifelong learning sector*. 3rd edition. Exeter: Learning Matters.

32 Reflective Practice and the Evaluation of Teaching

To evaluate something means to measure its worth or quality. In the FE sector, evaluation is a term that encompasses the different processes used to monitor and guarantee the quality of all of the different aspects of teaching and learning provision within a college. This might include resources, accommodation or even catering facilities, as well as the practice of the teachers and trainers. The quality of the teaching-learning process is all-important. It rarely emerges accidentally. Rather, it is a direct product of an effective teaching–learning partnership. That quality may vary from one period to another, and it is in the very nature of staff evaluation that problems, and their solutions, should be discovered. Evaluation of staff can help to maintain professional and college standards. College directors and staff bodies are aware of the significance of these standards and the importance of their being upheld. Students have an interest, too, in knowing that those who teach them are monitored regularly and effectively so that problems and difficulties arising in the classroom are not covered up and ignored.

Teaching staff understand the necessity of regularly updating their subject specialist knowledge, honing their skills and keeping abreast of a rapidly changing educational environment. This requires feedback, which will enable them to understand their successes and failures and to take steps to remedy any obvious shortcomings. New staff, in particular, will want to know to what extent they fit in with college requirements, and whether or not they are satisfying student expectations in relation to teaching and learning. College staff development programmes will require an element of feedback on performance targets and attainment, derived from formal and informal evaluation processes.

The three most common methods of evaluating staff performance in colleges are:

1 Self-evaluation.
   Self-evaluation is characterized by a process of self-generated feedback, developed from methodical self-scrutiny, analysis and criticism. It should be noted that this is not to be confused with reflective practice. Reflective practice constitutes a broader approach to professional learning that includes self-evaluation as just one component of a larger intellectual process, and is discussed in more detail below.

2 Professional peer evaluation.

Professional peer evaluation involves the attendance by colleagues of one or more classes delivered by the teacher so as to observe, criticize and evaluate her or his performance.

3 Student evaluation.

Student evaluation positions the student as a consumer, encouraged to give her or his opinions, in a structured manner, on a number of aspects of college provision.

These modes of evaluation can be used in conjunction with one another as part of an overall process of obtaining feedback and creating a basis for the examination of teaching standards.

Self-evaluation

This process is essentially an exercise in self-criticism, which is rarely an easy task. A list of questions should be drawn up prior to delivery of the lesson or lecture and should be answered as soon as possible after the end of the instructional event, and following a short period of reflection. The object of this exercise is the questioning of the effectiveness of instruction in relation to the desired learning outcome (Brown and Race, 1994). Self-questioning should take into account the following matters:

Self-evaluation questions

1 were my scheme of work and lesson plan adequate and well constructed, and did I adhere to the general direction laid out in these documents?

2 was my introduction effective in motivating and arousing interest? Did the students settle down swiftly?

3 did I make the key points with sufficient emphasis and was there any indication of student comprehension of these points?

4 given the amount of time available, was lesson content adequate? Did I divide the available time adequately and appropriately among the various outcomes/objectives?

5 was interest maintained throughout the session?

6 was my questioning appropriately placed within the overall plan and did the answers elicited assist in progress towards the instructional objectives?

7 did my summaries and recapitulations appear to be adequate?

8 were my teaching aids effective in assisting learning?

9 were class discipline and control adequate?

10 did any particular strengths or weaknesses appear in my presentation?

11 how should I deal with any perceived deficiencies?

This process of evaluation is not without its difficulties – self-diagnosis invariably involves problems associated with subjectivity and the unconscious repression of problems, with the ability to separate cause and effect, and with the capacity to note the intrusion into the instructional period of events totally outside one's control. Records of a self-evaluation should be kept and, where this is felt appropriate, should constitute the basis of a discussion with one's colleagues and section head. A self-evaluation should not be treated as a one-off event, but should be repeated at planned intervals so that progress can be noted.

Professional peer evaluation

Reputedly the most widely-used and productive type of staff evaluation, this process involves inviting one or two staff colleagues to observe a well-spaced series of lectures or lessons so as to offer constructive criticism and an overall survey of teaching strengths and weaknesses (Cohen and McKeachie, 1980; Shortland, 2004). Occasionally the instruction period is recorded on video with the assistance of the college staff development unit (or equivalent). The purpose of the procedure ought to be explained to the class; according to report, students accept it as an aid to the teaching-learning process.

The observers are given a lesson plan and a scheme of work in advance of the session, and are asked specifically to make a report based on their perceptions of the quality of instruction. The kinds of points upon which the observers would be expected to report include:

Peer-evaluation questions

1. In relation to the planning of the lesson:
    a. was it realistic in terms of objectives and desired learning outcomes?
    b. was it constructed on the basis of students' prior knowledge levels?
    c. was it based upon an appropriate awareness of time restraints?
2. In relation to the presentation of the instruction:
    a. did it show evidence of a clear structure?
    b. did it emphasize key points?
    c. did it utilize appropriate reinforcement techniques?
    d. were resources and audio-visual materials used in an appropriate manner?
    e. did it indicate an appropriate level of interaction between the teacher and the students?
    f. did it indicate unambiguously the instructor's competence in the subject-matter area?
    g. did the chosen teaching and learning techniques assist in the attainment of desired teaching outcome?

3   In relation to the instructor's teaching characteristics:
   a.   what are her or his obvious strengths? What are the areas of practice that need developing further?
   b.   what needs to be done so as to further develop those strengths and eradicate those weaknesses?
   c.   what matters have become apparent, during the observation, which need to be dealt with urgently?

The observers make a confidential written evaluation, which is discussed with the teacher with a minimum of delay (a necessary requirement of good feedback practice). Plans are made for further observation, and the instructor's colleagues, who are acting in the capacity of mentors, generally undertake to check carefully upon the level of progress seen as desirable in the light of their evaluation of teaching strengths and weaknesses.

Colleges tend to differ in how such observations are managed and timetabled. Some colleges operate complex programmes of observations of teaching and learning (OTLs) in which members of a central observation team carry out what are, in effect, mock Ofsted inspections, using the Ofsted Common Inspection Framework (CIF) as a template for the observations to be carried out. Inspection teams might consist of curriculum managers (or equivalent) and senior managers, possibly accompanied by members of the education and teacher-training team as well (although this latter practice, it is suggested, should be discouraged due to the potential for confusion between the teacher-educator's role which is in essence developmental, and the central observer's role which is in essence judgemental.

Student evaluation

This type of evaluation, which positions the students as consumers, presents the consumers' views of the teaching and learning process. Such an approach is used across the FE sector although its popularity among staff is far from widespread: at best it is described as 'interesting', although it tends to reflect 'feelings' among students rather than giving any indication of whether learning has taken place; at worst it is often characterized as flawed and emanating from the comments of those who, because of their relatively restricted experience, may lack developed powers of perception, comprehension and interpretation, all of which are demanded by the task of evaluation (Orpen, 1982).

Generally, the process takes the form of issuing end-of-course or end-of-term question-naires to students (either paper-based or online), who are invited to make their comments after the module or course has ended. The items comprising the questionnaire may be composed and arranged by the departmental head or senior management team. The teacher or trainer who is being evaluated rarely designs them. Students are asked to respond to questions regarding their perception of the teaching, how they have been assessed, the resources that they have been able to access and so forth. After the question-naires are collected, the comments are collated and an overall evaluation is presented to the teacher.

Evaluation in further education: A critical commentary

A number of aspects of the evaluation process within FE colleges have been critiqued by education researchers and writers. A number of the key concerns that are to be found within the literature are briefly outlined below:

1 The timing of evaluation
   There is now a general acceptance of the need for evaluation, but doubts persist as to its timing. Some college staff support the making of an evaluation immediately at the end of a lesson, so that memories of events are not allowed to deteriorate over time, while others feel the need for a period of reflection before committing themselves to recording their impressions. At the other end of the scale it has been argued that one cannot evaluate a teacher adequately until years after being taught by her or him (Epstein, 1981). However, in the interests of feedback, course management, staff development and systematic learning, continuous evaluation following the delivery of a module or unit would seem essential if standards of the teaching–learning process are to be maintained.

2 The student voice, and the student as consumer
   Many teachers and education researchers continue to question the positioning of students as consumers and of FE as a product, part of a wider phenomenon referred to as the marketization of FE (Newman and Jahdi, 2009). It is suggested that the introduction of a market ethos within the teacher-student relationship (as distinct from the market model which was introduced into the sector as a whole 20 years ago when colleges became independent corporations) has distorted the ways in which students understand, and hence evaluate, the role of the teacher. Indeed, for some commentators, what has been referred to (provocatively, but not entirely inaccurately) as the McDonaldization of FE (Bryan and Hayes, 2007; Ritzer, 1993), has led to the role of the teacher and the practice of teaching to be evaluated in terms of efficiency, uniformity and predictability: a model of evaluation that might be suited to industrial production, but not to education. The promotion of the student voice is an integral aspect of this model, and whilst many teachers agree that the student point of view needs to be heard and valued, the weight attached to it has distorted evaluation processes more generally. For some researchers, the very notion of the student voice,

reflected through end-of-term evaluations for example, is erroneous: students simply do not know enough to comment with any legitimacy on the teaching practices that they have been part of (Hayes, 2006).

An argument based on empirical research rather than philosophy can be found in research that has sought to establish the teaching and learning preferences of students in the FE sector (McQueen and Webber, 2009), and which suggests seven key areas that students look for in their courses:

- being able to say something when something is not understood
- mutual respect amongst students, and between students and teachers
- lessons that provide good preparation for assignments
- lessons that are interesting and inspiring
- regular feedback
- clarity of goals
- a positive atmosphere which shows enjoyment of learning.

3 Professionalism, managerialism and performativity
   Professionalism within the FE sector is, at the time of writing, an issue that causes considerable debate. The future role of the Institute for Learning (the professional body of teachers in the FE sector) is currently being debated, as is the creation of a new set of professional occupational standards for the sector and the establishment of a new FE Guild. These debates demonstrate the contested nature of professionalism in FE, which is increasingly seen as being imposed on the workforce rather than owned by them. Instead of professional values being written by members of that profession as a way of maintaining its standards, they are seen as being imposed on members as a form of control, reducing professional autonomy instead of enhancing it (Clow, 2001; Gleeson et al., 2005; Robson, 2003; Tummons, 2010a).

The notion that professionals are no longer to be left to practice without being constantly observed and controlled is linked to research research that has explored the FE sector from the linked perspectives of managerialism and performativity. Managerialism is an ethos of management within an organization where such management helps the organization in question to be as productive as it can possibly be, in as efficient a way as possible, overriding any alternative perspectives based on a professional ethos (Tummons, 2010a). Performativity is defined as a culture of workplace organization where management impose systems based around targets, accountability, and a blame culture (Avis, 2005). According to this perspective, the role of evaluation becomes less about a meaningful exploration of courses and curricula, and more about processes of surveillance and interference in the working lives of teachers. Evaluation procedures exist because teachers cannot be trusted to make sound and reliable value judgements. Rather, these judgements need to be generated and managed using systems that have been imposed on teachers, rather than created by them.

Moving beyond evaluation: The reflective practitioner

Reflective practice is a state of mind, a permanent pattern of behaviour. Being a reflective practitioner requires a constant, critical appraisal of teaching and learning, and of the teacher's work more generally. It is a way of exploring and picking apart all those aspects of teaching that get taken for granted. It is also a form of learning, enabling the teacher to extend and deepen her or his professional knowledge and understanding.

To reflect on practice involves much more than a simple evaluation of one's own teaching (as outlined earlier in this chapter). Instead, reflective practice requires the teacher to extend the scope of her or his enquiry beyond the classroom or workshop environments in which she or he teaches. For example, whilst a self-evaluation might lead a teacher to conclude that a lack of engagement on the part of a student might be related to the choice of teaching strategy that was made, the critically reflective practitioner might extent this analysis to consider broader factors. Examples might include: the reasons why that strategy was chosen and how this relates to the teacher's own preferred repertoire; whether or not the student is experiencing problems that would leave her or him disengaged no matter which teaching strategy had been chosen; or whether or not the resources that the strategy used embodied attitudes or values that the student might have found objectionable.

Theoretical approaches to reflective practice

Although writings on the subject are numerous, the key theoretical elements of reflective practice can be found reflected in the writing of a small number of key thinkers, whose work is outlined here:

- John Dewey
  John Dewey (1859–1952) was professor of philosophy at Columbia University. He wrote extensively on a range of issues relating to the education of teachers. His concept of reflective thinking was first set out in his 1933 book *How We Think*.

  Dewey was interested in the ways in which teachers went about solving problems. He argued that when encountering a problem, teachers engage in a process of reflective thinking, leading to learning, that would allow a solution to be found, tried out, and resolved. In fact, reflective thinking can only happen in these circumstances. To explain this process more fully, Dewey proposed a five stage model of problem solving:

1 Suggestions.

During this stage, some possible solutions to the problem that has been encountered are considered.

2 Intellectualization.

During this stage, the problem is defined questions are put forward that can lead to a solution.

3 Hypothesis.

During this stage, the teacher starts to put together a number of possible solutions to the problem. This stage is characterized by creative thought as the teacher reaches for and then decides upon a solution.

4 Reasoning.

During this stage, the solution that has been settled on is carefully thought about and reasoned over, perhaps involving reference to other sources of information.

5 Testing.

In this final stage, the solution to the problem is tested out in the real world.

Dewey did not intend for this model to be seen as a sequence. That is to say, it is not necessary for the teacher to start at Stage 1 and proceed to Stage 5 each and every time an unforeseen problem arises. Dewey acknowledged that in life, thinking and problem solving can never be as orderly as a five-point plan. Rather, he suggested that reflective thinking consisted of five recognizable elements, any combination of which might lead to problem solving.

- Donald Schön

  Donald Schön (1930–97) was professor of urban studies and education at the Massachusetts Institute of Technology. His specific areas of educational interest were adult and professional learning. He argued that professionals need to know more than can be learned from initial study: through professional experience, another kind of learning takes place which also generates knowledge. The process of reflection allows the professional to explore their professional experiences and the knowledge that has resulted from them. He proposed two forms of reflective practice in order to facilitate this: reflection-in-action, and reflection-on-action.

  Reflection-in-action is an instantaneous process, triggered immediately as the teacher solves a problem or encounters a dilemma during a teaching session. Reflection-in-action is found in that moment when the teacher, drawing on their experience, knowledge, skills and understanding of this and other situations, changes direction and decides to run the session differently, or to change the planned sequence of activities for that session, or to introduce something new. Reflection-on-action is a more conscious, deliberative process. When reflecting on action, the teacher needs to think critically about what has taken place, to analyze and evaluate the actions that were carried out, and to consider what might have happened if a different course of action had been chosen. It is a retrospective process (best carried out in a quiet and peaceful place (Boud, 2001)) that can be used by the professional to further develop his or her own professional knowledge.

- David Kolb
  David Kolb (born 1939) is professor of organizational behaviour at Case Western Reserve University, Ohio. Drawing on the work of John Dewey (above), he initially developed the four-stage model of experiential learning that bears his name in the 1970s, together with Roger Fry. In a later book, *Experiential Learning* (published in 1984), he expanded on this model (which also included a learning styles inventory). The four key elements of Kolb's experiential learning cycle are:

  1 concrete experience (doing something, having an experience of something)
  2 reflective observation (reviewing or reflecting on the experience)
  3 abstract conceptualization (applying theoretical knowledge to the experience)
  4 active experimentation (planning alternatives and trying them out).

  Kolb's model is simple to understand and straightforward to apply to learning situations: as such trainee teachers, when describing aspects of their own teaching practice, use it quite commonly. It is less common to see the model used as an approach to reflective practice, however (Duckworth et al., 2012). This is perhaps surprising as it is an example of a clearly understood theory of learning that integrates reflection within it.

- Stephen Brookfield
  Stephen Brookfield (born 1949) is currently a professor at the university of St Thomas in Minnesota. He has written widely about adult learning and teaching, and critical pedagogy and critical theory. In his 1985 book *Becoming A Critically Reflective Teacher*, he proposed a model for reflective practice that rested on four perspectives or critical lenses:
  - the point of view of the practitioner
  - the point of view of the students
  - the point of view of the practitioner's colleagues
  - the point of view of established theory, as found in relevant literature.

  The unpacking of assumptions such as 'student-led methods are always superior to teacher-led methods' is what characterizes critical reflection according to Brookfield. For example, a teacher working in FE might, quite understandably, be committed to a student-centred approach to learning. Such a commitment would obviously influence the tutor's choice of teaching and learning strategies. One commonly found approach would involve small groups of students working through a case study. From the point of view of the teacher, such student-led activities empower the students, encourage them to take responsibility for their own learning, and promote a facilitative approach where the students learn from each other, as well as from the teacher. However, some students may require a more structured, teacher-led pedagogy, and may not be ready for independent learning. Some students may interpret such strategies as a dereliction of duty. And some teachers may indeed employ such strategies because they have not made sufficient preparations for a session.

Criticisms of reflective practice

Reflective practice would appear to occupy a dominant position within teacher education for the FE sector. Readers of this text who are currently working towards a CertEd/PGCE or PTLLS/CTLLS/DTLLS award will have noticed that reflective practice constitutes a significant aspect of their curriculum. Readers who have completed their professional studies and are members of the Institute for Learning (IfL) will have noticed that reflective practice is positioned by the IfL, and others, as a key component of continuing professional development within the FE sector (Hitching, 2008; Scales et al., 2011).

Nonetheless, aspects of both the theory and application of reflective practice have been subjected to exploration and criticism by a range of researchers and writers (Ecclestone, 1996; Eraut, 1995; Jarvis, 2010; Keefer, 2009; Ixer, 1999; Scott, 2000; Tummons, 2011b). Some of the common themes that emerge from this body of literature are briefly discussed here:

1 The disputed nature of reflection itself
   There are many versions of reflective practice currently espoused in literature, but despite this proliferation of writing, the nature of the reflective process itself continues to be elusive. Taxonomies of reflective practice (technical reflection, critical reflection, reflection-in-action, reflection-on-action) arguably demonstrate nothing more than the lack of a clear and robust definition.

2 The disputed nature of learning through reflective practice
   Amongst the different writings on reflective practice, the ways by which professional learning or knowledge are encouraged or created remain obscure. This is problematic because the development of knowledge is positioned as a key benefit of the process. Some models of reflective practice suggest that it allows the teacher to develop their own theory. Both of these concepts rest on definitions of knowledge and of theory that lack specificity. Whilst distinctions between, for example, technical knowledge (formal, codified knowledge) and practical knowledge (informal, vernacular knowledge

that is difficult to describe) are well established in literature, the ways in which reflective practice contributes to knowledge building are less secure.

3 Problems in the assessment of reflective practice

Taking into consideration the arguments discussed above, it can be argued that reflective practice cannot be assessed because it is, simply put, impossible to assess something that cannot be properly described or defined. Reflective practice is such a nebulous concept that it cannot be summarized in outcomes/objectives. The many different ways in which teacher education curricula define reflective practice would appear to reinforce this view. Indeed, to attempt to assess students against such criteria would be invalid and unreliable because they would only by definition represent a partial and narrow definition of reflective practice. A further argument is that because reflective practice is summatively assessed, students on professional courses (not only teacher education) distort their reflective writing in order to meet assessment criteria, rather than write their reflections from a position of truthfulness (a particularly acute issue for those students who do not like to write in the first person and find it difficult or uncomfortable to expose their analyses to an assessor). In the process, the validity of the assessment of reflective practice is lost.

4 The difference between reflective practice whilst studying, and reflective practice whilst working

The formal, structured format of reflective practice that is presented during periods of initial professional development stands in stark contrast to the messy reality of the FE workplace. The prompts to reflective practice that are invariably embedded in assignment tasks and individual learning plans have no equivalent in the working lives of FE teachers who work in an increasingly complex and busy environment.

Pragmatic responses to reflective practice

The argument presented here is a pragmatic one, that reflective practice, whilst not without its problems, offers teachers a way of thinking about their professional practice, based on three key themes:

1 teachers can learn from their experiences

2 the knowledge that we acquire from our experience are useful to the teacher just as the knowledge to be gained from studying or reading is useful

3 the experience and knowledge that teachers acquire and reflect on in some way characterize the occupation of being a teacher as a profession.

With these issues in mind, the following template for encouraging reflective practice is proposed as a useful tool for the trainee teacher (Tummons, 2010a). This framework is not intended as a step-by-step programme: it is intended only to be a series of prompts.

- Identify the issue under discussion. This might be a specific incident in a session such as a learning activity that was not successful. It might be an issue that has cropped up in subsequent sessions, such as persistent disruptive behaviour.
- Have any actions been taken yet? How was the issue responded to?? What actions might need to taken in the immediate future and who will take them? Will someone other than the teacher be involved?
- Think about the issue in relation to past experience. Have similar issues been encountered in the past, and if so, how were they resolved?
- To what extent can the issue be explored using ideas in books or journals?
- Involve other professionals. This might be a colleague in the staffroom, a mentor, or a teacher-trainer. They may be able to help through the sharing of a similar experience of their own.
- Talk to the students. Are they able or willing to talk openly about the issue?

Reflective writing should not, by contrast, exhibit the following characteristics:

- Reflective writing should not consist of endless complaints about the lack of available resources, the attitude of colleagues or the perceived deficiencies of students without also including possible ways to change things, or at least to understand why things are the way that they are.
- Reflective practice should not describe lots of things that the teacher has done during teaching or training sessions without further evaluation or exploration.
- Reflective practice is not about engaging in self-absorbed contemplation at the expense of the wider world: it is not intended as an exercise in narcissism; nor is it intended as an exercise in navel gazing.
- Reflective practice is not only about identifying things that are going wrong and then trying to find ways to fix them. Reflective practice is about the entire span of professional practice, not just perceived deficiencies.

Summary: Reflective practice and evaluation in further education

Whilst it is commonly agreed that there is a need for the evaluation of the work of the teacher, the curriculum, the college and the wider FE sector, there is less agreement over how such evaluations should be carried out, who should carry them out, and what the consequences are of such evaluations for the teaching profession. Peer observations can be defined as supportive and developmental, but can also be seen as judgemental and compliant. Observations of teaching by managers can generate useful feedback but can also perpetuate the long-standing sense of a cultural divide between teaching staff and management staff in the FE sector (Wallace, 2002). Student evaluations are sometimes of questionable value and risk reducing educational provision to the level of a commercial transaction, something deeply opposed by many of the professionals who are working in the sector.

Reflective practice offers a partial response to the need for a profession to advance its own knowledge and skills base. The overarching idea that a reflective teacher is more likely to work to improve their practice is undeniably attractive: and yet it is difficult to avoid the fact that there is little meaningful research that demonstrates whether a teacher who claims to be reflective is 'better' or 'worse' than a teacher who claims to be unreflective.

Evaluation and reflection are, it is suggested, necessary and unavoidable aspects of the FE teacher's professional role. It is the case, unfortunately, that some aspects of these two practices cause problems – of varying degrees – to teachers who feel that they lack autonomy in some aspects of their professional lives. Nonetheless, it would be untenable to suggest that the kinds of processes that have been explored in this chapter should simply be abolished. The FE sector is large, complex and expensive (although it is the least well-funded education sector): it is important that everyone involved – students, parents, teachers, employers and even government ministers – has confidence in the quality of the provision.

Further reading

It has been argued in this chapter that reflective practice is a 'ever present' aspect of teacher-training in further education. As such, it is perhaps not surprising that although there are many books that focus on reflective practice, few of them provide a critical account of it. Amongst the many books that have been written about reflective practice, some are recommended here:

Moon, J. (2000), *Reflection in learning and professional development: theory and practice.* London: Routledge.

Roffey-Barentsen, J. and Malthouse, R. (2009), *Reflective practice in the lifelong learning sector.* Exeter: Learning Matters.

Scales, P., Pickering, J., Senior, L., Headley, K., Garner, P. and Boulton, H. (2011), *Continuing Professional Development in the Lifelong Learning Sector.* Maidenhead: McGraw Hill.

But for those who wish for a more critical account, the following book is strongly recommended:

Bradbury, H., Frost, N., Kilminster, S. and Zukas, M. (2009), *Beyond reflective practice: new approaches to professional lifelong learning*. London: Routledge.

And an excellent essay which is available online is:

Finlay, L. (undated), *Reflecting On Reflective Practice*. Available at: http://www.open. ac.uk/cetl-workspace/cetlcontent/documents/4bf2b48887459.pdf [accessed 15 May 2013].

PART 8

Intelligence and Ability: Issues and Debates

33 Conceptions of Intelligence

In this final part of the text we examine two questions which emerge from a study of the general level of cognitive functioning known as intelligence', and which are closely related to the theory and practice of teaching. The first question to be explored is: how is intelligence defined and assessed? The second is: what is the significance, for teaching and learning in the FE sector, of the ongoing debate surrounding 'nature versus nurture' in relation to the development of students' abilities?'

Educational researchers and psychologists differ as widely in their definitions of intelligence as in their definitions of learning. Indeed, these very difficulties have become an object of research in their own right (Sternberg, 1989). Such definitions have traditionally focused on intelligence as a cognitive function, the capacity of which is related to the student's ability to learn academic subjects. They include, typically: innate general cognitive ability; the ability to respond in present situations on the basis of cogent anticipation of possible consequences and with a view to controlling the consequences that ensue; the capacity to apprehend facts and propositions and their relationships and to reason about them; a hypothetical factor of wide generality that is presumed to underlie an individual's competence in performing cognitive tasks; the general ability common to all problem-solving abilities; and the aggregate or global capacity of an individual to act purposefully, to think rationally, and to deal effectively with her or his environment.

It is clearly the case that there are no definitive criteria of intelligence (and the definitions above can be further complicated through a consideration of the theories of multiple intelligences and emotional intelligence): it is a fuzzy-edged concept to which many features are relevant (Neisser, 1979). Nevertheless, there seems to be an element of general agreement among some psychologists on the nature of intelligence as displaying some type of capacity for rational responses to the stimulus of the environment – an essential feature of the processes of learning.

Doubts continue to be cast, however, on the very existence of the phenomenon of intelligence. Nor are such concerns only reserved for contemporary theorists and researchers: there is a long tradition of questioning what intelligence is. For example: if intelligence as a measurable capacity must at the start be defined as the capacity to do well in an intelligence test, then intelligence is what the tests test (Boring, 1923). At the same time, other researchers and teachers reject the possibility of the existence of a single generalized capacity responsible for a person's abilities, related to use of language, comprehension of symbols, perception of complex relationships and the solving of problems.

Towards the end of the twentieth century, concern with the implications of some aspects of intelligence theory and the procedures of intelligence testing spilled over from the teaching profession to the social and political arenas, producing much controversy. Many teachers questioned the very basis of intelligence theory which, they claimed, ignored the phenomenon of pupils of high ability scoring relatively low intelligence test (IQ test) marks, which often seemed to reflect disadvantaged backgrounds and restricted horizons, levels of expectation and achievement. Public anxieties mounted: the use of examinations to select children for school entry was widely perceived as being based on a dogmatic attachment to belief in an innate, fixed quantum of intelligence, allowing children to be classified according to their test scores. This was viewed as incompatible with egalitarian doctrines and aspirations and was held by some as providing a theoretical underpinning of a social hierarchy, which mirrored divisions resting on superior and inferior intelligence, in much the same way as the academic curriculum continues to be seen as superior to the vocational. At the time of writing, recent coalition government policies regarding selection to state-funded schools would seem to be reigniting these controversies. Further, some interpretations of intelligence theory were held to have given aid and comfort to the proponents of racialist doctrines. Finally, to add to the discomfiture of the psychometricians (who seek to measure intelligence), evidence was adduced which seemed to suggest the fraudulent manufacturing of data by one of the founding fathers of intelligence testing.

Nevertheless, the acceptance of the notion of intelligence testing (the measurement of the intelligence quotient – the IQ) remains widespread in colleges of FE as well as society at large. The tests are considered to provide a useful indicator of existing and potential levels of students' abilities. Some psychometricians have pointed out that intelligence tests do correlate significantly with educational achievement and occupational success and are useful, therefore, for purposes of educational and vocational guidance (Kline, 1996).

Concepts of intelligence

The development of theories of intelligence can be seen to have followed a similar path to theories of teaching and learning. Researchers have over time challenged the dominance of educational psychologists of the twentieth century through drawing on other traditions such as ethnography and anthropology. With these themes in mind, the following theorists should be of particular interest to teachers in FE.

- Charles Spearman (1863–1945)

  Charles Spearman was professor of psychology at University College, London. He propounded a two-factor theory of intelligence, which became highly influential in the practice of intelligence testing and the training of teachers (1923, 1939). Data collected from the many psychological tests he administered were interpreted as showing the existence of what was termed a 'g' factor – meaning general intelligence – a fundamental, quantifiable factor which entered into all cognitive processes, which was inherited, or at least inborn, and which could not be affected by training. It consisted of something of the nature of an energy, which served in common the whole cortex. He also identified an 's' factor, which recorded the effect of training (arguing that certain neurons in the brain become habituated to particular types of action), and which indicated the specific, unique information peculiar to the results of a given test and not related to any other test. It could be considered as the ability to grasp and use relationships swiftly and effectively. All mental tasks required the two kinds of ability or factors, general and specific, the former common to all types of these tasks, the latter being invariably specific to a given task.

  Spearman's analysis of intelligence was held to be of momentous importance. Here was a justification of intelligence testing, of educational theory and practice based on the concept of a fundamental, unchangeable, measurable reality to be found in the very structure of the human brain. (In his later work, Spearman suggested the existence of three additional general factors. The first of these was the 'p' factor, perseveration (the inertia of a person's mental energy). The second was the 'o' factor, oscillation (the extent to which mental energy fluctuates). The third was the 'w' factor, will (a motivational-personality factor which can be inferred from intelligence test achievement).)

  Spearman has been attacked for his belief that peoples' intelligence and abilities were fixed at birth and incapable of being developed or improved. The effect of his theories on social and political programmes concerned with education (which according to his theories, would be of no use) have also been criticized, as has his attempt to convert an abstract concept, intelligence, into a quantifiable entity (Gould, 1997).

- Cyril Burt (1883–1971)

  Cyril Burt was professor of psychology at University College London. His interpretation of data derived from tests of school pupils resulted in a four-factor theory, which was based on, and extended, Spearman's concept of intelligence (Spearman 1940, 1961, 1972). The theory provided an underpinning for the ideology from which the 11+ examinations for selection to grammar schools later emerged. Burt's four factors were: a 'g' factor and an 's' factor (both sharing the definitions established by Spearman), 'group' factors (relating to abilities classified according to their form or content) and 'accidental' factors (attributes of single traits measured on a single occasion). These accidnental factors were, however, not lodged in separate organs of the brain; they were merely convenient mathematical abstractions.

Education, according to Burt (and in contrast to Spearman), could affect the quality of 's' and 'group' factors, but could not affect the 'g' factor. (Burt argued that the 'g' factor was inherited, or at least inborn and could not be increased through education or training or any other acquisition of knowledge). A person's innate, all-round intellectual ability (the 'g' factor) was capable of being expressed numerically and therefore ranked. Burt regarded intelligence, fundamentally, as specifying certain individual differences in the structure of the central nervous system; these differences could be described in terms of histology (that is, the study of tissues).

Criticism of Burt's research has tended to stem from his fundamental hereditarianism (that is, the belief that heredity is of paramount significance in determining individual intelligence and behaviour). In recent years, however, it has been suggested that he falsified some of his data. As a result, considerable portions of his published findings are now viewed with some suspicion (Hearnshaw, 1979; Joynson, 1989; Mackintosh, 1995).

- Louis Thurstone (1887–1955)

  Louis Thurstone was president of the American Psychological Association and taught and researched at the University of Chicago. He was a pioneer in psychometrics (mental measurement) and established a specialist laboratory dedicated to the study of psychometrics at the University of North Carolina. He did not think that individuals possessed a single general intelligence. Instead, he argued that people possessed a number of different primary mental abilities (PMAs), independent factors of intelligence that different people possessed to different degrees (Thurston, 1924; 1938; 1947). PMAs, he argued, constituted the simplest units of intelligence (that is, they could not be further simplified or reduced). They included verbal comprehension, word fluency, computational skill, spatial visualization, associative memory, perceptual speed, and reasoning (by which he meant the ability to perceive and utilize abstract relationships, enabling an individual to put together her or his past experiences in seeking to solve new problems).

  Thurstone's research broke with the tradition established by Spearman in several ways. Firstly, he argued against the existence of general intelligence or a 'g' factor, claiming that his research results indicated that no such factor existed. Consequently, he argued that ranking peoples' intelligence on a scale (such as that resulting from a traditional IQ test) was erroneous. Instead, an individual should be described in terms of a profile of all of the PMAs which are known to be significant: this PMA profile would be unique to every person. He also argued that mental abilities were not fixed but could be trained. However, there was a limit as to what such training could accomplish: he argued that it would merely enhance innate differences, and he dismissed arguments relating to the impact of environmental factors on intelligence as mere sentimentality.

- Donald Hebb (1904–85)

  Donald Hebb was professor of psychology at McGill University in Canada and conducted research into brain science as well as human and animal behaviour. He made a distinction between two concepts applicable to the term 'intelligence'. What he termed 'intelligence A' was defined as a person's innate potential derived from the possession of a good brain and a good neural metabolism; 'intelligence B' was defined as, quite simply, the brain's actual functioning at any given time. 'Intelligence B', he suggested, was formed through a combination of 'intelligence A' together with the student's strategies and concepts emerging from her or his responses and reactions to the surrounding environment (Hebb, 1949). He argued in favour of intelligence tests, but suggested that they were only able to measure 'intelligence B'; 'intelligence A', by contrast, could never be measured directly.

- Joy Paul Guilford (1897–1987)

  Joy Paul Guilford began his research career as a psychologist within the United States Army Air Force, before moving to the university of Southern California to research and teach (indeed, much of his subsequent research was funded by the US Army and focussed on the non-completion of training programmes by Air Force trainees). Guildford sought to explain the structure of the human intellect in terms suggesting that intelligence is multifactorial (Guildford, 1967). He argued that what he termed an 'intelligent act' was comprised of three elements: operations, content and products. Operations are general intellectual processes, and include processes such as cognition, evaluation and memory. Contents are the broad categories of information which operations are applied to, and include (but are not restricted to): figural content (real world objects or information that can be seen, touched or listened to); symbolic content (content based on signs or symbols that carry meaning, such as letters of the alphabet); and semantic content (content based on abstract ideas and meanings). In general, Guilford contended, the content of any problem with which the student is faced will be of a symbolic nature, which requires operations, involving cognition and evaluation, which may produce a solution.

  Guilford's model has been criticized on several counts (Kline, 1996). The 'operations' category has been criticized on the grounds that it did not rest on any meaningful empirical research but was instead an intuitive classification. The 'products' category has been described as partial and incomplete. Thirdly, his work paid little attention to other – more empirically robust – research on cognitive processing. And finally, it would appear to be the case that most of the observations from which Guildford constructed his model involved an unrepresentative research group which was of above-average intelligence: army trainees.

- Raymond Cattell (1905–98)

  Cattell was a professor of psychology at the University of Illinois. Through his research, he distinguished a group of what he termed 'primary factors' which should be taken into account in studies of human ability. They included verbal ability, word fluency, meaningful memory, spatial and numerical abilities, perceptual speed, general motor coordination, and judgement. From these, he extrapolated that there are five fundamental capacities essential to human ability: visualization, fluency, cognitive speed, fluid and crystallized intelligence.

Crystallized intelligence, which (he argued) can be measured, is used to indicate the general effect of environmental experience on intellectual development. It involves knowledge and learned skills acquired through experience over time and can continue to develop throughout life. The testing of crystallized intelligence would need to be based upon culturally significant skills: hence, measures of this type of intelligence may differ according to time, place and cultural patterns. A second type of intelligence, termed fluid intelligence, which can also be measured, is used to indicate the influence of genetic, hereditable factors on intellectual development. It involves reasoning and insight and may be viewed in terms of pure ability (Cattell, 1966, 1971).

Cattell emphasized that both types of intelligence would be involved in assessments and other tasks. Measurements of fluid and crystallized intelligence can be of value, he claimed, in assessing academic and occupational achievement.

- Philip Vernon (1905–87)
  Philip Vernon was professor of psychology at the Institute of Education in London. He described intelligence in terms of a hierarchical structure, which comprises several abilities. At the top of the hierarchy is a general ability factor (similar to Spearman's 'g' factor). At the next level are major group factors: verbal-educational factors (involving the type of ability essential for successful learning in, for example, English or history) and spatial-practical (needed for successful performance in, for example, technical drawing). The next level comprises the minor group factors: these are subdivisions of the major group factors, and include verbal understanding, musical ability and manual ability. At the lowest level are highly specific factors. A student who is to achieve success in, say, a verbal test, requires a combination of the general ability factor, a less general verbal factor, appropriate kinds of verbal ability, and other abilities highly specific to the particular tasks involved in the test.

  Vernon noted many cases of significant differences in intelligence among children in the same family who had grown up in similar environments. He argued for a recognition of the significance of genetic endowment in any analysis and evaluation of intelligence, but stressed the importance for teachers and others of neglecting neither nature nor nurture in the furtherance of human development (refer also to the discussion in the following chapter).

- Howard Gardner (b. 1943)
  Howard Gardner is professor of cognition and education at Harvard University. His

structural theory of intelligence rejects the significance attached to the 'g' factor in the kinds of studies referred to above. He instead proposed the concept of 'multiple intelligences'. He originally theorized that there were seven intelligences: linguistic intelligence; musical intelligence; logical-mathematical intelligence; spatial intelligence; kinaesthetic intelligence; interpersonal intelligence; and intrapersonal intelligence (Gardner, 1983). He later added two further intelligences: naturalist intelligence; and existential intelligence (Gardner, 1991).

In general, multiple intelligences involve a competence which enables individuals to resolve problems and to acquire new knowledge. Gardner argued that rather than indicating fixed abilities, which might be measured, multiple intelligences reflected differing levels of potential (which could not be measured in the manner proposed by classical IQ testing) that should therefore become the focus of pedagogic activities in schools within formal educational institutions (Gardner, 2003).

Gardner's theory of multiple intelligences has been widely cited and is seen as being influential (Illeris, 2007). By reframing discussion away from a single intelligence (usually equated to academic/intellectual ability), he has, arguably, helped remove the elitism inherent in previous definitions of intelligence. The multiple intelligences that he has defined have the added attraction of being easily recognizable and applicable in a way that few other educational theories are able to manage. However, critics of multiple intelligences theory point out that although Gardner drew on evidence to support his theory, he did not actually carry out any empirical research in order to test his model (Sternberg, 1999), and his evidence was drawn from people who represented a very narrow socio-economic group (Hayes, 2010).

- Robert Sternberg (b. 1949)
  Robert Sternberg is professor of psychology at Oklahoma State University. He has interpreted the concept of intelligence in terms associated with the contemporary analysis of information processing. In general, information processing is perceived as involving five components (Sternberg, 1987):

  1 metacomponents are the higher-level processes that plan and 'take decisions' in situations involving problem-solving

  2 performance components are those processes used in the execution of a strategy of problem solving

  3 acquisition components are used in the acquisition of knowledge through learning

  4 retention components account for the retrieval of previously acquired information

  5 transfer components allow the generalization that results from transfer of learning.

Sternberg viewed the metacomponents (organizing, planning, decision-making, mental activities) as the all-important, overriding factors, which determine the extent and quality of a person's ability to acquire, interpret and utilize information presented by the environment. This inferred ability is to be regarded as intelligence.

- Daniel Goleman (b. 1946)

  Daniel Goleman, upon completing his PhD in psychology, became a science journalist rather than an academic and pursued his research in a more public sphere. Influenced by the concept of emotional intelligence initially outlined by Peter Salovey of Yale University and John Mayer of the University of New Hampshire (Salovey and Mayer, 1990), Goleman has written that people have two minds: the rational, and the emotional. Following the widening of the concept of intelligence established by Howard Gardner, Goleman has argued that emotions should be seen as being equally important to schooling and work as reason is. Importantly, however, Goleman does not offer a clear or unambiguous definition of emotional intelligence (Illeris, 2007); instead, he lists the characteristic of emotional intelligence, which include: self-awareness; self-control; empathy; conflict resolution, and cooperation.

  There is considerable disagreement amongst researchers and writers about the extent to which emotional intelligence is based on innate traits (that is to say, is located within the physiological make-up of the individual) or whether it is simply socially constructed (that is to say, the focus on behaviours such as self-control or empathy is a product of the contemporary wider social and cultural climate). These concerns, together with reservations regarding Goleman's work that echo criticism of Gardner (the lack of empirical research) have contributed to the development of alternative approaches commonly referred to as emotional literacy and emotional wellbeing. The latter is of particular interest to the FE sector, as it is increasingly linked to provision for students who have been labelled disaffected (Ecclestone, 2011; Ecclestone and Hayes, 2008).

Measuring intelligence: A brief account of IQ testing

The first intelligence test was developed in 1905 by the French psychologists Alfred Binet (1857–1911) and Theodore Simon (1873–1961), and reflected their belief that intelligence involved a goal to an individual's mental processes, the ability to create adaptable solutions to problems, and the ability to use selective judgement. Fifty-four items, ranging from simple verbal definitions to ingenuity problems, made up the test. Later, Lewis Terman (1877–1956, professor of educational psychology at Stanford University) drew on the work of the psychologist William Stern (1871–1938, professor of psychology at Duke University, USA), and constructed the index known as the 'intelligence quotient' (IQ). With the Binet-Simon test in mind, IQ is usually calculated as mental age divided by chronological age, multiplied by 100.

(Mental age is determined by an individual's score in a standardized intelligence test: thus, a nine-year-old child who achieves a score similar to that of an average 11-year-old child, is said, for purposes of the IQ calculation, to have a mental age of 11.) A score of 100 remains the average, with most scores being between 85 and 115. Scores over 145 were deemed to indicate someone who was 'gifted', and scores below 55 were deemed to indicate someone who was 'retarded'.

Controversies over IQ testing persist to the present day. On the one hand, there is research that indicates a correlation between IQ test score and achievement in formal education (Bee and Boyd, 2010). On the other hand, there is still no agreement as to whether IQ tests (or any other psychometric tests) are measuring an innate ability (which is called 'intelligence'), or are measuring environmental influences. A third possibility is that all that is being measured is the individual's capacity to take a particular form of test that rests on a specific and narrow theoretical foundation.

Attitudes in the colleges to the concept of intelligence testing are varied. It is contended by some staff that tests measure little, apart from some specialized skills (which can be taught and exercised for purposes of the test), that they place undue emphasis on verbal abilities, that there is a socio-cultural bias in their construction and interpretation, and that their importance in the educational process is overestimated. Evidence has emerged which suggests that the IQ may not be constant throughout a student's period of education and development (indeed, IQ tests are increasingly positioned as only appropriate for children). Further, some researchers believe that the development of some aspects of intelligence may cease on the attainment of adulthood, so that there may be only a limited value in attempting to measure IQ after that development has ended.

Among some college teachers will be found those who have rejected the IQ test as worthless (Evans and Waites, 1981). Intuitively, and understandably, they are suspicious of the claimed validity of a test which seeks to separate 'tested' and 'everyday' intelligence. There are plenty of anecdotes from teachers in FE concerning students who were successful in examinations or had a high IQ (an expression often used to describe students irrespective of whether the students have actually taken an IQ test) and yet were notoriously lacking in common sense.

College teachers who do accept the premise of IQ testing because of its predictive value, for example, include many who are aware of the difficulty inherent in any attempt to understand the essence of the elusive human characteristic which is being tested and evaluated. Most will keep in mind the importance for the teaching-learning process of a comprehensive assessment based on standardized tests. Their views will be reinforced by the reminder from Heim that valuable data relating to students capacities to learn can be derived from an IQ test which has been composed with skill, which provides results amenable to careful interpretation, and which is utilized together with other observations and procedures (Heim, 1987).

Summary: Intelligence – a nebulous concept?

How intelligence is understood has change over time. Two centuries ago, it was believed that the shape and size of peoples' heads provided a reliable indicator of intelligence (and, indeed, of other personality traits as well). For much of the last century, dominant modes of educational psychology have informed not only theories of learning but theories relating to knowledge and intelligence as well.

More recently, theories of learning have taken a social turn (as explored in Part 3 of this book). Alongside this shift, ideas about knowledge and intelligence have also begun to be reconsidered. What is referred to as 'intelligence' simply reflects social and cultural preferences for particular kinds of aptitude, and nothing more. The relative narrowness of definitions of intelligence reflects the interests of the people doing the defining, who in turn tend to represent a narrow social and cultural section of society. The theories of Gardner and Goleman represent a challenge to dominant views of intelligence, but at the same time also perpetuate them. They do not challenge the idea of intelligence per se: they simply seek to expand its definition. But if it is accepted that there is no such thing as a 'normal' or 'universal' form of cognition, and instead that there are different forms of cognition that are located in different social and cultural places, perhaps intelligence can similarly be seen as being relevant, and related, to the social and cultural places in which it is defined or looked for (Lave, 1988).

Further reading

Debates about what constitutes intelligence, skill or competence are rarely discussed in teacher-training textbooks. For those who wish to study these issues further, the following are all recommended:

Eraut, M. (1994), *Developing Professional Knowledge and Competence*. Abingdon: RoutledgeFalmer.

Polanyi, M. (2009), *The tacti Dimension*. Chicago: University of Chicago Press.

Schön, D. (1983), *The Reflective Practitioner: how professionals think in action*. Aldershot: Ashgate.

Sternberg, R. and Horvath, J. (1999), *Tacit knowledge in professional practice: researcher and practitioner perspectives*. Mahwah, NJ: Lawrence Erlbaum.

34 Nature, Nurture and Neuroscience

In this final chapter we sketch the outlines of two contemporary debates that continue to be of general interest to professionals across all sectors of education provision, including FE. The first debate to be considered is the nature-nurture debate. The second debate revolves around the emerging themes of neuroscientific research, which over recent years is beginning to have a pragmatic application in the workshop or classroom. It is not possible to provide an exhaustive survey of these arguments in a chapter of this size: however, it is hoped that a critical summary of recent debates can provide much for the FE teacher to reflect on as part of her or his own professional practice.

Nature or nurture?

The nature–nurture debate constitutes an ongoing controversy which has important implications for the very basis of all educational theory and practice. The debate turns on the relative contributions of heredity and environment to human psychological characteristics, such as intelligence (mindful of the problems that surround defining intelligence, as discussed in the preceding chapter). There are two arguments to consider. The first argument, characterized as biological determinism, argues that human intelligence is innate and unalterable. It is fixed at birth and cannot be altered through any form of external intervention. The counter-argument, characterized as environmentalism, argues that intellectual abilities are not fixed at birth, and that they can be modified by any number of nurturing interventions, including (of particular relevance to this textbook) parental/familial upbringing, and education. Teachers will recognize immediately that what is being debated cannot help influencing deeply the attitudes of society, its politicians, educationalists and legislators to the accepted functions of our educational institutions.

The biological determinist position

Most if not all teachers and trainers in FE colleges will have worked with students who have, during their course or programme of study, 'improved': that is to say, it is not simply the case that the student in question has passed the course or achieved the specified outcomes, but has effected an overall improvement in performance. According to the biological determinist position, there has been no real, measurable or fundamental improvement in the student's level of intelligence, which will have been inherited and cannot be altered. The teaching process may have improved some aspects of a student's capacities associated with the learning process, but it cannot affect intelligence (Gould, 1997).

The general position of biological determinism is exemplified in the views of the American educationist, Henry Goddard (1866–1957), who was professor of abnormal and clinical psychology at Ohio State University. Although in later life Goddard disowned many of his early writings, acknowledging that much of his early research was flawed (arguably, his work contributed to the emergence of mid-twentieth century scientific racism), he continued to argue that intelligence was fixed and innate, and that attempts at improving intelligence through formal educational processes would always be futile.

Other theorists shared this perspective. Charles Spearman (discussed in the preceding chapter) found himself unable to agree with educationalists and social workers who believed that a basic improvement in the mental capacity known as intelligence could be effected by specially-designed and intensive teaching programmes. Any such interventions could be in the nature of palliatives only, and fundamental capacities were not amenable to well-intentioned, but impossible, schemes designed for their alteration. Similarly, Cyril Burt (discussed in the preceding chapter) argued that there was a definite limit to what children would be able to achieve, that was inexorably set by the limitations of their innate capacity.

Burt's views led him to extrapolate from his data in ways which attracted much controversy. He argued, for example, that wide inequalities in personal incomes were largely (though not entirely) an indirect consequence of the wide inequality in innate intelligence. (Interestingly, many educational researchers and writers have effectively inverted this argument over recent years, and have demonstrated that the social and environmental backgrounds of wealthier families constitute a significant factor in determining the educational progress of the children from such families). Burt also argued that the small group of people endowed by nature with outstanding abilities should be nurtured so as to compensate for the general public's comparative ineptitude. Schools could do little to alter nature's work in the area of inherited intelligence.

The environmentalist position

Environmentalists are prepared to accept, in general, the heritability of characteristics and abilities, some of which are held to constitute intelligence. But they reject in its entirety the concept of 'biology as destiny' and will not accept the idea of an immutable genetic inheritance in relation to intellectual abilities. The very rationale of teaching rests in the presumption of nurture: that is to say, improving the quality of some inherited genetic traits. Teachers will probably be aware of the very considerable anecdotal evidence suggesting that individual IQ scores *can* be improved as the direct result of teaching. Some research suggests that it is possible to demonstrate that environmental factors can create differences as large as 38 IQ points (Kline, 1996). Indeed, empirical studies have underlined the significance of environment in determining IQ over a considerable perod of time:

- A study from the first half of the twentiwth century of the educational and social environments of identical twins concluded that differences in education and social environment produce undeniable differences in intelligence which cannot be ignored or denied (Newman, Freeman and Holzinger, 1937).
- A review conducted fifty years later of 111 separate studies giving 526 IQ correlations drawn from some 55,000 pairings of relatives, led the researchers to conclude that IQ has both a genetic and an environmental component, but that the proportion of each cannot be ascertained (Bouchard and McGue, 1981).

Neuroscience and education

A further challenge to notions of fixed or hereditary intelligence comes from neuroscience, a branch of scientific inquiry that has begun to attract an increasingly public profile over recent years. Neuroscience is the study of how the brain learns and remembers: as such, for the purposes of this book, it is important to note that neuroscience focuses on learning, but not on teaching. Neuroscientists explore the function of the brain at a molecular and cellular level, and also in terms of what are called brain systems which are the pathways in the brain that underpin, for example, the ability to speak and comprehend language (Goswami, 2004; Small, 2008; Tommerdahl, 2012). However, it is important to note that there is as yet no sound methodological process for conducting neuroscientific research in the workshop or classroom as opposed to the clinical laboratory, which for theorists who subscribe to anthropological and social theories of learning constitutes an area of significant difficulty in applying the findings of neuroscience to the real world of the school or college.

The brain grows in size fourfold from birth to adulthood, although the size and weight of adult brains can vary, as can the relative sizes of different brain structures.

For the purposes of this text, the most important theme to emerge is the concept of neuroplasticity or brain plasticity. In contrast to the older view that after an initial critical period of brain development during early childhood the adult brain becomes fixed, neuroplasticity remains a feature of the brain throughout adult life, and experiences through life (including formal education and training) can change both the way in which pathways and brain systems are organized, and also the actual shape of the brain. Environmental factors therefore do affect the development of the brain, but these are not necessarily permanent factors, and future environmental influences can further change the brain later in life.

Neuroscience has demonstrated a number of factors that are of interest to the FE teacher:

- The brain uses different regions for processing grammar and syntax (the ways in which sentences are constructed) on the one hand, and vocabulary and semantics (the ways in which meanings are constructed) on the other. In adults who are learning English later in life, the learning of syntax does not develop at the same speed as the vocabulary and semantics region, and the learning of grammar is shared across both brain regions.

- The brain uses different regions for mathematics. One region is used for operations relating to quantities (at a simple level, counting), whilst a second area is used for storing facts about numbers. An example of a fact about a number might be a times table, which is learned by rote rather than arithmetically. This area of the brain is also used for verbal sequences and repetition (such as learning a poem off by heart). A third region of the brain is activated when counting on one's fingers and performing calculations.

- A specific region of the brain is responsible for the recognition of common words in their written form. Reading involves an act of physical recognition of a word before processes relating to meaning (semantics) are activated in different parts of the brain. This region of the brain (that is, the word recognition region) would appear to be less active in people with dyslexia than in other readers.

- Different experiences impact on brain development in different ways. For example: the area of the brain that is responsible for spatial representation and navigation is enlarged in London taxi drivers; and musicians have enlarged brain areas relating to the hands that they use to play their instruments.

- When an individual is stressed, afraid or otherwise emotionally uneven, connections to the part of the brain that deals with problem-solving become impaired. A second part of the brain that assesses the value of information being received, also becomes impaired. This explains why learning may be impaired if a student is in an emotionally distressed state.

- Regular use of computers leads to changes in brain pattern in the areas of the brain associated with the integration of sensation (kinaesthetic or visual stimulus) and thought, and the areas associated with reading.

A brief note regarding neuromyths

The wider profile enjoyed by neuroscience has also had some unfortunate consequences that have resulted from public misunderstanding of the reports of scientific research. These misunderstandings are referred to as neuromyths (OECD, 2002). A number of neuromyths that will be familiar to practitioners in the FE sector are summarized here. It is perhaps a matter of regret that some of these can be seen to have directly influenced pedagogic practice in the FE sector in recent years.

- Left brain learning versus right brain learning.
  It is the case that some particular functions are divided between the left and right sides, or hemispheres, of the brain. However, the sheer volume of connections that exist between the two sides of the brain renders any attempt to divide functions between them meaningless. All of the cognitive functions that have been explored by neuroscience to date rely on both sides of the brain working together. The notion that a learning styles questionnaire can categorize learners according to brain pattern is, therefore, entirely erroneous.

- Male brains and female brains
  The description of the brain as either male of female was originally intended to signify differences in cognitive styles between men and women who, although sharing many aspects of cognition, diverged in some areas: for example, men appear to be better at understanding complex mechanical systems, and women appear to be better at communicating with and understanding others (Baron-Cohen, 2003). However, there are two important caveats to this. Firstly, this does not mean that women cannot understand complex mechanical systems or that men cannot communicate with and understand others. Secondly, this does not imply differences in brain shape, system or function.

- The Mozart effect
  The notion that listening to classical music – in particular, the music of Mozart – leads to temporary boosts in IQ scores has been shown to be fallacious. The broader notion that a multi-sensory or multi-stimulatory environment necessarily leads to more, and better, learning has also been demonstrated to be false. Any kind of environmental stimulation can cause the formation of new connections in the brain, but this does not predict a greater capacity for learning.

- Brain-based learning

  Brain-based learning purports to be a theory of learning that is based on the structure and function of the brain. It argues that traditional pedagogies inhibit the brain's 'natural' learning processes. However, the pedagogical strategies that it proposes (encouraging the active processing of learning by students, designing learning around students' interests, contextualize learning and focus learning on real life problems) are all found in other, longer-established theoretical frameworks such as constructivism, and the theory does not draw on neuroscience.

- Some people are 'naturally' talented and some people are not

  Expertise, particularly in playing sport or in playing a musical instrument, is often anecdotally referred to as a natural talent that is somehow innate and therefore incapable of acquisition by someone who does not have the correct physiological and psychological make-up. In fact, research has shown no innate condition relating to prowess or expertise in music. Rather, it is shown simply to be a product of intensive practice.

Nature, nurture and neuroscience – implications for teachers in further education

There is an impressive body of evidence, generated over time by a number of empirical research projects (some of which have been of a considerable scope and scale), that has helped to establish links between learning, and wider social, cultural and environmental factors. It is these wider factors rather than any innate 'ability' or 'intelligence' that are likely to have the greatest impact on the learning journeys and future opportunities of students in FE. Together with the challenge to fixed notions of intelligence offered by neuroscience and neuroplasticity, it is suggested that the following themes emerge from the current discussion:

- If the environment is right (which includes the motivation of the individual, the expertise of the teacher, a settled home life and so forth), there is no reason why any student cannot learn anything she or he wants to learn.

- Mindful of the challenges faced by students with specific needs or learning difficulties, there is no reason why a student cannot achieve in any area of the curriculum – vocational, technical, academic or professional. These curriculum areas are discriminated only on cultural and social grounds (the 'academic' being perceived as superior for purely arbitrary historical reasons).

- When a student complains that they are 'no good with books' or 'no good with doing practical tasks', such sentiments are in part responses to the ways in which the student has been labelled (Meighan and Harber, 2007). This label may have been attached to the student by a previous teacher, a friend or a family member. It may have been attached by the student her or himself, in response to prior experiences of education and training. There is no reason (beyond an undiagnosed learning difficulty, for example) why a student might not progress within either craft, technical or academic programmes of study should she or he wish to be given the opportunity: it is for the teacher to help establish the right environment in which learning can happen.

Summary: Innate ability or boundless potential?

The extent to which intelligence (however defined), ability or potential to learn is fixed or changeable continues to be debated by psychologists, neuroscientists, educationalists and teachers – and by government ministers as well. The arguments presented in this chapter represent a brief summary of a much more complex field of work. Nonetheless, the themes that emerge do give empirical credence to those teachers who espouse egalitarian and democratic pedagogies: that given the right chances and opportunities, students will succeed and will not only gain qualifications, but will also grow in self-esteem and cultural capital.

Further reading

Debates regarding neuroscience have entered the mainstream through books and media appearances by academics such as Susan Greenfield and Steven Pinker. These two authors on their own have authored a number of books on the subject suitable for the generally interested reader. For a closer focus on educational processes, however, the following are also recommended:

Goswami, U. (2004), Neuroscience, education and special education. *British Journal of Special Education* 31(4): 175–83.

Lave, J. (1988), *Cognition in Practice: Mind, Mathematics and Culture in Everyday Life*. Cambridge: Cambridge University Press.

OECD (2002), *Understanding the Brain*. OECD.

Sternberg, R. (1996), *Successful Intelligence*. New York: Simon and Schuster.

Thompson, R. (1985), *The brain: an introduction to neuroscience*. New York: Freeman.

Endnote

I have been working as a teacher-educator for about ten years: before then, I spent a further ten years working in adult and community education. Whilst at times the complexities and frustrations of working in the sector make me wish I was back working as a cycle mechanic again, it is the astounding level of professionalism that I invariably encounter that makes me happy to stay.

At the time of writing, colleges (and universities, in fact) are once again in a state of flux due to changes in government policy. Several years ago, I attended a lecture by Stephen Ball in London: he argued that governments spent a lot of time interfering in education because it was one of the few areas of public life that they could still actually affect. Certainly, much of what is currently happening seems to embody an illusion of procedural effectiveness as opposed to a coherent policy.

This edition of *Teaching in Further Education* shares the same central aspect as its predecessors: that the professional practice of teachers must always rest on not only meaningful and authentic practical experience, but also relevant and critical professional and theoretical knowledge. It is hoped that this current edition, despite the imperfections that will undoubtedly have crept through (and for which I take responsibility), will further contribute to this process.

Bibliography

Abercrombie, M. (1960), *The Anatomy of Judgement*. London: Hutchinson.

Adams, C. (2006), PowerPoint, habits of mind and classroom culture. *Journal of Curriculum Studies* 38(4), 389–411.

Adams, J. (1969), *Human Memory*. New York: McGraw Hill.

Aidman, E. and Leontiev, D. (1991), From being motivated to motivating oneself: a Vygotskian perspective. *Studies in Soviet Thought* 42(2), 137–51.

Alderfer, C. (1972), *Existence, Relatedness and Growth*. New York: Free Press.

Allen, M. and Ainley, P. (2007), *Education make you fick, innit? What has gone wrong in England's schools, colleges and universities, and how to start putting it right*. London: Tufnell Press.

Anderson, L. and Burns, R. (1989), *Research in Classrooms*. Oxford: Pergamon Press.

Armitage, A., Evershed, J., Hayes, D., Hudson, A., Kent, J., Lawes, S., Poma, S. and Renwick, M. (2012), *Teaching and Training in Lifelong Learning*, 4th edn. Maidenhead: McGraw Hill.

Armitage, A. and Renwick. M. (2008), *Assessment in Further Education*. London: Continuum.

Ashwin, P. (2009), *Analysing Teaching-Learning Interactions in Higher Education: accounting for structure and agency*. London: Continuum.

Atkins, L. (2009), *Invisible Students, Impossible Dreams: experiencing vocational education 14–19*. Stoke on Trent: Trentham Books.

Atkinson, J. (1980), *Introduction to Motivation*. New York: Van Nostrand.

Ausubel, D. (1968), *Educational Psychology: a cognitive view*. New York: Holt, Rinehart and Winston.

Avis, J. (2005), Beyond performativity: reflections on activist professionalism and the labour process in further education. *Journal of Education Policy* 20(2), 209–22.

—(2007), Engeström's version of activity theory: a conservative praxis? *Journal of Education and Work* 20(3), 161–77.

Avis, J., Orr, K. and Tummons, J. (2009), Theorising the work-based learning of teachers. In J. Avis, R. Fisher and R. Thompson (eds), *Teaching in Lifelong Learning: a guide to theory and practice*. Maidenhead: McGraw Hill.

Baddeley, A. and Hitch, G. (1982), Working memory. In G. Bower (ed.), *The Psychology of Learning and Motivation*. Waltham: Academic Press.

Bailey, B. (2004), Learning support workers in further education in England: a hidden revolution? *Journal of Further and Higher Education* 28(4), 373–93.

Barnes, L. (1994), *Teaching and the Case Method*. Harvard: Harvard Business Press.

Baron-Cohen, S. (2003), *The Essential Difference: men, women and the extreme male brain*. London: Penguin.

Barton, D. (1994), *Literacy: An Introduction to the Ecology of Written Language*. Oxford: Blackwell.

Barton, D. and Hamilton, M. (1998), *Local Literacies: Reading and Writing in One Community*. London: Routledge.

Barton, D. and Tusting, K. (eds) (2005), *Beyond Communities of Practice: Language, Power and Social Context*. Cambridge: Cambridge University Press.

Barton, D., Ivanič, R., Appleby, Y., Hodge, R., and Tusting, K. (2007), *Literacy, Lives and Learning*. London: Routledge.

Baumann, M. (2010), E-books: A new school of thought. *Information Today* 27(5), 1–4.

Beetham, H. and Sharpe, R. (eds) (2007), *Rethinking Pedagogy for a Digital Age: designing and delivering e-learning*. London: Routledge.

Berliner, D. (1990), If the metaphor fits, why not wear it? The teacher as executive. *Theory into Practice* 29(2), 85–93.

Bernstein, B. (1990), *Class Codes and Control IV: The Structuring of Pedagogic Discourse*. London: Routledge.

—(1996), *Pedagogy, Symbolic Control and Identity: Theory, Research, Critique*. Oxford: Rowman and Littlefield.

Biehler, R. (1993), *Psychology Applied to Teaching*. Belmont: Houghton Mifflin.

Biggs, J. and Telfer, R. (1987), *The Process of Learning*. New Jersey: Prentice-Hall.

Billett, S. (1996), Constructing vocational knowledge: history, communities and ontogeny. *Journal of Vocational Education and Training* 48(2), 141–54.

Black, P. and Wiliam, D. (1998), Assessment and classroom learning. *Assessment in Education* 5(1), 7–71.

—(2009), *Developing the theory of formative assessment*. Educational Assessment, Evaluation and Accountability 21(1), 5–31.

Bligh, D. (1998), *What's the Use of Lectures?* Exeter: Intellect.

Bloom, B. (ed.) (1956), *Taxonomy of Educational Objectives: Handbook I – The Cognitive Domain*. London: Longman.

Boring, E. (1923), Intelligence as the tests test it. *New Republic* (36), 35–7.

Bower, G. and Hilgard, E. (1981), *Theories of Learning*. New Jersey: Prentice-Hall.

Bredo, E. (1994), Reconstructing educational psychology: situated cognition and Deweyan pragmatism. *Educational Psychologist* 29(1): 23–35.

Briggs, A. (2000), Facilitating the role of middle managers in further education. *Research in Post-Compulsory Education* 7(1), 63–78.

Brooke, M.J. (2013), The alignment of skills and practice via active reading methodology. *Teaching in Lifelong Learning* 4(2), 5–13.

Brookfield, S. (2006), *The Skilful Teacher: on technique, trust and responsiveness in the classroom*. San Francisco: John Wiley and Sons.

Brosin, J. (1961), *Lectures in Experimental Psychology*. Pittsburgh: Pittsburgh University Press.

Brown, S. and Race, P. (1994), *Assess Your Own Teaching Quality*. London: Kogan Page.

Bryan, J. and Jayes, D. (2007), The McDonaldization of further education. In D. Hayes, T. Marshall and A. Turner (eds), *A Lecturer's Guide to Further Education*. Maidenhead: McGraw Hill.

Burke, A. and Rowsell, J. (2008), Screen pedagogy: challenging perceptions of digitial reading practice. *Changing English: Studies in Culture and Education* 15(4), 445–56.

Burt, C. (1940), *The Factors of Mind*. London: London University Press.

—(1961), Factor analysis and its neurological basis. *British Journal of Statistical Psychology* 14(1), 53–71.

—(1972), The inheritance of general intelligence. *American Psychology* 27(3), 175–90.

Clow, R. (2005), Just teachers: the work carried out by full-time further education teachers. *Research in Post-Compulsory Education* 10(1), 63–81.

Clow, R. (2001), Further education teachers' constructions of professionalism. *Journal of Vocational Education and Training* 53(3), 407–19.

Cobb, P., and McClain, K. (2006), The collective mediation of a high-stakes accountability programme: communities and networks of practice. *Mind, Culture and Activity* 13(2), 80–100.

Coffield, F. (ed.) (2000), *The Benefits of Informal Learning*. Bristol: The Policy Press.

Coffield, F., Moseley, D., Hall, E. and Ecclestone, K. (2004), *Should We Be Using Learning Styles? What research has to say to practice*. London: Learning and Skills Research Centre.

Cohen, E. and Lotan, R. (1990), Teacher as supervisor of complex technology. *Theory into Practice* 29(2), 78–84.

Cohen, P. and McKeachie, W. (1980), The role of colleagues in the evaluation of college teaching. *Improving College and University Teaching* 28(4), 147–54

Colley, H. and Jarvis, J. (2007), Formality and informality in the summative assessment of motor vehicle apprentices: a case study. *Assessment in Education* 14(3), 295–314.

Coombs, P. and Snygg (1959), *Individual Behaviour*. London: Harper and Row.

Cunningham, B. (2005), *Mentoring Teachers in Post-Compulsory Education*. London: David Fulton.

Curry, L. (1990), A critique of the research on learning styles. *Educational Leadership* 48(2), 50–6.

Daniels, H. (ed.) (1996), *An Introduction to Vygotsky*. London: Routledge.

Daniels, H. (2001), *Vygotsky and Pedagogy*. London: Routledge.

Davenport, J. (1993), Is there any way out of the andragogy morass? In M. Thorpe, R. Edwards and A. Hanson, A. (eds), *Culture and Processes of Adult Learning*. London: Routledge/Open University.

Davies, I. (1981), *Instructional Technique*. New York: McGraw Hill.

Davis, G. (1967), *Human Relations at Work*. New York: McGraw Hill.

Davydov, V. (1999), The content and unsolved problems of activity theory. In Y. Engeström, R. Miettinen, and R.-L.Punamäki (eds), *Perspectives on Activity Theory*. Cambridge: Cambridge University Press.

Dembo, M. (1981), *Teaching for Learning: applying educational psychology in the classroom*. Santa Monica: Goodyear Publishing Company.

Dixon, E. (2012), Building a model for online distance courses through social media and networks. *International Journal of Virtual and Personal Learning Environments* 3(3), 81–94.

Domjan, M. (1998), *Principles of Learning and Behaviour*. Pacific Grove, CA: Brooks/Cole.

Doyle, C. (1987), *Explorations in Psychology*. Pactific Grove, CA: Brooks/Cole.

Dreyfus, H. and Dreyfus, S. (1986), *Mind Over Machine: the power of human intuition and expertise in the age of the computer*. Oxford: Basil Blackwell.

Drucker, P. (1964), *Managing for Results*. London: Harper and Row.

Duck, S. and McMahan, D. (2012), *The Basics of Communication: a relational perspective*, 2nd edn. London: Sage.

Duckworth, V., Flanagan, K., McCormack, K. and Tummons, J. (2012), *Understanding Behaviour 14+*. Maidenhead: McGraw Hill.

Duckworth, V. and Tummons, J. (2010), *Contemporary Issues in Lifelong Learning*. Maidenhead: McGraw Hill.

Dyer, H. (1996), Where do we go from here? Issues in the professional development of learning support assistants. *Research in Post-Compulsory Education* 1(2), 187–98.

Eaton, G. (1982), *Learning from Case Studies*. New Jersey: Prentice-Hall.

Ecclestone, K. (1996), The reflective practitioner: mantra or a model for emancipation? *Studies in the Education of Adults* 28(2), 146–62.

Ecclestone, K. (2002), *Learning Autonomy in Post–16 Education: the politics and practice of formative assessment*. London: RoutledgeFalmer.

—(2007), Resisting images of the 'diminished self': the implications of emotional well-being and emotional engagement in education policy. *Journal of Education Policy* 22(4), 455–70.

Ecclestone, K., Davies, J., Derrick, J. and Gawn, J. (2010), *Transforming Formative Assessment in Lifelong Learning*. Maidenhead: McGraw Hill.

Ecclestone, K. and Hayes, D. (2008), *The Dangerous Rise of Therapeutic Education*. London: Routledge.

Edward, S., Coffield, F., Steer, R. and Gregson M. (2007), Endless change in the learning and skills sector: the impact on teaching staff. *Journal of Vocational Education and Training* 57(2), 155–73.

Eisner, E. (1967), Franklin Bobbitt and the 'science' of curriculum making. *The School Review* 75(1), 29–47.

—(1979), *The Educational Imagination*. London: Macmillan.

—(1970), *Curriculum Evaluation*. American Educational Research Association Monograph Series.

Engeström, Y. (1987*), Learning by Expanding: an activity-theoretical approach to developmental Research*. Helsinki: Orienta-Konsultit.

—(1993), Developmental studies on work as a test bench of activity theory. In S. Chaiklin, and J. Lave (eds), *Understanding Practice: perspectives on activity and context*. Cambridge: Cambridge University Press.

—(1999), Innovative learning in work teams: Analysing cycles of knowledge creation in practice. In Y. Engeström, R. Miettinen, and R.-L. Punamäki, (eds), *Perspectives on Activity Theory*. Cambridge: Cambridge University Press.

—(2001), Expansive learning at work: toward an activity theory reconceptualization. *Journal of Education and Work* 14(1), 133–56.

Engeström, Y., Miettinen, R. and Punamäki, R-L. (eds) (1999), *Perspectives on Activity Theory*. Cambridge: Cambridge University Press.

Epstein, J. (1981), *Masters: portraits of great teachers*. New York: Basic Books.

Eraut, M. (1994), *Developing Professional Knowledge and Competence*. Abingdon: RoutledgeFalmer.

Evans, B. and Waites, B. (1981), *IQ and Mental Testing*. London: Macmillan.

Evans, D. (1978), *Psychology: Dictionary of the Mind, Brain and Behaviour*. London: Arrow Books.

Falchikov, N. (2005), *Improving Assessment Through Student Involvement: practical solutions for aiding learning in higher and further education*. London: RoutledgeFalmer.

Fisher, R., Harris, A. and Jarvis, C. (2008), *Education in Popular Culture: telling tales on teachers and learners*. London: Routledge.

Fitts, P. and Posner, M. (1967), *Human Performance*. Wadsworth: Brooks Cole.

Fleck, N. and Law, F. (1988), *Effective Instruction*. Cambridge: ITRU.

Fontana, D. (1995), *Psychology for Teachers*. London: Macmillan.

Fuller, T. (ed.) (1989), *The Voice of Liberal Learning – M. Oakeshott on Education*. Yale: Yale University Press.

Gage, N. (1963), *Handbook of Research on Teaching*. Chicago: Rand McNally.

Gagné, R. (1983), *The Conditions of Learning*. New York: Holt-Saunders.

Gardner, H. (2003), Multiple intelligences after twenty years. Paper presented at the *American Educational Research Association*, Chicago.

Gee, J. (1996), *Social Linguistics and Literacies: Ideology in Discourses*, 2nd edn. London: RoutledgeFalmer.

Gee, J. (2003), *What video games have to teach us about learning and literacy*. Basingstoke: Palgrave Macmillan.

Gee, J. (2004), *Situated Language and Learning: a critique of traditional schooling*. London: Routledge.

Gerlach, V. (1980), *Teaching and Media*. New Jersey: Prentice-Hall.

Gleeson, D., Davies, J. and Wheeler, E. (2005), On the making and taking of professionalism in the further education workplace. *British Journal of Sociology of Education* 26(4), 445–60.

Gorard, S. and Smith, E. (2007), Do barriers get in the way? A review of the determinants of post–16 participation. *Research in Post-Compulsory Education* 12(2), 141–58.

Gossman, P. (2008), Teaching development – experience and philosophy (using the three Rs). *Teacher Education Quarterly* 35(2), 155–69.

Goswami, U. (2004), Neuroscience, education and special education. *British Journal of Special Education* 31(4): 175–83.

Gould, J. (2012), *Learning Theory and Classroom Practice in the Lifelong Learning Sector*, 2nd edn. London: Learning Matters.

Gould, S. (1997), *The Mismeasurement of Man*. Harmondsworth: Penguin.

Gregory, R. (1984), *Mind in Science*. Harmondsworth: Peregrine.

Gribble, J. (1983), *Literary Education: a revaluation*. Cambridge: Cambridge University Press.

Grint, K. (1999), *The Arts of Leadership*. Oxford: Oxford University Press.

Gronlund, N. (1981), *Measurement and Evaluation in Teaching*. London: Macmillan.

Guile, D. and Young, M. (1998), Apprenticeship as a conceptual basis for a social theory of learning. *Journal of Vocational Education and Training* 50(2), 173–93.

Haimann, T. and Scott, W. (1978), *Managing the Modern Organisation*. Boston: Houghton Mifflin.

Halliday, J. (1973), *Explanations in the Function of Language*. London: Edward Arnold.

Hargie, O. (1997) (ed.), *Handbook of Communication Skills*. London: Routledge.

Hargreaves, D. (2005), *About Learning*. London: Demos.

Harkin, J. (2006), Treated like adults: 14–16 year-olds in further education. *Research in Post-Compulsory Education* 11(3), 319–39.

Harlow, H. (1949), The formation of learning sets. *Psychological Review* 56: 51–65.

Harris S. R. and Shelswell, N. (2005), Moving beyond communities of practice in adult basic education. In Barton, D. and Tusting, K. (eds), *Beyond Communities of Practice: Language, Power and Social Context*. Cambridge: Cambridge University Press.

Harrow, A. (1972), *A Taxonomy of the Psychomotor Domain*. New York: David McKay.

Hearnshaw, L. (1979), *Cyril Burt, Psychologist*. London: Hodder and Stoughton.

Heim, A. (1987), *Oxford Companion to the Mind*. Oxford: Oxford University Press.

Herzberg, H. (1959), *The Motivation to Work*. New Jersey: John Wiley and Sons.

Highet, G. (1977), *The Art of Teaching*. London: Methuen.

Hill, C. (2007), *Teaching with E-learning in the Lifelong Learning Sector*, 2nd edn. Exeter: Learning Matters.

Hillier, Y. (2011), *Reflective Teaching in Further and Adult Education*, 3rd edn. London: Continuum.

Hillier, Y. and Thompson, A. (2005), *Readings in Post-Compulsory Education: research in the learning and skills sector*. London: Continuum.

Hitching, J. (2008), *Maintaining your License to Practice*. Exeter: Learning Matters.

Hodkinson, P. (2004), Research as a form of work: expertise, community and methodological objectivity. *British Educational Research Journal* 30(1), 9–26.

Hogben, H. (1972), The behavioural objectives approach: some problems and dangers. *Journal of Curriculum Studies* 4(1), 42–50.

Howarth, E. (1981), *The Structure of Psychology*. London: Allen and Unwin.

Huang, H-M (2002), Toward constructivism for adult learners in online learning environments. *British Journal of Educational Technology* 33(1), 27–37.

Illeris, K. (2007), *How We Learn: learning and non-learning in school and beyond*. London: Routledge.

Ingle, S. and Duckworth, V. (2013), *Enhancing Learning Through Technology in Lifelong Learning: fresh ideas, innovative strategies*. Maidenhead: McGraw Hill.

Ingleby, E., Joyce, D. and Powell, S. (2010), *Learning to Teach in the Lifelong Learning Sector*. London: Continuum.

Ivanic, R., Edwards, R., Barton, D., Martin-Jones, M., Fowler, Z., Hughes, B., Mannion, G., Miller, K., Satchwell, C. and Smith, J. (2009), *Improving Learning in College: Rethinking Literacies Across the Curriculum*. London: Routledge.

Ixer, J. (1999), There's No Such Thing As Reflection. *British Journal of Social Work* 29:513–27.

James, D. and Biesta, G. (2007), *Improving Learning Cultures in Further Education*. London: Routledge.

Jarvis, P. (ed.) (2006), *The Theory and Practice of Teaching*, 2nd edn. London: Routledge.

Jarvis, P. (2010), *Adult Education and Lifelong Learning: theory and practice*, 4th edn. London: Routledge.

Jarvis, P., Holford, J. and Griffin, C. (2003), *The Theory and Practice of Learning*, 2nd edn. London: RoutledgeFalmer.

Jephcote, M., Salisbury, J. and Rees, G. (2008), Being a teacher in further education in changing times. *Research in Post-Compulsory Education* 13(2): 163–72.

Jessen, A. and Elander, J. (2009), Development and evaluation of an intervention to improve further education students' understanding of higher education assessment criteria: three studies. *Journal of Further and Higher Education* 33(4), 359–80.

Joynson, R. (1989), *The Burt Affair*. London: Routledge.

Keefer, J. (2009), The critical incident questionnaire (CIQ): from research to practice and back again.

Kidd, R. (1975), *How Adults Learn*. New York: Association Press.

Klausmeier, H. (1975), *Learning and Human Abilities*. London: Harper and Row.

Kline, P. (1996), *Intelligence: the psychometric view*. London: Routledge.

Knight, P. T. and Yorke, M. (2003), *Assessment, Learning and Employability*. Maidenhead: Open University Press/Society for Research into Higher Education.

Knirk, F. (1986), *Instructional Technology*. New York: Holt, Rinehart and Winston.

Kolb, D. (1984), *Experiential Learning*. Englewood Cliffs, NJ: Prentice-Hall.

Koontz, H. (1985), *Management*. New York: McGraw-Hill.

Koriat, A. and Goldsmith, M. (1996), memory metaphors and the real life – laboratory controversy. *Behavioural and Brain Sciences* 19: 167–88.

Kress, G. (2003), *Literacy in the New Media Age*. London: Routledge.

Langford, P. (2005), *Vygotsky's Developmental and Educational Psychology*. Hove: Psychology Press.

Lefrancois, G. (1985), *Psychology for Teaching*. Stamford: Wadsworth Publishing.

Lave, J. (1988), *Cognition in Practice: Mind, Mathematics and Culture in Everyday Life*. Cambridge: Cambridge University Press.

—(2011), *Apprenticeship in Critical Ethnographic Practice*. Chicago: University of Chicago Press.

Lave, J. and Wenger, E. (1991), *Situated Learning: Legitimate Peripheral Participation*. Cambridge: Cambridge University Press.

Lemke, J. (1997), Cognition, context and learning: a social semiotic perspective. In D. Kirshner, and J. Whitson (eds), *Situated Cognition: Social, Semiotic and Psychological Perspectives*. London: Lawrence Erlbaum Associates.

Lillis, T. (2001), *Student Writing: Access, Regulation, Desire*. London: Routledge.

Lindblom, C. (1959), The science of muddling through. *Public Administration Review* 19(2), 79–88.

Lindsley, D. (1957), *Nebraska Symposium on Motivation*. Nebraska: Nebraska University Press.

Lovell, B. (1984), *Adult Learning*. London: Croom Helm.

Lowman, J. (1984), *Mastering the Techniques of Teaching*. New York: Jossey-Bass.

Lucas, N., Nasta, T. and Rogers, L. (2012), From fragmentation to chaos? The regulation of initial teacher training in further education. *British Educational Research Journal* 38(4), 677–95.

MacDonald-Ross, M. (1973), *Instructional Science*. Oxford: Elsevier.

Mace, C. (1973), *The Psychology of Study*. Harmondsworth: Penguin.

Mackintosh, N. (ed.) (1995), *Cyril Burt: fraud or framed?* Oxford: Oxford University Press.

Mager, R. (1962; 1984), *Preparing Instructional Objectives*. London: Pitman.

Malcolm, J. and Zukas, M. (2007), Poor relations – exploring discipline, research and pedagogy in academic identity. In M. Osborne, M. Houston and N. Toman (eds), *The Pedagogy of Lifelong Learning*. London: Routledge.

Marshall, H. (1990), Beyond the workplace metaphor: the classroom as a learning setting. *Theory into Practice* 29(2), 94–101.

Mather, K., Worrall, L. and Seifert, R. (2009), The challenging locus of workplace control in the English FE sector. *Employee Relations* 31(2), 139–57.

McQuail, D. (1984), *Communication*. London: Longman.

Meighan, R. and Harber, C. (2007), *A Sociology of Educating*. London: Continuum.

Meister, D. (1991), *Psychology of System Design*. Oxford: Elsevier.

Miettinen, R. (1999), Transcending traditional school learning: Teachers' work and networks of learning. In Y. Engeström, R. Miettinen, and R.-L. Punamäki (eds), *Perspectives on Activity Theory*. Cambridge: Cambridge University Press.

Miller, G. (1960), *Plans and Structure of Behaviour*. New York: Holt, Rinehart and Winston.

Mockler, R. (1972), *The Management Control Process*. New York: Prentice-Hall.

Mondy, J. (1983), *Management – Concepts and Practices*. Boston: Allyn and Bacon.

Morgan-Klein, B. and Osborne, M. (2007), *The Concepts and Practices of Lifelong Learning*. London: Routledge.

Nespor, J. (1994), *Knowledge In Motion: space, time and curriculum in undergraduate physics and management*. London: RoutledgeFalmer.

Norman, D. (1982), *Learning and Memory*. London: Freeman.

OECD (2002), *Understanding the Brain*. OECD.

Orpen, C. (1982), Student versus lecturer assessment of learning. *Higher Education* 11: 567–72.

Orr, K. and Simmons, R. (2010), Dual identities: the in-service teacher trainee experience in the English further education sector. *Journal of Vocational Education and Training* 62(1), 75–88.

Osborne, M., Houston, M. and Toman, N. (eds) (2007), *The Pedagogy of Lifelong Learning: understanding effective teaching and learning in diverse contexts*. London: Routledge.

Osgood, C. (1954), Psycholinguistics: a survey of theory and research problems. *Journal of Abnormal and Social Psychology*. 49(4), 1–203.

Paisley, R. (1980), *Progress in Communication Sciences*. Norwood, NJ: Ablex.

Papen, U. (2005), *Adult Literacy as Social Practice: more than skills*. London: Routledge.

Parsons, T. (1960), *Structure and Process in Modern Societies*. Glencoe: Free Press.

Passey, D., Rogers, C., Machell, J. and McHugh, G. (2004), *The Motivational Effect of ICT on Pupils*. London: Department for Education and Skills 4RP/2002/050–3.

Pennycook, A. (1985), Actions speak louder than words: paralanguage, communication and education. *TESOL Quarterly* 19(2), 259–82.

Popper, K. and Eccles, J. (1984), *The Self and Its Brain*. London: Routledge and Kegan Paul.

Popham, W. (1970), Probing the validity of arguments against behavioural objectives. In Kibler (ed.), *Behavioural Objectives and Instruction*. London: Allyn and Bacon.

Powell, S. and Tummons, J. (2011), *Inclusive Practice in the Lifelong Learning Sector*. Exeter: Learning Matters.

Pring, R., Hayward, G., Hodgson, A., Johnson, J., Keep, E., Oancea, A., Rees, G., Spours, K. and Wilde, S. (2009), *Education For All: the future of education and training for 14–19 year olds*. London: Routledge.

Raffe, D. and Spours, K. (2007), *Policy Making and Policy Learning in 14–19 Education*. Bedford Way Papers: Institute of Education.

Randle, K. and Brady, N. (1997), Managerialism and professionalism in the Cinderella service. *Journal of Vocational Education and Training* 49(1), 121–39.

Reece, I. and Walker, S. (2007), *Teaching, Training and Learning: a practical guide*, rev 6th edn. Sunderland: Business Education Publishers.

Ritzer, G. (1993), *The McDonaldization of Society*. Thousand Oaks: Pine Forge Press.

Robson, J. (2006), *Teacher Professionalism in Further and Adult Education*. London: Routledge.

Rogers, A. (2002), *Teaching Adults*, 3rd edn. Maidenhead: Open University Press.

Rogers, J. (2007), *Adults Learning*, 5th edn. Maidenhead: Open University Press.

Ryle, G. (1983), *The Concept of Mind*. London: Penguin.

Salmon, G. (2011), *E-moderating: the key to online teaching and learning*, 3rd edn. London: Routledge.

Salovey, P. and Mayer, J. (1990), Emotional intelligence. *Imagination, Cognition and Personality*. 9(3): 185–211.

Saunders, N. and Walstad, W. (1990), *The Principles of Economics*. London: McGraw Hill.

Savoy, A., Proctor, R. and Salvendy, G. (2009), Information retention from PowerPoint and traditional lectures. *Computers and Education* 52(4), 858–67.

Sayre, K. (1976), *Cybernetics and the Philosophy of Mind*. Michigan: Open Humanities Press.

Scales, P. (2013), *Teaching in the Lifelong Learning Sector*, 2nd edn. Maidenhead: McGraw Hill.

Scales, P., Pickering, J., Senior, L., Headley, K., Garner, P. and Boulton, H. (2011), *Continuing Professional Development in the Lifelong Learning Sector*. Maidenhead: McGraw Hill.

Scheffler, I. (1960), *The Language of Education*. Springfield, IL: Thomas.

Scheuermann, L. and Taylor, G. (1997), Netiquette. *Internet Research* 7(4), 269–73.

Schimmell, A. (1993), *The Mystery of Number*. Oxford: Oxford University Press.

Schön, D. (1983), *The Reflective Practitioner: how professionals think in action*. Aldershot: Ashgate.

Schramm, W. (1954), *The Process and Effects of Mass Communication*. Illinois: Illinois University Press.

Scott, G. (2005), Para-professionals in further education: changing roles in vocational delivery. *Management in Education* 19(3), 24–7.

Scott, M. (2000), Writing in postgraduate teacher training: a question of identity. In M. Lea and B. Stierer (eds), *Student Writing in Higher Education: New Contexts*. Buckingham: Open University Press/Society for Research into Higher Education.

Severin, W. (1988), *Communication Theories*. London: Longman.

Shain, F. and Gleeson, D. (1999), Under new management: changing conceptions of teacher professionalism and policy in the further education sector. *Journal of Education Policy* 14(4), 445–62.

Shannon, C. and Weaver, W. (1949), *The Mathematical Theory of Communication*. Illinois: Illinois University Press.

Sharp, P. (2001), *Nurturing Emotional Literacy*. London: David Fulton.

Shortland, S. (2004), Peer observation: a tool for staff development or compliance? *Journal of Further and Higher Education* 28(2), 219–28.

Shulman, L. (1986), Those who understand: knowledge growth in teaching. *Educational Researcher* 15(2), 4–14.

Simpson, E. (1966), The classification of educational objectives: psychomotor domain. *Illinois Journal of Home Economics* 10(4), 110–44.

Skinner, B. (1968), *The Technology of Teaching*. New York: Prentice-Hall.

Small, S. (2008), The neuroscience of language. *Brain and Language* 106(1), 1–3.

Smith, A. (1982), *Management Systems*. Birmingham: Dryden Press.

Smith, O. (1966), *Cybernetic Principles of Learning and Educational Design*. New York: Holt, Rinehart and Winston.

Snyder, I. (ed.) (2002), *Silicon Literacies: communication, innovation and education in the electronic age*. London: Routledge.

Solomon, N. (2007), Reality bites: bringing the 'real' world of work into educational classrooms. In Osborne, M., Houston, M. and Toman, N. (eds), *The Pedagogy of Lifelong Learning*. London: Routledge.

Spearman, C. (1923), *The Nature of Intelligence and the Principle of Cognition*. London: Macmillan.

—(1939), The Factorial Analysis of Ability II: Determination of Factors. *British Journal of Psychology* 30(2): 78–83.

Stanton, N. (1996), *Mastering Communication*. London: Macmillan.

Stenhouse, L. (1975), *An Introduction to Curriculum Research and Development*. London: Heinemann.

Stoner, J. and Freeman, R. (1989), *Management*. New York: Prentice-Hall.

Sugarman, L. (2001), *Life-Span Development: frameworks, accounts and strategies*. Hove: Psychology Press.

Taba, H. (1962), *Curriculum Development: theory and practice*. New York: John Wiley and Sons.

Tennyson, R. (1980), The teaching of concepts: a review of the literature. *Review of Educational Research* 50(4), 55–70.

Thomas, G. (2007), *Education and Theory: strangers in paradigms*. Maidenhead: McGraw Hill/Open University Press.

Thorpe, M. (1993), *Evaluating Open and Distance Learning*. Harlow: Longman.

Thurstone, L. (1924), *The Nature of Intelligence*. New York: Kegan Paul.

Tight, M. (2004), Research into higher education: an a-theoretical community of practice? *Higher Education Research and Development* 23(4), 395–411.

Tilles, S. (1963), How to evaluate corporate strategy. *Harvard Business Review* (July).

Tommerdahl, J. (2012), *Neuroscience and Education*. In J. Arthur and A. Peterson (eds), *The Routledge Companion to Education*. London: Routledge.

Tulving, E. (1983), *Elements of Episodic Memory*. Oxford: Open University Press.

Tummons, J. (2012), *Curriculum Studies in the Lifelong Learning Sector*, 2nd edn. Exeter: Learning Matters.

—(2011a), *Assessing Learning in the Lifelong Learning Sector*, 3rd edn. Exeter: Learning Matters.

—(2011b), 'It sort of feels uncomfortable': problematising the assessment of reflective practice. *Studies in Higher Education* 36(4), 471–83.

—(2010a), *Becoming a Professional Tutor in the Lifelong Learning Sector*, 2nd edn. Exeter: Learning Matters.

—(2010b), The assessment of lesson plans in teacher education: a case study in assessment validity and reliability. *Assessment and Evaluation in Higher Education* 35(7), 847–57.

Tummons, J. and Duckworth, V. (2012), *Doing your research project in the Lifelong Learning Sector*. Maidenhead: McGraw Hill.

Tusting, K. and Barton. D. (2003), *Models of Adult Learning: a literature review*. London: NRDC.

Tyler, R. (1949), *Basic Principles of Curriculum and Instruction*. Chicago University Press.

Verduin, J. (1978), *Adults Teaching Adults: principles and strategies*. Austin, TX: Learning Concepts.

Viskovic, A. (2005), 'Community of Practice' as a Framework for Supporting Tertiary Teachers' Informal Workplace Learning. *Journal of Vocational Education and Training* 57(3), 389–410.

Viscovic, A. and Robson, J. (2001), Community and Identity: experiences and dilemmas of vocational teachers in post-school contexts. *Journal of In-service Education* 27(2), 221–36.

Vygotsky, L. S. (1978), *Mind in Society: the development of higher psychological processes*. Harvard: Harvard University Press.

Walker, M. (2012), 'Encouragement of sound education amongst the industrial classes': mechanics' institutes and working-class membership 1838–1881. *Educational Studies* ifirst: DOI: 10.1080/03055698.2012.686694

Wallace, S. (2002), No good surprises: intending lecturers' preconceptions and initial experiences of further education. *British Educational Research Journal* 28(1), 79–93.

—(2011), *Teaching, Tutoring and Training in the Lifelong Learning Sector*, 4th edn. Exeter: Learning Matters.

Wallace, S. and Gravells, J. (2007), *Mentoring*, 2nd edn. Exeter: Learning Matters.

Wallis, J. (eds) (1996), *Liberal Adult Education: the end of an era?* Nottingham: University of Nottingham Continuing Education Press.

Warmington, P. (2011), Divisions of labour: activity theory, multi-professional working and intervention research. *Journal of Vocational Education and Training* 63(2), 143–57.

Welford, A. (1968), *Fundamentals of Skill*. London: Methuen.

Wenger, E. (1998), *Communities of Practice: Learning, Meaning and Identity*. Cambridge: Cambridge University Press.

Wenger, E., McDermott, R. and Snyder, W. (2002), *Cultivating Communities of Practice*. Boston: Harvard Business School Press.

Yeaxley (1929), *Lifelong Education*. London: Cassell.

Yunker, B. (1986), *Instructor's Resource Manual*. New York: Prentice-Hall.

Index